New Century, New Team
The 1901 Boston Americans

Edited by Bill Nowlin
Associate editors Maurice Bouchard and Len Levin
Photo editor Dan Desrochers

Society for American Baseball Research, Inc.
Phoenix, AZ

New Century, New Team: The 1901 Boston Americans
Edited by Bill Nowlin. Associate editors Maurice Bouchard and Len Levin. Photo editor Dan Desrochers.

Copyright © 2013 Society for American Baseball Research, Inc.

All rights reserved. Reproduction in whole or in part without permission is prohibited.

ISBN 978-1-933599-58-8
(Ebook ISBN 978-1-933599-59-5)

Design and Production: Gilly Rosenthol, Rosenthol Design

The Society for American Baseball Research, Inc.
4455 E. Camelback Road, Ste. D-140
Phoenix, AZ 85018
Phone: (800) 969-7227 or (612) 343-6455

Web: www.sabr.org
Facebook: Society for American Baseball Research
Twitter: @SABR

Table of Contents

Introduction: Bill Nowlin 1

Franchise Firsts: Bill Nowlin 8

Team Owner: George Somers: Fred Schuld 14

American League President Ban Johnson:
Joe Santry and Cindy Thomson 17

The Ballpark: Huntington Avenue Grounds:
Ron Selter 22

A Fuller Portrait of the First Home Game of the Franchise 34

Baseball in the New Century:
Following the Boston Americans in 1901:
Donna L. Halper 38

The Players

Ben Beville: Bill Nowlin 46

Jimmy Collins: Charlie Bevis 49

Lou Criger: Steve Krah 58

George "Nig" Cuppy: Charles Faber 62

Tommy Dowd: Bill Nowlin 66

Hobe Ferris: Dennis Auger 70

Frank Foreman: Jim Elfers 74

Buck Freeman: Eric Enders 81

Harry Gleason: Jack Morris 86

Charlie Hemphill: Paul Wendt 93

Charlie Jones: Frank Vaccaro 96

Win Kellum: Bill Nowlin 105

Ted Lewis: Rory Costello 109

Larry McLean: Mike Lackey 114

Fred Mitchell: Bill Nowlin 117

Frank Morrissey: Bill Nowlin 128

Freddy Parent: Dan Desrochers 133

George Prentiss: David Forrester 138

Osee Schrecongost: Bill Nowlin 144

Jack Slattery: Bill Nowlin 154

Chick Stahl: Dennis Auger 158

Jake Volz: Bill Nowlin 164

George Winter: Tom Simon 168

Cy Young: David Southwick 173

Personality: "Hi Hi" Dixwell:
Joanne Hulbert 178

Personality: Mike "Nuf Ced" McGreevy:
Pete Nash 182

1901 Boston Americans Season Timeline:
Bill Nowlin 199

By the Numbers: Dan Fields 253

Contributors 258

1901 - The First Year of the Boston Red Sox

It all had to start someplace. The team was known as the Boston Americans at first, to differentiate them from Boston's venerable National League team. But even just a few months before their first game, it was uncertain there truly would be a team—and on top of that, they didn't have a park in which to play. They didn't become the Red Sox until December 1907.

The team's first owner—at least on paper—was Charles Somers, but pretty much everyone knew who truly owned the team (and, for that matter, the American League.) That was Ban Johnson.

It all happened very quickly, almost unbelievably quickly. Just a few months before 1901 Opening Day there was no American League team designated for Boston. For that matter, the American League itself was more a draft plan than a true rival league. The speed with which league architect Ban Johnson built on the framework he had is breathtaking to recount. Somers was key. As Fred Schuld notes in his biography of Somers, the man was known as the "good angel of the American League" for his financial backing of Johnson and his crucial support in launching at least four of the eight teams in the league: Cleveland, Chicago, Philadelphia, and Boston. The placement of a team in Boston to go up against the National League's Boston Beaneaters came relatively late in the process of founding the new league. Initially, as Johnson's vision began to take shape, there had been no plan to field a team in Boston. A franchise was planned for Buffalo but with only months to go before the season would open, Johnson decided to go head-to-head in Boston instead, and once he did, he acted fast.

Boston was the eighth and final city selected as home for a club in the new American League. And once they decided to take on the National League in Boston, they had to find a place where they could play. Only by finding an appropriate site for a baseball field would the American League truly decide to place a team in Boston. Had Johnson and his associates not found a good location, the league would have placed its eighth club in either Buffalo or Indianapolis.

As he relied on Somers to help, Ban Johnson also enlisted Connie Mack's help in creating the American League—and Mack was initially involved in one way or another with not only his own Philadelphia Athletics, but also with the Boston team. In turn, Connie Mack looked to John S. Dooley and Hugh Duffy for assistance.

Connie Mack assisted the team in locating a suitable location for its first home ballpark, the Huntington Avenue Grounds.

The story, as Dooley set it down, went thus: In the fall of 1900, Johnson came to Boston to see if it were feasible to situate a charter American League franchise in a city already known for its passionate interest in baseball. He set up shop in the Old South building on Washington Street and sought out veteran baseball man Hugh Duffy, holding a number of meetings with him. Dooley was an enthusiast of the game and active in business in Boston. He sat in on a few of the meetings. Lining up the players would be easier than finding a suitable location for the ballpark. Duffy had previously considered a position as a principal with a group which could have frustrated any A.L. effort—a proposed American Association team to be placed across the river from Boston in Cambridge in an attempt to fend off an American League incursion. SABR researcher Doug Pappas found that the National League's Arthur Irwin had leased the Cambridge property in a pre-emptive move to try and keep out the upstart league, but the lease was structured such that it would expire if the property were sold. Duffy declined to join the effort to head off the A.L., arguing, "The grounds are too far out. They are in Cambridge and will not draw from Boston. Harvard students might patronize the club, but that is about all."¹

"I recall Peter Kelley, an old newspaper man, calling on me at my office," Dooley wrote in a brief account he typed up. Kelley was calling on behalf of Cleveland's Charles Somers, designated as the first president of the Boston American League club. Kelley himself "had an option on the old bicycle track across the Charles River in Cambridge, on a lease calling for a yearly rental of $5,000."² Mack and Clark Griffith had recommended the Cambridge location, but neither Johnson nor Duffy found it attractive. Johnson didn't want a Boston team playing anywhere but in Boston. He kept that sentiment to himself, sharing it only with the small circle of men trying to help situate the team.

Jack Dooley—John "Jack" Dooley (front row center) at a 1913 Winter League meeting with fans, players, ex-players and other baseball luminaries. Boston Royal Rooter Michael T. McGreevy sits to the left with his hat in his hand.

A location deemed more suitable, however, was a site on Huntington Avenue controlled by the Boston Elevated Railway Company. Duffy showed the site to Peter Kelley and they both recommended it to Johnson. Dooley recalled Durand Associates as the actual owners of the land, but they had leased it to the railway, which had envisioned building a terminal there. The car barn was no longer the cards, but the railway was holding out for a $10,000 a year rental.

Dooley was at the time working for the firm of J. R. Prendergast, brokers in cotton goods and yarn with offices at 87 Milk Street. Prendergast's brother Daniel was in charge of the real estate department of the Boston Elevated. Dooley learned that the terminal plan was off—it turned out there was an ordinance that prevented the construction of car barns on the land which, even though it had served as a dump, was still across the street from the opera house. He urged Duffy and Kelley to approach Dan Prendergast, offer $5,000 a year "and mention my name. Under no conditions, I said, were they to go higher than $5,000."

The offer was, Dooley said, "violently refused" and Daniel Prendergast called Dooley to complain about the "measly rental" the men had offered. "If you want my advice," Dooley says he told Prendergast, "I'd grab that $5,000 offer because they can get that wonderful site in Cambridge for that figure. You'd better grab them right now before they close with Cambridge."

Prendergast took the bit and a deal was struck. Dooley later told the *Boston Post*'s Gerry Hern, "I suppose I should be a little sorry for what I did to get the American League in here, but when I sit in Fenway Park these days, I figure maybe the good Lord will forgive me. It was in a good cause."

In 1956, Gerry Hern of the *Boston Post* wrote, "More than anyone, Jack Dooley is responsible for the American League obtaining the Huntington ave. grounds as their playing field."³ Had Dooley not helped out, there might never have been a Boston Red Sox. The February 2, 1901 issue of *The Sporting News* records the formal awarding of a Boston franchise to Somers. Three weeks later, the February 23 *Sporting Life* reported that Somers had said the American League would never have invaded Boston if the National League had acceded to its original request for recognition as a major league.

Boston it was, and just a little more than three months after the Boston franchise was announced, the Boston Americans were playing baseball at their first home: the Huntington Avenue Grounds.

Tim Murnane's view of the forthcoming 1901 season

Veteran Boston sportswriter Tim Murnane wrote an article in the *Boston Globe* the day after Boston's National League team had kicked off their home season with a win, but six days before the American League schedule had begun. He presented his views on baseball in Boston in 1901. His article ran under the headline "Play Ball!" in the April 21, 1901 issue of the *Globe*.

PLAY BALL!

Season of 1901 Will be a Strenuous One
Hub Has Two Chances in 16 for Honors This Year
Many New Names on List of Its Players
Only Real Thing in Playing Will Make Good
New Huntington Av. Grounds Nearly Done

Thirty years ago this spring Boston saw her first professional ball team, and from that day to this Boston has never missed a season with a first-class ball team in the leading baseball organization of the country, and is the only city to claim this distinction. Chicago comes next, having missed but once, owing to the big fire. The great fire in Boston also nearly cut Boston out of a ball team in 1872.

Twelve times have the local men brought home the championship and they have given, undoubtedly, the greatest exhibition of the game of any club in the country, notwithstanding the fact that the grounds have been a slight handicap in several ways.

Such remarkable ball players as Geo. Wright, Andrew Leonard, Ross Barnes, James O'Rourke, John Morrill, Jim White, John Burdock, Ezra Sutton, Billy Nash, Dickey, Johnson, Joe Hornung, John Manning, Jim Whitney, Tommy Bond, Charlie Buffinton, Lew Brown, Curry Foley, and A. G. Spalding did their best work at their famous old grounds before the reconstructed league of 10 years ago flooded the country with new faces, but with no better ball players nor any half, as popular with the public.

Then came such players as Kelly, Clarkson, Duffy, McCarthy, Nichols, Lowe, Long, and an army of the best players the game could produce, until Boston has been given the privilege of cheering for the cream of the profession, until nothing but a winner will satisfy the followers of the sport in this vicinity.

Championships will often kill the game in some cities, as was the case in Providence, Detroit, Baltimore, and many other places. Boston, however, is not one of those cities, neither is Chicago nor New York, and yet there are no cities that insist so constantly as the three last-named that the team shall be a winner.

This season Boston will have two chances out of 16 for honors in baseball. The league club will start off with an experiment, and yet, with so many unknown players, surprises are no doubt in order. The new men are little known, with the exception of Kittridge and De Montreville, and the team, as a whole, looks light at the bat, a serious thing in the national league, where you must hit to make runs.

The triumvirs will not be content with a weak team, should the present aggregation fail to make good, but will keep on hustling for talent that can play baseball, and there are a number of good ones yet in the minor leagues.

The team this season will contain no less than seven college players, and is altogether the finest-looking club ever photographed in Boston uniforms. That doesn't mean, however, that they can play ball as well as they dress, although the greater number are known as the real thing in baseball.

Manager Selee will have a rough road to hoe this season to build up the Boston team, and I doubt if this modest manager will ever again be as lucky in picking up clever young talent as in the past, when he made several successful deals without having seen the men work.

Selee has the knack of keeping the players good-natured, and this will count for much this year of roast from the fans, for it will be a year of bitter likes and dislikes in the three cities where two clubs are located.

The National league boys are now at it, and will not be seen here again until May 2, when they return for a two-months' stay.

The American league will start the ball a-rolling the coming week, and there is much speculation as to what showing they will make in the east. Boston will be at Baltimore and Washington at Philadelphia.

Both Baltimore and Philadelphia are fully ripe for the new order of things, and the boys on the press of those cities are whooping things up in good style — which counts for much at the go-off, or until the teams show weakness, when they gradually become lobsters, and loyalty for local favorites is at a discount.

Jimmy Collins is quite confident that his boys will do well. With a strong list of pitchers he would surely be in it, but there is the question.

The Boston fans have faith in Collins, who is one of the biggest favorites ever connected with the Boston club. His name is mentioned more often than all the other players who have done to the American from

Top, left to right: Fred Mitchell, pitcher; Ambrose Kane; Tommy Dowd, left field.
Middle row: Charlie Hemphill, right field; Freddy Parent, shortstop; Kit McKenna, pitcher; Hobe Ferris, second baseman; Win Kellum, pitcher; Nig Cuppy, pitcher; Buck Freeman, first baseman.
Bottom row: Osee Schrecongost, catcher; Lou Criger, catcher; Larry McLean, first baseman; Jimmy Collins, third baseman; Cy Young, pitcher; Chick Stahl, center field.

this city. I never knew what a favorite this player was until this spring, when even the best friends of the old league can say nothing but good for Jimmy Collins. Some doubt his ability to manage a successful ball team, but wish him the best of luck.

The Boston club has given up all hope of getting back any more of its players and has made no effort in that direction since it landed Vic Willis. Chick Stahl is the only man it would go after.

I am fully convinced that Stahl has made up his mind to keep away from the league; in fact he was the only player at Charlottesville to openly express himself against his old employers, and that he did in no uncertain way. Still I have heard ball players declare themselves in the most vigorous manner and the next day come to terms with the very men they had roasted. It will be interesting to watch the future work of the Boston league officials in this direction, for they are satisfied that every man they hold an option on belongs to them by every right.

The public, however, in this city as well as all over the country, is sick of this jumping, and once the season begins we will see but little of it.

The American league will not be seen here until May 8. By that time the new stand will be ready.

The bleachers are all up, and the finishing touches are going on with the grand stand. The field looks much larger than the South End grounds, and the spectators have a splendid view from every seat. I doubt if there will be more satisfactory ball grounds in this country after they have been completed than these grounds on Huntington av.

The Americans will have a great opening, as the fans are anxious to see the new team.

The boys must now loosen those salary arms, and the fan will again have a chance to hand up that half and quarter to get inside the fence to see the stars of the profession, and a lot of newcomers.

T.H.M.

The Huntington Avenue Grounds

Ron Selter's article in this volume goes into depth regarding the team's first home ballpark. The park was constructed with astonishing celerity. As he notes, plans for the park were completed in February 1901 and groundbreaking was on March 7. The park itself was open for business for the first home game, on May 8. Not everything was ready on time; the *Boston Herald* mentioned that the dressing room for the players (what we now call the clubhouse) was not completed and the players had to change into their uniforms elsewhere.

They had a couple of other problems, too, on the actual opening day—May 8. Using a bit of the parlance of the day, the *Herald* explained, "The Boston players had no easy jump to reach the grounds. They let New York in the morning, did not reach Boston until 2 o'clock, and did not have time to partake of dinner, so they fought their first game on empty stomachs." One wouldn't want a team playing on full stomachs, but

First Spadeful - Baseball dignitaries gather on March 7, 1901 for the groundbreaking ceremony of the construction of the Huntington Avenue Grounds. Prepared to remove the first shovel of dirt at the former Huntington Carnival Lot is Arthur "Hi-Hi" Dixwell, Boston's "Chief Crank", surrounded by the likes of Mike Sullivan, former pitcher and Massachusetts State Senator, the Roxbury Royal Rooters, including Charlie Lavish and Michael T. McGreevy, and *Boston Globe* reporter Timothy Murnane. The park opened two months later serving as the home field for the Boston Americans through the 1911 season.

apparently this train in 1901 didn't have an adequate dining car. And the team didn't even have their own bats, according to the *Boston Post*. Sports that they were, the Athletics allowed the Bostons to use their bats, too.

The team had come from Washington where they had played on May 7. The first ten games of the 1901 season were played on the road. They were:

Date	Location	Score
April 26	Baltimore	Baltimore 10, Boston 6
April 27	Baltimore	Baltimore 12, Boston 6
April 29	Philadelphia	Philadelphia 8, Boston 5
April 30	Philadelphia	Boston 8, Philadelphia 6 (in 10 innings)
May 1	Philadelphia	Philadelphia 14, Boston 1
May 2	Philadelphia	Boston 23, Philadelphia 12
May 3	Washington	Washington 9, Boston 4
May 4	Washington	Boston 10, Washington 2
May 6	Washington	Boston 9, Washington 5
May 7	Washington	Boston 7, Washington 3

Thus, after starting off losing four of the first five games, the Bostons completed their initial road trip with a 5-5 record, coming back to Boston even in wins and losses.

Something else the Americans faced in returning to Boston was the competition. The National League team, established in Boston since 1876, wasn't going to arrange their schedule to accommodate the upstarts, the team which had lured away many of its popular players: manager/third baseman Jimmy Collins, outfielders Chick Stahl and Buck Freeman, and pitchers Cuppy and Lewis, credited with 21 of the Beaneaters' 66 wins in 1900. The 1900 team had four players who hit over .300; Collins and Freeman were two of the four (and Stahl had hit .295.) The two top RBI men on the 1900 Beaneaters had been Collins (with 95 RBIs) and Stahl (with 82.)

The Nationals had opened their 1901 season at home, on April 19, with a definitive 7-0 shutout of the New York Giants. Attendance was reported at 6,501. Five-year veteran pitcher Ted Lewis sat on the Beaneaters bench — but he hadn't yet decided for which team he would play. The team's South End Grounds sported a new fence in left field.

After planting the flag with their home opener, the Boston Nationals went on the road for five games, alternating losses and wins and returning home with a 3-3 record to play games on May 3 and 4 against the Giants (again) and games on May 6 and 7 against the Brooklyns, the Superbas. They split those, too. Both teams thus had 5-5 records before they went head-to-head in Boston for the first time, on May 8. The Nationals had played five home games, drawing a total of 8,000 fans over the four games after Opening Day.

The Americans drew over 11,025 fans to their home opener. The Nationals drew almost precisely half that amount — 5,500. Details regarding attendance in the first eight games where the two teams squared off face-to-face are in the timeline. The scales tilted even more heavily in favor of the new team.

The two games on May 8 were quite different games. The one played by the Nationals at the South End Grounds was a dramatic 7-6 win for the home team which took 12 innings to fight out. Brooklyn scored two in the first, and Boston scored once. In the sixth, Brooklyn scored another, but Boston came back with two to tie it. Then Brooklyn scored yet again in the seventh, taking a one-run lead, only to have Boston score twice in the eighth and take the lead for the first time in the game. Brooklyn scored two in the top of the ninth and the advantage tilted back their way, but Boston scored one to tie it in the bottom of the ninth.

Scene on Beacon Street, Boston, February 1901. In another section of the city, construction was underway on building the Huntington Avenue Grounds.

Boston Nationals Infield of 1900
Clockwise from left, second baseman Bobby Lowe, first baseman Fred Tenney, shortstop Herman Long and third baseman Jimmy Collins. Collins became player/manager for the 1901 Americans.

And Boston won it in the bottom of the 12th on three consecutive singles.

The one played by the Americans at the Huntington Avenue Grounds was one-sided. Indeed, the *Globe* intoned, "The game was one of the poorest ever played in this city by the visiting team….The work of the Quakers was worth about 3 cents on the dollar." While Cy Young held the Athletics scoreless through the first six innings, his Boston Americans scored four times in the first, once in the second, once in the third, three times in the fourth, and twice more in the fifth. Poorly played by the Philadelphians, perhaps (they committed six errors, but Boston made four), but most home crowds take a certain pleasure in seeing their team rolling up a 12-0 lead. The final score was 12-4.

The season was off and running. The Americans won their second home game, too, then ran into a five-game losing streak. It was their longest losing streak of the season, but coming when it did was perhaps not the best timing. They won the final game of their first homestand, for a 3-5 record, and then set out on the road. It was a 6-6 road trip. Their second homestand began with five wins. There was a loss to Detroit, and then Boston won its next nine games. It was a 15-2 homestand. That's the sort of thing that makes an impression. The team concluded their second stint in the city with a 29-18 record after Cy Young's 4-2 win over Washington on June 25. They were just one game out of first place, behind Chicago. The Boston Nationals were in fifth place (24-22), though only four games behind the league-leading Pirates.

The 1901 timeline presented elsewhere in this book provides a look at the complete season through its conclusion and a look ahead to 1902.

Notes

1 *Boston Herald*, January 29, 1901.
2 Dooley's papers were made available to the author by his daughter Katherine Dooley in 2001.
3 *Boston Post*, May 13, 1956.

Some Franchise Firsts—An Overview

By Bill Nowlin

The first spring training and the first home runs

The very first games the Boston Americans played against an opponent preceded the regular season. They came in spring training. The team trained in Charlottesville, Virginia and the team never left its Charlottesville base. The first 12 members of the team showed up on April 1 to begin the first spring training of the franchise and held a light workout on the grounds of the local YMCA. Four more players arrived the following day and that constituted the full contingent, as the plan was to field 14 players on the roster. Though the term "racially diverse" would not be used at the time, there were both black and white spectators at some of the early workouts.

There were a few intrasquad "regulars vs. subs" games and a lot of bad weather. The April 18 *Boston Globe* reported that manager "Collins is disappointed with the south as a training ground." In addition, the *Globe* remarked that the team was "unfortunate in not having any strong team in this section against whom they can play."

The only two teams the club played against opponents were both shutouts, so Boston concluded its first spring training with an aggregate score of 36-0.

4/5 @ Charlottesville VA: Boston 13, University of Virginia 0
4/11 @ Charlottesville VA: Boston 23, University of Virginia 0

The first game was clearly an easy win, but the second one was even more lopsided. It was in the second of the two games that the first home runs in franchise play were hit. Both came in the April 11, 1901 exhibition game against the University of Virginia team, the 23-0 win. The homers were hit by Jimmy Collins and Hobe Ferris.

Tim Murnane covered spring training for the *Boston Globe* and it's likely he who wrote the account: "Everyone but Hemphill hit the ball. Ferris led with a home run and two singles. Close behind came Parent, with two screeching doubles and a single, and Dowd with four singles. Collins lifted the leather over the palings, besides singling."

It's virtually certain that the pitcher who surrendered the first homer was Stearns, since he pitched into the fifth—by which time Boston had already scored at least 17 runs. Stearns was Virginia's first baseman, who "tried his hand at twirling, and the professionals batted him all over the lot" according to the *Washington Post*.

Franchise Firsts

All of the first ten games in franchise history were away games, played on the road. The first two games were April 26 and 27, 1901 against Baltimore (the team that became the New York Highlanders in 1903, later known as the New York Yankees). Boston lost both of its two games against the future Yankees, and lost its first game against Philadelphia as well, before winning for the very first time in a 10-inning game, 8-6, on April 30. Here are some of the firsts rung up *before* the team found its way to its home park, the Huntington Avenue Grounds. All firsts happened in the April 26 game unless otherwise noted.

First franchise game: April 26, 1901 (Baltimore Orioles 10, Boston Americans 6)

Starting pitchers: "Iron Man" Joe McGinnity (Baltimore) vs. Win Kellum (Boston)

Managers: Jimmy Collins (Boston) and John McGraw (Baltimore)

First pitch by a Boston pitcher: Win Kellum

First hit off Boston pitching: leadoff batter John McGraw doubled to right field

First run scored off Boston pitching: "Turkey Mike" Donlin followed McGraw's double with a triple to right. 1-0, nobody out and Donlin on third.

First base on balls issued by Boston pitching: Kellum walked Jimmy Williams, the third batter up in the first inning.

First strikeout: Win Kellum struck out Cy Seymour in the first, the first out recorded by Boston.

First out by a defensive player: Buck Freeman recorded the putout when Jim Jackson followed Seymour's strikeout with an out at first base

First Boston batter: Tommy Dowd, who grounded out to the Baltimore pitcher, 1-3.

First Boston hit: Jimmy Collins, who doubled in the top of the fourth

First Boston run scored: Jimmy Collins

First RBI: Buck Freeman, who singled in Jimmy Collins in the fourth

First multiple-hit game: Collins and Criger both had two hits for three total bases apiece

First double: Collins, in the fourth inning

First triple: in the sixth game of the season, May 2, Chick Stahl tripled in the third inning

First home run: in the fourth game of the year, on April 30 in Philadelphia, Buck Freeman hit a two-run homer off Billy Milligan in the top of the ninth to send the game into extra innings.

First player to hit two home runs in the same game: Buck Freeman (June 1, 1901 in Chicago) — Freeman was the first to do so in the American League.

First Boston batter to work a base on balls: Buck Freeman, in the second inning

First hit by a Boston pitcher: Win Kellum

First extra-base hit by a Boston pitcher: Ted Lewis, on May 2

First Boston pinch-hitter: Larry McLean, who doubled, batting for Kellum in the top of the ninth.

First futile Boston rally: Despite scoring two runs in the eighth and three in the ninth, Boston still lost the game, 10-6.

First double play by Boston: Parent to Freeman, in the bottom of the first

First triple play: August 7, 1901 at Baltimore: Roger Bresnahan of the Orioles hit into a 1-5-2-6-1 triple play. With runners at the corners, he bunted to Boston pitcher Ted Lewis, who looked to third and had the runner, Steve Brodie, caught off the bag. Lewis threw to third baseman Jimmy Collins. In the meantime, the runner on first base had run all the way to third and the batter to second base, but when Brodie was forced back toward third in a rundown, the other runners both had to retreat. Brodie was tagged out at the plate by catcher Osee Schrecongost, who fired the ball to shortstop Freddie Parent. He tagged Jim Jackson at second and then threw to Lewis, who tagged Bresnahan before he could get back to first.

First stolen base: none in the first two games, but Dowd walked and stole second in the first inning on April 29, then stole third and scored on a bad throw to third — all before the second batter completed his at-bat.

First Boston catcher to throw out a baserunner: unclear. It was either April 29 or 30, 1901. Criger got an assist on April 29, but contemporary news accounts don't make it clear how he earned it. He had three assists in the April 30 game, and two of them were throwing out runners. In the third inning, Criger threw out Phil Geier.

First Boston error: Jimmy Collins

First win by a Boston pitcher: Cy Young, beating the Athletics, 8-6, in 10 innings on April 30, 1901, despite giving up 12 hits and walking one.

First loss by a Boston pitcher: Win Kellum pitched a complete game loss, 10-6, on April 26.

First spring training game: April 5, 1901, at Charlottesville VA: Boston 13, University of Virginia 0.

First midseason exhibition game: April 28, 1901 at Weehawken NJ: Boston 5, Weehawken 2.

First extra-inning game: April 30, 1901 at Philadelphia, an 8-6 win in 10 innings.

First postponement: May 5, 1901 due to rain.

Finally, home to Boston

After scoring 79 runs in its first 10 games (but only recording a 5-5 mark on the road), the team played its first home game on Huntington Avenue, on May 8, 1901. Cy Young won a 12-4 victory over the Philadelphia Athletics.

A few other franchise firsts

First ejection: Buck Freeman on May 11, 1901, by umpire John Haskell. Nabbed off second base after doubling in the bottom of the second inning, Freeman "ran at the umpire and grabbed him by the two shoulders." His ejection may have spelled the difference in a 3-2 loss to Washington. Freeman was later fined $10.

First shutout: a 4-0 loss to the Washington Senators, in Boston, on May 15, 1901. It capped the first sweep by an opponent in a series in Boston, as the Americans lost four games in a row to Washington.

First shutout win: May 25, 1901 at Cleveland, a six-hit 5-0 shutout by Ted Lewis.

First sweep of a homestand of more than two games: June 7-11, 1901. Boston swept all five games from the visiting Milwaukee team. Between June 17 and 20, Boston swept five games in a row from the visiting White Sox. In fact, Boston beat Chicago every one of the 10 games that the White Sox played in Boston in 1901. And beat Milwaukee every one of the 10 games the Brewers played in Boston. Chicago won the pennant but Milwaukee came in last.

First postseason game: an exhibition game held on September 30, 1901 at the Huntington Avenue Grounds: Boston Americans 7, Chicago White Sox 5.

Ballparks

The team has only had two home ballparks in its century-plus history, though a handful of home games were played at Braves Field in days long gone by.

Huntington Avenue Grounds

The first home of the Boston Americans (from 1908, the Red Sox) was the Huntington Avenue Grounds. Many ballparks of the era were simply known as "league park" or the "National League grounds," but the ballpark where the Red Sox first began was the Huntington Avenue American League Base Ball Grounds. It was constructed very quickly, on the former Huntington Carnival Lot, with groundbreaking on March 7, 1901. Longtime Boston baseball fan Arthur "Hi Hi" Dixwell turned the first shovelful of dirt. The first home game for Boston was played on May 8, just two months later. Dixwell threw out the first pitch.

Boston already had a major-league team—the National League's Boston Beaneaters. The competition between the Americans and the Nationals was accentuated by the proximity of the two parks. It was approximately 600 feet as the crow flies from home plate at the South End Grounds to home plate of the Huntington Avenue Grounds. It was even closer between the outside perimeters of the two parks. In between lay the tracks of the New York, New Haven and Hartford Railroad and a couple of repair sheds used to service the trains.

When the Red Sox later moved to Fenway Park in 1912, they moved less than half a mile away from the Huntington Avenue Grounds, effectively just across the Muddy River and the Fens.

The architect of the American League, Ban Johnson, had a willing financier in Cleveland magnate named Charles Somers, who not only provided initial funding for the Cleveland Indians but the Boston Americans as well. Somers was active in shipping on the Great Lakes, in coal, and in lumber. Frederick Lieb writes that Somers also advanced $10,000 to Charles Comiskey to help him finance the Chicago White Sox and "was Connie Mack's original backer" in the Philadelphia

Athletics. So Somers had his financial fingers in *four* of the eight original American League clubs. Connie Mack, owner of the Athletics, was involved with the Boston Americans, too; he headed the small group selected to find a suitable site for the AL's Boston franchise. They visited possible locations in Cambridge, Charlestown, and Boston, but finally settled on a site not far from the National League park, the South End Grounds.

The site was owned by Durand Associates and leased to the Boston Elevated Railway Company. Mack's committee (which comprised Hugh Duffy and Tommy McCarthy) asked John Dooley to speak with his partner in the J. R. Prendergast Company, a cotton brokerage. Daniel Prendergast was also a director of Boston Elevated Railway, and Dooley recalls an old newspaperman named Peter Kelley coming to his office on behalf of team owner Charles Somers to ask that Prendergast help convince the railway company to accept a ballpark on the site. Dooley says he prevailed upon Prendergast to have the Elevated accept the offer of $5,000 for the rights to use the land. It was Connie Mack who signed the lease on the Huntington Avenue land.

John Dooley was involved in many Boston baseball booster organizations, from the Royal Rooters to the Winter League to the Half Century Club and, finally, the Bosox Club. He was father to loyal and longtime devoted Red Sox fan Lib Dooley.

To say the site was unimproved was an understatement. It was, in the words of Ed Walton, "no more than an expansive wasteland made up of heavily weeded bumps and lumps." It had been used as a circus lot—even the temporary home to Buffalo Bill's traveling Wild West Circus—when a show would come to town. There was a fairly large pond on the property that children would splash into during summer months from a number of chutes they would slide down, as a water slide. In the winter, of course, people could ice skate there, but this was no high society skating pond. The area was largely bounded by rail yards, a huge Boston Storage Warehouse behind the length of the left-field bleachers, some stables, breweries, and a pickle factory. The United Drug Company was situated near enough to the park that one could often smell the chemicals at work. Oddly, perhaps, the opera house was across the street.

The park had a very large footprint. It seated around 9,000 fans at first; more seating was added in later years. On the busiest days, several thousand more simply watched from the field itself, standing behind ropes, necessitating a change in ground rules for the day. Typically, a fair ball hit into the crowd was ruled a double, but the rules did vary some from day to day. It was 350 feet to the left field corner, 440 feet in left-center field, and some 530 feet to straightaway center. Right field was close, though, just 280 feet down the line. An expansion in 1908 pushed the right-field fence out to 320 feet, but took center field out to a staggering 635 feet. After terming it "the most mis-shapen of all the big league ballparks," Michael Gershman further emphasized the unusual center field as "the most challenging in major league history, since it featured hip-high weeds and was dotted with slippery patches of sand left over from the circus. In addition to being vast, center field sloped uphill and was made even more treacherous by the presence of a sizable tool shed in deep center." The shed was in play, though by the time any ball might have traveled that far, the batter would surely have himself an inside-the-park home run. [Gershman, *Diamonds*, p. 70]

A statue of Cy Young is positioned today on the Northeastern University campus on the very spot understood to be where the pitcher's rubber had been, facing toward home plate some 60 feet, six inches away.

The field was indeed a rough one, and Philip Lowry's *Green Cathedrals* also noted the "large patches of sand in the outfield where grass would not grow." The facility itself was striking, "built with expanded metal and roughcast cement, with a light grey tone. The roof rested on columns 28 feet in the air, hipped on all four sides," in the words of Alan E. Foulds, who quoted the *Boston Globe* as saying the structure was "covered with granite felting, toned to a soft crimson." The interior was all of pine. There were three sections of grandstands arranged in a semi-circle, each seating nearly 800 people, and large bleachers at each end. A brand new facility, the park lured patrons away from the less-attractive South End Grounds.

There were limitations, though. Gershman quotes an Associated Press article which said the "wooden seats were rickety, soot from trains in neighboring yards filled the area, and the saloon next door was a beacon for bored players — during the games."

It worked, though, and from the very first day, fans flocked to the Huntington Avenue Grounds rather than its older neighbor, the South End Grounds. It didn't hurt that the American League franchise priced its tickets at half-price (25 cents instead of 50 cents), and that Jimmy Collins and several of the National League stars had been lured to the new league.

Huntington Avenue Grounds — firsts before the home crowd

First home game: May 8, 1901 (Boston Americans 12, Philadelphia Athletics 4)

All firsts cited here happened in the May 8 game, unless otherwise noted.

Starting pitchers: Cy Young (Boston) and Bill Bernhard (Philadelphia); Cy Young got the first win.

Managers: Jimmy Collins (Boston) and Connie Mack (Philadelphia)

First pitch: Cy Young

First out recorded: Athletics leadoff batter Jack Hayden, who grounded out to third base, Collins to Freeman.

First strikeout: Cy Young struck out the second batter in the inning, Phil Geier.

First hit: Dave Fultz (a two-out single) off Cy Young in the first inning.

First Boston batter: "Buttermilk" Tommy Dowd

First Boston hit: Tommy Dowd, a first-inning leadoff single to left field

First Boston bunt: Charlie Hemphill, to sacrifice Dowd to second. Hemphill reached safely on a Philadelphia error, one of nine Athletics errors in the game.

First run scored: Tommy Dowd, in the bottom of the first

First RBI: Jimmy Collins, who drove in Dowd with a single

First home run: Buck Freeman, also in the bottom of the first inning, an inside-the-park homer that got by Geier in center. Freeman tripled and singled later in the game.

First triple: Charlie Hemphill in the fourth inning, his first of two triples on the day

First Boston double: Jimmy Collins smacked a double in the bottom of the first inning of the May 9 game.

First hit by a Boston pitcher: Cy Young, singling to lead off the second inning after Boston had scored four runs in the first.

First extra-base hit by a Boston pitcher: Cy Young tripled into the crowd in the fifth.

First double play by Boston: Parent to Ferris to Freeman (6-4-3), in the second inning

First stolen base: Charlie Hemphill (Freeman was caught stealing in the third)

First Boston catcher to throw out a baserunner: Lou Criger threw out Fultz trying to take second base in the top of the first inning.

First Boston error: Buck Freeman, third inning

First run scored off Boston pitching: an unearned run in seventh inning off Young, marring the 11-0 shutout he had going.

First ceremonial first pitch: General Arthur "Hi Hi" Dixwell

Umpire for the first home game: John E. Haskell

First base on balls issued by Boston pitching: none in the first home game, but Nig Cuppy walked one batter in the May 9 game.

First hit batsman: Doc Powers hit by Cuppy on the same date — May 9, 1901.

First wild pitch: Philadelphia pitcher Chick Fraser, also on May 9, 1901.

First crowd to go home disappointed: May 11, 1901, in the third home game for the franchise, Washington beat Boston, 3-2.

First shutout: Washington pitcher Watty Lee on May 15, 1901.

First shutout win for the home team: Cy Young on July 6, 1901, shutting out Washington, 7-0.

First grand slam: the first one hit at Huntington Avenue was hit on July 8, 1902 by Philadelphia's Harry Davis, part of a 22-9 Athletics win.

First grand slam by the Boston Americans: on July 25, 1902, Jimmy Collins hit a ball "to the clubhouse" for an inside-the-park four runs in the fourth off Jack Harper of the St. Louis Browns. The phrase appears not to refer to a particular clubhouse — the Huntington Avenue Grounds clubhouses were underneath the grandstand behind home plate — but to be a generic phrase of the day meaning a very long drive.

First balk: as best we can tell, it came from Boston's Tom Hughes on July 10, 1903.

First ballpark vendor memorialized in print

The first vendor at a Boston American League game memorialized on a newspaper page remains anonymous. Of the May 8, 1901 opening game, the *Boston Globe* noted, "It was a regular holiday attendance and the peanut man was in high glee as he sailed his paper bags among the joyous throngs in the bleachers."

Coda for the Huntington Avenue Grounds

The last game at the Huntington Avenue Grounds was an 8-1 win for Patsy Donovan's Red Sox over the Senators, pitched by Charley Hall before a small October 7, 1911 gate of 840 fans. Carl Cashion was the losing pitcher. The last batter up was Kid Elberfeld. He hit into a force out.

The last run scored (and the last RBI) came on the last home run hit in the park, an inside-the-park home run hit by Boston's Joe Riggert off Charlie Becker in the bottom of the eighth.

The Red Sox began to play at Fenway Park in April 1912. Even though the Huntington Avenue ballpark had only been used for 11 seasons, it was already the oldest park in use in the American League — only because the Tigers played their last 23 games of 1911 on the road, last playing at Bennett Park on September 10.

After the move to Fenway Park, Roger Abrams writes, the Huntington Avenue Grounds ballpark was demolished and the lot on which it stood reverted to occasional use for traveling circuses and shows, such as annual visits by the Ringling Brothers and Barnum and Bailey circus. Abrams reports that the Reverend Billy Sunday, himself a former ballplayer, "built a terracotta brick and steel structure on the field for his evangelical crusades of 1916 and 1917. The new building had a capacity of 18,000 and cost $45,000 to erect. More than 1.5 million people attended Sunday's riveting sermons, almost sixty-five thousand of whom came forward to declare themselves converted."[1]

Notes

1. Roger Abrams, *The First World Series and the Baseball Fanatics of 1903* (Boston: Northeastern University Press, 2003), 181. Incidentally, there was a time that Babe Ruth, Billy Sunday, and the Red Sox were all on the same field. It came on April 4, 1919 when Sunday was holding a tent revival on the property adjacent to the Red Sox spring training site at Plant Field in Tampa. Sunday was invited to throw out the first pitch. Babe Ruth, leading off Boston's second inning, hit a home run off George Smith that measured 508 feet. Ruth later signed the ball and presented it to Sunday. The Babe was not converted.

Charles Somers

by Fred Schuld

Once called the "good angel of the American League," Charles Somers was much more than one of the league's founding members; he was also its principal financier. A shy, unassuming man who made his fortune in the coal business, Somers brought major-league baseball back to Cleveland in 1901, and also helped the junior circuit establish clubs in Chicago, Philadelphia, and Boston. At one point, the free-spending magnate was part-owner of four of the league's eight franchises. "[Somers's] faith in Ban Johnson and his open checkbook were the legs upon which the American League learned to walk," writer Franklin Lewis observed in 1949. "Without them, there would be no American League today." Yet Somers's enthusiasm for the national pastime also led to his downfall, as the magnanimous yet meddlesome owner failed to lift his Cleveland franchise into contention. Bankrupt by the end of his 16-year tenure, Somers was obliged to sell off his biggest star before his creditors forced him out of major-league baseball for good in 1916.

Charles W. Somers was born on October 13, 1868, in Newark, Ohio, the only child of Joseph Hook and Philenia McCrum Somers. Joseph Somers worked in the coal-shipping business, and in 1884 the family moved to Cleveland, where Joseph established the J.H. Somers Coal Company. Under Joseph Somers's stewardship the company became very successful, opening numerous mines in Ohio and Pennsylvania. After attending business school, Charles began working for his father, though he soon ventured out on his own. He later described his first years in the business world this way: "Kept store for my father. Went on the road as a salesman. Got into the coal business on my account. When I could not buy outright attractive mining properties, I managed to obtain them by lease. Kept at it for ten years. Then sold out." At the age of 31 he was worth $1 million. The young millionaire returned to his father's coal operation as general manager.

But the budding coal magnate had bigger dreams, and an avid interest in the national pastime. A fan of the

Charles Somers.

Cleveland Spiders of the 1890s, Somers joined forces with John F. Kilfoyl, a local haberdasher who was interested in reviving major-league baseball in Cleveland after the Spiders were dropped from the National League when it was reduced from 12 teams to eight after the 1899 season. Approached by Ban Johnson, Somers and Kilfoyl bought the Grand Rapids, Michigan, team of the Western League and moved it to Cleveland in 1900. When Somers's father learned that his son was preparing to invest in the new American League, he discouraged him, warning Charles not to associate himself with "such a foolish and unprofitable thing as baseball." Undeterred, Charles disregarded his father's advice.

Kilfoyl became the nominal president of the new club, while Somers served as vice president of both the Cleveland franchise and the American League. Using his quiet leadership and deep pockets, Somers strengthened the fledgling circuit at a critical moment in its history. In the first three years of the American League, Somers loaned or spent close to $1 million on other American League franchises. He helped Connie Mack establish a team in Philadelphia and financed the principal owner, Ben Shibe, with a substantial loan for a new ballpark. Shibe had been worried about investing in baseball in Philadelphia with so much National League opposition, but Somers wired Ban Johnson: "We will cure Shibe of his shyness. Tell Connie Mack to find the grounds and I'll put up the money."

Somers also loaned Charles Comiskey money to build a new grandstand for his ballpark in Chicago, and when the Buffalo franchise was transferred to Boston, he founded the American League team there after no local purchasers came forward. Upon assuming control of the Boston franchise in 1901, Somers temporarily transferred his Cleveland ownership to Kilfoyl. During his two-year stewardship of the Boston Somersets, as sportswriters referred to the team, Somers lured stars Jimmy Collins and Cy Young away from the National League, thereby immediately establishing a strong competitor for the Boston National League team. In 1902, Somers was able to reassume his co-ownership of the Cleveland franchise after selling his Boston interests to Henry J. Killilea, a Milwaukee lawyer.

During the Somers era, the Cleveland Naps, as they were known after their manager and star second baseman Nap Lajoie, annually boasted one of the league's most talented rosters. In addition to Lajoie, the Naps were anchored by stars such as Bill Bradley, Elmer Flick, Addie Joss, and Joe Jackson. Yet a frustrating string of injuries and bad luck prevented the Naps from winning the pennant, and as the disappointing seasons mounted for the franchise, Somers became more actively involved in the club's day-to-day operations. In mid-1910, Kilfoyl sold his interest in the club, leaving Somers as the team's sole owner.

During the next six years, Somers earned a reputation as one of the game's most meddlesome owners, as the Cleveland franchise cycled through six managers from 1909 to 1915, but finished with a winning record only

A more dapper Somers.

twice. In 1912 Somers drew the ire of his players when he traded the team's popular manager, George Stovall, to the St. Louis Browns and replaced him with Harry Davis. Davis never had a chance to succeed with his disgruntled players. With the team in sixth place on September 1, Davis resigned and Somers hired 28-year-old center fielder Joe Birmingham as his playing manager.

The club's nadir came in 1914, when Cleveland finished in last place with a record of 51-102, and manager Birmingham's authority was publicly challenged by former manager Lajoie, who had resigned from that post in 1909 but continued as the team's second baseman. The following year, Somers sold Lajoie to Philadelphia and a poll by the sportswriters christened the franchise the Indians, but the changes did not bring success. After the Indians got off to a slow start, Somers ordered Birmingham to play right fielder Joe Jackson at first base, a move the manager resisted. Somers also criticized many of Birmingham's in-game decisions, declaring that the manager was using the hit-and-run too much and not bunting enough. "I own the club and its success means much to me, probably more than any other man in Cleveland," Somers told a reporter. "That being so, why should I not take an interest in its management and offer a word of advice now and then when I thought such advice was needed." Twenty-eight games into the 1915 season, Somers forced Birmingham's resignation and replaced him with Lee Fohl, but the disheartened club continued to struggle, finishing in seventh place.

Despite the club's on-field failures during this period, the franchise also enjoyed a few triumphs. In 1909, Somers renovated dilapidated League Park, replacing the old wooden structure with a steel-and-concrete edifice. In 1911 he successfully petitioned the Ohio General Assembly to allow Sunday baseball, making Cleveland the third American League franchise (following St. Louis and Chicago) to host legal Sunday baseball. In 1912, Ernest Barnard, Somers established the first farm system in baseball history, with franchises in Ironton, Ohio; Waterbury, Connecticut; Toledo; New Orleans; and Portland, Oregon. Perhaps because the venture did not prove a success (although the system did eventually produce pitchers Jim Bagby and Stan Coveleski), Banard and Somers's invention was largely ignored, until Branch Rickey introduced the modern farm system with the St. Louis Cardinals in the 1920s.

By then, however, Somers had long since departed the major-league scene. Financial difficulties proved to be the undoing for this self-made millionaire. An economic downturn in 1914 caused his coal business and lake shipping investments to lose large amounts of money. It was bad timing for Somers, who also had to pay his players higher salaries to compete with the Federal League. Making matters even worse, the Indians finished dead last in the standings and at the turnstiles that year. In January 1915, with Somers owing debts of $1.75 million, a consortium of his creditors took control of the Indians and his minor-league clubs, though leaving Somers nominally in charge of team operations. Desperate for money, in August 1915 Somers traded Joe Jackson to Chicago for three players and $31,500 cash, but the infusion of money was not nearly enough to pay his debts. After the season, the bankers gave Somers an ultimatum: "Get rid of the ballclub or we'll get rid of it for you." So early in 1916, Charles Somers, the man whom Ban Johnson would later credit for making "the American League's ambitious dreams become actual realities," was out of major-league baseball.

Somers was divorced from his first wife, Cora, in 1906, and later that year remarried a 22-year-old model, Elsie J. Hubbard. Later divorced again, he spent his post-baseball years with his third wife, the former Mary Alice Gilbert, and an adult daughter, Dorothy, from his first marriage. He died at his island summer home at Put-in-Bay, Ohio, on June 29, 1934, after a lingering illness, and was buried at Lake View Cemetery in Cleveland. At the time of his death, the 65-year-old Somers had rebuilt his personal fortune to more than $3 million.

Note

This biography originally appeared in David Jones, ed., *Deadball Stars of the American League* (Washington, D.C.: Potomac Books, Inc., 2006).

Sources

Lewis, Franklin. *The Cleveland Indians*. (New York: Putnam Books, 1949).

Lieb, Frederick G. *The Boston Red Sox*. (New York: Putnam Books, 1947).

Murdock, Eugene. *Ban Johnson: Czar of Baseball*. (Westport, Connecticut: Greenwood Books, 1983).

Cleveland Plain Dealer, Cleveland Leader, Cleveland News, Cleveland Press. Various issues 1900-1915.

Cleveland Plain Dealer, Cleveland News, Cleveland Press. Obituary articles June 29-30, 1934.

Ban Johnson

by Joe Santry and Cindy Thomson

THE MOST POWERFUL figure of the Deadball Era, Ban Johnson's rise to prominence in the national pastime was as improbable as it was meteoric. Relying neither on athletic renown (his amateur catching career was abruptly cut short by a thumb injury) nor inherited wealth (he dropped out of law school to become a journalist), the talented Johnson maneuvered his way into becoming president of the Western League in 1893, then skillfully transformed the fledgling circuit into one of the most formidable minor leagues of the late nineteenth century. At the turn of the twentieth century, Johnson renamed the Western League the American League, declared major league status, and then succeeded in challenging the one-league supremacy of the National League. Johnson's triumph marked a turning point in baseball history, cementing the modern two-league system and setting the stage for the unparalleled financial successes of the coming years.

The catalyst for these momentous changes was a jowly, arrogant man whose outward demeanor seemed so cold, so unsympathetic, that one observer suggested Johnson had been "weaned on an icicle."[1] Autocratic and humorless, Johnson almost single-handedly administered the American League during his tenure, drafting schedules, signing players and shifting franchises as he saw fit. Following the peace agreement with the National League in 1903, Johnson also became the most powerful force on the three-man National Commission that oversaw the sport, in the process making more than his share of enemies among the ownership ranks in both leagues. To writer Bob Considine, Johnson was "a ruthless dreamer who lived and died believing that baseball was perfected in order to serve him as a gigantic chess board on which to move his living pieces."[2] Yet there could be no denying his enduring impact on the sport. "His contribution to the game," Branch Rickey once observed, "is not closely equaled by any other single person or group of persons."[3]

Byron Bancroft Johnson was born in Norwalk, Ohio, on January 5, 1864, the fifth of six children of Alexander Byron and Eunice C. Fox Johnson. Shortly after Ban's

Ban Johnson, ca. 1910.

birth, the Johnsons moved to Avondale, Ohio—then a Cincinnati suburb, though today it is part of the city—where A.B. Johnson served as a prominent school administrator. The elder Johnson, who hoped his son would continue the family lineage of educators and ministers, was irritated when Ban ignored his studies to run off to play baseball as a youth. After graduating from preparatory school, Ban showed a lack of focus in his studies, bouncing from Oberlin College to Marietta College to the University of Cincinnati Law School, where he would remain for less than two years. At Marietta, the big, sturdy Johnson gained a reputation as a fearless catcher on the school team, manning his position without a glove, mask, or chest protector. Not surprisingly, a thumb injury ended his baseball career. At the time of the injury, his experience consisted of a handful of games with the semipro Ironton, Ohio team while on vacation from school.

When Johnson dropped out of law school midway through his sophomore year in 1886 to take a job as sportswriter at the Cincinnati Commercial Gazette at $25 a week, his father hit the roof. The paper's legendary editor, Murat Halstead, was finally able to convince Ban's father that journalism was an honorable profession. When sports editor O. P. Caylor left the Cincinnati paper to take a similar position in New York, Halstead named Johnson to the job.

Johnson soon earned a reputation for his knowledge of sports and willingness to speak his mind. From the beginning, he didn't back down from volatile topics of the day. For example, he was a champion of the Players League in 1890, which alienated, among others, Indianapolis Hoosiers owner John Brush. However, his strong opinions won him the friendship of others, such as star first baseman Charles Comiskey, who had joined the Players League.

When the Players League folded after 1890 and the American Association dissolved into the National League the following year, a new circuit, the Western League was created in 1892. The progressive new league was the brainchild of Jimmy Williams, a Columbus, Ohio, attorney. Williams was one of the founding fathers of the American Association and the minor league International Association and was named president-secretary-treasurer of the new league.

The circuit got off to a shaky financial start, however, and Williams was forced to close down the league in July, 1892. In the fall of 1893, members of the disbanded league sought to rekindle the circuit, but Williams begged off, claiming he could no longer take charge of keeping the league afloat financially. Comiskey, remembering his old friend, suggested Johnson to committee members Denny Long of Toledo and James Manning of Kansas City. That November, Ban Johnson was named President-Secretary-Treasurer of the Western League and given a salary of $2,500 a year.

In order to boost league attendance, Johnson crusaded against rowdiness in the league, supporting his umpires with better pay and backing up their rulings on the field with stiff penalties for bad behavior. Under

L to R: Ban Johnson, Massachusetts Lt. Gov. Curtis Guild, and Gen. Charles Taylor, publisher and owner of the Boston Globe, Opening Day at the Huntington Avenue Grounds, April 18, 1904.

Johnson's able stewardship, the league became more profitable over the rest of the 19th century. In 1897 the circuit drew nearly one million fans, with the top clubs in Kansas City, Milwaukee, and St. Paul drawing better than some National League franchises.

When the National League voted to scale down from twelve to eight teams prior to the 1900 season, Johnson saw his big opportunity. Shifting the St. Paul club to Chicago and the Columbus franchise to Cleveland, he changed the league's name to the American League. The following year, Johnson declared his organization a major league and abandoned the circuit's western roots, moving franchises into National League territories in Boston and Philadelphia, as well as Baltimore and Washington, cities the National League had abandoned the year before.

The newly named American League waived the National League's $2,400 salary cap and enticed 111 players from the National League to jump to the new venture, including top stars Cy Young, Napoleon Lajoie, and John McGraw. Before the 1902 season, Johnson transferred the Milwaukee club to St. Louis to compete head-to-head with the Cardinals, and continued his raid on National League rosters, coming away with more big name players, including sluggers Ed Delahanty, Jesse Burkett, and Elmer Flick. The results were impressive: in 1902 the American League outdrew the National

League by more than 500,000 fans. In the four cities home to franchises in both leagues, the upstart American League outdrew the National League in all of them by wide margins.

Clearly outmatched, the hapless National League owners finally sued for peace following the 1902 season, and the resulting truce between the two leagues reaffirmed the principle of the reserve clause and the sanctity of contracts. A three-man National Commission was appointed to settle disputes, with Johnson, the National League president, and Cincinnati Reds executive Garry Herrmann, a friend of Johnson's, picked to chair the new governing body. While Herrmann was hardly Johnson's puppet, as he is often portrayed, his close relationship with the American League president did help Johnson to cement his power.

As chief executive of the American League, Johnson extended his efforts to stamp "rowdyism" out of the game. Supporting his umpires with a firm hand, Johnson swiftly punished players and managers who crossed the line. Johnson's tactics were not always successful. When Johnson and Baltimore manager John McGraw clashed over the skipper's unsportsmanlike behavior on the diamond during the 1902 season, McGraw jumped to the New York Giants and took many Orioles with him. Baltimore was able to complete the season only because owners from the other AL teams contributed players from their rosters. After the 1902 season, Johnson moved the Orioles to New York, where they would in time become the most successful franchise in the history of the sport.

The American League grew and prospered under Johnson. He dealt with each problem with a firm hand. Whether it was the Tigers striking over Ty Cobb's suspension in 1912 or floating loans to teams to strengthen the league, the obstinate Johnson usually got his way. He became so powerful he even changed the outcome of the 1910 batting race when the results did not suit him.

But it was Johnson's arrogant manner and dictatorial inclinations, which eventually led to his downfall. During the last five years of the Deadball Era, four controversial rulings paved the way for the demise of the National Commission and fractured the ownership ranks of the American League into pro-Johnson and anti-Johnson camps.

In 1915, the National Commission ruled that George Sisler was the property of the American League's St. Louis Browns. As a 17-year-old, Sisler had signed a contract with the Akron club of the Ohio-Pennsylvania League. Akron was part of the vast farm system of Bobby Quinn and the Columbus Senators of the American Association. Sisler decided instead to attend the University of Michigan.

While in college, Sisler's contract was transferred to the parent club and Quinn sold it to the Pittsburgh Pirates. Sisler's coach at Michigan was Branch Rickey. Rickey became the manager of the Browns in 1913, and when Sisler was ready to turn pro, Branch represented the youngster in a legal battle to sign a contract with St. Louis. Rickey's argument was that because Sisler

Charles Somers with Ban Johnson.

Ban Johnson seems to enjoy the moment, ca. 1922.

was a minor when he signed the Akron contract, his father's signature was required to make the contract binding. Johnson and Herrmann agreed, and Sisler became a Brown.

Barney Dreyfuss, owner of the Pirates, cried foul and vowed to destroy the National Commission. Cubs owner Charles Murphy, disgruntled after a Commission decision, was quoted by I.E. Sanborn in the Sporting News as saying he wanted the entire commission disbanded. His suggestion would later be partially fulfilled. Sanborn claimed that Murphy wanted, ". . . a non partisan, none [sic] baseball body of three or five men, among them an ex judge or two, appointed for life to adjudicate all the disputes now coming before the commission."[4] It was the first nail in the coffin.

In 1917, the next nail was driven when Atlanta of the Southern Association sold pitcher Scott Perry's contract to the Braves. Perry jumped the team to play semipro ball. The National Commission ruled that Atlanta could resign Perry for $2,000. The Crackers then sold the journeyman pitcher to the A's. When Boston objected, the National Commission awarded Perry's contract to Philadelphia. Once again, the American League had won a contract dispute, leaving some to wonder if the National League could ever win a case brought before the Commission.

Contract dispute number three came before Johnson in 1919, when the American League president awarded pitcher Jack Quinn to the Yankees instead of the Chicago White Sox. Johnson's action effectively ended the life-long friendship with his drinking buddy Comiskey. Gradually over the years, the men who had shared the same Chicago office for nearly two decades became bitter enemies.

Later that season, star pitcher Carl Mays of the Boston Red Sox jumped the team and refused to return. The Red Sox traded Mays to the Yankees after Johnson ruled that Mays first had to return to Boston and serve a suspension before he could be traded. The Yankees owners Jacob Ruppert and Tillinghast Huston got a temporary restraining order allowing Mays to pitch for New York. Divided over the issue, the league split into the "Loyal 5" (St. Louis, Philadelphia, Cleveland, Detroit, and Washington) versus the "Insurrectionists" (New York, Boston, and Chicago). The Insurrectionists controlled the five-man Board of Directors and stripped Johnson of much of his power.

The owners met, voted in a new board, and reinstated Johnson. The New York owners then bombarded Johnson with lawsuits. Late that year things got so ugly that the Insurrectionists gave the league a one-week ultimatum. If an agreement could not be reached, the Yankees, Red Sox and White Sox would join a 12-team National League. The twelfth team would be the first of the Loyal 5 to jump. If no team moved, the National League planned to place a team in Detroit. Finally, Frank Navin, the Detroit owner, brokered a peace agreement, albeit a tenuous one. Johnson now was required to answer to the owners.

A few months later a story broke centering on suspicion that Comiskey's Chicago White Sox had thrown the 1919 World Series to gamblers. Johnson took some pleasure over his former friend's embarrassment. But when he tried to ride in and save the situation, the owners balked. To restore integrity to the game, baseball's magnates decided to replace the National Commission with an all-powerful commissioner.

Judge Kenesaw Mountain Landis was chosen for the position. Landis had limited baseball experience, but he was every bit as stubborn as Johnson, who opposed Landis's appointment. Over the next several seasons, Johnson had little interaction with Landis, concerning himself solely with league matters.

But in 1927, enraged that his authority had been undermined by Landis in the Ty Cobb-Tris Speaker gambling scandal, Johnson locked horned with the commissioner. In response, the judge gave an ultimatum to the owners, Johnson or Landis. The American League owners voted 7-1 to strip Ban of his powers, but allowed him to retain his title. Phil Ball of the Browns was the lone dissenting vote.

After three meetings on July 8, 1927 at the Belmont Hotel in New York, a sick and sullen Johnson passed his scribbled resignation through his hotel door to Ruppert. His resignation would take effect at the end of the season.

Johnson was still owed $320,000 for the balance of his contract running eight more years, but he refused to take any money for work not performed. As Branch Rickey once said, "The making or amassing of money was not part of Ban Johnson's life. He lived for the American League and the game of baseball."[5]

Ban and his wife of over 30 years, Jane Laymon, retired to Spencer, Indiana. Their marriage had not produced any children. His retirement years were spent fund raising for Marietta College and promoting baseball in Mexico. In his final interview, Johnson stated that major league baseball should extend coast-to-coast. Even near the end of his life, he was still 25 years ahead of his time.

Johnson died of diabetes on March 28, 1931 in St. Louis. He was buried in Riverside Cemetery, in Spencer.

Note: An earlier version of this biography originally appeared in David Jones, ed., *Deadball Stars of the American League* (Washington, D.C.: Potomac Books, Inc., 2006).

Sources

Appel, Marty and Bert Goldblatt. *Baseball's Best - The Hall of Fame Gallery*. McGraw-Hill Book Company, 1974

Barrow, Edward Grant with James M. Kuhn. *My Fifty Years in Baseball*. Coward-McCann, Inc., 1951

Hubbard, Donald. *The Red Sox Before The Babe*. McFarland and Company, Inc., Publishers, 2009

Lewis, Franklin. *The Cleveland Indians*. G.P. Putnam's Sons, 1949

Lieb, Fredrick G. *The Boston Red Sox*. G.P. Putnam's Sons, 1947

Murdock, Eugene C. *Ban Johnson, Czar of Baseball*. Greenwood Press, 1982

Santry, Joseph M. *Grazing Through Columbus Baseball*. 2004

Seymour, Harold. *Baseball - The Golden Age*. Oxford University Press, 1971

Seymour, Harold. *Baseball - The Early Years*. Oxford University Press, 1960

Spink, J. G. *Judge Landis and Twenty-Five years of Baseball*. Thomas Y Crowell Company, 1947

Stout, Glenn and Richard Johnson. *The Red Sox Century*. Houghton Mifflin Company, 2000

For this biography, a number of contemporary sources, especially those found in the subject's file at the National Baseball Hall of Fame Library were used.

Notes

1 The identity of this observer is unknown.

2 "Mr. Mack" *Life Magazine*, August 9, 1948, page 95.

3 Branch Rickey with Robert Riger, *The American Diamond: A Documentary of the Game of Baseball* (New York: Simon and Schuster, 1965), p.23

4 *The Sporting News*, January 18, 1912

5 Branch Rickey with Robert Riger, *op. cit.*

Huntington Avenue Baseball Grounds
Boston AL: 1901-11

By Ron Selter

BEFORE THE 1901 season the ballpark called Huntington Avenue Baseball Grounds was built for the AL Boston franchise (the team, later called the Red Sox, was known for the first seven seasons as the Boston Americans). The ballpark site was located at Huntington and Rogers Avenues, in the Roxbury section of Boston, and was just North, across the railroad tracks and yards, from the National League's Boston park, the South End Grounds. The Huntington Avenue site had previously been used as a temporary location for carnivals and traveling circuses, and as a result the area was dubbed the Huntington Carnival Lot.[1] The site was leased by Charles Somers, who in addition to being the owner of the Cleveland franchise in 1901, was the financial backer of the Boston American League entry.[2]

The story of the selection of the site and the acquisition of the lease is told in Bill Nowlin's recent book *Red Sox Threads*:

> Connie Mack, owner of the Athletics, was involved with the Boston Americans, too; he headed the small group selected to find a suitable site for the AL's Boston franchise. They visited possible locations in Cambridge, Charlestown, and Boston, but finally settled on a site not far from the National League park, the South End Grounds. The site was owned by Durand Associates and leased to the Boston Elevated Railway Company. Mack's committee (which comprised Hugh Duffy and Tommy McCarthy) asked John Dooley to speak with his partner in the J. R. Prendergast Company, a cotton brokerage. Daniel Prendergast was also a director of Boston Elevated Railway, and Dooley recalls an old newspaperman named Peter Kelley coming to his office on behalf of team owner Charles Somers to ask that Prendergast help convince the railway company to accept the site. Dooley says he prevailed upon Prendergast to have the Elevated accept the offer of $5,000 for the rights to use the land. It was Connie Mack who signed the lease on the Huntington Avenue land.

To say the site was unimproved was an understatement. It was, in the words of Ed Walton, "no more than an expansive wasteland made up of heavily weeded bumps and lumps." It had been used as a circus lot—even the temporary home to Buffalo Bill's traveling Wild West Circus when a show would come to town. There was a fairly large pond on the property that children would splash into

Aerial panoramic view spanning the Huntington Avenue Grounds in a 1911 game against the Detroit Tigers. Fans ring the outfield in front of the packed grandstands forming a human fence. The South End Grounds where the Boston Rustlers (Braves) played is visible above the upper right field stands.

during summer months from a number of chutes they would slide down, as a water slide. In the winter, of course, people could ice skate there, but this was no high society skating pond. The area was largely bounded by rail yards, a huge Boston Storage Warehouse behind the length of the left-field bleachers, some stables, breweries, and a pickle factory. The United Drug Company was situated near enough to the park that one could often smell the chemicals at work.³

Plans for the park were completed in February 1901, and called for a covered grandstand and uncovered bleachers located down the first and third base lines. Total seating capacity was to be 9,000 patrons.⁴ Groundbreaking for the park was March 7, 1901. The structure of the grandstand was built with expanded metal and roughcast concrete.⁵ The rest of the park was built of wood, and the roof rested on 28 foot columns. There were four entrances to the park—two on Huntington Avenue and two on Rogers Avenue. One of the two entrances on Huntington Avenue, the one

Fans approaching this Huntington Avenue entrance to the Grounds and those exiting a carriage ponder purchasing 5 cent bottles of Dr. Swett's Root Beer. A large crowd is inside the park, with fans also seated on the fence running along entrance path.

near the left-field corner, was the access point for a wide walkway into the park which was at an angle to both the left-field foul line and the Huntington Avenue fence. This diagonal walkway thus limited the left-field distance and made the left-field dimension necessarily less than the distance from home plate to the Huntington

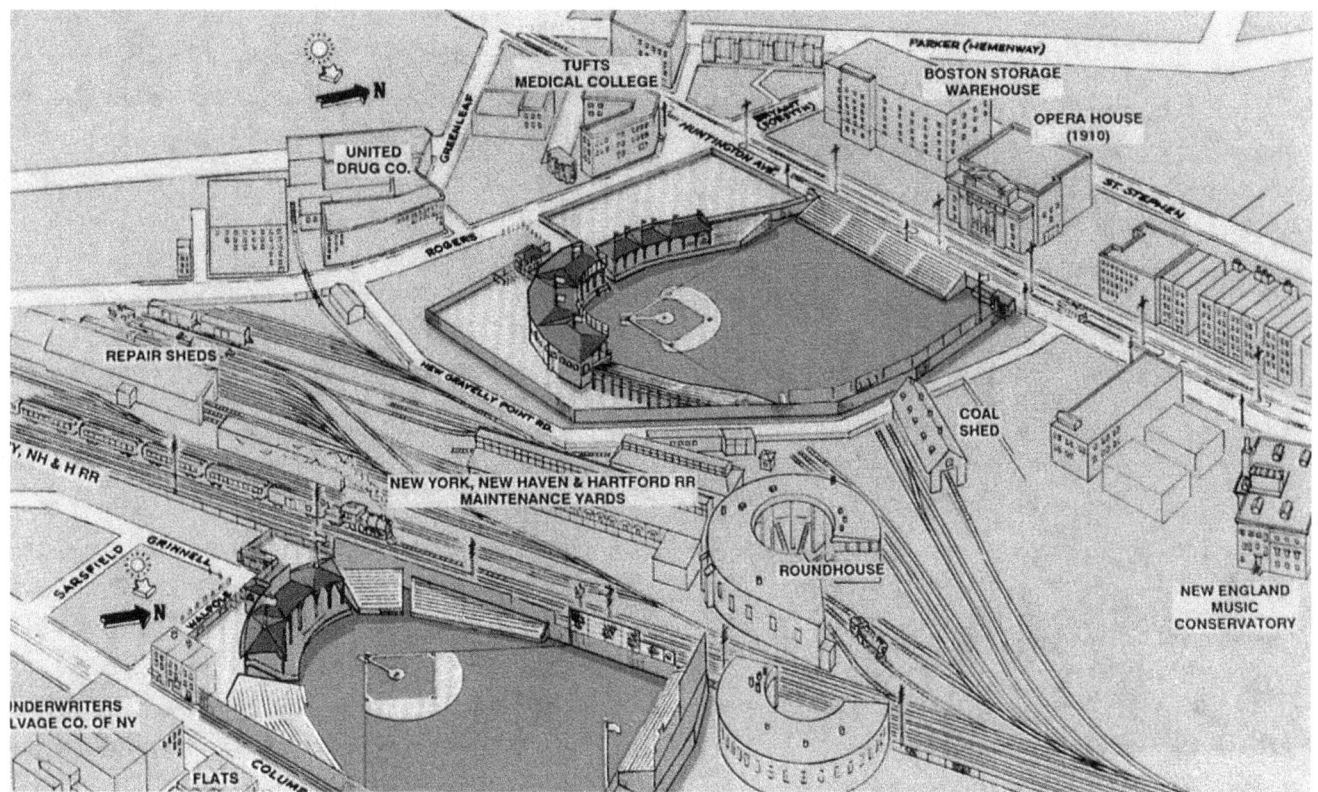

Close Competition - Not only did the newly formed Boston team of the American League lure away five popular players from the hometown National League squad, they also built their ball field across the railroad tracks from the Boston Beaneaters' (Braves) South End Grounds III (bottom, left-center). The adjacent parks were the closest in the big leagues.

Avenue fence. There was a sloping embankment in left field in front of the Huntington Avenue fence that started about 50 feet in front of the fence and was used to accommodate standee overflow crowds. At the time of the 1901 opening of the park, there were no stands or bleachers in the outfield. The grandstand and home plate were in the southwest corner of the park site. An odd feature of the park was a large in-play tool shed located in center field. In addition there was an in-play scoreboard mounted above the fence in right-center field.

After the 1904 season, a rectangular set of bleachers was added in left field.[6] These bleachers ran from a short distance left of the center-field corner to nearly the junction of the entrance walkway fence and the Huntington Avenue fence. These bleachers did not, because they could not, run all the way to the left-field foul line. These bleachers consisted of 14 rows of seats, and had a low fence in front, and this last feature contributed to a number of bounce home runs into the left-field bleachers starting with the 1905 season. The addition of these left-field bleachers increased seating capacity by an estimated 3,500 seats. According to the *Boston Globe*—the park's total capacity, reported as 9,000 when the park opened in 1901, was now surprisingly reported to be about 17,000. The next change to the ballpark was before the 1909 season. A 1909 game account by the writer for the *Chicago Tribune* included the observation, "President Taylor (of the Boston Red Sox) improved the park—new bleachers in CF, and moved the press box to the roof".[7] There was no mention of any increase in seating capacity. The next expansion was before the 1910 season and involved the extension of the third-base bleachers into fair territory in left field. This new section of seating crossed the left-field foul line at about a 45-degree angle and extended to within 20-25 feet of the pre-existing left-field bleachers. Having two set of bleachers referred to as left-field bleachers starting with the 1910 season, led in the newspaper game accounts to numerous ambiguous references to home runs hit into the "left-field bleachers".

The Red Sox stayed at Huntington Avenue Grounds until the end of the 1911 season, when they moved into one of the first classic ballparks—Fenway Park. The Red Sox took the sod with them from Huntington Avenue Grounds to use in the infield at Fenway Park.

The Basis of the Park's Configurations and Dimensions

Unlike the case with many other early Deadball Era ballparks, there is no shortage of dimensional data for Huntington Avenue Baseball Grounds. The problem is that the available dimensional data have the unfortunate characteristic of being in substantial disagreement. The configurations and dimensions shown below are in part estimates and in part are based on park diagrams. Where possible, ballpark photos have been used to confirm or disprove reported dimensions. The listed outfield dimensions for Huntington Avenue Grounds were taken from *Green Cathedrals*.[8] They are:

1901 LF 350, LC 440, CF 530, RF 280
1908 LF 350, LC 440, CF 635, RF 320

The original plans for the building and the configuration of Huntington Ave Grounds, as reported in the *Boston Globe*, included a park diagram and outfield dimensions.[9] This article and diagram gave the park's dimensions as LF 350 feet, CF 530 feet, and RF 320 feet. One limitation of this diagram is that the diagram did not extend to the right-field fence. The diagram ends in left-center field at the 32-degree point along the Huntington Avenue fence, and also ends along the right-field foul line about 75 feet before the right-field corner. The

An anxious fan standing wearing a bowler hat spots a photographer in the stands along the third base line. View of field during this ca 1903 game show outfield walls with grassy incline, designated for standing room crowds during big games.

Boston rooters gathered at the Huntington Avenue Grounds centerfield, on rooftops, and seated on the outfield fence to see the Boston Americans play the New York Highlanders (Yankees) in a pivotal doubleheader in 1904. Boston went on to clinch the pennant from New York on the last day of the season.

alignment of the right-field fence was derived from a 1904 photo in the *Boston Globe*.[10]

In this photo, the fence at the back of the angled first-base bleachers extends, at an angle of noticeably more than 90 degrees to the foul line, into fair right field for about 30-40 feet. At this point there is a kink in the fence to the left as one moved away from the right-field corner. A second photo of the park, taken for the 1903 World Series, also shows the right-field fence from the foul line to past the kink.[11] The right-field fence beyond the kink, to meet the left-field fence at the center-field junction (at a home plate-center field distance of 530 feet), must have been aligned at 95 degrees to an extension of the right-field foul line. A new diagram on a larger scale was drawn using all of the above data. All subsequent ballpark dimensions, were derived using this diagram.

The 1908 center-field distance of 635 feet, listed in *Green Cathedrals*, can only have been correct if the park was expanded towards the east and the right-field fence realigned at much more than 95 degrees to the foul line. In addition, as the center-field bleachers were added for the 1909 season, the center-field dimension of 635 feet could have existed for only that one season.

The 1901 right-field dimension of 280 feet listed in *Green Cathedrals* bears closer examination. In the seven seasons that the Huntington Ave Grounds right-field dimension of 280 feet was said to be in effect (1901-07), there were a grand total of only four home runs hit over the right-field fence. This works out to be a rate of 0.6 over-the-fence home runs to right field per season. By comparison, the right-field distance at Columbia Park (Philadelphia AL) was 280 feet. At Columbia Park in the 1901-08 seasons, home runs over the right-field fence averaged 9.8 per season — some 16 times the rate of comparable home runs at Huntington Avenue Grounds. Thus, in addition to being contradicted by the 1901 listed right-field dimension, the home run data show that it is most unlikely that the right-field dimension at Huntington Avenue Grounds was ever 280 feet.

The left-field bleachers, built before the 1905 season, were located on the Huntington Avenue Grounds diagram based on a photo and story in the *Boston Globe*.[12] From this photo the left-field bleachers were determined to be 14 rows deep with a narrow walkway in front just behind a short fence. The depth of these bleachers was estimated at 27 feet, at ground level. The front of the bleachers if extended to the left-field foul line would have intersected the foul line at a distance

Fans sit on top of outfield wall at the Huntington Avenue Grounds during a Boston Red Sox - Detroit Tigers game ca. 1910.

of 348 feet from home plate. The horizontal extent of the left-field bleachers was estimated from the photo in the *Boston Globe*. The left end of the bleachers was about 20 feet to the right of the junction of the walkway fence with the Huntington Avenue fence. The right end of the bleachers extended to nearly dead center field.

The park diagram, with the left-field bleachers added to it, was used to estimate the dimensions for the 1905-08 time period for left field and center field (right field was unchanged during the life of the park). The location of the center-field bleachers added for the 1909 season was based on two factors: (1) game accounts of inside-the-park home runs hit "to the flagpole" during the 1910 season—which establishes that the flagpole was still in play, and (2) photos that showed the location of the flagpole to be in front of the right side of the center-field fence. Therefore the center-field bleachers must have been located behind the flagpole. The location and extent of the left-field bleachers, added for the 1910 season by the extension of the third-base bleachers, was based on a photo in *Diamonds*.[13]

The new 1910 left-field distance of 305 was derived from a story in the *Boston Post* where sportswriter Paul Shannon commented that the LF distance at the then new Fenway Park would be 19 feet more than left field at Huntington Ave Grounds.[14] The left-field distance at Fenway Park when it opened in 1912 has been found to have been 324 feet. Adding the third-base bleachers to the park diagram such that they cut the left-field foul line 305 feet from home plate established the location of the front of the bleachers. These bleachers extended about 50 feet past the foul line into fair left field. Park data and dimensions for Huntington Avenue Grounds are shown below:

Dimensions (From Park Diagrams)

Years	LF	SLF	LC	CF	RC	SRF	RF
1901-04	350	388	433	530	412	365	320
1905-08	350	360	402	530	412	365	320
1909	350	360	402	456	412	365	320
1910-11	305	360	402	456	412	365	320

Average Outfield Distances

Years	LF	CF	RF
1901-04	393	470	366
1905-08	370	457	366
1909	370	441	366
1910-11	363	441	366

Fence Heights (from Green Cathedrals and estimated from photos)

Years	LF	CF	RF
1901-04	14	14	14-28*
1905-08	6-14	6-14	14-28*
1909	6-14	6-14	14-28*
1910-11	3-14	6-14	14-28*

* The 28-ft. fence height was only at the scoreboard mounted above the RF fence

Capacity: 9,000 (1901-04), 12,500 (1905-08 est.), 14,000 (1909-11 est.)
Park Size - Composite Average Outfield Distance: 410 (1901-04), 398 (1905-08), 392 (1909), 390 (1910-11)
Park Site Area: 6.3 acres
Deadball Era Run Factor: 102 (Rank: AL 8)

The Impact of the Park's Configurations and Dimensions on Batting

In the park's original 1901-04 configuration, Huntington Avenue Grounds, along with Baltimore's Oriole Park IV, was the largest park in the American League. Unlike today where large parks (adjusted for altitude in the case of Coors Field) are known as pitchers parks, Huntington Avenue Grounds was average or above average in every offense category except doubles (see data in the Batting Park Factors table below).

In 1903 the American League adopted the foul-strike rule—foul balls with less than two strikes on a batter would now be counted as strikes. Despite this rule change which reduced overall batting average in the AL by about 15 points, the home batting average for the 1903 Boston Americans increased from .280 in 1902 to .296 in 1903. The batting average park factor, 98 in 1901, and 97 in 1902, jumped to 108 for 1903. One possible contributing factor is that the negative impact of the adoption of the foul-strike rule affected Huntington Avenue Grounds much less than the other AL ballparks. Another indirect contributing factor was the elimination of Burns Park in Detroit and Oriole Park IV in Baltimore. Unlike in 1902 Burns Park, which was an extreme hitter's park (with a batting average park factor of 116), was not used in 1903. When the Baltimore franchise was transferred to New York, Oriole Park IV (with a 1902 batting average park factor of 108) was replaced by Hilltop Park in New York (1903 batting average park factor of 97). As these two changes made the other American League parks worse for hitters, the batting average park factor for Boston's Huntington Avenue Grounds and the other AL parks increased. However, these two factors are believed to be only partial explanations with no explanation having been found for the entirety of the large increase in the Huntington Avenue Grounds batting average park factor.

The large outfield dimensions at Huntington Ave Grounds turned hits that would have been doubles at other parks into triples and inside-the-park home runs (IPHR). With the generous outfield dimensions in the park's original configuration, nearly all (97 %) of the home runs were IPHR, as over-the-fence (OTF) home runs were rare—there only four such home runs. Despite being the biggest park in the AL, Huntington Ave Grounds managed to post the third-highest home run park factor in the 1901-04 time period (only Washington 1901-03 at 189, and New York 1903-04 at 208 had higher home run park factors).

The effect on batting of the installation of the left-field bleachers for the 1905 season was noticeable, but generally not very substantial. The 1905-09 park factors decreased slightly for batting average, on-base, and slugging. The park factor for doubles increased slightly, while triples decreased (156 to 132) as one would expect with the shorter left field and left-center field dimensions. The small decrease in the batting average, on-base percentage, and slugging park factors may have been due to the poorer batters background that resulted from the new outfield bleachers that extended into center field. One noticeable effect of the installation of the new left-field bleachers was more home runs and more OTF home runs (an impressive sounding 425 % increase in OTF home runs—but still amounting to only four per season), most of which (15 of 21) were of the bounce variety. Thus the left-field bleachers led to the number of bounce home runs increasing from less than one per season (1901-04) to about four per season (1905-08). Nearly all of the bounce home runs hit in the 1905-08 seasons were hit into the left-field bleachers.

For the 1909 season, with the construction of CF bleachers, the proportion of IPHR declined to 58% of the total vs. 82% in 1905-08. The extension of the third-base bleachers into left field starting with the 1910 season led to lower 1910-11 park factors for batting average, on-base percentage, and slugging. The park factor for doubles increased, while the triples park factor decreased (132 to 82), as one would expect with the shorter left-field dimension. At the same time total OTF home runs and OTF home runs to LF increased sharply. OTF home runs (excluding bounce home runs) were 2.0 per season in 1905-09 and 18.5 in 1910-11. OTF home runs to left field went in the same time periods from 1.25 per year to 15 per year.

As would be expected with the shorter left-field and center-field dimensions, the proportion of IPHR dropped again, this time to 47% of the 1910-11 total home runs. In addition the successive changes in configurations led to changes in the distribution by field of IPHR—the proportion to center field increased with each change in configuration. The home run and batting park factor data are shown below in three tables:

Home Runs by Type at Huntington Avenue Baseball Grounds

Years	Total	OTF	Bounce	IPHR
1901-04	158	4	1	154
1905-08	113	20	15	93
1909	31	13	9	18
1910-11	88	47	10	41

Bounce: Bounce Home Runs (a subset of OTF)
IP: Inside-the-Park
OTF: Over-The-Fence (Includes Bounce)

Inside-the-Park Home Runs by Field at Huntington Avenue Baseball Grounds

Years	Total	LF	LC	CF	RC	RF	Unknown
1901-04	154	15	11	69	35	20	4
1905-09	111	7	6	60	20	17	0
1910-11	41	3	1	25	8	4	0

Batting Park Factors at Huntington Avenue Baseball Grounds

Years	BA	OBP	SLUG	2B*	3B*	HR*	BB**
1901-04	101	101	104	71	156	139	105
1905-09	97	98	100	89	109	169	100
1910-11	95	98	98	103	82	191	108

* Per AB
** Per Total Plate Appearance (AB+BB+HP)
The Home/Road data for 1901 is from the Official AL Day-by-Days.

1901 Home/Road at Huntington Avenue Base Ball Grounds

1901 BOS AL		G	AB	H	2B	3B	HR	BB	HP	TPA	BA	OBP	SLUG	2B/AB	3B/AB	HR/AB	BB/TPA
	HOME	69	2347	672	68	67	21	181	26	2554	.286	.344	.399	.0290	.0285	.0089	.0709
	ROAD	69	2519	681	115	37	16	150	22	2691	.270	.317	.364	.0457	.0147	.0064	.0557
	YR	138	4866	1353	183	104	37	331	48	5245	.278	.330	.381				
TBB	YR	138	4866	1353	183	104	37	331	47								
1901 BOS AL OPP		G	AB	H	2B	3B	HR	BB	HP	TPA	BA	OBP	SLUG	2B/AB	3B/AB	HR/AB	BB/TPA
BOS PARK		69	2355	561	56	64	18	144	24	2523	.238	.289	.339	.0238	.0272	.0076	.0571
OTHER PARK		69	2319	617	116	41	15	150	15	2484	.266	.315	.371	.0500	.0177	.0065	.0604
	Total	138	4674	1178	172	105	33	294	39	5007	.252	.302	.355				
TBB	YR			1178			33	294									
1901 BOS AL & OPP		G	AB	H	2B	3B	HR	BB	HP	TPA	BA	OBP	SLUG	2B/AB	3B/AB	HR/AB	BB/TPA
BOS PARK		69	4702	1233	124	131	39	325	50	5077	.262	.317	.369	.0264	.0279	.0083	.0640
OTHER PARK		69	4838	1298	231	78	31	300	37	5175	.268	.316	.368	.0477	.0161	.0064	.0580
											.977	1.002	1.005	.552	1.728	1.294	1.104
										OPC Ratio	.980	1.002	1.004	.585	1.584	1.248	1.090

In the above data TBB stands for Total Baseball.

TPA: Total plate appearances-excludes SF and SH.

Home Run Log 1901 Huntington Ave Baseball Grounds

Date	DH	Batter/Team	Pitcher/Team	Field	Inn	On	Out
5-8		Buck Freeman BOS	Bill Bernhard PHL	CF	1	2	1
6-11		Hobe Ferris BOS	Bill Reidy MIL	CF	8	1	UNK
6-11		Buck Freeman BOS	Bill Reidy MIL	CF	1	1	2
6-11		Charlie Hemphill BOS	Bill Reidy MIL	LC	8	0	0
6-12		Freddy Parent BOS	Ed Siever DET	LC	7	0	2
6-14		Doc Casey DET	Win Kellum BOS	CF	3	0	UNK
6-14		Joe Yeager DET	Win Kellum BOS	CF	3	0	UNK
6-17	1	Buck Freeman BOS	Jack Katoll CHI	CF	1	2	1
6-17	2	Frank Isbell CHI	Cy Young BOS	RF	2	0	0
6-19		Freddy Parent BOS	Roy Patterson CHI	LF	6	1	0
6-20		Billy Sullivan CHI	Cy Young BOS	CF	2	1	UNK
6-21		Erve Beck CLE	Ted Lewis BOS	CF	6	0	1
6-21		Pete Dowling CLE	Ted Lewis BOS	RF	5	0	1
6-22		Chick Stahl BOS	Bill Hart CLE	CF	7	1	UNK
7-3		Buck Freeman BOS	Harry Howell BAL	RF	8	2	UNK
7-4	2	Cy Seymour BAL	Ted Lewis BOS	RC	1	1	2
7-4	2	Jimmy Collins BOS	Frank Foreman BAL	RF	8	1	1
7-4	2	Hobe Ferris BOS	Frank Foreman BAL	RC	8	1	1
7-6		Chick Stahl BOS	Watty Lee WAS	RC	1	0	1
7-10		Harry Davis PHL	Ted Lewis BOS	RF	4	0	UNK
8-9	2	Jimmy Williams BAL	Fred Mitchell	CF	1	1	2
8-10		Steve Brodie BAL	Ted Lewis BOS	CF	2	0	UNK
8-12	1	Chick Stahl BOS	Bill Bernhard PHL	LF	3	0	2
8-19		Chick Stahl BOS	Bert Husting MIL	CF	3	0	2
8-20		Chick Stahl BOS	Pink Hawley MIL	RC	4	2	UNK
8-23		Buck Freeman BOS	Harry McNeal CLE	RC	1	1	2
8-24		Erve Beck CLE	Ted Lewis BOS	RF	7	0	UNK
8-24		Candy LaChance CLE	Ted Lewis BOS	CF	4	0	UNK
8-28		Jimmy Barrett DET	Ted Lewis BOS	RC	7	2	2
9-16	1	Jimmy Collins BOS	Casey Pattern WAS	LF	6	0	UNK
9-16	1	John Farrell WAS	Ted Lewis BOS	RC	1	1	0
9-16	2	Bill Coughlin WAS	George Winter	CF	6	1	UNK
9-23	1	Tommy Dowd BOS	Joe Yeager DET	LF	5	2	2
9-23	1	Kid Gleason DET	Cy Young BOS	CF	6	1	UNK
9-28	1	Tommy Dowd BOS	Bert Husting MIL	UNK	3	0	1
9-28	2	Jimmy Collins BOS	Bill Reidy MIL	UNK	1	0	2
9-28	2	Jimmy Collins BOS	Bill Reidy MIL	RC	5	2	1
9-28	2	Bill Friel MIL	Jake Volz BOS	UNK	6	1	2
9-28	2	Davy Jones MIL	Jake Volz BOS	CF	2	0	UNK

Team Codes:

BAL Baltimore
BOS Boston
CHI Chicago
CLE Cleveland
DET Detroit
MIL Milwaukee
PHL Philadelphia
WAS Washington

Field Codes:

CF Center
LC Left Center
LF Left
RC Right Center
RF Right

DH = Double Header
1 "Morning" Game
2 "Afternoon" Game

Reflecting the large outfield at the Huntington Avenue Grounds, every home run hit at the park in 1901 was an inside-the-park home run. The 1901 configuration at the ballpark was the same for the first four seasons (1901-04). In those seasons, there were 160 HRs in total. Six were over the fence and 154 were IPHR. The ones hit over the fence were clearly the exception.

Fans relax on the right field corner grass at the Huntington Avenue Grounds, ca. 1903.

The dedicated Boston rooters stand along the grassy knoll along the leftfield fence during the October 8, 1904 Boston Americans doubleheader game against the New York Highlanders (Yankees) before a packed crowd of 28,040 fans. In 1905, bleachers were installed in this section to accommodate the overflow crowds.

The crowd leaving the Huntington Avenue Grounds line up in the walkway along the 3rd base line wall, many to board the awaiting Huntington Avenue trolleys after doubleheader between Boston and Cleveland on Bunker Hill Day in 1903.

A Cleveland batter runs toward first during doubleheader at the Huntington Avenue Grounds on Bunker Hill Day in 1903.

The Huntington Avenue Grounds field lined with delivery wagons of the Hotel & Railroad News Co. in 1911. To the left are the covered grandstands along the third baseline. Behind the vehicles, centered and to the right, are leftfield grandstands additions from 1905. These upgrades included a new entry to the park from Huntington Avenue and also provided a spacious ladies' retiring room, two smoking rooms for the gentlemen, and two new refreshment booths. The Boston Storage Warehouse (L) and Boston Opera House (far R) are shown in the background.

The Boston Americans and Washington Senators marching out to centerfield during the 1904 Opening Day ceremonies at the Huntington Avenue Grounds, celebrating Boston winning the first World Series in 1903. Perched above the outfield fence in right field is the Pureoxia Ginger Ale scoreboard. Additional larger scoreboards were added in this area later that year.

Views from the leftfield grandstand area of the Huntington Avenue Grounds infield and surrounding in October 1904

Changes in baseball rules and Huntington Avenue Grounds configurations and dimensions affected batters statistic during the short history of park. Above is an isolated field-level look of 1910 Red Sox players along the third baseline in a panorama of the team and Washington Senators.

This 1904 image of the Huntington Avenue Grounds clearly shows just how expansive was the outfield in the first park where the Red Sox played.

Fans gather in the outfield during the April 19, 1910 Patriots Day Game at Huntington Avenue Grounds. Fans pack the centerfield bleacher seats, erected in 1909.

A Chicago White Sox batter approaches home plate in a 1903 game at the Boston Americans ball field.

Full House - Boston enthusiasts gather in front of the empty first base dugout (far right with white background) for the October 3, 1903 World Series Game against the Pittsburgh Pirates at the Huntington Avenue Baseball Grounds. The players shifted from the dugout to benches and positions along the first base line adjacent to the fans.

Notes

1. Alan E. Foulds, *Boston's Ballparks & Arenas* (Northeastern University Press Boston MA, 2005), 28.
2. *Boston Globe*, January 23, 1901.
3. Bill Nowlin, *Red Sox Threads* (Burlington MA: Rounder Books 2007).
4. *Boston Globe*, February 3, 1901.
5. Alan E. Foulds, op. cit., 32.
6. *Boston Globe*, March 29, 1905.
7. *Chicago Tribune*, September 17, 1909
8. Philip J. Lowry, *Green Cathedrals*, (New York: Addison-Wesley, 1992 ed.), 109.
9. *Boston Globe*, January 23, 1901.
10. *Boston Globe*, September 15, 1904.
11. Eric Enders, *Ballparks Then And Now* (San Diego CA, PRC Publishing Ltd. 2002), 25.
12. *Boston Globe*, March 29, 1905.
13. Michael Gershman, *Diamonds-The Evolution of the Ballpark* (Houghton Mifflin Co., Boston MA, 1993), 100.
14. *Boston Post,* April 9, 1912.

A Fuller Portrait of the First Home Game in Red Sox Franchise History

"The diamond shone in the sun like a great canvas of freshly spread green paint, the uniforms of the home team were as spotless as a just-from-the-wrapper ball and the great crowd seethed with good nature."
– Tim Murnane

NO ONE WOULD know them as the Red Sox until mid-December 1907. They wore blue stockings until the 1908 season. But the May 8 game was the first regular season home game in franchise history. The *Boston Globe* headline read AMERICAN LEAGUE MEN GIVEN ROYAL WELCOME BY 11,500 ROOTERS. Auspicious Christening of Huntington Av. Grounds - Philadelphias Prove Easy Victims — Local Team Strikes A Winning Gait. The story by T. H. Murnane seems worthy of inclusion in this volume:

It was the birth of a major league baseball club for Boston.

Eleven thousand five hundred persons went to dedicate the new grounds on Huntington av and cheer for the members of Capt Collins' team.

The day was an ideal one for sport and the large crowd were the essence of good nature. It was a regular holiday attendance, and the peanut man was in high glee, as he sailed his paper bags among the joyous throngs on the bleachers.

With new grounds, and practically new teams, the lovers of the sport were not too particular about the style of ball played, so long as the home team came out victorious.

The members of the new club who had gained honor in the National league were early recognized and applauded. The welcome to Napoleon Lajoie, the captain of the Athletics, and to Capt James Collins, was the most cordial.

With the welcome hand for the Boston captain came flowers to the home plate; one piece, a wreath of jacqueminot roses on a stand, with a red silk ribbon marked "success," and another a horseshoe five feet high of mixed flowers, mostly yellow jonquils.

The flowers slightly expressed the great regard the lovers of baseball both in the profession and out have for the lad from Buffalo, the greatest third baseman of this or any other age, and as unassuming as the little sprig of maidenhair fern that trailed from the flowery horseshoe.

In the second row of seats in the grand stand, back of the home players, sat Mr Charles W Somers and his charming wife. They had come from Cleveland to see the opening of Mr Somers' new enterprise, and must have thought pretty well of the Boston weather man, who had furnished such perfect conditions for the opening of the American league.

In the crowd were clergymen, business men, professional people, ex-ballplayers, old-time fans, and an army of fresh recruits and many who had not seen a game for years.

People were there from Bangor, Me, Newport, R.I. and about every city between those points, including Col

Panorama of a Boston Americans game at the Huntington Avenue Grounds. An overflow crowd rings the infield and the outfield. Circa 1903.

A near capacity crowd of over 11,000 filled the Huntington Avenue Grounds on Opening Day. Amongst the cheering local diehard fans were the Royal Rooters, a Boston Americans fan club. The Rooters in this 1903 photograph are shown seated in their special designated section in foul ground, providing closer proximity to the action.

Osgood of Lewiston, the sincere friend of the game for 30 years, and as warm a supporter as ever.

The large crowd was handled in an admirable manger by manager Jos. Gavin.

Two tally-ho coaches drove in through the center-field gate and across the field. The first contained Col Thomas F. McCarthy, the famous old ballplayer, and a party of live sports, and the second carried Charley Kelley, Dan Daley and their friends.

The crowd gathered early at the grounds, where the Boston cadet band gave them an excellent concert. Small flags were distributed by Prof Chas. Green among the crowd, and the stars and stripes gave a pretty effect.

A new feature in baseball was the megaphone man, who announced the change of players and other interesting facts that the crowd were anxious to learn.

At the close of a waltz melody three Boston players in white uniforms emerged from the players' dressing rooms and spread out for a little triangle practice. They were the first players to appear, but were not recognized by the crowd and were given but a weak sendoff.

The tallest one was slugger McLean, the six-foot-four catcher, the others were Schreckengost and Jones. These boys will be treated with more warmth when they show their real mettle, as the Boston fan is rather slow to warm up to a new man.

The next man out was "Parson" Ted Lewis. The other players soon followed, among them many who were unknown to the crowd.

The game was one of the poorest ever played in this city by the visiting team. The home team hammered the weak pitching all over the field until the crowd cried to have Bernard [sic] taken out. The home team put up a good all-round article of ball.

The work of the Quakers was worth about 3 cents on the dollar. Even Lave Cross made a bad mess of things. In the outfield Geier and Hayden couldn't judge a fly or stop a grounder.

Cy Young was in the points for the locals and held the visitors down to a few scattered hit for seven innings, when he found the game was a walkover and threw over straight ones to save that good right wing.

In the early part of the game he was serving up curves that made the ball look as small as butterfly eggs to the

Arthur Dixwell throws out the ceremonial first ball. *Boston Globe* illustration, May 9, 1901.

Quakers. Criger was doing some nice work behind the stick, and the crowd thought of that old Cleveland leader, brave Pat Tebeau.

Chick Stahl was given a round of applause when he first went up to the plate. Chick wrenched his side and retired from the game in favor of Jones in the fifth inning. The outfield was soft, and the players often lost their footing.

Hayden opened the game with a slow roller to Collins and was thrown out at first, Geier fanned and Fultz chipped off the first safe hit. A fine throw by Criger nipped Fultz, while headed for second.

Tommy Dowd opened for Boston with a fine single to left. Hemphill bunted to Cross and the ball was fumbled. Stahl sacrificed. Then came Capt Collins with a single and Dowd scored.

Freeman drove a liner to center and thanks to Geier got in a home run. Parent was thrown out by Cross. Criger sent one up to right field, where it was muffed. As Lewis tried for second, he was thrown out.

Lajoie got a fine sendoff when he went to the plate and cracked out a single. Seybold hit to Parent, who with Ferris and Freeman got in a fast double play. Cross was thrown out at first.

Young opened with a single. Down also singled, and Hemphill made it three of a kind. Stahl then flew out to left. Dowd was thrown out in trying for third on the play, and Collins sent a long fly to left.

With two out in the third Bernhardt [sic] got one through Freeman's feet. Hayden doubled when [the word should have been "then] Geier flew out to Ferris.

Freeman opened with a single, only to be thrown out when trying to steal second. Parent got first on Hayden's muff. Ferris singled and Criger put one in a safe spot, scoring Ferris.

Fultz led off with a single in the fourth and Lajoie got one through the infield. Then three men went out on flies and the home team got in three more runs on a fine triple by Hemphill, singles by Stahl and Ferris and a triple by Buck Freeman.

The fifth and sixth were played in quick order, as far as the visitors were concerned at the bat, Bernhardt [sic again] and Saybold [sic] putting in singles with two out.

The home team scored two runs in the fifth on triples by Young and Dowd, the ball going into the crowd. Parent and Criger singled in the sixth, but failed to get past second.

The visitors scored one run in the seventh. Lockhead going to first on Parent's fumble, to second on a put out and home on a single by Hayden. Boston scored one in this inning on a triple by Hemphill and Collins' single.

Larry got his men worked up in the eighth. Fultz and Lojoie singled and jogged home on a fine triple by Saybold [sic]. A long fly allowed the latter to come in.

Each team got in a safe hit in the ninth, but the life had long since left the game.

AMERICAN LEAGUE MEN GIVEN ROYAL WELCOME BY 11,500 ROOTERS.

Auspicious Christening of Huntington Av. Grounds—Philadelphias Prove Easy Victims—Local Team Strikes a Winning Gait.

Boston Globe illustration showing Opening Day 1901.

The same teams play today at the Huntington-av grounds, and Connie Mack promises to wake up his Quakers.

There was what we might call a "period piece" which followed the game story and boxscore in which one "Darkhue White"— a fictional character who spoke in what was once called "Negro dialect" offered his observations on the game. We will not reproduce that text here.

There were some "Echoes of the Game" which offered additional observations on the day, and we will offer those here.

—Bill Nowlin

Echoes of the Game

Everything inside the high fence was as new as this spring's tulip. The diamond shone in the sun like a great canvas of freshly spread green paint, the uniforms of the home team were as spotless as a just-from-the-wrapper ball and the great crowd seethed with good nature.

Friends of Lajoie were up from the Androscoggin, and those of them who knew how to put the proper pronunciation on his name passed it around for the benefit of those who call him "Lay-joy." He left an enduring reputation in Lewiston, but really his team should assemble its better playing qualities, for the game was decidedly too easy for the home club.

Among other new things was the shrinkage in the bags of peanuts and the new style of slam-banging them into the bleachers when a purchaser high up on the benches tossed down a nickel. That was half the fun. Money was thrown away for the sport of seeing the swiftly-thrown bags burst.

Backward as the season is, six straw hats in all the jauntiness of a cocked-on-the-side position, limed up amid the sea of soft felts and hard derbies. In striking contrast was the millinery of the ladies, which, sprinkled amid the black, brown, gray and white somberness of the male head covering, warmed up the interior of the grand stand and seemed to rob the east wind of half its chill.

Just a dash of Tabasco was thrown into the game before the final inning, and the visitors saved themselves from a bad defeat.

Arthur Dixwell, seated down among the scorekeepers and telegraph operators, wafted memory back to the days when sensational plays and close finishes were greeted with cracker snapping "hi hi's."

Baseball in the New Century: Following the Boston Americans in 1901

By Donna L. Halper

It was Tuesday, January 23, 1901, about 1:20 P.M., and a major news story broke: Great Britain's Queen Victoria had died. She had been ill for several days, and her death was not unexpected, but for much of the day people had begun to gather in "Newspaper Row," that part of lower Washington Street where most of Boston's major dailies had their offices; they hoped to confirm what had up until then been only a rumor. The *Boston Herald* claimed to have gotten the story first, and initially there were conflicting reports, causing some confusion at several of the other newspapers: Was she still clinging to life or had she really died? Finally, the story was verified and all of the newspaper bulletin boards confirmed it: The popular queen was dead.[1] Throughout the year the scene would be repeated as breaking news unfolded: When Patrick Donahoe (a leader in Boston's Irish Catholic community and the editor of the *Pilot*) died at age 90 in March, and when President William McKinley was assassinated by an anarchist in September, crowds thronged to Newspaper Row, seeking confirmation and expressing their sorrow.

For the *Herald*, as well as the *Boston Globe*, the *Post*, the *Morning Journal*, and the other newspapers on Newspaper Row, the procedure for spreading any breaking story was the same: As soon as telegraphers received the information, usually transmitted to them in Phillips code (a specialized version of Morse code used by the press), they transcribed it; reporters then began writing the story up for the next edition of the newspaper; a headline was posted on a chalkboard in front of the newspaper's office, as crowds gathered to read the latest information; and if it was a big enough story, newsboys (who waited in Pie Alley, a narrow lane off Washington Street, to pick up the newspapers the moment an "Extra" edition was ready) spread around with copies of the paper, providing all the details to an eager public. Meanwhile, people who were lucky enough to live or work in proximity to Newspaper Row came by on their lunch hour, or whenever they heard that there might be breaking news. Over the previous 15 years, lower Washington Street had become known as a gathering place: For example, crowds could be seen there during presidential elections, and partisans booed or cheered as the results were posted. Crowds also came to

Boston Journal office, ca. 1909.

Boston Globe building on Washington Street ca. 1906.

Newspaper Row during important sporting events. In 1897, when boxer Gentleman Jim Corbett fought Bob Fitzsimmons, several Boston newspapers reported large numbers of fans standing in front of their office to find out who was winning. There was considerable shock and consternation when Corbett was defeated.[2] Although the street was always congested and noisy, the benefits outweighed the discomforts: If you wanted up-to-the-minute headlines, lower Washington Street was definitely the place to be.

But Newspaper Row was not just where you got the latest news, long before your friends in the suburbs did. In March 1901 Newspaper Row itself became a national story: Late Friday night, March 15, a fire broke out at 248 Washington Street, the building that housed the *Boston Daily Advertiser* and the *Evening Record*. It seemed to have started in the pressroom, and it spread quickly; firemen and trucks arrived within minutes, but it was not an easy fire to put out. As thick, black smoke filled the building, the night-shift workers tried desperately to get out, but many could not even see the fire escape. As crowds on the street below watched in horror, they saw some of the men break windows and try to climb out of the burning building. A few were able to jump to an adjoining roof and escape the flames. Fire trucks with ladders were able to reach some of the men, while others were eventually able to find the fire escape and get to safety. But three men were not so fortunate. After the fire was finally put out, their bodies were found. Early reports said eight other men were injured, including two of the firefighters; later, some sources reported as many as 11. The building itself was destroyed, suffering over $150,000 in damage. Fortunately for everyone at the *Globe*, which was next door, its building sustained only some water damage. Without hesitation, the editors offered the *Advertiser* and *Record* staff a place to work and publish their newspapers.[3] For the next several days, hundreds of curiosity seekers came to Newspaper Row to look at the ruined building, while witnesses to the events talked about what they had seen. Even after a tragedy, everyone who could get to Newspaper Row wanted to be there.

It is interesting for modern researchers to examine the reporting from different turn-of-the-century newspapers. We see how intensely the newspapers competed for scoops, but they also competed in other ways: for daily readers, of course, but also for the size of the crowds that gathered in front of their bulletin boards. Reporters would also mention in their stories how their paper got the details of a story first, or posted it first, or had it right when others had it wrong. In the Queen Victoria story, for example, the *Herald* was quick to point out that other newspaper bulletin boards had printed rumors, and then had to rely on the *Herald* to get the story straight.[4]

And that brings us to the baseball season, which began in April. There was a new professional league, and for the first time, Boston had two major-league teams—one in the National League and one in the new American League. How the fans would react to this development was an open question. The *Boston Journal*'s Walter S. Barnes, Jr. wondered about which team the fans would support, and whether fans even cared about the "war between rival leagues"—would they support the Nationals or the new team, the Americans? Or perhaps they would support both? Only time would tell.[5] Meanwhile, the newspapers kept the fans up to date on the progress being made with the new Huntington Avenue Grounds, as well as making sure everyone had realistic expectations for the new team. Not every Boston newspaper followed sports closely: The *Post*, for example, was as likely to cover whist, checkers, rowing, horse shows, and yacht races as it was to cover baseball, and some days, the *Evening Record* had no sports coverage at all. But for the most part, in a town that was crazy for sports, fans knew that their favorite paper would keep them up to date.

Where today the Boston American League franchise is the Red Sox (the name the team has used since 1908), and the former Boston National League team became known as the Braves (the name they adopted in 1912), the newspapers of 1901 generally called the American League team the Boston Americans, and the Boston National League franchise was known as the Boston Nationals. And often, when reporting the story, a baseball writer would just call the team "the Bostons." (You would know which team from the context of the story, and from mentions of the league the team played in.) For those who followed either (or both) of the teams, getting news about the games was a far different procedure compared with how quickly and easily it is done in our Internet age. For one thing, back then there was no expectation of instant information. If you could not attend a game in person, you had only a handful of options. The most devoted fans (and those whose schedules permitted it) would stop by Newspaper Row, to see if any scores had been posted on a newspaper's bulletin board. One of the advantages of hanging around lower Washington Street was that a reporter hurrying in to file a story might sometimes give the waiting fans a piece of news about a game that had just concluded. In a few cases, there were what today would be called "super-fans" who had developed a friendship with someone in the sports department of their favorite

Eager boys are ready to deliver the *Sunday Globe* in this Lewis Wickes Hine October 1909 image, taken at 5 A.M. in front of the *Boston Globe* office on Newspaper Row.

Sports reporters J. C. Morse, with hat, and Tim Murnane, with silver hair and mustache.

newspapers, like the *Journal* and *Post*, also provided good coverage); these newspapers were a lifeline for eager fans. In 1901 most of the Boston newspapers cost 2 cents during the week (the *Evening Record* and the *Post* were bargains at 1 cent each, while the voice of the upper class in the city, the *Boston Evening Transcript*, cost 3 cents); the Sunday edition of some of the newspapers cost a nickel, since that edition was considerably larger: For example, both the *Boston Globe* and the *Boston Herald* had between 12 and 14 pages during the week, but between 40 and 50 pages—including expanded coverage of sports, the arts, society, the "funnies" (what we today call comic strips), and various syndicated features—on Sundays, thus explaining the higher price.

Speaking of the fans, the language of the newspapers was somewhat different in 1901 from the language used today. The people who followed their favorite team were not always called *fans* yet. This word was still new—so new that some newspapers put quotes around it, as the *Boston Journal* did with the headline: "Surfeit of Baseball: Conflicting Dates and Double-Headers for the 'Fans' This Week."[7] While the word *cranks* was beginning to fade in popularity, it was still frequently used as a synonym for the most passionate followers of baseball. And *rooters* was also in common use.[8] The rookies on a team were called *Yannigans*. Sportswriters were often referred to as *sporting writers*, and the editor of the sports pages was thus the *sporting editor*. And while a majority of the newspapers were now referring to baseball (one word), some—including the *Journal*, would sometimes still print it as two words: base ball. (On the other hand, some things were the same as today. To cite one example, the press box was still the press box, and reporters sat there taking notes about the game.)

newspaper; these fans might go in and visit that writer, to ask about their favorite team or discuss a rumor about a player retiring or being traded.[6] Usually, though, the writers were busy and the bulletin boards were the best source for the latest scores and information.

For the fans who could not stand outside the offices of their favorite newspaper, the other option was waiting for the next edition of the newspaper to come out. Telephone service was not yet widely available (although a few cities had limited service, and several newspapers, including the *Globe*, made use of it), so you could not call your friends to ask if they'd been to the game. And since there was also no radio to listen to, newspaper coverage was especially important. Some newspapers became known for their thorough sports reporting (the *Globe* and the *Herald* were two of the best, and other

Automobiles were gaining in popularity, although they too had a different name: some newspapers had begun to refer to them as automobiles, and drivers as "automobilists."[9] But the terms "horseless vehicle" and "horseless carriage" were still popular expressions.[10] Baseball writers, however, who often traveled to road games along with their favorite telegrapher, went by train, then the most common means of long-distance transportation. Baseball teams, of course, took advantage of the railroads as well. And whether at home or on the road, sometimes the baseball writers took a sports cartoonist with them. While photographs of the players did appear in the newspapers, it was often a staff artist or a cartoonist who provided illustrations about some aspect of the day's game. In 1901 a number of the newspaper cartoonists were anonymous members of the paper's art department, but there were several exceptions. One was Wallace Goldsmith, a sports cartoonist for the *Herald* (who would later work at the *Globe*). Another well-respected sports illustrator was H.G. "Howard" Laskey of the *Globe*.

Many of the reporters were also anonymous: Where today the idea of a byline, telling us who wrote the story, is common, that custom had not entirely taken hold in journalism. A few reporters who had longevity at their newspaper might be given a byline; but it was not a common practice, and even many of the bylined reporters tended to use only their first two initials and last name. Among the sports reporters whose names were well known in 1901 were two men from the *Boston Journal*—Walter S. Barnes, Jr. (often in print as W.S. Barnes Jr.) and Peter F. Kelley. Both Barnes and Kelley also wrote about other sports, but during the baseball season, they provided in-depth reporting on the games from both leagues. Also well-known and admired was the baseball editor for the *Boston Herald*, J.C. Morse (Jacob, better known as Jake). Morse was one of the few Jewish sportswriters in Boston at that time; he came from a family well-known in Boston for its philanthropy. He was also respected for his knowledge of the business side of baseball, and he could cover amateur or college sports as thoroughly as he covered the pro teams. The most famous baseball reporter in town, though, was the *Globe*'s Timothy H. "Tim" Murnane, who sometimes wrote as THM (everyone knew who that was) or as T.H. Murnane. The dean of Boston's sportswriters, he was a player before joining the *Globe* in 1888, and like his friend and fellow baseball writer Jake Morse, Murnane's insights on the game were often sought by newspapers in other cities.[11] (In addition to being friends and colleagues as sportswriters, Murnane and Morse were business associates, serving as executives in the New England League: Murnane was its president and Morse was the league's secretary.)

Today, whether we live in the city or the suburbs, we are accustomed to seeing professional sports dominate the coverage in the newspapers but in 1901 even the cities with a major-league team did not necessarily focus on it exclusively. In fact, back then, not every major newspaper had a sports page (or had one only for their Sunday edition); and even among those that did, you were just as likely to see high-school and college sports, or sports like cycling, horse racing, and golf given as much attention as what the pro baseball teams were doing. Where today a number of the suburban newspapers have reporters who cover pro sports (for example, the *Quincy Patriot Ledger* regularly has a reporter at Boston Red Sox home games), at the turn of the 20th century many suburban papers completely ignored professional sports, unless a well-known citizen made a trip to see a game. Weeklies like the *Milton Times* or the *Arlington Advocate* covered only high-school and amateur sports. As for the suburban dailies, the *Quincy Daily Ledger* (then a separate paper from the *Quincy Patriot*) printed the professional baseball standings but seldom wrote about the games or the players; occasionally the paper might print a syndicated piece, such as one by the *New York Tribune*'s George E. Stackhouse.[12] For the most part, though, both Quincy newspapers reported mainly on the amateur leagues and the doings of the high schools in the area. The *Lowell Sun* regularly tried to cover stories from both

Newspaper Row, Boston, showing *Boston Journal* office ca. 1906.

the local (including the city's team in the New England League) and the professional realms. While its main focus was on area teams and players, the newspaper used syndicated columnist Ben Tavis, as well as anonymous Associated Press reporters to get the news about the pro teams. In fact, when the Boston Americans made their debut in Baltimore, the story of how the team played (and lost) was on page one in the *Sun*.[13]

Surprisingly, although the *Lowell Sun* treated the first game as a page-one story, not every Boston newspaper did; most placed it on an inside page. For example, the *Herald* and the *Globe* put it on page 8.[14] Considering that Tim Murnane of the *Globe* had championed the idea of an American League team in Boston, the page 8 coverage was puzzling. Once the Boston Americans made their home debut, the *Globe* went all-out in its coverage, with a full page of baseball news and a large sports cartoon from H.G. Laskey.[15] However, even the home debut did not land the team on page one in most of the newspapers: the *Post* was one of the exceptions, while the *Herald* placed the story, including a cartoon by Wallace Goldsmith, on the same page as other sports stories — page 8.[16]

As a Boston Americans' fan in 1901, you were especially eager for any interesting news about the players and the league. The baseball writers understood that the fans wanted to feel as if they were getting inside information, and each man tried his best to provide it. Some sports reporters concluded their daily column with a special segment that contained short observations about the team, and also answered questions the fans had sent in. The *Boston Evening Record* called this "Baseball Gossip," and while the game summaries tended to be "just the facts," the comments in "Baseball Gossip" were in a far more conversational tone, as if the writer was talking to the readers about some mutual friends: "There seem to be a few sparks of baseball left in old Cy Young yet. Eh?"[17] Some of the *Record*'s sports columns had no byline, but others were signed by F.A. (Francis) Frost. Over at the *Boston Journal*, the column was "Base Ball Notes" (the *Journal* continued to spell it as two words for much of the season) and Peter F. Kelley sometimes wrote it; his comments were about not just the Boston Americans but about baseball in general — National League, minor leagues, trade rumors, whatever he thought the fans would want to know. It was similar to Tim Murnane's *Globe* column, which he called "Baseball Notes." (One big difference, however, was that Murnane was much more outspoken about what he thought was wrong with baseball — given his many years in the game, he had the stature to comment about poor umpiring or players who did not give their all.) The *Herald* at first used the name "Baseball Gossip" for their sports commentary, and it was probably Jake Morse who wrote it; later in the season, it was renamed "Around the Bases." In some of the columns, the *Herald* also reprinted the remarks of sportswriters from other cities, a practice known as the "exchange"—every day, newspapers in one city would send copies of their paper to newspaper offices in other cities, and an "exchange editor" would then select items that seemed noteworthy. One in particular seemed as if it could have been written yesterday: Abe Yager of the *Brooklyn Eagle* remarked that Boston's "cranks" were the most well-versed in all

Sports cartoonist Wallace Goldsmith.

of the technicalities and rules of baseball, such that "they keep tabs on every play, tell the players how they ought to field and bat, and when an error is made, assure the unfortunate bungler that if he had done this or that thing, it would have been different."[18] As anyone who listens to sports-talk radio knows, some things have not changed.

While society was still very traditional, a growing number of women had begun to follow baseball and wanted to attend the games. The Boston Americans decided to make it easier for female baseball fans to do so, and began a series of "Ladies Days," when female fans were admitted free (general admission was 25 cents) as long as they had a male escort. This idea met with great success, and it became a regular event, with a Ladies Day at least once a month. As the *Herald* noted after one such occasion in early July, "The attendance of ladies is always large on days that are complimentary in their honor."[19] And while the reporters seemed accepting of having more women in the stands, they could not resist the temptation to poke some fun at the lack of understanding some women seemed to have about the rules of the game. When pitcher Cy Young was running the bases, one female fan quoted as saying, "It's too bad to make that big man run that way."[20]

The first season was exciting for the loyal fans of the Americans, but the final month brought disappointment, as a long Western road trip yielded only four wins; the Boston baseball writers remarked upon the team's weak hitting, and said the Americans had played better during the first half of the season. Still, the team finished the season with a winning record, 79-57, although that wasn't good enough for a pennant. Tim Murnane was among the reporters who noted that the team had some flaws, but he praised the manager, Jimmy Collins, for having gotten the most out of the players, and thought the season could certainly be considered a "big success."[21] Walter S. Barnes, Jr., who had wondered at the beginning of the season whether the fans wanted or would support a new team, now had his answer. He wrote that "President Charles W. Somers and the American League are to be congratulated upon the success of the season just closed at the Huntington Avenue grounds. It took courage to invade a National League stronghold like Boston with a new venture.... The Boston [American League] Club became a popular institution from the start, and maintained its popularity with an amazing steadiness."[22] It had been a very entertaining season, but other sporting events were taking place, and on Newspaper Row, people were already gathering to await the results and talk sports with other fans. As the Boston Americans' season came to a close, large crowds were coming to find out who won the America's Cup yacht race between the Columbia and the Shamrock II. Soon there would be college football, and perhaps some news about offseason baseball trades. On Newspaper Row, there was always something to talk about, and the daily newspapers would continue keeping the fans informed.

Notes

1   "Told by the Herald," *Boston Herald*, January 23, 1901, 9.

2   "Scene in Newspaper Row Yesterday," *Boston Journal*, March 18, 1897, 3.

3   "Three Men Dead, Eight Injured," *Boston Globe*, March 16, 1901, 1, 4; "Newspapermen Leaped for Life," *Cleveland Plain Dealer*, March 16, 1901, 6.

4   "Told by the Herald," *Boston Herald*, January 23, 1901, 9.

5   " 'Play Ball' the Slogan of the Week," *Boston Journal*, April 14, 1901, 14.

6   "Surplus Players," *Boston Globe*, January 22, 1901, 3.

7   *Boston Journal*, August 19, 1901, 3.

8   "American League Men Given Royal Welcome By 11,500 Rooters," *Boston Globe*, May 9, 1901, 4.

9   "Boston's Feminine Automobilists," *Boston Herald*, May 10, 1901, 6.

10 "Boston's First Big Race for Horseless Vehicles," *Boston Post*, June 16, 1901, 9.

11 "Tim Murnane's Pointers," *Boston Globe*, May 29, 1888, 5.

12 "Baseball Managers," *Quincy Daily Ledger*, May 11, 1901, 3.

13 "10,000 People Saw Baltimore Win From the Bostons," *Lowell Sun*, April 27, 1901, 1.

14 "Baltimore Beats Boston in the American, 10 to 6," *Boston Herald*, April 27, 1901, 8; "Run to the Good," *Boston Globe*, April 27, 1901, 8.

15 "American League Men Given Royal Welcome by 11,500 Rooters," *Boston Globe*, May 9, 1901, 4.

16 "Boston Americans Cheered to Victory," *Boston Post*, May 9, 1901, 1, 5; "A Home Victory at the New Grounds," *Boston Herald*, May 9, 1901, 8.

17 "Baseball Gossip," *Boston Evening Record*, May 9, 1901, 7.

18 "Baseball Gossip," *Boston Herald*, May 11, 1901, 8.

19 "Washington Dies Hard," *Boston Herald*, July 6, 1901, 4.

20 "Duffy's Nine Bumps Into Another Iceberg of Hard Luck," *Boston Herald*, August 21, 1901, 4.

21 "No Hope Now," *Boston Globe*, September 19, 1901, 7; "Eight Games," *Boston Globe*, September 23, 1901, 4.

22 "Boston Americans: Remarkable Average and Aggregate Attendance at Home Games," *Boston Journal,* September 30, 1901, 3.

Ben Beville

By Bill Nowlin

CLARENCE BENJAMIN BEVILLE was a pitcher on the first-year team of Boston's American League franchise. A native Californian, Beville was born in Colusa township on August 28, 1877. His father, William T. Beville, was a bookkeeper in the tax collector's office, and later in the sheriff's office. William's wife, Luta Beville, looked after three children at home: Virginia (9 at the time of the 1880 Census), Willie May (age 6), and young Clarence. William had come from Virginia and his wife from Missouri, both of them having parents from two different states as well. They both had arrived early enough in the area that on Ben Beville's passing, the *Colusa Daily Times* obituary referred to his parents as "pioneer Colusans."[1]

William Beville was a Confederate soldier who had served in the 8th Virginia Cavalry, but made his way to California after the Civil War. He was named Deputy County Clerk in Colusa County in 1868 and served as Under-Sheriff from 1870 for a number of years, interrupted only by a four-year term as County Assessor. In 1886, he was elected Colusa County Sheriff. He and Lutie also owned a 20-acre apricot and peach orchard.[2]

Ben himself is said to have been a Spanish American War veteran.[3]

In the 1900 Census, William was listed as a clerk and Clarence as a laborer. It was in 1900 that he began his brief baseball career. Controversy preceded him to Boston.

Beville first played in 1900 for the Oakland Oaks (California League), but the *Los Angeles Times* on February 2 described the right-hander as a "star twirler of the Oaklands, but is now debarred from the California League for jumping his contract and signing with the Montana aggregation"—by which the newspaper referred to the Butte Smoke Eaters of the Montana State League.

He played some right field for San Bernardino in the winter league, in February 1901, and some left field in

Photograph of Ben Beville with Lowell.

March, batting .162 at the end of the Southern California Baseball League season, which ended in March. He also pitched for the San Bernardino team. In April, he pitched for Lagoon, Utah, in the Inter-Mountain League, though posting a disappointing 0-3 record.

He was signed by Detroit, though saw no action with the Tigers because manager George Stallings "didn't have any room for him" and he was released on May 7 to the Boston Americans.[4] The *Chicago Tribune* picked up on the story after he joined Boston and ran the headline "Collins Gets New Pitcher" saying he was "at least ten pounds overweight and will not be in form for some days."[5] He's officially listed as standing 5-feet-9 and weighing 190 pounds.

The *Boston Herald* had told readers that "Connie Mack tried to get him" and right after he reported, the *Herald* declared him a "likely looking chap."[6] Beville debuted for manager Jimmy Collins on May 24, and he pitched acceptably, but the Bostons were shut out by the Tigers in Detroit, 3-0. Beville "did pretty good work," declared the *Globe*. He allowed three runs in three different innings on seven hits and five walks, and hit a batter, but suffered as much as anything on account of absent-minded play and three errors by the Boston defense. The *Globe* said he was "not hit hard, but was as wild as a hawk." At the plate, he was hitless in four at-bats. The *Herald* called him a "comer" and said he was "a strapping big fellow, with plenty of speed and a fine drop ball, and he kept the Detroits guessing throughout, but the errors behind him and Miller's fine pitching gave the Tigers a rather easy victory."7

Six days later, on May 30, Beville started again in the morning game of a Memorial Day doubleheader in Chicago. He walked the first two batters but escaped further damage in the first. An error behind him gave the White Sox a baserunner to lead off the second. There followed a walk and then a double down the third-base line past Collins. "Beville lost his bearings completely here," reported the *Chicago Tribune*. He threw eight straight balls, and was yanked from the game in favor of Cuppy. The *Boston Globe* wasn't any kinder, offering a subhead "Beville Goes to Pieces Almost at Start of First Game." Boston lost, 8-3.

In the fifth inning of a game on June 2 in Milwaukee, umpire Haskell banished both Jimmy Collins and Buck Freeman, so Dowd was brought in from left field to play third and two pitchers were inserted as fielders—Cuppy in left and Beville at first base. Ben came through well enough at the plate, with a 2-for-3 game, though he made an error in the field. With the score 4-2 in favor of Boston after eight innings, Beville kicked off a two-out rally in the ninth with a double into the crowd in left field. Parent hit a home run, and the hits just kept coming. Beville came up a second time and doubled again. They were the only two hits he ever had—and in the process he set a record that still stands today for the most doubles in an inning. It's been tied by several others, including six other Boston batters. Before the third out could be secured, Milwaukee had given up nine runs. Earlier in the game, in the sixth, Beville had walked and come around to score. Not a bad day at all—but he was released on June 10 when Boston prepared to bring in George Winter, whose

Beville, far left back row with the 1902 Lowell baseball team. Other notable team members include former Cleveland Naps outfielder, Louis Sockalexis (front row, fourth from the left, glove in hand), the first Native American, and first recognized minority, to perform in the National League. In the back row, forth from the left, is Fred Lake who played five years in the majors, and managed both Boston teams; the Red Sox in 1908 and 1909, and the Doves (Braves) in 1910.

Ben Beville illustration.

debut on the 15th was the first of 213 appearances for Boston.

Beville finished his major-league career with an 0-2 record and a 4.00 earned-run average. His teammate Cy Young was 33-10 for Boston in 1901.

By July 1, Beville was found pitching in Lewiston, Maine, for the New England League's Lowell Tigers. He pitched in 18 games, but appeared in 44 — his .282 bat perhaps more productive than his pitching. He did have his moments, though, such as the one-hitter he threw against Nashua on July 16.

His last year in Organized Baseball was 1902, when he played for both Lowell and the Haverhill Hustlers, with a 3-2 record.

There was another Beville — Monte Beville — who played around the same time (1903 and 1904 for the Highlanders and Tigers), but he was a catcher and first baseman from Indiana and the two were not related.

The 1910 Census shows Beville still living at home with his parents, his father a bookkeeper in the tax collector's office but Ben (still listed as Clarence) at age 32 as a laborer doing general work. By 1920, he was himself working as a bookkeeper in a law office, and still living with his parents on Fremont Street in Colusa. At some point, Beville worked as an agent for the I.R.S.

A bit embarrassing for someone working in a law office was his arrest in 1924. Beville (listed in the newspaper as a former internal revenue service agent) pled guilty in U. S. District Court on conspiring with three others to pose as Federal officers and "raided" the house of H. H. "Happy" Sanders, removing 324 cases of liquor from the Sanders home. Judge Frank H. Kerrigan dubbed taxicab George Miller the "master mind of the outfit" and sentenced him to two years in the Federal penitentiary at Leavenworth, saying that he wished the law permitted him to impose a longer sentence. The other two conspirators were Joseph Udell and Jack Romain, known as the "New York kid." All four impersonated government officers. Udell was sentenced to 20 months, while Romain got 15 months at McNeill's Island. Both Romain and Beville served as government witnesses.[8]

In 1930, despite his guilty plea in 1924, Beville was working as a police officer in a steel works in the Pittsburg area of California's Contra Costa County. Bill Lee's *Baseball Necrology* says that Beville worked for a number of years for the government at Pittsburg and that he died from alcoholic poisoning on January 5, 1937, in the Veterans Hospital at Yountville.

Sources

In addition to the sources cited in Beville's biography, the author consulted the online SABR Encyclopedia, retrosheet.org, and Baseball-Reference.com. Thanks to Dan Desrochers, Charles Yerxa, Joe Williamson, and Joe and John Morton.

Notes

1. *Colusa Daily Times*, January 8, 1937.
2. E-mail from Joe Williamson to Charles Yerxa, December 18, 2012.
3. *Colusa Daily Times*, January 8, 1937.
4. *San Diego Union*, May 24, 1901 and *Cleveland Leader*, May 8, 1901.
5. *Chicago Tribune*, May 16, 1901.
6. *Boston Herald*, May 8 and May 22, 1901.
7. *Boston Herald*, May 25, 1901.
8. *Woodland Daily Democrat*, October 8, 1924.

Jimmy Collins

By Charlie Bevis

The initial third baseman enshrined in the Baseball Hall of Fame, Jimmy Collins was an outstanding fielder and above-average hitter during his 14-year major-league career in the Deadball Era. As the first manager of the Boston franchise in the American League, Collins gained widespread acclaim when he led the team to consecutive pennants in 1903 and 1904 and victory in the inaugural 1903 World Series.

Collins was a businessman in a baseball uniform. In an interview with the *Buffalo Evening News* just a few weeks before his death, he gave writer Cy Kritzer an encyclopedic recall of his salary levels as a ballplayer, practically gloating about once earning $18,000 in one year, but yet, as Kritzer related, "he couldn't recall once during the interview the size of his batting average in any one season."[1] It wasn't just about acquiring money, though. Collins used his baseball income to develop a real-estate business by building multifamily rental housing, which provided his income after his playing days.

James Joseph Collins was born on January 16, 1870, in the village of Suspension Bridge in Niagara Falls, New York, the second of four children of Irish immigrants Anthony and Alice Collins. The family moved in 1872 to Buffalo, where Anthony Collins worked as a policeman for three decades, rising to the rank of captain.

The Collins family first lived in Buffalo's Irish-American neighborhoods in the southern section of the city. Irish-Americans were then the distinct minority in Buffalo, as they tussled for economic and political power with the dominant German-Americans on the East Side and the native-born Americans on the West Side. Collins's father tutored him well in how to work effectively within the three ethnic groups that controlled life in Buffalo.

After receiving his early education in Catholic parochial schools, Collins attended St. Joseph's College in downtown Buffalo. Despite the use of "college" in its name, St. Joseph's was more like an advanced high school,

Jimmy Collins as player/manager of the Boston Americans in 1903, when the team won the first World's Series.

more akin to a prep school today; its successor is a high school, St. Joseph's Collegiate Institute. Collins graduated from St. Joseph's in 1888 with a diploma in commercial studies, acquiring a business education that he put to good use in the coming years. After graduation Collins worked as a clerk in the Black Rock station of the Delaware, Lackawanna and Western Railroad, just a few blocks north of his parents' new residence on Niagara Street in Buffalo's native-born-American-dominated West Side.

The teenaged Collins honed his baseball skills by playing for amateur teams organized by the social clubs in Buffalo. In 1889 and 1890 he played outfield for the Socials, a team made up of Irish-Americans, which helped maintain ties to his old neighborhood. For the 1891 and 1892 seasons, though, Collins played third base for the North Buffalo team, based in the Black Rock section of the city, where he made the difficult decision to forsake his Irish-American ties with the Socials and forge new relationships with the men in his new neighborhood. Soon baseball changed his perspective on life and Collins abandoned his father's traditional Irish-American value that deified job security.

When Jack Chapman, the manager of the Buffalo minor-league team in the Eastern League, offered Collins the chance to play professional baseball in May 1893, he left his secure job with the railroad for the uncertain life of a ballplayer and what he hoped would be greater income potential in the future. After starting out at third base, Collins played mostly shortstop for Buffalo during the 1893 season, finishing with a respectable .286 batting average, but an erratic .863 fielding average. When Chapman put Collins in the outfield for the 1894 season to minimize his fielding lapses, his batting average improved to .352 (among the league's top ten hitters) and he led the league with 198 hits.

In November 1894 the Boston ballclub in the National League paid $500 to obtain the services of the 5-foot-9, 178-pound Collins from the Buffalo ballclub as insurance should one of its outfielders stage a lengthy holdout in salary negotiations. Jimmy Bannon did hold out, so Boston manager Frank Selee put Collins in right field on Opening Day. After 11 games, though, the right-handed hitting Collins was clearly a less than adequate substitute for Bannon, as he was hitting barely .200 and had committed four errors. When Boston finally signed Bannon, Collins was expendable, so he was sold to the last-place Louisville team for $500 in a transaction characterized as a "loan" that was really a recall option.

Collins played in the outfield during his first few games with Louisville, before manager John McCloskey suddenly pressed him into service at third base midway through the May 31 game at Baltimore after the Louisville third baseman had committed four errors. The legend of Collins's first major-league game at third base, like so many baseball legends, grew over time so that the more recent retellings—that he told Baltimore's Hugh Jennings, "Bunt 'em down to me and I'll show you something," and then threw out four bunters in a row—bear only a partial resemblance to the 1895 facts.[2] The bunters Collins threw out were fewer than four and occurred two months later (on July 28) after he became the regular third baseman in mid-June.

Since Collins flourished at third base in Louisville, Boston decided to exercise its recall option in August to have him temporarily fill in for an injured infielder. Collins, however, balked at returning to Boston. The brash Collins looked to leverage the situation and get a better deal from Boston, telling baseball writers that if he couldn't stay with Louisville he'd retire from baseball and return to his railroad job in Buffalo. Boston relented and instead recalled Collins for the 1896 season.

After Boston traded its incumbent third baseman, Billy Nash, to Philadelphia in November 1895 to make room for Collins in the Boston infield, Collins showed tremendous chutzpah in his salary negotiation with Arthur Soden, the principal owner of the Boston ballclub. The strong-willed Collins thought the Nash trade gave him a negotiation advantage, so he held out for a higher salary until April 1896. Since the National League was a monopoly and the reserve clause in the player contract bound the player to a team until released, ownership had the upper hand in player negotiations. Collins learned a hard lesson that he had little leverage over ownership and finally agreed to a salary of $1,800 for the 1896 season. After performing well as the Boston third baseman in 1896, Collins was offered a salary increase to $2,100 for the 1897 season. Collins, however, felt he should be paid the unofficial salary maximum of $2,400. As he had been the year before, he was a holdout, but he eventually accepted Soden's offer, which was four times the $500 average pay of an American worker.

Continual disagreements over money soured Collins's relationship with the Boston ballclub and led to his highly publicized departure from the National League after the 1900 season. Collins had an easier time negotiating back home in Buffalo and in Louisville, where there was a more ethnically tolerant climate among the Irish-Americans, German-Americans, and native-born populations than the environment he found in Boston. There was a fundamental difference in ethnic relations in Boston, where the Irish didn't just clash with the native-born Brahmin aristocracy over political, religious, and economic issues but indeed were the underbelly of society. In the 1890s the Brahmins (Soden included) controlled virtually everything in Boston, and considered Irish-Americans like Collins as simply pawns in their world.

In 1897 during Boston's drive to the National League pennant, Collins matured into a graceful fielder and a consistent line-drive hitter who could find the outfield gaps. He became a fan favorite among the changing nature of the spectators at the South End Grounds, dubbed the Royal Rooters, who were middle-class businessmen that were displacing the gentlemanly crowd as ballpark spectators. In late September, more than 100 Rooters traveled to Baltimore to watch the Boston team play a crucial series there, where Collins, with a leech on his face to heal a swollen eye, led the team to victory in the series. Three days later Boston clinched the pennant.

While Collins finished the 1897 season with a .346 batting average, his real value was his ability to produce runs. Although the RBI statistic hadn't yet been invented, a retrospective determination indicates that Collins would have had 132 RBIs in 1897, second among all National League batters. With the regular season over, Collins moved on to the supplemental income opportunities of the postseason. After the anticlimactic rematch with Baltimore in the Temple Cup series, Collins played for the All-America Baseball Team in a cross-country tour with the Baltimore team, where he observed Boston manager Frank Selee as businessman turn a profit on the itinerant baseball venture.

Collins quietly negotiated a contract with Soden to be paid the $2,400 salary maximum for the 1898 season. After three years as a National League ballplayer, the 28-year-old Collins had reached the pinnacle of his profession. However, because the National League owners lengthened the baseball season by 22 games to play 154 games in 1898, Collins felt duped by Soden, since Collins actually received just a minimal pay increase on a per-game basis.

Boston went on to capture a second consecutive National League pennant in 1898, as Collins compiled a .328 batting average, seventh highest in the league, and led the league with 15 home runs. Collins, who didn't take kindly to having a boss, responded well to manager Selee's approach to leave the ballplayers alone to play the game, a managerial style Collins adopted in the future. By now Collins had developed a stellar reputation as baseball's best fielding third baseman, because he had a quick eye, good dexterity, extensive range, and a strong throwing arm. Collins covered a lot of territory at third base, not just bunts and groundballs but also snagging many pop flies in foul territory and in short left field.

At a team testimonial in October 1898, Selee received a $2,500 check from Soden to share with the players, as a "gratuity" for winning the pennant. It must have galled Collins to receive a "tip" as if he were a Pullman Car porter. It was one more signal to Collins that his income potential was very limited by working for the Boston ballclub. Indeed, he had no success in securing a salary increase for the 1899 and 1900 seasons.

During the winter of 1900 Collins made an investment to take advantage of the explosive future growth he saw in the nascent South Buffalo neighborhood, to which Irish-Americans had begun moving from the inner city. Collins purchased a house lot and made plans to construct a rental unit on it. This was the first of many properties Collins purchased as he planned to live off the rental income as a self-employed person during his post-baseball years.

Collins doubtless saw no benefits in a future with the Boston National League ballclub. Given the penurious ways of the Boston owners, he was likely to face a decrease in salary as age took its inevitable toll on his playing skills. He had no chance to succeed Selee as manager and had been passed over as captain. One ray of hope for Collins to get an increased salary was the formation of the Players Protective Association in 1900. Collins was one of Boston's player representatives in the fledgling players union, but he was also looking out for his own interests. After attending two union meetings that summer and seeing no action on the compensation front, Collins took matters into his own hands.

Jimmy Collins, ca. 1902.

In March 1901 Collins became the manager, captain, and third baseman of the Boston team in the new American League, which Ban Johnson had established as a second major league to compete against the monopolistic National League. Collins justified jumping leagues at the time by saying, "I have given the National league people my best efforts for several years past and often asked them for more money, knowing that I was worth it, but until now they have turned a deaf ear to all my requests. ...I saw a chance to better myself and took it."[3]

Since Collins was motivated by money and displeased with his history of salary negotiations with the Boston Nationals, he was willing to take the risk of switching over to the Boston Americans. The possible failure of the new baseball enterprise and of being blackballed by the National League were not big risks to the 31-year-old Collins; he could simply fall back on his real-estate venture and connections in Buffalo. Collins was not only pleased that he could be a manager in the American League, but he was also intrigued that former ballplayers could also be part-owners, as exemplified by Connie Mack in Philadelphia.

Collins was handsomely compensated for jumping leagues. His contract with the Boston Americans called for a $3,500 annual salary for three years, nearly a 50 percent increase over his $2,400 salary for the 1900 season, with no reserve clause to restrict his freedom to negotiate with other teams thereafter. This $10,500 package was a key aspect of the deal for Collins, so that he'd have additional capital to invest in his real-estate business. Charles Somers, the owner of the Boston club, agreed to add a personal guarantee concerning the salary payments, to negate Collins's risk if Soden took legal action to try to enforce the reserve clause that he thought legally bound Collins to the National League ballclub. Collins was also a nominal owner of the Boston Americans, being awarded a few shares of stock in the club.

The timing of Collins's switch to the American League was impeccable from a cultural perspective, coinciding with the rise of Irish-American political power in Boston. John Fitzgerald, a member of the Royal Rooters, was a congressman in Washington (and soon would be mayor of Boston), while Patrick Collins became the second Irish-American mayor of Boston. From 1902 to 1905, two men named Collins were the toast of Boston among the city's Irish-American citizens: the mayor and the baseball manager.

Collins piloted Boston to a second-place finish in 1901 and to third place in 1902, while producing .332 and .322 batting averages, respectively, as the team's third baseman. Because the Royal Rooters followed Collins and transferred their loyalty, the Americans outdrew their rival Nationals at the ballpark, becoming the more popular team in Boston. Collins seized the opportunity to renegotiate his contract each year, nearly doubling his 1901 salary by the beginning of the 1903 season.

Collins was successful as a baseball manager because he extended to the baseball diamond his general contracting skills from his house-building activities in Buffalo, where he had to depend on highly skilled, motivated workers to build well-constructed houses for him. In this fashion, Collins adopted the same philosophy that his former manager, Frank Selee, had used during his five years with the Boston Nationals: find good ballplayers and let them do their jobs without interference. Because he was able to motivate his players through his on-the-field activities as a third baseman, Collins was more of a leader "among" men than a leader "of" men. It was the "we're all in this together" attitude that enabled Collins to win two American League pennants as player-manager and lead his team to victory in the first modern-day World Series.

Offsetting these positive attributes as manager, Collins had several flaws, primarily that he stayed too long with veteran players and failed to adequately mix in younger players to prepare the team for the future. His problem with handling aging ballplayers was compounded by his weakness in talent evaluation, which stemmed in large part from his inability to build an effective network of contacts to acquire new talent in that pre-farm-system era.

While he continued to perform as a third baseman in Boston for five more seasons, Collins focused more on the leadership functions of his job and his activities to improve the stature of the American League and its president, Ban Johnson. Two developments in 1903 elevated Johnson's gratitude to Collins for making the new league a success: the peace conference between the two leagues in January 1903 and the first modern-day World Series in October 1903. Both developments solidified Johnson's stature as an influential baseball executive, and they enabled Collins to enjoy several more years of financial prosperity as well as indulgence by Johnson as his reward for jumping leagues in 1901.

When the Boston Americans secured the American League pennant in September 1903, new Boston owner Henry Killilea and Pittsburgh owner Barney Dreyfuss agreed to play an interleague postseason series in October. The agreement provided for the owners to share revenue from the games, but did not include a provision to pay the ballplayers. Since the contracts of the Boston players expired at the end of September, Killilea had foolishly entered into a contract to play a postseason series without securing the services of the Boston ballplayers. Collins exploited Killilea's poor business judgment to negotiate a great deal for the ballplayers. They got not just 75 percent of Boston's portion of the shared revenue under the World Series agreement, but 75 percent of *all* of Boston's net revenue from the series.[4]

After Boston lost three of the first four games of the best-of-nine-games postseason series, Collins led the team, accentuated by the Royal Rooters' incessant singing of the song "Tessie," in a comeback to win the next four games to become the World Series champion. In the eyes of the sporting public, the victory over the National League established the legitimacy of the American League. At the time Collins believed these postseason games to be merely meaningless exhibitions to generate additional income, based on his experience in 1897 with the Temple Cup series and the All-America tour. However, he took advantage of the national belief that the 1903 World Series determined baseball supremacy. Indeed, the vast majority of his wealth garnered from major-league baseball between 1904 and 1908 was the direct result of his national acclaim from Boston's 1903 World Series victory.

After the World Series victory, Collins negotiated a new three-year guaranteed contract with Killilea, who was seeking to retain his services so he could sell the ballclub, which paid Collins a $10,000 annual salary and had a profit-sharing arrangement equal to 10 percent of the club's profits over $25,000.[5] In April 1904 John I. Taylor, the son of *Boston Globe* publisher Charles Taylor, became the new owner of the Americans. Collins's clash with the inexperienced Taylor led to a testy feud that eventually led to Collins's departure from the Boston Americans three years later.

Collins led an aging Boston team to a second consecutive pennant in 1904, in a neck-and-neck battle with the New York Highlanders in the first installment of the longstanding rivalry between the Boston Red Sox and New York Yankees. Unlike 1903, when Boston participated in the first modern-day World Series, the 1904 championship had no similar culminating event, as the National League champion New York Giants refused to play such a series. Although Taylor honored the profit-sharing provision in Collins's contract, the $8,000 payment on top of Collins' $10,000 salary stuck in the owner's craw.

An article in the *Boston Globe Magazine* in January 1905 portrayed Collins as an up-and-coming businessman. Accompanying the article was a portrait of Collins dressed in a suit, white shirt with raised collar, cravat loosely knotted at the neck, with a watch fob draped across his breast. He looked like any well-to-do Boston Brahmin, not a baseball player. Three photos of his rental properties in Buffalo were also included. "For several winters he devoted his time to looking after the new buildings he was erecting," writer Tim Murnane wrote of Collins's dedication to this business venture, "and even now with several fine pieces of real estate, he has planned for two more new houses."[6] Collins was now more businessman than ballplayer, which accelerated Taylor's dislike for him.

Collins also displayed more hubris during the 1905 baseball season, indicating that he believed the Boston Americans were *his* team, not Taylor's. Collins had run the baseball operation for three years without any direct oversight by the ballclub's absentee out-of-town owners before Taylor became the owner, and had successfully engineered a second straight pennant-winning season in 1904 without Taylor's assistance. This was the dark side to the soft-spoken but ambitious Collins.

Taylor took a more active role in the team for the 1905 season, seeking to remedy the team's injury and age issues, not by providing the resources to Collins so that he could fix the situation, but rather by fancying himself as a recruiter of baseball talent to rescue the team on his own. Not only did Taylor's signings do nothing to improve Boston's chances for victory on the baseball field (the team finished in fourth place), they intensified Collins's smoldering animosity for Taylor. While hidden from the public during the baseball season, the feud spilled onto the sports pages in December.

In a late December meeting in Buffalo with Ban Johnson, Collins leveraged his favorable relationship with the American League president to push him to honor the verbal commitment made back in 1901 for

Jimmy Collins helps hoist the World's Championship banner early in the 1904 season.

"Safe" - Posed action shot of Collins at second base at the Huntington Avenue Grounds, ca. 1904. It appears Collins was a bit rushed for the photo shoot still wearing dress footwear, not his baseball spikes. The original photograph was taken by *Boston Globe* photographer Edmunds E. Bond, with a colorized version appearing in the 1907 Morgan Stationery Co. of Cincinnati "Red Belt" postcards series.

Collins to eventually obtain an ownership interest in an American League ballclub. Johnson then exiled Taylor to Europe for a six-month vacation. The timing was perfect to take advantage of John Fitzgerald's becoming mayor of Boston in January 1906 as the city's first American-born Irish Catholic mayor, to increase the influence of the Royal Rooters among Irish-Americans and take advantage of transportation improvements (train connections and automobiles) that would bring suburban spectators to the Americans' Huntington Avenue Grounds.

Although Johnson temporarily assumed the role of Boston owner, Collins was the acting president of the Boston ballclub. To reflect his new duties, Collins extended his guaranteed contract for two more years, through the 1908 season. At the same time, he made his first investment in a baseball organization when he became a one-third owner of the minor-league Worcester, Massachusetts, club in the New England League.

With Taylor out of the way for the 1906 season, Johnson gave Collins a tryout as president. However, just when he was on the cusp on moving from the baseball diamond to the executive suite, three factors combined to derail Collins from achieving his ultimate goal in professional baseball. First, Collins discovered that he just wasn't good at the job of being an executive, which changed his relationship with the ballplayers. Second, the early success of his investment in the Worcester ballclub nudged him to modify his goal to be a minor-league owner rather than one at the major-league level. Third, Collins, a 36-year-old bachelor, looked to marry his longtime girlfriend.

Over a two-year span following consecutive American League pennants, Collins plummeted from revered hero to reviled bum. A 20-game losing streak in May 1906 sank the team into last place, where it stayed for the remainder of the season. On July 1 Collins abruptly left the team and made his fateful decision to stop performing all his duties for the Boston ballclub to focus on his personal future. He made just two brief returns to the team during the summer. On August 29 the front-page headline in the *Boston Globe* told the whole story: "Capt. Jimmy Collins No Longer at Helm: Indefinitely Suspended by Boston American League Club." After Collins' several absences without leave, Johnson used the term "desertion" in the press announcement.

Collins's decision to desert the Boston Americans was a disaster. He struck out at buying into ownership in the Buffalo and Providence ballclubs of the Eastern League, believing the asking prices to be too inflated to justify the investment. By December Collins was negotiating to return to Boston as its third baseman for the 1907 season, since he had a guaranteed contract to play through 1908 with the Boston Americans. Because Taylor, now back from his extended European vacation, was legally obligated to pay Collins whether or not he played, he agreed to take Collins back as a player, but not as manager.

During the winter of 1907 Collins secretly married Sarah E. "Sadie" Murphy before he left for spring training. The news of the marriage wasn't reported in the Boston newspapers until after he was traded on June 7 to the Philadelphia Athletics, when old friend Connie Mack agreed to take on Collins and his contract to bolster the A's infield to make a run at the pennant. By August Philadelphia had climbed from fourth place to first place, but then lost the pennant after a late September swoon. In August 1908 Mack excused Collins from the team's season-ending road trip so he could try out some minor-leaguers at third base to replace Collins in 1909, which gave Collins some time to contemplate his next step in baseball and enjoy some family time with his newborn daughter, Agnes.

For the 1909 season, Collins had to settle for being player-manager of the Minneapolis Millers in the American Association. Early in the season, however, Collins suffered an off-the-field tragedy when 8-month-old Agnes died in Buffalo. Collins returned to Buffalo to console his distraught wife, who was now four months pregnant, and made arrangements for Sadie to return to Boston so that she could be with her family for the next five months of her pregnancy. In early July Minneapolis moved into first place, but faded down the stretch to a third-place finish. Just before the season ended, Collins received word from Boston that his daughter Kathlyn had been born.

Now living with his family in Boston, not Buffalo, Collins sought a position near Boston. In October 1909 he was hired as the manager of the Providence team in the Eastern League, which was owned by Charlie Lavis, a former Royal Rooter. He lasted only a season and a half at Providence, being fired in June 1911; his passive managerial style didn't produce results in an era dominated by intimidating managers. Collins's hope to become the majority owner of a minor-league ballclub was dashed, as prices continued to skyrocket at what turned out to be a height of popularity of minor-league baseball. In January 1912 his daughter Claire was born and Collins sold his one-third interest in the Worcester ballclub and left Organized Baseball.

Settling into Boston was challenging for Collins. During his days as a popular player-manager, he had managed to navigate the ethnic stratification between Boston's Brahmin society and its Irish-American underclass. Now, as just another former ballplayer, he couldn't establish himself in business in the city. Collins was even rebuffed when he tried to become the baseball coach at an Irish-American institution, Boston College. In 1914 the family moved back to Buffalo, where Collins purchased a house in South Buffalo near his rental properties and settled into a quiet life as a real-estate mogul.

In 1922 Collins was appointed president of the Buffalo Municipal Baseball Association, in the wake of a corruption scandal in the Buffalo Parks Department, which sent to prison the former head of the city's amateur baseball leagues. Collins served 22 consecutive terms as president of the muni-league, during which he helped to expand the opportunity for thousands of youngsters to develop their baseball talents in the city-run amateur leagues, a vast improvement over the former system of social-club leagues in which Collins had played that could accommodate only a few hundred players.

As muni-league president, Collins's reputation as a great major-league ballplayer spread among a new generation of baseball fans and sportswriters in western New York. John Meahl, the commissioner of the Buffalo Parks Department, was not bashful about profusely praising Collins as baseball's "greatest third baseman of all time."[7] As a result of Meahl's promotional efforts, Collins's baseball reputation soon spread beyond regional newspapers into national publications. During the 1920s his name regularly surfaced as the third baseman picked for the various all-time teams selected by famous ballplayers and sportswriters. When *The Sporting News* published a long biographical sketch of Collins in 1933, the baseball weekly reinvigorated the fabled 1895 story about his exceptional fielding of bunts by the infamous Baltimore Orioles.[8] Ten years later this legend became the centerpiece of a campaign to put Collins in the Baseball Hall of Fame.

Collins's real-estate business reached its zenith of prosperity during World War I, before suburban flight in the 1920s changed the neighborhood, real estate prices peaked in 1926, and then mortgage defaults during the Great Depression resulted in property foreclosures. In 1927 Collins sold his home; he and his wife began renting apartments, before they moved in with their oldest daughter, Kathlyn. By 1935 Collins's real-estate business had imploded and he earned an income as an employee in the Buffalo Parks Department. Despite his financial reversals, Collins continued to gracefully serve as an ambassador for Buffalo athletics in his unpaid role as muni-league president.

Collins died on March 6, 1943, in Buffalo and was buried in Holy Cross Cemetery. Two months before Collins passed away, *Buffalo Evening News* sports editor Bob Stedler began a press campaign to have Collins elected to the Baseball Hall of Fame at the next BBWAA election in January 1945. Even with a heavy dose of electioneering by Stedler, Collins polled only 49 percent of the vote, far short of the required 75 percent. But that spring the Old-Timers Committee unanimously selected Collins for enshrinement in the Hall of Fame.

Jimmy Collins's legacy in baseball is much more than his batting and fielding exploits during the Deadball Era. As a star player, first manager, and the public face of the nascent Boston Americans, Collins put the franchise, valued by *Forbes* in 2012 at $1 billion, on a solid foundation. He delivered two pennants in the team's first four years and victory in the 1903 World Series, and thus should be remembered as the patron saint of today's Red Sox Nation.

Sources

Charlie Bevis, *Jimmy Collins: A Baseball Biography* (Jefferson, North Carolina: McFarland, 2012).

"Daguerreotypes: James J. (Jimmy) Collins," *The Sporting News*, July 27, 1933.

Cy Kritzer, "Late Jimmy Collins, the 'King of Third Sackers,' Became Hot Corner Star by Ability to Handle Bunts," *The Sporting News*, March 11, 1943.

Tim Murnane, "His Winter Pastime Collecting Rents," *Boston Globe Magazine* section. *Boston Globe*, January 15, 1905.

Fred O'Connell, "Boston's Baseball Idol: Jimmy Collins, Manager and Captain of the World's Champion Club." *Washington Post*, September 11, 1904.

Bob Stedler, "Jimmy Collins, Buffalo's Baseball Immortal, Dies," *Buffalo Evening News*, March 6, 1943.

Notes

1 Cy Kritzer, "Late Jimmy Collins, the 'King of Third Sackers,' Became Hot Corner Star by Ability to Handle Bunts," *The Sporting News*, March 11, 1943.

2 Charlie Bevis, *Jimmy Collins: A Baseball Biography* (Jefferson, North Carolina: McFarland, 2012), 33-35.

3 *Boston Globe*, March 10, 1901.

4 Bevis, *Jimmy Collins*, 113, 120-121.

5 Ibid., 7.

6 Tim Murnane, "His Winter Pastime Collecting Rents," *Boston Globe Magazine* section. January 15, 1905.

7 *Buffalo Express*, December 6, 1922.

8 "Daguerreotypes: James J. (Jimmy) Collins," *The Sporting News*, July 27, 1933.

Lou Criger

By Steve Krah

Feisty, slender, and packing a strong, accurate throwing arm, the smarts to call pitches for the winningest pitcher of all time, and the resiliency to last despite facing many physical ailments, catcher Lou Criger was regarded by his peers as one of the best backstops of the Deadball Era. At 5-feet-10 (some sources say six feet) and 165 pounds, Criger made an inviting target for bigger opponents, but the slender receiver took the punishment and held his ground. "Many players tackled Criger because he looked like a weakling," said Louie Heilbroner, who managed him in St. Louis before the respected receiver jumped to the American League. "But Criger would fight any six men on earth in those days, and if someone didn't pull them apart, Lou would lick all six by sheer perseverance."

A 1910 newspaper account described Criger as having light chestnut hair, porcelain colored eyes, a countenance something like Julius Caesar's, and so slight that he "looks anything but athletic." But looks can deceive, as Criger proved by using his arm and his cunning as weapons worthy of journalists' praise. Wrote Boston writer and former player Tim Murnane, "Criger is the man who can turn back the fleetest base runner, a man who can nip the boys at first and third unless they are ever on the alert. Criger is the backstop that never drops a ball that he can reach, and who can throw harder and quicker to second than any catcher in the profession. … I would like to see some one pick out the equal of Criger."

Louis Criger was born on February 3, 1872, on a farm just south of Elkhart, Indiana, to Charles Criger, a cooper originally from the Mecklenburg region of Germany, and Lovina (Stutsman) Criger. Lou had five brothers, one of whom, Elmer, pitched in the minor leagues, winning 22 games with Jackson of the Southern Michigan League in 1909 and earning a place with Los Angeles of the Pacific Coast League. In 1890 Lou Criger pitched for the Elkhart Lakeviews. The following year,

Lou Criger joined the Elkhart Truths in 1891.

he moved behind the plate, where he became a mainstay for the newly organized Elkhart Truths.

After spending five seasons playing for Elkhart, Criger was signed by the Michigan State League's Kalamazoo Kazoos in 1895. The next year he began the season with the Fort Wayne Farmers of the Inter-State League, splitting his time between left field and catcher and typically batting third or fourth in the lineup. One of his Fort Wayne teammates was R.C. Grey, whose brother Zane, a semipro player, went on to fame as an author of Western fiction.

Criger joined the Cleveland Spiders at the end of 1896, going hitless in five at-bats. He began 1897 year as a third-string catcher for the Spiders, but when he finally

Lou Criger, 1899.

got a chance to play, he dazzled observers with his powerful throwing arm, gunning down all six would-be Louisville base stealers on June 22, 1897. Criger took great pride in his throwing; he often sounded like a pitcher when he discussed his technique. "Now the way I throw the ball, it rotates backward and has an upward tendency, while some catchers throw with the thumb exposed and that gives it the downward effect, like the billiard draw shot, a ball that hurts to catch," he told the *St. Louis Post-Dispatch* in 1909.

In 1898 Criger became the Spiders' primary receiver, appearing in 82 games behind the plate and batting a modest .279 with one home run. That turned out to be the best offensive performance of the right-handed batter's career. A classic example of the good-field, no-hit catcher, Criger batted just .221 during his 16-year-career, and never collected more than 22 extra-base hits in a single season. He played because of his stellar defensive work and his close relationship with Cleveland ace right-hander Cy Young.

From 1897 to 1908, wherever Young went, Criger joined him: with Cleveland in 1897 and 1898, St. Louis in 1899 and 1900, and the Boston Americans from 1901 to 1908. During those 12 seasons Young won 283 games, and Criger was behind the plate for most of them. As *Sporting Life* put it in 1908, "What battery still serving in the major leagues has more inseparable service than the firm of Young and Criger?" In 1910 Young called Criger "the greatest catcher that ever stood behind the plate." But catching the burly hurler took its toll. Recalled his son, Harold Criger, in 1988, "I remember when the ball hit the mitt, it sounded like a pistol shot, and when dad was home, he soaked his hand in hot water, and it was red as fire. Sometimes he put a slice of beefsteak in his mitt for more padding, and Cy beat it to bloody shreds." After the two parted ways — Boston traded Criger to the Browns in December 1908 — Young talked to the *St. Louis Post-Dispatch* about what the 1909 season might be like without Lou. Said Young, "In Criger, St. Louis will get one of the greatest catchers that ever donned a glove. I've pitched to him so long than he seems a part of me, and I am positive no one will suffer from the departure more than I. Lou is a great student of the game and knows the weaknesses of every batter in the league. So confident am I of his judgment that I never shake my head. It means that I have to learn a great deal about the batters, features to which I had heretofore paid no attention."

This 1904 spring training photo shows Criger with Hugh Duffy and umpire Tim Hurst.

The battery of Lou Criger (L) and Cy Young (R), at the Huntington Avenue Grounds, ca. 1905.

Criger was behind the plate for some of Young's greatest games, including his perfect game against the Philadelphia Athletics at the Huntington Avenue Grounds on May 5, 1904, and his no-hitter against the New York Highlanders at Hilltop Park on June 30, 1908. Criger also caught all 20 innings of Young's famous duel with Rube Waddell on July 4, 1905. In 1903 the backstop was behind the plate for every game of Boston's eight-game triumph over the Pittsburgh Pirates in the first modern World Series. Twenty years after that success, Criger revealed that he had turned down a $12,000 offer from a gambler named Anderson to call "soft pitches" during the Series. In 1923 Criger, believing he was dying of tuberculosis, hired an attorney to file an affidavit with American League president Ban Johnson, who went public with the incident. Johnson, impressed with Criger's honesty, personally established a pension that helped Criger and other players after their playing days.

During his playing career Criger endured his share of bumps and bruises, a subject about which the catcher was particularly sensitive. While recuperating from a damaged finger during the 1901 campaign, Criger told *Sporting Life*, "They are very solicitous about my health. Just tell them for me that I am feeling perfectly well. I am out of the game just now with a bad finger, but will be in all right, and think I am good for many more years of ball playing before I quit. Every now and then someone sends me a clipping in which it is stated that I am not well. It is extremely annoying, not only to me, but to my folks." Nonetheless, Criger became so associated with injury that he later became a spokesman for the Elkhart-based Dr. Miles' Anti-Pain Pills.

With batterymate Cy Young nearing the end of his career, Criger was traded to the St. Louis Browns in December 1908 for catcher Tubby Spencer and $5,000 (some sources say $4,000). In one season with St. Louis, Criger batted just .170 with two extra-base hits in 212 at-bats. After the season Criger was again traded, this time to the New York Highlanders for pitcher Joe Lake and outfielder Ray Demmitt. Criger appeared in only 27 games for the Highlanders and batted just .188. The following year he played briefly for Milwaukee of the American Association and was player-manager for Boyne City of the Michigan State League. In 1912 Criger returned to the American League as pitching coach for the Browns. The 40-year-old played in one game when both Browns catchers got hurt.

Criger married the former Belle Louise Wolhaupter in 1893. They and their six children lived in Elkhart until 1909, when the family moved 22 miles northeast to a 40-acre farm at Bair Lake, Michigan. There, he spent many an offseason hunting and fishing with his ballplaying friends. In 1914 Criger developed tuberculosis in his left knee, and the following year his leg had to be amputated above the knee. In failing health, Criger moved to Nevada in the early 1920s and in 1924 relocated to the arid climate of Arizona, spending winters in Tucson and summers in Flagstaff. The family ran a bakery in Tucson. In 1920 Criger's son Rollo, also a catcher, joined the St. Louis Cardinals but never appeared in a game.

Criger died on May 14, 1934, in Tuscon and was buried in Evergreen Cemetery in that city. A Northern Indiana SABR chapter was named for Criger in the spring of 1998.

Note

This biography originally appeared in David Jones, ed., *Deadball Stars of the American League* (Washington, D.C.: Potomac Books, Inc., 2006).

Sources

Sporting Life

Elkhart Truth

St. Louis Post-Dispatch

Jeanette Criger Done (granddaughter and family historian)

George "Nig" Cuppy

By Charles F. Faber

Cuppy, with the Boston Nationals, 1900.

BECAUSE OF HIS dark complexion, he was called Nig.[1] For the same reason, some sportswriters referred to him as the Cuban Warrior or the Cuban Hero. But Nig Cuppy was not African-American or Cuban. He was a first-generation American, son of immigrants from Bavaria.

George Maceo Koppe was born on July 3, 1869, in Logansport, Indiana, fourth of the eight children of Christina Stieffenheffer Koppe and Christian Koppe. Christina came to the United States in 1845. Christian immigrated five years later. The couple married in 1856. In 1880 the family, including 11-year-old George, was living in Eaton, Ohio, where Christian worked as a brick and stone mason. Later they returned to Indiana. Christian and Christina were living apart in Jasper County in 1900. By this time George was no longer living at home. After playing baseball for independent clubs in Indiana, George started his career in Organized Baseball at the age of 20 with the Dayton (Ohio) Reds of the Tri-State League in 1890. His baseball name became Cuppy, the phonetic spelling of the German name Koppe. It is not clear when he acquired the nickname Nig. In 1891 Cuppy divided his time between two clubs in the New York-Pennsylvania League, Jamestown, New York, and Meadville, Pennsylvania. The right-handed pitcher won 21 games that season and found time to play 17 games in the outfield.

On April 16, 1892, the 22-year-old Cuppy made his major-league debut with the National League Cleveland Spiders. His first major-league win came in his first start, on April 23. He bested Cincinnati Reds starter Billy Rhines, who was knocked out of the box in the first inning. Cuppy allowed five earned runs on eight hits and six walks with a wild pitch as his mates beat Cincinnati 14-5 at League Park. The 5-foot-7, 160-pound hurler had an outstanding rookie season, winning 28 games against 13 losses and posting an earned-run average of 2.51, fourth in the league. He was second on the team in wins, an accomplishment that happened many times. For each of his first five seasons, Cuppy ranked second in wins among Cleveland pitchers, always behind future Hall of Famer Cy Young. During those five years, 1892-1896, Cuppy and Young combined for 279 wins, the most of any two teammates in the majors over that span. In 1894 Cuppy led the National League in shutouts. A good-hitting pitcher, he scored five runs in an 18-6 win over the Chicago Colts on August 9, 1895. Cuppy pitched a complete game in that contest, one of the 224 times in his career that he finished what he started.

Cuppy was known as a slow pitcher, not only for the number of off-speed pitches he threw, but also because of the time he took between deliveries, which many hitters found frustrating. Newspapers of the day took delight in describing Cuppy's actions in the pitcher's box. One reporter wrote, "It is really amusing to those in the stands to witness the maneuvers of this little twirler with the swarthy complexion and pearly teeth. He fondles the ball, rubs it on the back of his neck, grins at the batsman, and then stops to adjust his cap and hitch up his trousers. He does all this several more times before he delivers the ball to the batsman."[2]

In addition to his slow pitch, Cuppy also threw a jump ball, that is, a rising fastball. The elimination of the pitcher's box and lengthening of the distance to the plate in 1893 may have been at least partly responsible for a decline in his performance during the 1893 season, but he recovered in 1894.

According to the *Cleveland Press*, one day in 1894 Cuppy announced that he was going to spring a surprise on fans and players alike at that afternoon's game. When the game began Cuppy walked out into the pitcher's box wearing a glove on his left hand. Other fielders had worn gloves before, but this was believed to be the first time in history that a pitcher had used a glove. By the end of the season use of the glove had been adopted by other pitchers.[3]

During his first six seasons in the majors, Cuppy had five 20-win seasons. (He collected 17 victories in the exception, his "poor" 1893 season.) In 1897 his arm gave out. He won only ten games that season and never came close to 20 again. During Cuppy's tenure with Cleveland, the club consistently finished in the first division, including three seasons in second place, but they captured no pennants.

On March 29, 1899, Cuppy was transferred to the St. Louis club. (The St. Louis Browns were expelled from the league before the start of the 1899 season. The Robison brothers, who owned the Spiders, were allowed the St. Louis franchise without having to relinquish the Spiders. They took the best players from the 1898 Browns and Spiders and made an "A" team which stayed in St. Louis. The "B" team went to Cleveland, which went 20-134, drawing fewer than 10,000 fans for the season.) After playing second fiddle to Cy Young for so many years, was Cuppy now freed from comparisons with his more famous teammate? No. Young also joined St. Louis that season. However, Cuppy was sold to the Boston Beaneaters on May 23, 1900, and did not appear in a game for St. Louis that season. For the only time in his major-league career, Cuppy did not pitch on the same team as Young. With an 8-4 record, Cuppy won

Cuppy Image—A Welcomed Return to Boston

There are limited photograph of the Boston Americans players taken during their inaugural season. This 1901 picture depicts Sox pitcher George "Nig" Cuppy in a wind-up pitching motion during a Holsinger Studio photo shoot in Charlottesville, Virginia during Boston's first spring training.

This rare sepia-toned cabinet photograph was pilfered from the Michael T. "Nuf Ced" McGreevy Collection at the Boston Public Library in the 1970's. Fortunately, in 2011 an observant baseball collector who had purchased the image at an auction website, noticed Boston Public Library stamp. He arranged for its return to the delight of the Boston Public Library, baseball fans, and historians.

twice as many games as he lost that year, but he was far from the pitcher he had been in his heyday.

In 1901 as the American League gained major-league status, Cuppy joined a host of National Leaguers jumping to the new circuit. Among the jumpers was Cy Young. Both pitchers joined the Boston Americans. Cuppy and Young were teammates for one last time. This time Cuppy did not play second fiddle to Young; he was much further behind the maestro, ranking fourth in wins among the Boston pitchers with only four victories compared with Young's 33. Cuppy's four wins were outnumbered by his six losses, giving him the only losing season of his career.

The Americans' manager, Jimmy Collins, made an effort to speed up the pitcher's notoriously slow delivery. With the hyperbole that permeated sportswriting in that era, a reporter for a Cleveland newspaper wrote:

"Collins has served notice on Pitcher Cuppy that one and one-half minutes is the limit of time which will be allowed him in delivering the ball. Cuppy in the national league was noted as the living picture twirler. He assumed seventy-seven imposing and statuesque poses while in the act of delivering the ball, the poses melting into one another 'til the whole performance was like watching a kinetoscope picture with the machine slowed down. The bleachers used to take delight in rising and counting in unison from the time Cuppy received the ball through all the convolutions in his frame and the divers and sundry positions he assumes until with an Ajax-defying-the-lightning attitude he finally lets the ball go. ... Collins has given one of his young players the task of standing behind Cuppy as he warms up in practice. The youngster is armed with a long hatpin and at the count of eight if the ball isn't delivered, Cuppy receives a jab."[4]

Whether the manager's efforts speeded Cuppy's delivery is unknown. What is known is that it did not improve his effectiveness. During the season he was released, and his career on the big stage was over. Cuppy made his final major-league appearance on August 7, 1901, at the age of 32. His finale was a 10-4 loss to Joe McGinnity of the Orioles at Baltimore. A Logansport newspaper reported that Cuppy retained counsel in preparation of a lawsuit against the Americans for salary allegedly owed him. At the request of the club he went to Boston to enter negotiations on the matter.[5] The outcome of the negotiations was not reported.

Cuppy was noted for his bubbling good nature and his fondness for harmless practical jokes. Once he announced he was going to build a 22-story hotel in Logansport. It would be so luxurious that it would make the famed Palace Hotel in San Francisco look like a wrecked shanty on the Wabash. The absurdity of locating such a building in a small Indiana town did not register with the public. Cuppy received more than 100 letters in his mailbox. There were applications for positions as manager, clerk, cashier, and bellboy; inquiries from builders, architects, and dealers in hotel furnishings. Cuppy answered every letter. This was to be a $10,000,000 project he said. He was going to pay himself one million as manager. None of the job applicants was good enough; none of the drawings submitted by builders or architects was satisfactory; the furnishings were not elegant enough.[6]

After leaving the majors, Cuppy returned to Indiana, where he pitched for and managed an Elkhart semipro club in 1902. For some time he and his former catcher Lou Criger ran a billiard parlor, appropriately called The Battery. Later he entered the retail tobacco business. The 1910 census showed George Cuppy, the owner of a cigar store, living in Elkhart. Cuppy was an excellent trapshooter, who scored well in tournaments.[7]

Cuppy died of Bright's disease on his farm near Elkhart on July 27, 1922, at 53. He was buried at Rice Cemetery in Elkhart.

George "Nig" Cuppy was only a minor contributor to the Boston Americans in 1901. Unfortunately for him, he was released before the end of the season and was no longer around when Boston won the World Series in 1903. He never got to celebrate a league championship. However, he had posted 162 major-league victories against just 98 losses, which is certainly worthy of celebration.

Acknowledgement:

The kindness of Trey Strecker in sharing information about Cuppy's life and career is deeply appreciated.

Sources

Cuppy's file at the National Baseball Hall of Fame

Rich Eldred, "George Joseph Cuppy," in *Baseball's First Stars*, Robert L. Tiemann and Mark Rucker, eds. (Cleveland: Society for American Baseball Research, 1996), 46.

David Nemec. *Major League Baseball Profiles, 1871-1900*, vol. 1. (Lincoln: University of Nebraska Press, 2011), 40-41.

www.ancestry.com.

www.Baseball-Reference.com.

www.NewspaperArchive.com

Notes

1. Such a derogatory nickname would be unacceptable today, but nicknames based on physical characteristics were common in the early 20th century. Native Americans were routinely called "Chief"; deaf players were "Dummy." Some of the better known examples include: Chief Bender, Three-Finger Brown, Nig Clarke, Fats Fothergill, and Dummy Hoy.
2. *Logansport* (Indiana) *Pharos-Tribune,* August 8, 1900.
3. *Cleveland Press,* November 17, 1906.
4. *Cleveland Press,* June 19, 1901.
5. *Cleveland Press,* September 14, 1901.
6. *Logansport Daily Reporter,* September 14, 1908.
7. *New York Times,* April 28, 1919.

Cuppy depicted on tobacco card, 1893.

Tommy Dowd

By Bill Nowlin

AFTER NINE YEARS in the major leagues, Tommy Dowd's tenth and last season of big-league baseball was with the Boston Americans in the very first year of the new franchise, 1901. This was the team that became the Red Sox. Dowd was, in fact, the first player to ever play for the team, the leadoff batter in the top of the first inning of the Americans' first game. The game was played at Baltimore on April 26, 1901. Dowd had turned 32 six days earlier. This was Thomas Jefferson "Buttermilk" Dowd, born on April 20, 1869, in Holyoke, Massachusetts. He was the first ballplayer for the franchise who was born in the Commonwealth of Massachusetts, and the only player for the Red Sox clearly named for a United States president. And he played every single game of the 1901 season.

Dowd, the left fielder, led off that first game by grounding right back to the Baltimore Orioles' pitcher, Joe McGinnity, and was thrown out at first base. He was 1-for-5 that first day, singling in the top of the eighth and driving in Lou Criger. Boston lost the game, 10-6. Dowd also had the first stolen base for the new team. There were no thefts in the first two games, but Dowd walked and stole second in the first inning of game No. 3, on April 29, 1901, then stole third and scored on a bad throw to third — all before the second batter completed his at-bat.

In Boston's first home game, played on May 8 at the Huntington Avenue Grounds, Dowd earned a number of firsts. He was the first batter to play before the home crowd, and he got the first hit in Boston, a first-inning leadoff single to left field. He was sacrificed to second, and scored the first run when Jimmy Collins drove him in with a single. The final score of the game was 12-4 over the Philadelphia Athletics.

Dowd played Brown University baseball from 1888 to 1891. A brief article in the March 6, 1891, *Boston Globe* said that "T. J. Dowd, second baseman of the Brown University team, has been signed by the Boston Athletic Club team." This was the American Association team known as the Boston Reds, not to be confused with the National League's Boston Beaneaters. The American Association approved the contract the next day. Dowd played his first game for the Reds in Baltimore on April 8, in front of 5,000 fans. The Reds played under manager Arthur Irwin. Dowd "made a beautiful running catch in the ninth inning, for which he got a round of cheers."[1] He played right field and batted ninth, after the pitcher. He was 1-for-4 and scored a run, but Baltimore won, 11-7. The *Brown Alumni Magazine* wrote that the *Globe*'s Tim Murnane had called him "the best center fielder he'd ever seen, especially for his skill at sprinting back on a ball over his head and then turning left or right for the catch. For years Dowd held the unofficial record time for circling the bases." He was fast; he stole 366 bases during his years in the majors.

Dowd also attended other colleges as well, and studied law at Georgetown. In that 1891 debut season, he appeared in four games for Boston with just the one hit and the one run, in 11 at-bats. He was then sold (or loaned) to the Washington Nationals. Dowd was a hit in Washington. The April 27 *Boston Globe* quoted the *Washington Post*: "Tommy Dowd owns the town, and can have all the earth but Italy for the asking." He'd gone from the team that finished first—the Reds—to the team that wound up finishing last. He was the Senators' regular second baseman, appearing in 112 games. His .259 was a few points above the team average. Dowd played in 1892 for Washington as well, getting into 144 games and hitting .243. This time, his average was four points above the team's. He was released in November and was signed on December 1 by the St. Louis Browns, for whom he played the next four-plus seasons. The release and sign appears to have been part of a prearranged deal; the August 6, 1989, issue of *Sporting Life* wrote that St. Louis executive Chris Von der Ahe had seen Dowd in action and after "becoming stuck on his playing, bought his release from Washington." But by mid-1898 he was seen to have "retrograded rather than advanced."

Beginning in 1893, the National League was a 12-team league. Dowd was never on teams finishing in the top six. His batting average fluctuated from .282 in 1893 (when he mostly played left field) to .271 (1894, when he was the right fielder) to .323 (right field) to .265 (back to his original position at second base). His best year without a doubt was 1895 (the .323 season), when he drove in a career-high 74 runs.

The Browns were a team that had managerial instability, to say the least. Bill Watkins was the skipper in 1893 and Doggie Miller was in 1894. There were four managers in 1895: Al Buckenberger, Chris Von Der Ahe (for one game), Joe Quinn, and Lou Phelan. The 1896 team topped even that, with five managers: Harry Diddlebock, Arlie Latham (three games), Von Der Ahe (two games), Roger Conner (under whom the team was 8-37), and Tommy Dowd, who oversaw 25 wins against 38 defeats. Dowd's work was regarded highly, at least at first, in *Sporting Life*. The August 15, 1896, issue saw a "great improvement" in the team during his first couple of weeks on the job. "Roger Conner as manager lacked firmness," the publication opined. "There is none of that nonsense now. Dowd, in addition to being a tip-top ball player, has a good head. He has taken advantage of his opportunity and possesses an education above the average. It was Dowd's original intention to become a lawyer. His studiousness now stands him well in hand."

Dowd was the first of four managers in 1897. "He Will Hustle Hard to Keep the Browns out of Last Place" was the subhead in a March 20 *Sporting News* article titled "Tommie's Task." It was, the paper added, "a task that would dismay many men." In fact, it did. The Browns posted a record of 6-22 before Dowd was relieved of his duties, surrendering them to Hugh Nicol. After appearing in 35 games, Tommy was traded on June 1 to the Philadelphia Phillies for Bill Hallman, Dick Harvey, and the princely sum of $300. He finished the season, batting .292 to the .262 he'd hit for St. Louis, reverting back to right field. On November 10, the Phillies traded him back to St. Louis, but as part of a much larger trade, one involving two played named Cross going in opposite directions: Lave Cross, Dowd, Jack Clements, Jack Taylor, and $1,000 was the package for the Browns, who swapped Monte Cross, Red Donahue, and Klondike Douglass.

Dowd played second base in 1898, hitting .244—just three points below the team average. The Browns finished last in the league standings. He stayed with St. Louis until March 29, 1899, when he was part of a group of 15 players assigned to the Cleveland Spiders. (The St. Louis club had gone into receivership and the assets were sold at a sheriff's auction for a sum in excess of $70,000. The sale included all the stands of Sportsman's Park and the lease held on the ground, and a number of ballplayers.)[2]

The team in St. Louis changed its name to the Perfectos. On March 29, the following ballplayers were all assigned to the Cleveland Spiders: Kid Carsey, Jack Clements, Lave Cross, Dick Harley, Bill Hill, Jim Hughey, Harry Lochhead, Harry Maupin, Joe Quinn, Jack Stivetts, Willie Sudhoff, Joe Sugden, Suter Sullivan, Tommy Tucker, and Tommy Dowd.

The Perfectos did improve as a team, reaching fifth place. The Spiders finished last, with the unbelievably bad record of 20-134, finishing 84 games out of first place. Their center fielder, Dowd, scored a team-leading 81 runs, batting .278, but drove in only 35 runs. He led the team in stolen bases with 28.

Dowd was out of the majors in 1900, working for more lucrative pay at a laundry business in Holyoke, then playing for Chicago and Milwaukee of the American Association, which by then had reverted to minor-league status. On March 29, 1901, Dowd signed with the Boston Americans and returned for the one final year.

Holyoke was his home. He was born there and he died there. He is buried there at Calvary Cemetery. Both parents had come to the United States from Ireland. Jeremiah Dowd was a brick mason or bricklayer (he used both terms) and did some farming. His wife, Mary (Lynch) Dowd, was listed in the 1870 Census as "keeping house." It would have been a full-time job. At the time of that year's census, when Tommy was 1 year old, he had older brothers Michael, John, Jeremiah, and Eddie, and an older sister, Mary. But the Dowd parents weren't finished yet. After Tommy was born, they added Kate, Lawrence, and Theresa to the Dowd brood. Michael and John became bricklayers, too. Mary became a dressmaker and Theresa a schoolteacher. Thomas became a professional ballplayer.

He was right there at the beginning of franchise play, on April 1, 1901 when Jimmy Collins and 11 members of Boston's brand-new American League club began their first workout of their first spring training, at Charlottesville, Virginia, with two hours of light practice on the grounds of the local YMCA. Collins, Stahl, Freeman, Dowd, Hemphill, Schrecongost, Jones, McLean, Mitchell, Kane, McCarthy, and Connor joined in the session. Cuppy, Criger, Parent, Ferris, Kellum, and McKenna reported the following day. Perhaps the first sign of exceptions for Red Sox superstars was set — Cy Young was training in Hot Springs and due to report on Opening Day in Baltimore.

Dowd had a standout game in the second spring training game, a 23-0 win over the University of Virginia nine on April 11. It was only the second game the team ever played. Tim Murnane covered spring training for the *Globe* and it's likely he who wrote the account: "Everyone but Hemphill hit the ball. Ferris led with a home run and two singles. Close behind came Parent, with two screeching doubles and a single, and Dowd with four singles. Collins lifted the leather over the palings, besides singling."

Dowd's last major-league games were both on September 28, 1901, in the final day's doubleheader. He was 1-for-5 and 2-for-3. For the season he batted .268 — close to his .271 career mark — with three home runs and 52 RBIs. Boston wrapped up the first year of the franchise with two high-scoring wins over Milwaukee, 8-3 and 10-9. (Jack Slattery, the only Boston native playing for the Americans that year, made his major-league debut as Boston's catcher in the first game. He went 1-for-3, and then was injured in the eighth.) Dowd homered for Boston in the first game. The second game perhaps didn't offer the best competition. "Both pitchers worked wretchedly," wrote the *Washington Post*. Manager Jimmy Collins hit two homers for Boston, but it was Hobe Ferris who won it in the bottom of the seventh with a two-run triple. Then the umpire (games in this era often had just one), Tommy Connolly, called the game due to darkness. Boston wound up the year with a six-game winning streak but finished four games behind the first-place White Sox. They drew three times as many fans as the Boston Nationals. The team that would become the Red Sox was here to stay.

Tommy Dowd had aspirations for 1902 and applied to the National Association for a franchise in Milwaukee but his request was referred to committee.[3] He went to the minor leagues in 1902, playing for the snappily-named Amsterdam-Gloversville-Johnstown Jags (in the Class B New York State League). There was a method to his seeming madness, though: He owned the club, and also managed it. And batted .287 in 404 at-bats, and 94 games. Alas, the team finished last, 29-72.

The next year Dowd played for two clubs — 55 games with the Baltimore Orioles in the Eastern League and 33 games as player and sometime manager in Nashua, New Hampshire — a team without a name. One of his fellow outfielders was Moonlight Graham. With the

Orioles he played under two future Hall of Famers, Wilbert Robinson and Hugh Jennings, and hit .228. In Nashua, B-level ball in the New England League, he hit .276. He was busy in 1904, too, but without any extra duties, playing Class B ball for both the New Orleans Pelicans (Southern Association, 30 games, .256) and then, right in his own hometown, the Holyoke Paperweights (Connecticut State League, 82 games, .241).

In the spring of 1905, Dowd coached the Williams College baseball team in Western Massachusetts during the school year, then managed in Burlington, Vermont, the rest of the year.

In 1906 and 1907 he returned to the Paperweights, as player-manager, running the team for part of 1906 (and hitting .270) but hitting only .216 in his final year as an active player. Though not successful at the plate, he led the 1907 team to the Connecticut State League pennant.

The next three seasons, Dowd managed exclusively. He raised hopes in Hartford in 1908, assuming the reins there. George E. Cox wrote before the season got under way, "The players, upon reporting, will be given a 'treatment' in the Dowd method which has been so successful in other cities where applied in the past. No laggards, says Dowd, will be tolerated on the team. He adds that he will demand that every player give his best efforts, but will not ask anything more than he is willing to do himself. The fans in this city like this sort of talk."[4] He didn't last the year as manager.

In 1909 and 1910, Dowd managed the New Bedford Whalers of the New England League, placing sixth the first year (after coaching at Williams again) and winning the League pennant the second. In March 1911, he was involved in a controversy regarding a case of farming player George Walsh between Boston's National League team and the Whalers, which the National Commission found objectionable, adding in its report, "This is but one of many violations of the laws of organized base ball by the New Bedford Club within the past year. The same unlawful and irregular tactics were employed by its offices in the Temple and Ulrich cases."[5]

Dowd and Organized Baseball parted company, but Tommy kept busy, coaching independent baseball teams, Williams College, and Amherst College, too. Among the players he is credited with discovering were Chick Evans and Rabbit Maranville.

On July 2, 1933, the body of a man was found in the Connecticut River near Holyoke. Two days later, Dowd's brother Jeremiah identified the body as that of Thomas Dowd. The death certificate ruled his death as due to accidental drowning.

He was single and had been retired since December 1914. He is said to have "fallen upon unfortunate days" for some unspecified period of time prior to his death.[6]

Sources

In addition to the sources noted in this biography, the author also accessed the online SABR Encyclopedia, Retrosheet.org, and Baseball-Reference.com.

Notes

1 *Boston Globe*, April 9, 1891.

2 *Boston Globe*, March 18, 1899.

3 *Sporting Life*, January 25, 1902.

4 *Sporting Life*, April 25, 1908.

5 *Sporting Life*, March 25, 1911.

6 *Hartford Courant*, July 6, 1933.

Hobe Ferris

By Dennis Auger

AT 5-FEET-8 AND 162 pounds, slick-fielding second baseman Hobe Ferris looked the part of a light-hitting middle infielder, an initial impression supported by his lifetime .239 batting average and .265 on-base percentage. But looks can be deceiving, as Ferris was one of the hardest hitters in the American League. Twenty-eight percent of the right-hander's 1,146 career hits went for extra bases, a ratio exceeded only by 10 other American Leaguers during the Deadball Era, and higher than such renowned sluggers as Ty Cobb, Frank Baker, Elmer Flick, and Jimmy Collins. During his nine-year major-league career, Ferris ranked in the league's top five in triples and home runs three times each. Defensively, Ferris was widely regarded as one of the best fielding second basemen of his time, and led the league in putouts twice, assists twice, and double plays once during his seven years with Boston. "At his best," the *Washington Post* observed in 1908, "[his defense] made Larry Lajoie look like a second-rater." A fierce competitor and notorious umpire baiter, the hot-tempered Ferris was later described by sportswriter Fred Lieb as a "rough and tumble old time player that could take it and dish it out."

Hobe Ferris, with the 1903 World Champion Boston Americans.

Most sources record Ferris as being born on December 7, 1877, in Providence, Rhode Island. However, the Rhode Island State Archives have no record of his birth, and census records indicate that Albert Sayles Ferris was actually born in England, as were his parents, and immigrated to the United States in 1879. Having developed his baseball skills on the Providence sandlots, Ferris advanced to the next level by playing for a team in North Attleboro, Massachusetts, in 1898. One day the shortstop was missing, so Hobe, "with one side of his face swollen with a toothache," filled in and handled 22 chances perfectly, a feat that won him a starting position. Having kept himself in fine shape by playing polo during the offseason, Ferris reported to Pawtucket of the New England League in 1899. Despite an initial batting slump, he finished with a .295 average and won accolades for his fielding. In 1900 the infielder joined Norwich in the Connecticut League, where he played shortstop and batted .292 with 31 extra-base hits.

Before the 1901 season Ferris was drafted by the Cincinnati Reds, but instead jumped to the American League to play for the Boston Americans. That same offseason, shortstop Freddy Parent signed with the club, and Ferris shifted to second base. It was initially a rough transition for Ferris, who committed 61 errors in 1901, the second highest total by a second baseman in American League history. (That same year, Detroit second baseman Kid Gleason committed 64 errors.) At the plate, the 23-year-old Ferris batted .250, drove in 63 runs, and led American League rookies with 15 triples.

The next year, 1902, Ferris again drove in 63 runs while hitting eight home runs (tied for seventh best in the league) and 14 triples. His glove work also showed signs of improvement, as he committed 22 fewer errors in the field and showed brilliant range. In one June contest,

Ferris recorded 11 putouts, and on another occasion he accepted 26 chances in two consecutive games.

But it was Ferris's numerous run-ins with umpires that garnered the most attention. In May he tangled with umpire Jack Sheridan and received a three-day suspension from American League president Ban Johnson. "Ferris deserves his suspension, and while it will hurt Collins' club, I am glad of it," wrote Peter Kelley of the *Boston Journal*. "We do not want any of the John McGraw biz in Boston, and the sooner that certain players become reconciled to that fact, the better it will be for Boston baseball lovers. I hope this will be a lesson for Hobe, for if he behaves, he will make a big name for himself."

Ferris never reformed his ways, but he remained an integral part of the Boston club as it captured the 1903 American League pennant. In August the second baseman's defense led to two victories in a doubleheader against St. Louis. "When the Browns broke into a rally Hobe cut them down with a triple play in one game and worked a double in the next that thrilled 19,000 fans," one account said. "Retiring five men on two chances is quite an achievement for one day." For the season Ferris batted an unimpressive .251, but hit a career-high nine home runs and scored a career-best 69 runs. In the Americans' World Series triumph over Pittsburgh, Ferris recovered from a poor showing in the first game, in which he made two errors (and briefly raised suspicions that Boston had thrown the game), to make a spectacular unassisted double play on a Honus Wagner line drive in Game Two, preserving a 3-0 Boston victory. In the eighth and final game, Ferris drove in all three Boston runs off Deacon Phillippe to secure the franchise's first world championship.

In 1904 Ferris slumped badly at the plate, as his batting average dipped to .213, but he figured prominently in Boston's narrow victory in the American League pennant race, scoring from second base on a fly ball and error in a showdown end-of-season series with the New York Highlanders to give Boston a 1-0 victory. It was the final team triumph of Ferris's major-league career, as the aging Boston roster unraveled from 1905 to 1907. Still in his prime, Ferris continued to post low batting averages but ranking among the league leaders in extra-base hits and providing Gold Glove-caliber defense at second base. He also continued to make headlines whenever his nasty temper flared on the ball field, as occurred on September 11, 1906.

In that afternoon's game against the Highlanders at New York's Hilltop Park, Boston outfielder Jack Hayden took a leisurely route on a fly ball hit to short right field, which Ferris himself failed to go after, and the result was an inside-the-park home run. Returning to the bench at the end of the inning, Ferris initiated a vile verbal attack on Hayden for what he perceived as lackadaisical play. Hayden in turn landed three stingers to Hobe's jaw. After their teammates separated them, Ferris braced himself on a rail and thrust his foot into Hayden's face, knocking out several teeth. The fisticuffs continued and eventually both players were arrested. Neither pressed charges, but in response to what one reporter called "the most disgraceful affair ever predicated by any ball players on the ball field," Ban Johnson suspended Ferris for the remainder of the season. For his part, Hobe declared, "I suppose I'm a fool for being in earnest and trying to win, but that is my way. I can't

Ferris in posed photograph, ca. 1901.

Double play combination, Hobe Ferris (front) with Fred Parent, ca. 1901.

help it." Ferris lasted one more season in Boston before owner John Taylor dealt him to the St. Louis Browns in a six-player trade. Explaining the move, Taylor suggested that Hobe had "outlived his usefulness."

With the Browns Ferris enjoyed perhaps his best season as a professional in 1908, as he posted career highs in batting (.270), on-base percentage (.291), and RBIs (74). Because Jimmy Williams was already established at second base, Ferris shifted to third, where he combined with shortstop Bobby Wallace to form what one writer called "the stonewall defense." Hobe adjusted very well to his new position, and led the American League's third basemen in putouts, double plays, and fielding percentage. Browns manager Jimmy McAleer was effusive in his praise of Ferris: "I have been in the game a long while, but I have never seen a man play such remarkable ball for a team as has Ferris for us. ... You never see him that he is not hustling."

The 1909 campaign, however, was a disappointment, as Ferris's average plummeted to .216. He claimed he had a difficult time getting in shape, and as his season deteriorated, his frustration level spiraled to the point that a sportswriter sarcastically wrote that Ferris "has a sweet disposition when he is not getting his share of base hits." In a game against Washington he hit a fly ball to left, and as he returned to the dugout complained to Tom Hughes, the Washington pitcher, "I ought to have killed that one." The hurler retorted, "You hit like an old woman." Hobe applied "a few choice names to Hughes, who was willing to stop the ball game while he got at Ferris. Umpire Egan, however, waved him back and prevented hostilities."

After the 1909 season Ferris was released to Minneapolis of the American Association, where he produced respectable numbers for three seasons as his playing time gradually decreased. He spent the 1913 season with St. Paul in a utility role before drawing his release. Ferris played one season for Wilkes-Barre of the New York State League before that club, too, released him. *Baseball Magazine* clarified the reasons for Hobe's decline: "Ferris is let out because he has slowed up both with arms and legs—finds it hard to make the throw to first, hard to stoop quickly for fast grounders."

By 1920 Ferris, his wife, Helena, and their daughter, Natalie, had established roots in Detroit, where Hobe worked as a mechanic and occasionally played for semipro teams. As the years passed, however, Ferris became obese. On March 18, 1938, he came across a newspaper account of ex-Tiger Fatty Fothergill's hospitalization. As he informed his wife of this story, Ferris died of a heart attack. He was 60 years old.

Note

This biography originally appeared in David Jones, ed., *Deadball Stars of the American League* (Washington, D.C.: Potomac Books, Inc., 2006).

Sources

Newspapers

Boston Globe

Chicago Tribune

Evening Times (Pawtucket)

Los Angeles Times

New York Times

Providence Journal

Washington Post

Books, Articles

Anderson, David. *More Than Merkle*. (Lincoln: University of Nebraska, 2000).

Browning, Reed. *Cy Young: A Baseball Life*. (Amherst: University of Massachusetts, 2000).

Carter, Craig, ed. *The Sporting News Complete Baseball Record Book 2001.*

DeValeria, Dennis, and Jeanne DeValeria. *Honus Wagner*. (Pittsburgh: University of Pittsburgh, 1998).

James, Bill. *All-Time Major League Handbook*. 2nd ed. (STATS, 2002).

James, Bill. *The New Bill James Historical Baseball Abstract*. (STATS, 2001).

Masur, Louis. *Autumn Glory*. (New York: Macmillan, 2003).

Neft, David, Richard Cohen, and Michael Neft, eds. *The Sports Encyclopedia: Baseball 1999*. (New York: St. Martin's Press, 1999).

Palmer, Pete, and Gary Gillette, eds. *The Baseball Encyclopedia*. (New York: Barnes & Noble, 2004).

Phelon, W,A., "The Month's Parade." *Baseball Magazine*, April 1915.

Reichler, Joseph. *The Baseball Encyclopedia*, 6th ed. (New York: Macmillan, 1985).

Reichler, Joseph. *The Great All-Time Baseball Record Book*. (New York: Macmillan, 1981).

Stout , Glenn, ed. *Impossible Dreams*. (Boston: Houghton Mifflin, 2003).

Stout, Glenn, and Richard Johnson. *Red Sox Century*. (Boston: Houghton Mifflin, 2000).

Thorn, John, Pete Palmer, and Michael Gershman. eds. *Total Baseball*, 6th ed. (New York: Total Sports, 1999).

Tourangeau., Richard. Remembering Opening Day a Century Ago." *The National Pastime*, Volume 22, pp. 19-24, 2002.

Ward, John. "The Keystone Kings." *Baseball Magazine*. October, 1914, pp. 43-48.

Other Resources

Hobe Ferris's file at the National Baseball Hall of Fame

Rhode Island State Archives

Heritage Quest

Frank Foreman

by James Elfers

FRANCIS ISAIAH "MONKEY" Foreman's life began and ended in Baltimore, Maryland. In between he played virtually everywhere in the Northeast and Midwest and seemingly forever. He was one of 19 men who played in four major leagues: the Union Association, the American Association, the National League, and the inaugural seasons of the American League. His minor-league career took him through seven leagues, primarily in the East and Midwest.

Known throughout his career as a comedian, Foreman may not have had the temperament for umpiring in the major leagues, a task he performed briefly on the major-league level in the twilight of his big-league career. He looked like the stereotypical 19th-century baseball player as he wore a well-maintained handlebar mustache which, at least according to Hollywood, was *de rigueur* for the day. He stood an even 6 feet tall and weighed 169 pounds. Fulfilling another stereotype of left-handed hurlers, Foreman was something of a flake and was always good for a joke or a laugh. His nickname came from one of his favorite on-field impersonations. So well did he impersonate a simian that *Sporting Life* was led to comment, "Frank Foreman should dispose of his inimitable impersonations. His portraiture of the monkey has a tendency to strengthen the Darwinian Theory."[1]

Frank's younger brother, John Davis "Brownie" Foreman, followed him to both the major leagues and the umpiring ranks. His father, George Washington Foreman, was born in 1837 and worked as a steamfitter, cotton mill worker, and engineer. His mother, Anne Elizabeth, was born in either 1841 or 1843. According to a distant cousin of the family, Suzanne De Vier, and Ancestry.com, there were three children in the family. Frank had an older brother, Joseph E. Foreman, born around 1860, who was employed as a machinist—the very same work that Frank sometimes engaged in when not playing ball. There was also a sister, Ella May, born in 1881.

Born during the Civil War, on May 1, 1863, Frank grew up in the Woodbury section of Baltimore. He and John, 12 years younger, grew up playing on the city's lots where both boys distinguished themselves. Frank played for the local nine, the Woodbury Baseball Team. Though he tried all the positions, it soon became clear that pitching was his forte. A teammate and friend described a game from 1882 or 1883: "I think the last game I played with him was on the Huntingdon grounds against the pastime club.... Foreman struck out 16 men in that game."[2]

Around this time Frank married a local girl, Annie Bates Barton. Like him, she was of English extraction on both sides of her family.[3] The marriage lasted until

Annie Foreman died in 1950. At the age of 21 he became a professional when he joined the Chicago/Pittsburg franchise of the upstart Union Association. The Union Association was the brainchild of Henry V. Lucas, a St. Louis railroad millionaire. Lucas went to war with the established National League and American Association and those leagues' oft-opposed reserve clause. He attempted to lure big names to the new venture but was largely unsuccessful. Baseball historian Bill James maintains that, in retrospect, the UA should not be considered a major league. He notes that not even the *Spalding Guide* of 1885 considered the UA among the major leagues of the previous season. Of all the players of UA only about 40— including Foreman— had any sort of career after 1884. Illustrating James's point is the league's tendency for signing greenhorn players such as Frank Foreman.[4]

The Union Association was a woefully organized league. The strongest and only talented team was Lucas's own St. Louis Maroons. Every other team in the league was a decided also-ran. The Chicago and Baltimore franchises were both owned by A.H. Henderson, a Baltimore mattress manufacturer. Foreman parlayed the Baltimore connection he shared with the team's owner to land his contract with the Chicago Browns. Thus it was that he made what is considered his major-league debut on May 15, 1884.

Illustrating that perhaps Foreman was too green for even this maiden league, he had a thoroughly mediocre 1-2 pitching record with a 4.50 earned-run average. Mediocrity would be the hallmark of Foreman's career: He ended his tour of the major leagues with a 96-93 record.

Not a lot of people saw Foreman pitch in Chicago. Because the UA was noncompetitive, the National League White Stockings easily outdrew the Chicago Browns and forced them to relocate from the Windy City to the Smoky City in August. Once in Pittsburg, the Browns were renamed the Stogies.

Demonstrating the fly-by-night nature of the Union Association, Foreman next played with a second franchise that was part of the UA's musical-chairs season. Dropped by the Browns, he ended up with the Kansas City Cowboys. Until June 1 the Cowboys' spot in the Union Association's standings had been occupied by the Altoona, Pennsylvania, Mountain City. After compiling a 6-19 record Altoona, the smallest city to ever host a major-league franchise, folded and was replaced by the Kansas City Cowboys, who became the city's first major-league team.

Foreman was either given his outright release or traded to Kansas City. In any event he was on the mound for Kansas City on June 19 when they appeared in Chicago. He pitched for his new team against his old teammates and was completely ineffective in a 7-1 loss. Dropped after the one game, Foreman returned to Baltimore, but not for long. Within days he had journeyed to nearby Lancaster, Pennsylvania, where he joined the Ironsides of the Eastern League. Piecing together how good a player he was is difficult because the league's statistics are incomplete. Playing primarily in the outfield, Foreman was also given a chance to pitch. He started 15 games, completed 14, and had a 5-9 record in 120⅔ innings with an ERA of 2.24. Not bad at all for a 21-year-old rookie. But Foreman's actual statistics may be quite different due to the incompleteness of the statistics.

After wintering in Baltimore, Foreman found work in the 1885 season with the Baltimore Orioles of the American Association. Before he was dropped in late June, he had his first winning season, 2-1 with a 6.00 ERA. He also put in a two-game appearance with the Newark Domestics of the Eastern League. He acted strictly as an outfielder and got just seven at-bats. After the season Foreman managed and served as an instructor at a roller rink. (1885 was a banner year for roller skating. In 1884 ball bearings had been added to roller skates, creating the modern roller skate. For the first time virtually everyone could skate with minimal effort or athleticism. This kicked off a worldwide craze for four-wheeled relaxation. Rinks popped up everywhere from the smallest country hamlets to the largest cities. Foreman got in on the ground floor and profited handsomely.[5])

Foreman claimed that skating kept him in shape but by 1887 the fad had abated somewhat and Foreman sought work again in baseball. He played for both the Mansfield and Columbus Buckeyes in the Ohio State League. He appeared in eight games, seven as a pitcher. According to baseball-reference.com, he won one game for each team and lost three for Mansfield and one for Columbus. At home in 1888 he was scouted by fellow Baltimore resident Thomas York, manager of the Albany (New York) Governors of the International Association, and easily landed a position on the team. Foreman's appearance with Albany, if the statistics are to be believed, was one for the ages. He appeared in 42 games in the outfield and 39 on the mound (he probably played in the field on some days on which he also pitched). He went 9-24 with a 2.96 ERA on a truly terrible team. The team went 18-87, meaning that Foreman won half of his team's games! His batting, on the other hand, was an abysmal .199. His workhorse heroics must have appealed to the Orioles, who needed pitching, so in 1889 Foreman was back with the team. He had turned down several offers from teams in both the American Association and the National League to play in his hometown.

In a remarkable turnaround, 1889 was be one of the finest seasons Foreman ever had. As part of the Orioles' rotation he pitched 414 innings, won 23 games and lost 21 with an ERA of 3.52. Demonstrating a knack for wildness, Foreman led the league with 40 hit batsmen and walked 137. He started 48 games and completed 43. His wildness caused *Sporting Life* to assert, "Frank Foreman is not quite up to the standard of Association pitchers"[6] — a characterization that neatly summarized his entire career.

In March 1890 Foreman's contract was purchased by the Cincinnati Reds of the National League. One negative was that it took him away from his batterymate, Tom Quinn, probably the most effective catcher Foreman had ever been teamed with. *Sporting Life* noted: "Foreman is most effective when Quinn catches him."[7]

Before agreeing to the contract with the Reds, Foreman passed up a chance to join with disgruntled players who were moving to the upstart Players League. He flirted with an offer from the Philadelphia team, going so far as to accepting an $800 advance from the Athletics. Only personal intervention from the Reds president kept him in the National League.[8] The final destination of the Athletics advance is lost to history.

In Cincinnati Foreman stayed with his young family in a boarding house only a few blocks from the boarding house where team manager Tom Loftus and several teammates roomed. The Queen City was the only other place besides Baltimore where Foreman lived for any length of time.

He was not entirely happy with the Reds. He really missed Tom Quinn. "Frank Foreman would like to go back to Baltimore for the sake of having Tommy Quinn catch him. He says, 'Unless a pitcher is receiving cooperative assistance from his catcher he suffers from a terrible handicap.'"[9] The loss of Quinn resulted in a severe dropoff in his skills. His final results for the season were a 13-10 record with a 3.95 ERA. Despite his gripes about missing Tommy Quinn, Foreman had a pretty good first season in the National League. While he racked up more walks and fewer strikeouts, the competition was tougher. He started 24 games and completed 23 of them, something for anyone to be proud of.

Once the season was over, Foreman found himself in a low-stress job, no doubt set up by the Reds. He worked in Stern's Clothing store for $80 a month. Alluding to possible family troubles, *Sporting Life* mentioned that "Frank Foreman's family have gone to Baltimore and Foreman would not mind getting back there himself. He seems imbued with the idea that his room in Cincinnati is preferred to his company."[10] As it turned out he spent most of the offseason in Cincinnati apart from his family. Eventually he did return east, finding work as a machinist in Woodbury.

Desperate to return to the baseball in the Baltimore area, Foreman jumped his contract with the Reds to sign for $300 a season less to play with Washington of

Frank Foreman, from Sporting Life 1889.

the American Association. His 1891 season with Washington was a bit of a step down from Cincinnati. He won 18 games and lost 20 with a 4.34 ERA, pitching 345⅓ innings. Like other pitchers he had to adjust to a new longer pitching distance of 60 feet 6 inches, an increase of 10 1/2 feet. The increased distance and his extensive pitching took a toll on Foreman's arm, however, and he complained of arm trouble throughout the following season.

Evidence of arm trouble is seen in his statistics. Completely ineffective in 1892, he appeared in only 11 games for Washington, now in the National League, winning two and losing four before he was traded to Baltimore (then in the National League), for whom he pitched in four games and lost three without a win. He also played five games in the outfield for Baltimore. He ended the season with Buffalo of the Eastern League strictly as an outfielder and hit .267.

Foreman kept himself in baseball shape. On May 13, 1893, *Sporting Life* reported, "Pitcher Frank Foreman says this is the first year since 1890 that he has not had a sore arm. He practices at Union Park in Baltimore every day."[11] The paper also said he would be given a trial by the Giants. Foreman was quite full of himself in 1893: "Pitcher Foreman who is free to sign with any club writes from Woodbury, Baltimore, that he is in the best condition. Far better, in fact, than at any time last season. He thinks he could hold his own against all comers in the big leagues this season."[12]

Foreman did in fact end up with the Giants in 1893, for two games with a record of 1-0 but a nightmarish ERA of 27.00. When not working on his pitching, Foreman once again managed his skating rink. He was out of Organized Baseball completely in 1894 as his arm was completely useless. In 1895 he recovered enough to turn in an 11-14 record with a 4.11 ERA for eighth-place Cincinnati. He batted .309 with seven doubles, two home runs, and 11 RBIs. Despite his sore arm, this season may have been his best. His earned-run average was the best on the Reds' pitching staff.

After the season Foreman found a novel way to keep himself in shape. Already an adept roller skater, he added ice skating to his résumé. The brand-new North Avenue Rink was a wonder of 19th-century technology. Wrote the *Baltimore Sun:* "The building is of brick with a graystone front and iron roof, and is 75 feet by 300 feet. The skating surface is 55 feet by 250 feet on a foundation resting solidly on the ground. Seven consecutive floors were laid with interlinings of waterproof paper and wool. On this foundation is built a seamless pan, which contains the artificially frozen ice for skating. Over three and one-half miles of one and one-half inch pipe are laid throughout the pan. This is covered by four inches of water, which is frozen solid to 100 tons of ice in 37 hours."[13] The day the *Sun* ran this article the rink hosted the first ice hockey game played in the US on an artificial surface when players from Johns Hopkins University challenged the Baltimore Athletic Club to a match.

The 1896 season in Cincinnati was a turnaround. Either Reds coach Buck Elwood or Denver's coach McGlone (sources vary) developed an exercise regime that was credited with bringing Foreman "back to life again."[14]

The process hardly seems revolutionary. Foreman described it thusly: "Just take and rub your arm in a brisk manner. Then let cold water run on it for fifteen or twenty minutes, hold it under the hydrant. Then give it another good rub and that will help it."[15]

However primitive the treatment seems today, there is no doubt that it worked wonders. In 1896 Foreman had perhaps his best major-league season so far: 14-7 with a 3.97 ERA. He appeared in 27 games, started 22 and completed 17. The Reds were much improved, especially on the mound. The third-place team's ERA was 3.67, second best in the league. (Younger brother Brownie was briefly a teammate. He appeared in four games, winning one and losing three. It marked the end of his abbreviated playing career.)

For his efforts Frank thought he deserved a big pay raise, but the Reds thought differently. At the close of the season he remained the only unsigned Red, and in 1897 he was with the

Indianapolis Indians of the Western League. There Foreman put together the two best seasons of his professional career. The Reds must have kicked themselves when they saw the Western League box scores. In 43 games in 1897 Foreman went 30-9 in 332 innings with a 1.87 ERA. The next season, 1898, was a bit of a drop-off but still impressive, especially since Foreman was now 35 years old. He won 24 games and lost 11. In both seasons he also played the outfield, batting .225 and .231. After those seasons Baltimore and Louisville, among other teams, wanted Foreman but couldn't land him. The main problem was the contract he had signed with John T. Brush, owner of the Indians. No one wanted to pay Brush the money to buy out his contract.

In protest, Foreman sat out the entire 1899 season. He worked at the skating rink and hung out with the legendarily rowdy Orioles. He was part of the circle of high-living, hard-partying Birds including Wilbert Robinson, Ned Hanlon, and John McGraw. He was a regular at Robinson's bowling alley. (Late in life Foreman claimed to have been the first man to bowl 200 in a duckpin game.)

After Foreman refused to report to Indianapolis for spring training in 1900, the Indians' manager, Bill Watkins, dropped him from the team. Watkins was convinced that Foreman was through. Foreman proceeded to sign with the Springfield, Massachusetts, Eastern League team on May 1. He was released on July 8. (League records are incomplete and his statistics have not been unearthed.) Within a few days the 37-year-old had signed with Buffalo of the nascent American League.

Not yet a major league, Ban Johnson's brainchild was marking time until it emerged to challenge the monopoly of the National League. Foreman seemed to have found a home by Lake Erie. His pitching did not go so well; he won seven and lost six with a 5.38 ERA. The Lake Erie nine finished seventh in the eight-team league. There was talk of Foreman's taking over as manager in 1901, but Ban Johnson dumped Buffalo in favor of placing a team in Boston. It was from the Bisons that the nucleus of the Boston Americans was drawn.

The lure of managing was too much to resist, so in the offseason Foreman began a stint as coach for Gettysburg College in Pennsylvania. There he coached a local boy, Eddie Plank. Foreman is said to have told the youngster, "If you follow my instructions closely I'll make you one of the greatest southpaws in the country."[16] Foreman recommended Plank to Connie Mack. With the Athletics Plank became a starter in 1901 and was the first left-hander to win 300 games. In 1946 he was enshrined in the Baseball Hall of Fame. Plank always credited Foreman for his major-league career.

Foreman was still not through with baseball. On April 27, 1901, he signed with the Boston Americans. He appeared in exactly one game for the Americans. He pitched in Washington on May 3, 1901, going the distance in a losing effort. He surrendered eight earned runs on eight hits and two walks. Not surprisingly, on May 16 Foreman was dropped from the roster. His outing on the mound, as bad as it was, did indeed count as an official appearance in his fourth major league. While 18 other men share this distinction, few have had as odd a trajectory as Foreman. At the age of 38 he gave no thought to hanging up his spikes. He was nothing if not persistent and stubborn. He signed with the Orioles on June 16, determined to show that perhaps Boston had given up on him too soon. Pitching like a man much younger, Foreman became a part of the Orioles' rotation and put together a solid season. He went 12-6, with an ERA of 3.67, a hair above the league ERA of 3.66. Proving that he was still a workhorse, he started 22 games and completed 18. In 1901, at least, Father Time had been defeated.

If this were fiction, the 1901 season would have been Foreman's last—a final hurrah worthy of the dime novels of the day. But as the 1902 season began, Foreman's 40-year-old body and arm were once again a part of the Orioles. This season Father Time had the upper hand. As the second oldest player in the American League, he went the distance in two games but lost both. His ERA at 6.06 was almost doubled from 1901. *Sporting Life* covered Foreman's dismissal by John McGraw in its May 24 issue.[17]

Still feeling that he had something to offer baseball, Foreman spent the rest of 1902 bouncing between three teams in two leagues. In rapid succession he played for and was released by Omaha, Colorado Springs, both of the Western League, and Kansas City of the American Association, the city where he had played in his rookie season 18 years previously. After this Foreman could no longer deny that his day had passed.

Having had experience as a fill-in major-league umpire in 1895 and 1901, Foreman spent 1903 trying to hack it as a professional umpire. It was not necessarily the best fit. Umpiring has always been a thankless job, even more so at the turn of the 20th Century. Foreman may have been too gregarious for umpiring. He started out in the American Association, just a rung below the majors. His name dots the box scores of *Sporting Life* throughout the 1903 season. He was regarded as a fairly good umpire by the publication even though he did not always maintain a cool head, calling the police in at one point in a game to restore order.

In 1904 Foreman was making noises about pitching again. In April *Sporting Life* reported, "Frank Foreman persists in declaring that he can still pitch, and he is trying himself out with the Baltimore Eastern Leaguers."[18]

In May the journal had the following one-line notice: "Frank Foreman, the veteran pitcher, has signed with the Roxborough (Pa.) Independent club."[19] Roxborough is a prosperous suburb of Philadelphia, close enough to Baltimore to go home on offdays. Foreman's last two years in baseball were by far the saddest part of his long story. By 1905 he was playing for anyone who would have him. He ended up with Holyoke in the Massachusetts amateur leagues. He did about as well as one might expect a 42-year-old to do, and he was cut from the team. Yet this was still not the end. Having been cut by Holyoke he was signed by the Meriden Silverites of the Connecticut State League. Amazingly, Foreman had worked his way back into Organized Baseball, just barely. The Connecticut State League was a Class B league, equivalent to the very low minors today. He was abysmal, going 4-10 primarily against players young enough to be his sons. At this point even Foreman had to admit that it was over.

His final major-league totals after 11 years of service stood at 96-93 with a 3.97 ERA. His lifetime batting average stood at .224 with nine home runs.

For the next few years Foreman kept himself in the game by scouting for various teams, though he never made a discovery on a par with Eddie Plank. (Foreman's sons, Elmer E. and J. Barton Foreman, both pitchers like their dad, also pursued baseball careers. Neither reached the major leagues. By 1910 Elmer had made it as high as Reading in Class A ball. J. Barton Foreman signed with Jacksonville of the South Atlantic League in 1911.)[20]

In retirement at last, Foreman returned to Baltimore and held several jobs. At various times he ran ice-skating and roller rinks. Like many former ballplayers of his era he owned a billiard hall. Foreman ran the Fayette pocket billiard parlor on 223 West Fayette Street, not far from where he played ball as a youngster. He resided at 1410 Union Avenue, where in 1945 he and Annie celebrated their 63rd wedding anniversary. Although the census recorded Foreman's occupation from 1900 through 1930 as machinist or clerk, his obituary makes no mention of these jobs. Instead it focused upon his career in ice and roller rinks. Aside from their sons, Frank and Annie had two daughters, Helen and Frances.

Foreman was the oldest living major leaguer in 1957. He was 94 when he died on November 19 of that yer. He had been ill for 18 months. During that time he gave interviews to various reporters about his career and long life. He told *The Sporting News* in an interview that it included in his obituary the following tall tale: "A faint heart is one of the big causes of sore arms. In the old days we were ready to pitch every day. I never had a sore arm."[21]

Foreman is buried in St. Mary's Episcopal Cemetery, in the same neighborhood where he was born.

Notes

1. *Sporting Life* June 22, 1895 6.
2. Unattributed press clipping from Foreman's player file at the National Baseball Hall of Fame.
3. Letter to Lee Allen from Ted Baldwin in Foreman's Hall of Fame file.
4. James, Bill. *The New Bill James Historical Baseball Abstract*. (New York: The Free Press, 2001).
5. For a look at roller skating in the 1880s see: http://www.suite101.com/content/shall-we-rinkulate-a124550
6. *Sporting Life,* April 3, 1890, 4.
7. *Sporting Life,* July 3, 1889, 3.
8. Press clipping from Foreman's Hall of Fame player file
9. *Sporting Life,* January 24, 1891, 3.
10. *Sporting Life,* December 31, 1891, 6.
11. *Sporting Life,* May 13, 1893, 2.
12. *Sporting Life,* February 15, 1893, 6.
13. *Baltimore Sun,* December 27, 1894, quoted at http://scottywazz.blogspot.com/2010/01/baltimore-hockey-history-first.html
14. *Sporting Life,* December 28, 1895, 6.
15. Press clipping dated 12-27-1895 in Foreman's Hall Of Fame player file.
16. "Veteran Plank Bids Game Farewell," undated press clipping in Foreman's Hall of Fame player file.
17. *Sporting Life,* May 24, 1902, 7.
18. *Sporting Life,* April 30, 1904, 13.
19. *Sporting Life,* May 21 1904, 3.
20. This information is gleaned from reports in *Sporting Life.*
21. *The Sporting News,* November 27, 1957, 46.

Buck Freeman

By Eric Enders

THE FIRST LEGITIMATE home run hitter in baseball history, Buck Freeman escaped the coal mines of Northeastern Pennsylvania to become one of the premier sluggers during the first decade of the American League. Freeman won seven home run titles during his professional career, and his astonishing 25 homers for the Washington Senators in 1899 shocked the baseball world. After jumping to the Boston Americans, Freeman played a key role in that club's capture of the 1903 World Series and 1904 pennant. Umpire Tim Murnane called Freeman "the batting wonder of the age."[1] The *Washington Post* agreed: "Modern base ball has never produced his like," a *Post* reporter wrote. "Even the eagle-eyed Anson, the slugging Brouthers of the falcon-eye, the mighty Tip O'Neill… all move back a niche in the game's history, and make room for one who is their master."[2] Freeman broke the single-season home run records in the New England League, Eastern League, and American Association, while nearly doing the same in both the American and National leagues. During his peak from 1899 through 1905, Freeman led all major-league players with 77 home runs, outdistancing his nearest competitor, Nap Lajoie, by 28.

John Frank Freeman was born on October 30, 1871, in Catasauqua, Pennsylvania, near Allentown, to Irish immigrants John and Annie Freeman. The elder John Freeman, born in Ireland at the height of the potato famine, emigrated to Pennsylvania in 1865. When young John was 8 years old, the family moved to coal mining country near Wilkes-Barre, where first the father and later the son found work at what was reputed to be the largest coal breaker in the world. Young John lied about his age to get the job, and worked his way up from slate picker to — at age 12 — the more glamorous job of mule driver. Much to the dismay of his parents, John found he liked baseball more than the mines, and starred as a pitcher on various local semipro teams. In 1891 the Washington Statesmen of the major-league American Association gave Freeman a trial, but the 19-year-old

Buck Freeman led the 1901 team with 114 RBIs. He is shown here with the 1903 Americans.

southpaw quickly earned his release by walking 33 batters in five games.

Back in Wilkes-Barre, Freeman began pondering the sage advice given him a few years earlier by Bud Fowler, the first African-American player in professional baseball, who had reportedly witnessed the 16-year-old Freeman hit two home runs in an 1888 sandlot game. "I never gave batting a thought until Fowler tipped me off," Freeman said. "You have pretty good control of the ball for a left-handed pitcher, kid," Freeman claimed Fowler told him. "But batting is your hold. Keep on practicing with the stick. It will get you more money."[3] Freeman pitched for Wilkes-Barre's Eastern League squad in 1893 before moving on to Haverhill, Massachusetts, where in 1894 he destroyed the New England League in his first season as a full-time hitter. Buck won the batting title at .386, while clubbing 34 home runs (including four in one game) and driving in a whopping 167 runs. After a brief stint with Detroit in 1895, the latter half of that year found Freeman in

Toronto, where he would spend four seasons. Buck's "wicked bat made the hearts of the Eastern League pitchers quake with craven fear," according to one reporter.[4] The free-swinging Freeman slugged 20 homers for the Toronto Canucks in 1897 and a league-record 23 in 1898.

At the conclusion of the 1898 Eastern League season, Toronto manager Arthur Irwin took over as skipper of the NL's Washington Senators. He took five of his best players with him to Washington, including Freeman, who was given a month to "make good" or be sent back to the minors. On September 14, after a seven-year absence from the major leagues, Buck made his National League debut and in his second at-bat, drove the ball deep into the right-field bleachers for his first major-league homer. Freeman impressed the Washington press corps by hitting the ball hard six times in eight at-bats during his debut doubleheader. "Freeman has a free, natural swing," the *Washington Post* reported. "His position at the bat indicates a natural hitter."[5] Buck turned in a two-homer game five days later, and his .364 average and .523 slugging percentage during his 29-game trial eliminated any possibility of returning to Toronto.

Unlike almost every other hitter of the day, Freeman's batting style was to swing from the heels, and for the fences. Umpire Pop Snyder compared Freeman's batting approach to the pugilistic style of then-World Heavyweight Champion Bob Fitzsimmons. "When Fitz drives one of his pile-driver favorites into the enemy the blow is supported by the force of the body," Snyder said in 1898. "Freeman seems to push his full weight against the ball… he meets the ball about half way in a well-gauged, sweeping stroke. But his knack of meeting the ball is supported by a keen, correct eye for judging the angles."[6] Freeman, an amateur boxer himself, was no doubt flattered by the comparison to the heavyweight champ.

In 1899 Freeman became the talk of baseball, clouting an unheard-of 25 home runs in his first full major-league season. He also batted .318, slugged 25 triples, scored 107 runs while driving in 122, and even stole 21 bases during what still stands as one of the greatest rookie seasons in baseball history. Reds manager Buck Ewing called the rookie "one of the greatest batsmen that ever came into the League." John McGraw publicly lusted after Freeman's services, calling him "the best developer of heart disease among pitchers." Meanwhile, Irwin, Freeman's manager, claimed that half of Buck's homers had come on hit-and-run plays, and praised him as "one of the best natural batsmen I have ever seen." Not everyone was so pleased, however. The 1900 *Spalding Guide* virulently denounced Freeman without ever mentioning him by name, excoriating "sluggers" whose "sole object was to hit it out of sight." The *Guide* concluded that a good slap hitter was "worth a dozen of your common class of home-run hitters."

Although the *Washington Post* predicted that "his triumph at skirting the bases for homers will stand as a red-letter record for many a season to come," Freeman's 25 round-trippers were not technically the major-league record.[7] In 1884, Chicago's Lakefront Park boasted distances of 180 feet to the left-field fence and 196 feet to right. Four White Stockings took advantage of these cozy dimensions to post 20-homer seasons, led by Ed Williamson with 27. Until 1899, they were the only four 20-homer seasons in major-league history, and because of their illegitimate nature, Freeman's mark of 25 in 1899 was widely considered the standard until Babe Ruth arrived.

Freeman didn't need short porches to pad his home-run totals; he was noted for holding distance records at several different ballparks. In 1899, Buck slugged what Ned Hanlon and others described as the longest home run ever hit at Brooklyn's Washington Park. "The ball sped far over a canvas awning in the right center corner of the lot," the *Washington Post* reported, "and was picked up by a small boy on the opposite side of the street, in front of a row of tenement houses half a block from the grounds."[8] Although Freeman claimed the pitch was eight inches outside, he still had enough plate coverage to pull it to deepest right field. Meanwhile, in Louisville that year, a Freeman drive hit the wall of a distillery 50 feet behind the outfield fence. In Washington, he smashed two opposite-field drives off

L to R: Jimmy Collins, Fred Parent, Hobe Ferris, and Buck Freeman with the 1901 Bostons.

the distant left-field scoreboard. On August 20, 1903, Freeman became the first man ever to hit the ball completely out of Chicago's South Side Park. And at Philadelphia's Columbia Park, he once hit a ball so far that it reportedly sailed out of the stadium, over several houses, and through an open second-story window.

As part of the National League's contraction from 12 teams to eight before the 1900 season, the Washington club went out of business. On February 9, 1900, owner J. Earl Wagner sold off eight of his best players, including Freeman, Bill Dinneen, and Shad Barry to the Boston Beaneaters for $8,500. Freeman, who made a point of never engaging in holdouts, immediately agreed to a $2,000 contract with Boston for 1900. Even the Boston papers called Washington's dumping of Freeman and the others "the rankest offense ever perpetrated on a sport-loving public."[9]

Freeman batted a solid .301 in 1900, but did not get along with Beaneaters manager Frank Selee, who, like the *Spalding Guide*, abhorred Buck's power-hitting ways. "I know the Boston public like to see Freeman in the game, as he is likely to hit the ball very hard at times," Selee said. "But this style of play is not a winner, for when Freeman is dangerous the pitchers keep the ball away from him, and his hitting counts for little. He is a poor fielder, thrower, and base runner." Although previous observers in Washington had called Freeman's outfield defense "above average," Selee's comments were the start of a bad defense rap that would follow Freeman the rest of his career. Meanwhile, Boston's season spun out of control, with the franchise posting its first losing season in 14 years. "The Boston team is now playing every man for himself, and floundering about like a ship without a rudder," Tim Murnane wrote in the *Boston Globe*.[10] The "Napoleon-like" Selee pounced upon Freeman as a scapegoat, leaving him off the traveling squad for a late-season road trip and insulting him in the press: "I have often thought of playing [Freeman] at first and trying Tenney in the outfield," Selee said, "but brains are needed in the infield."[11]

It was no surprise, then, that Freeman chose to jump to the fledgling American League in 1901 rather than play for a manager who openly despised him. In March, Buck signed a contract with the Boston Americans and rebounded to have one of his best seasons, ranking third in the AL batting race at .339 while finishing second to Nap Lajoie in homers (12), RBIs (114), and slugging percentage (.520). Freeman also contributed several game-winning hits in the ninth or extra innings, helping the Americans to a second-place finish in their inaugural season. Freeman posted equally strong numbers in 1902, finishing second with 11 homers while leading the AL in extra-base hits (68) and RBIs (121).

Ballplayers of Freeman's day shunned conditioning and weight training, often believing that it would make them muscle-bound and restrict their movements. "The successful ballplayer never hardens his muscles," Ty Cobb wrote in 1913. But Freeman was a notable exception. Indeed, he was a forerunner of the power-hitting workout gurus of the 1990s. A dedicated member of the local gym in his offseason home of Wilkes-Barre, Freeman kept himself in shape by walking 12 miles a day in addition to weightlifting, parallel bars, boxing, and other activities. "What work I have done as a batsman I owe in large measure to my exercise in the gymnasium," Freeman said, "which… developed the muscles that come into play when I hit the ball."[12]

Freeman also carefully studied the mechanics of hitting, adapting his stance to get as much of his weight behind the swing as possible. "I gather myself for a swing, and, as a rule, take a forward step in order to place myself at such an angle that the whole weight of my body moves at once in the same direction as the bat."[13] This approach to hitting was enhanced when Freeman began playing for Irwin, who spent long hours in Toronto teaching the dead pull hitter how to hit for power to the opposite field. Freeman was also an expert at intentionally fouling off pitches he didn't like — a practice which, though commonly accepted today, was illegal during Buck's career. On August 15, 1899, umpire Hank O'Day enforced the little-used rule against Freeman, calling a strike against him (foul balls did not yet count as strikes) for intentionally fouling off a Cy Young pitch.

In 1903 Freeman was the best hitter on Boston's World Championship team, winning his second consecutive RBI title with 104 while also pacing the league in home runs (13), extra-base hits (72), and total bases (281). He thus became the first hitter ever to lead both the National and American leagues in home runs, later to be joined by Sam Crawford, Fred McGriff, and Mark McGwire. That October, Freeman played a key role in helping Boston win the inaugural World Series, batting .290 with three triples in the eight-game Series. Freeman continued to bludgeon opposing pitchers in 1904, leading the league with 19 triples while finishing second in RBIs (84) and tying for second in homers (7).

In 1905, however, the 33-year-old Freeman slipped dramatically, his batting average dropping 40 points to .240, while he failed to finish among the league leaders in home runs for the first time since 1898. In 1905 he also ended his impressive streak of playing 541 consecutive games and 5,431 consecutive innings, the latter a record which would stand until broken by Cal Ripken in 1985. In 1906 Freeman's downhill slide continued, as he posted a .302 on-base percentage with only one homer in 436 plate appearances. When Freeman started off the 1907 season 2-for-12, Boston gave up on him, selling him to the Washington Senators on April 24 for the waiver price of $1,000. But four days later, before Freeman played in a single game for Washington, the Senators sold him to Minneapolis.

Although the origin of his nickname is unknown, Freeman's popularity was such that later players with that surname were automatically dubbed "Buck". "Some day—but not in our generation," *Baseball Magazine* wrote in 1913, "it will be possible for a man named… Freeman to escape being called 'Buck.'"[14] This phenomenon proved especially confusing in 1907, when there were three Freemans on the Minneapolis Millers, with the others dubbed "Buck II" and "Buck III" by the press. But the original Buck separated himself from the crowd, posting a .335 average while taking advantage of Nicollet Park's 279-foot right-field fence to set a new American Association record with 18 homers. Freeman returned to Minneapolis in 1908, but his season ended in late July when he dislocated his right shoulder sliding into home plate. Despite playing only half a season, his ten homers were still good enough to tie for the league lead.

Freeman recovered from the injury to serve as a player-manager in the outlaw Susquehanna League in 1910

Buck Freeman image from 1900 Sporting News supplement.

and 1911, and in 1913 he embarked on a lengthy minor-league umpiring career. After a game on August 9, 1913, the rookie arbiter was mobbed by 2,000 angry fans in Wilmington, Delaware. As a squad of a dozen policemen rushed him off the field, Buck was pelted with a hail of stones and bricks, several of them hitting him on the head. With Freeman still under police escort, the mob trailed him from the ballpark to a local saloon and then a trolley stop, where Freeman was finally able to board a car and escape safely. Unbowed by the riot, Freeman umpired for the next 13 years in the Tri-State League, Canadian League, International League, American Association, and even, apparently, a brief stint in the Negro Leagues. (An umpire named Buck Freeman is known to have worked the 1924 Negro League World Series. Since Freeman was an active minor-league ump at the time, and since the Negro Leagues used white umpires then, it was almost certainly the same Buck Freeman.)

During his offseasons, though he didn't need the money, Freeman kept in shape by working as a stoker in the boiler room of a local silk mill. He spent much of his time cockfighting, and became well known as a breeder of fighting birds, keeping a flock of more than 100 gamecocks in his barn. Even a 1937 police raid on a cockfight at Freeman's home did not deter him. "I'd walk 20 miles to see a good cockfight," he once said.[15] In October 1906, Freeman purchased the New Haven Blues of the Connecticut League; by 1910 the team had been renamed the Prairie Hens. After his retirement from umpiring, Freeman scouted for the St. Louis Browns from 1926 to 1933, then managed an outlaw team in Bloomsburg, Pennsylvania, for two years. After the 1935 season Freeman retired to the modest hillside home in the Georgetown section of Wilkes-Barre where he resided with his wife, the former Annie Kane (whom he had married in 1895), and their six sons. A well-known local institution, Freeman enjoyed regaling youngsters with tales from his playing days. "In Wilkes Barre he was just like Babe Ruth," one of those youths recalled years later. "Every kid in town knew him."[16] Buck Freeman died of a stroke in Wilkes-Barre on June 25, 1949, at age 77. He is buried at Evergreen Cemetery in nearby Shavertown.

Sources

Scott Labenski. Unpublished biographical sketch of Buck Freeman. 2004.

Boston Globe

Chicago Tribune

New York Times

Sporting Life

Washington Post

Notes

This biography originally appeared in David Jones, ed., *Deadball Stars of the American League* (Washington, D.C.: Potomac Books, Inc., 2006).

1 *Washington Post*, October 2, 1899.
2 *Washington Post*, October 15, 1899.
3 Ibid.
4 *Washington Post*, September 14, 1898.
5 *Washington Post*, September 15, 1898.
6 *Washington Post*, October 3, 1898.
7 *Washington Post*, October 2, 1899.
8 *Washington Post*, October 19, 1899.
9 *Washington Post*, February 12, 1900.
10 *Boston Globe*, October 5, 1900.
11 *Washington Evening Star*, October 12, 1900.
12 *Washington Post*, October 15, 1899.
13 *Washington Post*, October 15, 1899.
14 William A. Phelon, "The Decline and Fall of the Left Handed Batter," *Baseball*, July 1913.
15 Scott Labenski, "Buck Freeman bio," unpublished biographical sketch of Buck Freeman. 2004.
16 Ibid.

Harry Gleason

By Jack Morris

ON THE SURFACE, Harry Gleason's career wasn't noteworthy. He played a total of 274 major-league games over five seasons with a career batting average of .218. He was an everyday starter in only one of those seasons. But there's so much more to Gleason's story.

Gleason was almost killed by a beanball thrown by future Hall of Famer Rube Waddell. He fought with his team's hometown fans during one game and was arrested after another game for defying New York's Blue Laws. Despite his minuscule offensive output, he perpetually fought with ownership over pay, getting placed on Organized Baseball's suspended list several times.

Gleason was very short, even by Deadball Era standards. Reference books list him at 5-feet-6 and 160 pounds. However Alfred Spink, in his 1911 book, *The National Game*, listed him as 5-feet-3, 145 pounds. In describing him, the press often called him "midget" or "little"—sometimes both in the same sentence. He was also a dead ringer for his famous older brother, William, better known as Kid. "Harry is the very picture of his brother in every possible way and many address him for his brother," wrote the *Utica Herald-Dispatch*. Early in his career, he earned the nickname Kid or Kidlet for this reason.[1]

On the field Gleason was a fan favorite almost everywhere he played because of his hustle and baseball smarts. He was "one of the brainiest players in baseball" and was often described in the press as "heady" and "clever."[2]

He was forever looking for greener pastures. He jumped from team to team, from league to league with frequency. Trying to keep track of it was probably confusing for the fans during his career, let alone for historians of today.

Harry Gilbert Gleason was born on March 28, 1875, in Camden, New Jersey. He was the seventh of nine children born to William and Ellen (Ivins) Gleason. His

Gleason with the St. Louis Browns in 1905.

father was a railroad man, working himself up from freight hand to superintendent of the Pennsylvania Railroad's West Jersey & Seashore railyard in Camden. Five of Gleason's brothers eventually worked there as well.[3]

Harry, however, followed in the footsteps of his brother Kid, who was nine years his senior. He played baseball at Camden High School for two years. After high school he played right field for the Camden town team. In 1897 the *Philadelphia Inquirer* wrote that Gleason "played a beautiful game in right field" and that he "promises to get in the push with his brother."[4]

With his brother's recommendation, Tom Burns, former major leaguer and manager of the 1897 Springfield, Massachusetts, team in the Eastern League, signed Gleason to a contract for 1898.[5]

The *Springfield Republican* called Gleason "a valuable acquisition" and said he had "showed to wonderfully good advantage" in training camp. He initially practiced at shortstop but when the regular season started he mostly played second base.[6]

Springfield struggled throughout the season. Mired in last place at the end of May, the team suffered low attendance and ownership missed payment to some of the ballplayers as a result. Gleason, a utility fielder, left the team until he was paid.[7]

Gleason wasn't setting the world on fire either. His defense and versatility (in addition to second base, he also played 19 games at shortstop and three in right field) made him a popular player, but his hitting was terrible. He ended the season with a .199 batting average.

Still, Springfield brought him back the next season despite cleaning house on most of the 1898 team. New manager Tom Brown played Gleason solely at second base in 1899. But Gleason, unhappy with his pay, jumped his contract on June 14. The *Springfield Republican* implied that Gleason was dishonorable with respect to "baseball dealings." The team placed him on the suspended list. In his 26 games with Springfield, Gleason did hit better, batting .230.[8]

There is a Gleason who appears in box scores for the Mount Holly, New Jersey, town team after Gleason left Springfield. This may be where Harry played for the rest of the 1899 season.[9]

Sporting Life reported that Springfield had reserved Gleason for the 1900 season for "disciplinary purposes." If Gleason wished to play in Organized Baseball, he would have to work it out with the management. So in April 1900, Gleason signed with Springfield again.[10]

This time he played third base for the Ponies. Instead of leaving the team in midseason, Gleason was sent down to Meriden in the Connecticut State League after he batted just .232 in 26 games. "He is a nice little fellow," wrote *Sporting Life*, "but his stick work is poor."[11]

At Meriden, Gleason played shortstop and managed to hit a respectable .251 in 66 games. But the league was at the lowest rung of the Organized Baseball ladder. Gleason could not be demoted any lower. Remarkably, he was playing in the major leagues by the end of the following season.

In 1901, Gleason signed with the Utica Pentups of the New York State League. The *Springfield Republican*, after watching Gleason demand money but not perform for parts of three seasons, sarcastically wrote about the signing, "Those who know his record here and the high value he set upon his services will be surprised that he is not in one of the big leagues."[12]

Yet the Utica press welcomed Gleason with open arms. The *Utica Daily Press* wrote that Gleason was a "cracking good short stop" and that Utica manager Wally Taylor "thinks very highly of him." For once, Gleason proved the predictions right. In what was easily the best hitting season of his career to that point, he batted .284 in 99 games.[13]

In fact, he played so well in Utica that it was arranged that he would report to Boston to play for the Americans once the New York State League season ended. When Gleason finally reported to the team, he was inserted into just one game, on September 27, as a replacement for player-manager Jimmy Collins at third base in Boston's 7–2 win over the Milwaukee Brewers. He got his first major-league hit, a single off Ned Garvin, in his only official at-bat. He also stole a base and started a double play.[14]

Boston held onto Gleason for spring training the next season. Utica wanted him back but Boston manager Jimmy Collins wouldn't let him go. Gleason "has made a very favorable impression upon [Collins]," wrote the *Utica Herald-Dispatch*. Rumors also popped up that Connie Mack wanted Gleason for the Philadelphia Athletics.[15]

Gleason, however, stayed with Boston and made the Opening Day roster as one of two utility infielders. In all, Gleason played in 71 games in 1902. Boston utilized him mostly at third base, where he played in 35 games. He also played 23 games in the outfield as well as four games as a second baseman. Though he batted only .225, on May 16 he hit the first of his three major-league home runs, off Philadelphia's Snake Wiltse. He also led all American League pinch-hitters with three hits in eight at-bats, good for a .375 average. Additionally, for making the big leagues, he was rewarded with a pair of diamond-studded cuff buttons by his Camden friends during a July 11 game against the Philadelphia A's.[16]

All in all, things were going very well for Gleason. "Little Harry Gleason has established himself as a prime favorite here," wrote the *Boston Globe*. "He is always in the game, is quick in all departments and never lets up. The crowd is quick to applaud such a player upon any provocations."[17]

In the offseason, rumors abounded that both the Baltimore Orioles and the Philadelphia A's wanted Gleason, but Gleason was in Macon, Georgia, with Boston when the 1903 training camp began. This marked one of the strangest periods of Gleason's baseball life.[18]

Boston had decided that Gleason wasn't in its plans for the 1903 season. The Americans planned to audition John O'Brien and George Stone for the utility-player job. Essentially Boston gave Gleason to Charles Comiskey and his White Sox team for nothing. It was up to Gleason to work out his contract, but Gleason wasn't going to go without a fight. In March the first reports of Gleason's going to the White Sox hit the press. Yet he never left Macon despite assurances to Comiskey from Boston owner Henry Killilea, manager Collins, and Gleason himself that he would report to White Sox camp in Mobile, Alabama. The White Sox were desperate for a third baseman, having lost infielders George Davis, Sam Mertes, and Sammy Strang to the National League. Yet Gleason stayed with Boston, practicing with the Americans throughout camp.[19]

American League president Ban Johnson weighed in finally, awarding Gleason to Chicago, but added, "He cannot be compelled to play in Chicago but if he consults his own interests he will do so. There is no room for him on the Boston team." At some point, Gleason did report to the White Sox. He worked out for Comiskey and was offered a contract at "pretty steep terms." But Comiskey balked when Gleason demanded that back pay be included in the contract.[20]

So Gleason stayed with Boston, practicing with the team. When Hobe Ferris was hurt late in spring training, Gleason filled in at second base. He traveled north with the team and, despite persistent reports that he was going to Chicago, he played in six games at the opening of the regular season, two as a second baseman.[21]

Finally, on May 16, Gleason was purchased for $1,000 by the Columbus (Ohio) Senators of the American Association. Columbus owner T. J. Bryce was trying to build a powerhouse and wasn't averse to paying for it. *Sporting Life* called the move "another bold stroke" by Bryce to put together a championship team. The bold stroke didn't pay off for Bryce, however. Gleason, in 70 games, hit but .143. It was by far the worse batting performance of his career.[22]

After the season Columbus traded Gleason and "a bunch of cash" (one report mentioned $1,000) to the St. Louis Browns for Bill Friel, Benny Bowcock, and Joe Martin. Browns second baseman Dick Padden had injured his thumb toward the end of the season, and Gleason was seen as an insurance policy in case it didn't heal in the offseason.[23]

Padden's thumb did heal in time for spring training but Gleason had such a good camp that the Browns kept him as a utility fielder. Gleason "is playing a great game at second," wrote *Sporting Life* in March. "[Browns manager Jimmy] McAleer is well pleased."[24]

Gleason didn't play much but when he did get into the starting lineup, he made the most of it. When shortstop Bobby Wallace went down with an injury, Gleason played so well that he was one of the "most popular players" on the Browns.[25]

Gleason's season came to an end on August 2. On that day, he replaced the injured Padden in the lineup against Philadelphia. Gleason was having a great day, lashing two hits including a triple against future Hall of Famer Rube Waddell. His third time up, he came to bat in the bottom of the sixth with no outs and a run in. Waddell threw one of his hard "inshoots" and hit Gleason in the back of the head, behind his left ear.

Harry Gleason with the 1902 Boston Americans.

When it struck his head, it sounded like it had hit the bat. Gleason "fell like a log, unconscious."[26]

The players rushed to Gleason's side, Waddell being one of the first. Dr. Max C. Starkloft, the former St. Louis city health commissioner, was called out of the grandstand to attend to Gleason. Played was stopped for 10 minutes, while Gleason lay at home plate. "Father Tracey, who was in the grand stand, hurried to the side of his parishioner, and with a wide Panama, fanned the stricken gladiator."[27]

With Waddell carrying Gleason at the shoulders and the Browns' Mike Kahoe taking his legs, Gleason was carried to the bench. Blood was running from his nose and ears. He was semiconscious. Two players tore a clubhouse door off its hinges and, using it as a makeshift stretcher, carried him into the clubhouse. An ambulance eventually arrived to transport Gleason to St. Louis's Missouri Baptist Sanitarium.[28]

The next day he was reported to be in "critical condition suffering from a concussion of the brain." By chance, Gleason's mother, Ellen, was traveling that day from Camden to St. Louis to visit him. It was a stopover on a cross-country trip to see her daughter, who was ill, in California. Another visitor to Gleason was Waddell. When the game had resumed that day, there was a noticeable difference in the level of play between the two teams. "Rube was completely unnerved."[29]

On August 5 Gleason was "rapidly recovering." He spent almost two weeks in the hospital, eventually feeling good enough to leave. On August 15, thirteen days after the beaning, Gleason was in uniform for the Browns and practiced for 15 minutes. His only complaint was a "faintness at irregular intervals."[30]

But those proclamations were obviously a brave front because three days later Gleason announced his retirement from baseball. The left side of his head was in a "constant state of numbness" and his right arm and shoulder "were almost useless." "I think my time on the diamond is over," Gleason told the *Philadelphia Inquirer*. He added that the doctor had advised him to retire.[31]

Despite his pronouncement, Gleason stayed with the team. And on October 3 he entered a game in the eighth inning in a 3–0 win over New York when Padden was thrown out of the game for arguing a call.[32]

After the season Gleason moved to California for the winter, living with relatives in Oakland. The *St. Louis Republican* reported that he was playing second base for Portland in the Pacific Coast League. The PCL season ran into November that year.[33]

When the 1905 spring training camps opened, Gleason was again a holdout. He and a group of his teammates were upset with the contracts that were offered them. "A mutiny is rife in the ranks" of the Browns, wrote the *Washington Post*. Eventually the Browns signed the disgruntled players with pay increases. Gleason signed for $1,500 with the provision that his pay would be increased if he could remain a regular all season.[34]

Before he signed, there were rumors that Gleason might be traded to the White Sox, but that was quickly denied by Charles Comiskey. "I had one dose of Gleason when Boston gave him to me," said Comiskey. "I do not want another."[35]

For the first time in his major-league career, Gleason was handed the starting job. The extremely popular player played third base for most of the season. But despite his hustle and defense, his batting left much to be desired. For the year, he batted only .217 in 150 games. On October 8, 1905, he played the last major-league game of his career.

The Browns were disappointed with Gleason. "Gleason is a fairly good player," wrote the *Cleveland Plain Dealer* after the season ended, "but did not come up to expectations at all times last year."[36]

Rumors swirled about Gleason's next destination. Earlier in the season Hughie Jennings, manager of the Baltimore Orioles, was supposedly interested in Gleason. In October the New York Highlanders expressed interest. Finally, the outlaw Tri-State League was reported to want Gleason.[37]

In February 1906 the Browns sold Gleason, along with Joe Sugden, to the American Association's St. Paul (Minnesota) Saints. St. Paul wanted Gleason to play shortstop for the team, but Gleason wasn't about to take a pay cut just because he was sent down. He refused to report to St. Paul and signed with the Tri-State League, which played baseball outside the aegis of Organized Baseball. The league was paying top dollar for talent and Gleason was more than happy to play with them, even if it meant he was placed on Organized Baseball's blacklist.[38]

Before he reported to camp, he worked all winter for the Pennsylvania Railroad in Camden under his brother Walter, who was a yardmaster. An accident, though, almost cost him his life and he resigned immediately.[39]

Gleason played the next four seasons in the Tri-State League and before almost every season there was a dispute over which team in the league owned his rights. Part of the fault belonged to the league, which was loose on its signing rules, but part of the blame belonged to Gleason, who was always trying to cut the best deal possible for himself, even if he had already had a deal in place.

Gleason played the next four seasons in the Tri-State League and before almost every season there was a dispute over which team in the league owned his rights. Part of the fault belonged to the league which was loose on its signing rules but part of the blame belonged to Gleason, who was always trying to cut the best deal possible for himself, even if he had already had a deal in place.

In all, he played with Williamsport (1906-1907), Trenton (1908), Wilmington (1908), Harrisburg (1909), and York (1909), with a 36-game stint in 1908 with the Jersey City Skeeters of the Eastern League. In 1907 the Tri-State League moved under Organized Baseball's umbrella. That meant salaries would come down to the other minor leagues' levels. There was much conjecture about players like Gleason, who were on Organized Baseball's blacklist and whether they would be allowed to play. In the end, all the players were allowed to play but at reduced salaries.[40] There were several other significant events for Gleason while he played in the Tri-State League.

On the morning of May 12, 1906, Gleason was married to Christine Wilhemine Carstens of Philadelphia, at the parsonage at St. Stephen's Lutheran Church in Lancaster. He then played in a game that afternoon against Lancaster. According to newspaper accounts, he had "a great game." After the game, he left with his bride on a "western trip."[41]

After the 1907 season a new outlaw league, the Union League, was being formed. The league organizers' objective was to become a third major league. Rumors swirled that Gleason had signed a contract with the Washington team. He even attended the Union League's spring meeting in Philadelphia. He was to play second base for the team in the coming season. But the league collapsed, leaving Gleason no choice but to go back to an Organized Baseball team.[42]

In 1909, while playing for a terrible Harrisburg team, Gleason had an altercation with a Harrisburg fan. On July 13, in the middle of a game at Harrisburg that the home team would lose to Lancaster, 11–3, Gleason punched the fan, who was sitting in a car beyond the bleachers. The fan had been heckling all during the game and after the sixth inning Gleason had had enough. Two days later, Gleason left Harrisburg for good.[43]

And soon after that incident, Gleason left the Tri-State League for good. After a short stint with a Hagerstown, Maryland, semipro team at the end of the 1909 season, Gleason moved on to New York State League. At the beginning of the 1910 season, he was with the Utica Utes but didn't play well. By June 13, he was batting only .154, so Utica released him. However, an injury to Utica shortstop Louis Hartman kept Gleason on the team a little while longer. On June 28 he was sold to the Binghamton (New York) Bingoes.[44]

In late August, after returning to the team after tending to his sick wife, Gleason was one of several players and coaches arrested after Binghamton and Albany attempted to play a Sunday game in Colonie, New York, in opposition to the Blue Laws in that city.[45]

While with Binghamton, Gleason managed to pull his batting average up to .219 by season's end. He returned for the 1911 season but batted only .218, playing in 123 games. With little prospects for a light-hitting 36-year-old in Organized Baseball, Gleason retired for good after the season.

Even before he retired, Gleason had worked in the winters at a shoe company. His maternal grandfather, Isaac H. Ivins, had been a shoemaker, and Gleason no doubt learned the trade from him. By 1911 Gleason was vice president of the Union Shoe Manufacturing and Repair Company of Philadelphia. According to his World War I draft card, which was filled out in 1918, he listed his occupation as shoe repairing and wrote that he was self-employed. He moved to Haddonfield, New Jersey, sometime in the 1910s, and in 1915 his wife, Christine, gave birth to their son, William Carstens Gleason. He and Christine later had a daughter, Pauline.[46]

Tragically, Christine died in 1928. By 1930 Gleason was remarried to a widow, Ena Griffing, who was 15 years his junior. According to the 1930 US Census, he had become an undersheriff in the Camden Sheriff's Department. He remained an undersheriff until he retired.

On October 21, 1961, after a three-day stay in West Jersey Hospital in Camden because of an infected appendix, Harry Gleason died at the age of 86.[47] He is buried at Locustwood Memorial Park in Cherry Hill, New Jersey.

Notes

1 Baseball-Reference.com ; Alfred H. Spink, *The National Game, Second Edition*. (Carbondale, Illinois: Southern Illinois University Press, 2000), 226.; *Williamsport Gazette & Bulletin*, May 25, 1906; *Sporting Life*, July 18, 1902; *Utica Herald-Dispatch*, May 2, 1902; *Worcester Daily Spy*, May 26, 1903.

2 *Altoona Mirror*, February 1, 1910; *Utica Herald-Dispatch*, April 25, 1910; *Sporting Life*, July 10, 1909; *The Sporting News*, April 11, 1903.

3 *Sporting Life*, April 7, 1906.

4 Typed two-page biography in Gleason's Hall of Fame file; *Philadelphia Inquirer*, May 2, 1897.

5 Burns didn't manage the 1898 Springfield team. The Chicago Orphans hired him away from Springfield for the 1898 season. *Philadelphia Inquirer*, February 26, 1898.

6 *Springfield Republican*, April 8, 1898.

7 *Springfield Republican*, June 19, 1898.

8 *Springfield Republican*, February 4, 1899; *Boston Globe*, June 17, 1899; *Springfield Republican*, July 5, 1899.

9 *Philadelphia Inquirer*, July 9, 1899.

10 *Sporting Life*, September 16, 1899.

11 *Sporting Life*, June 16, 1900; *Sporting Life*, June 23, 1900.

12 *Springfield Republican*, March 29, 1901.

13 *Utica Daily Press*, March 19, 1901.

14 *Utica Daily Press*, September 7, 1901.

15 *Utica Herald-Dispatch*, May 2, 1902; *Utica Sunday Journal*, May 18, 1902.

16 Bob McConnell and David Vincent, *SABR Presents the Home Run Encyclopedia.* (New York: Macmillan, 1996), 564; Paul Votano, *Stand And Deliver: A History of Pinch-Hitting.* (Jefferson, North Carolina: McFarland & Co., 2003), 24.; *Sporting Life,* July 18, 1902.

17 *Utica Herald Dispatch,* August 20, 1902—The *Herald Dispatch* was quoting from an article that ran in the *Boston Globe.*

18 *Utica Herald Dispatch,* August 14, 1902; *Philadelphia Record,* May 2, 1902.

19 Hubbard, Donald *The Red Sox Before the Babe: Boston's Early Days in the American League, 1901-1914.* (Jefferson, North Carolina: McFarland & Co., 2003), 39; *Sporting Life,* March 14, 1903; *Sporting Life,* March 28, 1903.

20 *Sporting Life,* March 28, 1903; *Sporting Life,* May 23, 1903.

21 *The Sporting News,* April 11, 1903.

22 *Philadelphia Inquirer,* May 18, 1903; *Sporting Life,* May 23, 1903.

23 *Cleveland Plain Dealer,* November 15, 1903; *Boston Journal,* November 17, 1903;

24 *Sporting Life,* March 26, 1904.

25 *Sporting Life,* July 2, 1904.

26 *Philadelphia Inquirer,* August 3, 1904; *St. Louis Republican,* August 3, 1904; *Boston Globe,* August 3, 1904.

27 *Philadelphia Inquirer,* August 3, 1904; *St. Louis Republican,* August 3, 1904.

28 *Philadelphia Inquirer,* August 3, 1904; *St. Louis Republican,* August 3, 1904.

29 *St. Louis Republican,* August 3, 1904; *Philadelphia Inquirer,* August 3, 1904.

30 *St. Louis Republican,* August 5, 1904; *Philadelphia Inquirer,* August 20, 1904; *St. Louis Republican,* August 16, 1904.

31 *Philadelphia Inquirer,* August 20, 1904.

32 *St. Louis Republican,* October 4, 1904.

33 *Seattle Times,* November 6, 1904; *St. Louis Republican,* November 11, 1904.

34 *Cleveland Plain Dealer,* March 28, 1905; *Washington Post,* March 29, 1905; *Sporting Life,* April 29, 1905; *Sporting Life,* May 6, 1905.

35 *Auburn Bulletin,* April 12, 1905.

36 *Cleveland Plain Dealer,* December 19, 1905.

37 *Sporting Life,* May 27, 1905; *Washington Post,* October 25, 1905; *Trenton Evening Times,* November 17, 1905.

38 *Washington Post,* February 9, 1906.

39 *Sporting Life,* April 7, 1906.

40 *Cleveland Plain Dealer,* December 25, 1906.

41 *Philadelphia Inquirer,* May 13, 1906.

42 *Sporting Life,* March 3, 1908; *Washington Times,* March 21, 1908.

43 *Harrisburg Patriot,* July 14, 1909; *Harrisburg Patriot,* July 16, 1909.

44 *Trenton Evening Times,* June 13, 1910; *Sporting Life,* June 25, 1910; *Utica Observer,* June 29, 1910; *Binghamton Press,* June 30, 1910.

45 *Syracuse Post-Standard,* August 29, 1910.

46 *Sporting Life,* April 20, 1911; Ancestry.com. *World War I Draft Registration Cards, 1917-1918* [database on-line]. Provo, Utah:Ancestry.com Operations Inc., 2005.

47 State of New Jersey Death Certificate in Gleason's Hall of Fame file.

Charlie Hemphill

By Paul Wendt

AT HIS BEST, Charlie Hemphill was a strong-armed, fleet-footed outfielder and solid hitter who drew walks. In 1910, *The Sporting News*'s Alfred Spink described him as "a cracking good batsman and when right is a hard man to beat." At his worst, however, Hemphill was a poor fielder known to misjudge balls in the air, and an inattentive baserunner. Hemphill's career was also marred by several bouts with dissipation. After his major-league career was over, drinking cost him his managerial post with the Atlanta Crackers and his chance for a long career in the minor leagues. Hemphill is in the "All Deadball Era" outfield for both the Browns and Yankees, reflecting a weakness of both teams.

Charles Judson Hemphill was born in Greenville, Michigan, on April 20, 1876, to Frederick and Louisa Hemphill, natives of Canada and probably recent immigrants. Three of his grandparents were born in Ireland, one in England. During Charlie's childhood, Frederick worked as an engineer, while his wife stayed at home, raising the couple's four sons. Two of them, Charlie and Frank, would play in the major leagues.

Charlie played for Saginaw in 1895-96, missed the 1897 season with Dayton because of illness, but was reserved for 1898 and played with Grand Rapids from late that season until June 1899, when he was acquired by St. Louis. He made his major-league debut on June 27 against the Philadelphia Phillies. Batting third and playing center field, Hemphill fouled out, then hit a home run off Wiley Piatt in a 6-4 victory. In eight games, he posted a .389 on-base percentage, but was benched because of his terrible fielding. Playing three times more that season, he finished with five errors in 10 games as an outfielder for a glaring .750 fielding average. In August Hemphill was transferred to the Cleveland Spiders, who were en route to the worst record (20-134) in major-league history. When judged against the low standards set by his teammates, Hemphill acquitted himself well in Cleveland, rapping out a .277 batting average in 55 games, of which the

Hemphill with the 1902 St. Louis Browns.

Spiders won only three. His fielding remained problematic; for the year he posted an abysmal .837 fielding percentage.

The Cleveland franchise folded at the end of the season, and Hemphill was transferred back to St. Louis for the 1900 campaign. But with the team's roster overcrowded with players, Hemphill sat on the bench for the first three weeks of the season before the Cardinals loaned him to the Kansas City Blues of the American League, then in its final season as a minor league. Hemphill joined the Blues on May 10 and soon established himself as the club's leadoff batter and center fielder. Despite his late arrival, Hemphill led the league in triples and ranked fourth in runs scored and batting average. On June 30, according to the *Chicago Tribune*, "Hemphill, who has never been suspected of being a phenomenal fielder, robbed the White Stockings of what appeared to be a certain victory" by making "three of the greatest catches ever made."

St. Louis reserved him for the 1901 season, but Hemphill jumped his contract to sign with the Boston Americans. The *Boston Globe* introduced Hemphill as "the poorest outfielder in the league," but it was his hitting that proved to be the biggest disappointment. Dropped from second to fifth in the batting order in early June, Hemphill finished the year with a .261 batting average and a .332 slugging percentage, both figures worse than all but two of the 24 American League outfielders who played more than half their team's games that season.

Despite standing 5-feet-9 and weighing 160 pounds, no better than average size for his day, Hemphill was often described as big by contemporary sportswriters, perhaps by some illusion of build or the way he wore his uniform. A left-handed batter and thrower with good speed but no special talent for using it either on the basepaths or in the field, Hemphill boasted below-average power at the plate and failed to distinguish himself as a hitter, a shortcoming that, coupled with his defensive failures, made him expendable. He went unsigned after the 1901 season, became a free agent and in February 1902 joined the Cleveland Bronchos, a bad team rapidly on the rise. At the start of the season, Hemphill was used as a substitute in right field for the injured Zaza Harvey. He batted .266 in 25 games before drawing his release. He quickly signed on with the St. Louis Browns, where he became the club's regular right fielder and number three hitter. Hemphill enjoyed one of his best seasons with the 1902 Browns, leading the team in batting average (.317), slugging percentage (.447), triples (11), home runs (6), and stolen bases (23).

The following spring, Hemphill reported to Sportsman's Park "a trifle fat," according to one reporter. During a four game preseason series with the Cardinals, Hemphill could be seen running around the park "five or six times as a flesh reducer." After the series, one writer noted that "Hemphill is a hard worker who is often guilty of stupid baserunning." And weak hitting. By August, Hemphill was benched, then suspended for "dissipation," and finished the year under a doctor's care in Youngstown, Ohio. For the season he batted .245 with only 12 extra-base hits in 383 at-bats.

Despite spending part of his offseason boiling out in Hot Springs, Arkansas, in 1904 Hemphill again reported for duty out of shape, and finished the year with a .256 batting average in 114 games. The following offseason St. Louis farmed him out to the St. Paul Apostles of the American Association, where the left-hander rediscovered his hitting stroke. At season's end, Hemphill led the circuit in batting average (.364) and hits (204), a performance that earned him another chance with the Browns in 1906.

Batting in the top third of the St. Louis order, Hemphill showed significant improvement at the plate over his 1904 totals, and finished the year with a .289 batting average, 62 RBIs, 33 stolen bases, and a career-best 90 runs scored. In better shape, Hemphill also spent 114 of his 154 games patrolling center field, where he used his improved foot speed to offset his other defensive shortcomings. The following year, however, Hemphill was mediocre at best, batting .259 with 38 RBIs and 66 runs scored in 153 games. That November the Browns traded him, along with Fred Glade and Harry Niles, to the New York Highlanders for Jimmy Williams, Hobe Ferris, and Danny Hoffman.

Joined by Jake Stahl and Willie Keeler in the outfield, Hemphill played center field for the Highlanders and made 1908 the best season of his major-league career. In addition to his .297 batting average, he stole a career-high 42 bases and drew 59 bases on balls, also a career best, to give him a .374 on-base percentage, third best in the American League. Meanwhile, the Highlanders, who started out the year 16-8, finished the season with a ghastly 51-103 record, a collapse that sportswriter

Charlie Hemphill with the New York Highlanders, ca. 1909.

Francis Richter characterized as "the most cruel disappointment of major-league history."

Hemphill's 1909 campaign was marred by illness. Vaccinated twice that spring for smallpox after teammate Hal Chase was quarantined in Atlanta, Hemphill played the opening game of the season, then went home with a sore throat. Sidelined with an illness rumored to be, by various media accounts, smallpox, tonsillitis, tuberculosis, and diphtheria, Hemphill eventually returned to the lineup but batted poorly and finished the season as the team's fifth outfielder. Despite his .243 batting average, however, Hemphill posted a solid .357 on-base percentage in 216 plate appearances.

Back in the starting lineup in 1910 after Keeler retired, Hemphill split his time between right and center fields and held the leadoff spot for three months before his poor hitting again relegated him to the bench. He finished the year with a .239 batting average, but once again posted an excellent on-base percentage (.350), thanks to 55 walks. In 1911, his last season in the major leagues, Hemphill played in only 69 games but batted .284 with a .397 on-base percentage, thanks to 37 walks in 244 plate appearances. Though it went mostly unappreciated at the time, Hemphill had transformed himself into a very different hitter by the end of his major-league career. Before he joined the Highlanders, Hemphill's walk rate had hovered around 7 or 8 percent each season. In 1908, his first in New York, he walked more than 10 percent of the time, and in his final three seasons he reached base via the walk nearly 15 percent of the time. Unfortunately, he also had lost what little power he once had, collecting a mere 25 extra-base hits in 879 plate appearances over the same period.

Hemphill started out the 1912 campaign as player-manager of the Atlanta Crackers of the Southern Association. After a fair start, the team slipped into last place by July 15. Everything unraveled for Hemphill during a weekend series with New Orleans, when he drank too much to play in the Saturday game. When he did not report for a game in Montgomery on July 22, he was summoned home, deposed as manager, suspended as a player, and peddled to clubs in the American Association. Kansas City was interested; Columbus made the purchase.

He lasted only a week with the Senators before management suspended him "for failure to get into condition" and complained to the National Commission for refund of the $1,500 purchase price. Columbus was eventually awarded $250, the difference between the purchase price and the next best offer Atlanta had for Hemphill. He spent the rest of the season playing for Youngstown of the Inter-State League, though he remained Columbus property. Sold to St. Paul in the offseason, Hemphill spent the winter boiling out in Hot Springs. In April 1913 the National Commission denied Hemphill's request for 60 days of back pay that he claimed the Atlanta and Columbus clubs owed him from 1912. After a hot start, Hemphill faded during the summer and was suspended again on August 27 for "failure to keep in condition" and "failure to report at the park for that day's game."

Many old ballplayers moved up during the Federal League years but Charlie Hemphill moved briskly down. In 1914 he batted .277 for St. Paul and .225 for New Orleans. In 1915 he appeared in 15 games for Youngstown, batting .119. By then Hemphill was also making his offseason home in Youngstown with his wife, Theresa (whom he had married in 1905), and their three children.

By 1930 the family had moved to Detroit, where Hemphill worked as an automobile ironmaster. He died there on June 22, 1953, at the age of 77.

Note

This biography originally appeared in David Jones, ed., *Deadball Stars of the American League* (Washington, D.C.: Potomac Books, Inc., 2006).

Sources

For this biography, the author used a number of contemporary sources, especially those found in the subject's file at the National Baseball Hall of Fame Library.

Charlie "Theory" Jones

By Frank Vaccaro

ON JULY 1, 1907, the *Washington Times* ran a photo of .300-hitting Washington center fielder Charlie Jones. The caption read: "One of the Most Valuable Outfielders in the World." For Jones, it was the pinnacle of a checkered career: streaks and brilliant fielding balanced by vast slumps. Jones shared endless batting theories with anyone who'd listen but, in the end, the theories were benched.

Known as Theory Jones, he had an excuse for everything. His most famous theory was that he would not swing at a first pitch, so every pitcher he faced threw it in nice and easy for strike one.[1] He used a short and heavy bat, into which he pounded nearly a hundred tacks. The tacks added weight to the bat and, he lectured, were proof against cracking.[2] Not that he swung at the ball … he flat-footed stabbed at it after posing gorgeously with the bat.[3] He beat out bunts and squibbers for at least half his safeties. Jones looked like the worst-hitting pitcher in the league, often taking three straight seemingly easy pitches before heading to the bench without a murmur.[4]

Born on June 2, 1876, and raised in Butler, Pennsylvania, about 35 miles north of Pittsburgh, Charles Claude Jones was the youngest of at least 17 children born to John L. and Margaret Jones. John Jones worked as a farmer and a house painter.[5] In 1897 Charlie enrolled in nearby Grove City College, where the baseball team featured as many as 11 future major leaguers.[6] Jones was the fastest and his teammates once placed him on a track to run against a rabbit. Another time, after beating the larger Washington & Jefferson College, the celebrating players slipped into the armory at Sharon and fired off a few rounds. Rhody Wallace, Terry Turner, Frank Smith, Spike Shannon, Mal Eason, Doc Marshall, and the Hemphill brothers were all on the roster.

The only Grove City player not to make the majors was Charlie's good friend Teddy Radcliffe, and the Browns had a string on him in 1902 before he became chronically ill. Jones, Radcliffe, and another buddy,

Charlie Jones with Washington, 1907.

Rube Waddell, played ball together, schooled together, and joined the Knights of the Golden Eagle, a strong semipro team in Butler.[7] Jones and many of the Grove City players also appeared on the team. When Pat Donovan's Pittsburgh Pirates stopped for an exhibition game that summer, Jones ran to get Waddell off farm chores, and introduced him to the Pirates manager.

Early in 1898 Jones signed with the London, Ontario, team in the International League, a loop comprising teams in Ontario and Michigan. He batted .262 with poor fielding marks in a handful of games and was released to George Sleeman's independent Chatham team. Waddell jumped Detroit and joined Jones for several early summer weeks. The International League folded on July 7 and Sleeman, a millionaire Guelph brewer, hustled his charges into a patched-up four-team Canadian League that was born on July 11. Chatham finished dead last. Jones batted .238 and fielded .883, poor marks even for that company. *Sporting Life* called

Chatham "a mediocre class of amateurs … laughingstock to the entire community,"[8] and Jones "liable to strike out daily with the bases loaded."

Chatham dumped Jones in favor of 18-year-old Sam Crawford the next season, and Jones was back with London. There he enjoyed two straight seasons of .290 or higher and London finished first twice. Schoolmates Radcliffe and Frank Hemphill also played and Jones was labeled "a fast man with a good arm" who "will command the attention of minor managers."[9] Jones and Hemphill were tied for the league lead in homers with five. When the league folded on July 5, London remained intact and played one month as an independent. On August 6 the team, along with a boatload of Canadian fans, traveled to Detroit for a Simcoe Day doubleheader. George Stallings, manager of the team in the fledgling American League, picked up Jones and Hemphill on a handshake.[10]

Jones sat on the bench for a few days before replacing injured right fielder Ducky Holmes in midgame on August 12. Jones hit a double off Frank Foreman in an easy win that brought Detroit third place. His first high-level minor-league home run came off left-hander Harvey Bailey against Minneapolis in the team's small, alternate Sunday park in the Detroit suburb of Stillwells. But his value as a fielder became immediately clear and Jones regularly started in place of each of Detroit's three slow ex-major-league outfielders. Arthur Irwin, a scout who was looking for players for a possible American Association team in Boston (a stillborn venture propped up by National League interests), traveled to Detroit to see Jones and came away impressed, saying , "Detroiters believe they've landed a capital fielding prize."[11]

Stallings approached Jones and a few other players before the final pay envelope with a 1900 Detroit contract. Stallings called it a formality, but Jones noticed that the contract was for 1901 and the players "started a small riot." Stallings insisted that was a typo and the contracts were amended.[12] Jones remained in Detroit the offseason, plying his necessary non-baseball trade: interior painting and wallpapering.[13] On January 28, 1901, American League president Ban Johnson announced that the league was "major" and the baseball war with the National League was on. Jones and hundreds of other players suddenly became the jealously-guarded property of their respective leagues. In mid-March, Jones was handed to the Cleveland team. Charles Somers, at the moment a principal stockholder of both Boston and Cleveland, switched Jones to the Boston Americans on March 21.[14]

Spring training for new manager Jimmy Collins in the new AL was three weeks of fungoes and exercise on the Charlottesville campus of the University of Virginia. Jones showed off his loping stride, fly-ball-tracking ability, and powerful arm. Beat writer Jacob Morse quickly sized him up: "Certainly one of the most graceful players I ever saw."[15] But Jones caught the measles and was bedridden when the season opened.[16] Grove City alumnus Charlie Hemphill became Boston's inaugural right fielder. When Nap Lajoie spiked Hemphill and Chick Stahl bruised his ribs, Collins used Jones for nine starts. But Jones, 30 pounds underweight, played weakly and opened his major-league career 1-for-21.[17] On May 20 Collins posted a list of 14 players for a three-week Western road trip. Jones, having been given fair consideration, was not on the list.[18] He was likely headed for assignment in the New England League.

Scouting in the East, Denver player-manager Tom Brown induced Jones to jump to the 1900 Western League champs.[19] On June 12, 1901, Jones made his first appearance in Denver, where the deep outfield grass could be four feet high, and where a young grizzly bear sat chained near the ticket office. Jones whacked an inside-the-park home run to the flagpole in deep center field. Jones and Denver were a good fit. Teddy Radcliffe was the team's shortstop. The friends were a good-looking duo and women went to Broadway Park in droves to fawn on them. Jones married Lucille P. Bugge after the season, and within a year had two daughters, Margaret and Katherine. Radcliffe didn't marry in his Denver years and, it was reported, about 30 women sat near third base to cheer him on every game.

Still weak from the measles, Jones started slow and then exploded. In last place on July 21, Denver played .920 ball for a month and finished over .500. Jones's fielding was "the daily sensation."[20] It seemed every week he made a catch described as "the greatest catch ever seen." On September 8 he gunned out five runners from left field. "Jones is fast becoming a favorite with the local public," the *Denver Post* wrote. "[H]e hits well, fields great, and runs the bases like a deer."[21] In September Oakland of the California League offered to borrow Jones, Kid Mohler, and Henry Schmidt for play into November. Denver owner D.C. Packard OK'd the loan of Mohler and Schmidt, but denied the loan of Jones. When Jones found out, he went AWOL on Labor Day and sulked in a tavern.[22]

In the offseason Jones contracted to work in Golden, Colorado, as an interior painter. On January 16, 1902, perhaps still bitter about being denied a chance to play on the coast, Jones jumped to the Milwaukee American Association franchise, an embarrassment for the Western League, which also had a Milwaukee team. Jones's letter to new manager Billy Clingman was published by the *Milwaukee Daily Journal*: "I am with the American Association, first and last." Jones insisted he couldn't be scared into honoring his Denver reserve claim. Two months later he did just that, sheepishly signing back with Denver as Packard reimbursed a $100 advance.

Back to his normal playing weight of 165, Jones had a spectacular 1902. He did miss most of spring training when his father died, but again hit over .360 through July, including a 34-for-73 tear in which Denver played .800 ball.[23] At one point he hit four home runs in five games during a 15-game hitting streak. Weeks could go by with the intense Jones quietly filling his position, never even murmuring to umpires on called third strikes. From time to time he ran in from the outfield with rallying cries — a memorable one: "Are we playing 'One Old Cat'?" The 1902 Western League saw the entire first division within 1 1/2 games of one another with days to go: "A blanket might cover the four teams," the *Denver Post* wrote.[24] The Grizzlies bolstered their great home winning percentage with a 22-2 spurt and speared first place on September 11. They kept it until the final weekend, only to be eliminated on the final day.

The first draft of a new and updated major- and minor-league National Agreement would not be finalized until mid-1903. In the confusion Jones was advised to remain with Grizzlies a third season and he did. It was a disappointing year. He started in a slump and struggled in August as the entire team saw a 50-point batting decline. Oddest of all, he batted .120 against known left-handed pitchers while his average against right-handers remained normal. Jones was known to experiment with left-handed batting throughout his career. June 20 he was moved to the leadoff position and did have a resurgence, but Denver was 15 games back in early July and under .500 for good at the end of the month. On September 5 his mother died. While Jones was in Pennsylvania for the funeral, White Sox owner Charles Comiskey, backed by a new National Commission ruling, demanded immediate possession of Jones and Gus Dundon as per a November signing.[25] The boys still ignored the ruling and finished the year out West, but were corralled by Commie in the cold months.

Fielder Jones, star White Sox center fielder, held out all of spring 1904 and Charlie Jones was used as center-field insurance. He played the first five games of the year for the White Sox, batting seventh, throwing out baserunners, and generally impressing. Fielder signed during that fifth game. It was suggested that Charlie's good play forced Fielder to come back sooner for less, and Comiskey spoke well of Charlie after the stint. Nevertheless Chicago shipped him, strings attached, to the St. Paul Saints. Jones insisted that the reserve clause be stricken and it was. The St. Paul press called Jones "taciturn" and said he was "an unobtrusive stealthy sort of player, in the game all the time."[26] But when Jim Jackson hit a game-winning home run right after Jones joined the team, the *St. Paul Globe* observed, "(C)ool, calm, undemonstrative Jones shot through the crowd and hugged and kissed the chunky little right fielder like a long lost brother."[27]

Charlie Jones, 1905.

For the first time Jones played center field regularly, batted leadoff and more than re-earned his throwing reputation with 42 assists; nearly half were obtained during one July homestand. Now a bona fide terror on the basepaths, Jones amazed fans by squirreling out of rundowns. He stole bases on catcher return throws, after being picked off, and sometimes while the pitchers simply stood in the set position. On July 14 against Toledo, he stole second and third on pickoff throws to first and second bases. St. Paul's pennant hinged on a brawl-filled three-game sweep of Columbus at Columbus, concluding August 15. From there the team soared but Jones batted .199 in 40 games, pulling a .322 average down to its final .287. He visited the Minneapolis State fair during this stretch and fans there recognized him and demanded he act as a steer judge making Jones late to that day's game. A costume "farce" played September 15 was touted as a "good-bye for fans." Each player dressed up: Kelley as an Oriental, Jackson as a vaudeville hobo, and catcher John Sullivan as a Zulu. Jones was a "Coy Country Maiden" and he played the whole game holding his skirt down. A gleeful press noted that he threw just like a girl.

Jones's defensive emergence was noted by Milwaukee manager Joe Cantillon. He made a tremendous catch at St. Paul's Lennon Field on June 30, off the bat of Milwaukee's George Stone. Playing shallow, Jones rocketed to the flagpole and crashed into the fence to make the grab. A catch on September 9 against Kansas City was touted as "the greatest catch in history."[28] Playing big Bill Massey in right center field, Jones cut across the outfield and caught the drive while bouncing off the left-center-field scoreboard. A number of Jones's catches were labeled as "the greatest ever" yet seem to have been forgotten within a few years. Was Jones simply the first great outfielder to disdain the two-handed catch? A simulated action photo used in 1909 has Jones leaping up with one gloved hand. In any case, Cantillon told Ban Johnson that Jones "was the best all around player in the AA." Ban Johnson, with a financial interest in the Washington team, wanted Charlie Jones.

Jones's interior painting and papering business boomed in Denver amid a flurry of offseason machinations to sign him for 1905. Jones, adamant that he would never play for Washington, belonged at various moments to St. Paul, Milwaukee, Toledo, and Denver. After the National Commission awarded him to Washington on January 9, Jones's stance softened on reporting. "I would be a fool to do otherwise. I am in baseball to make a living." He took his family to Washington and rented Gene Demontreville's house.

Washington offered less pay than St. Paul. The reluctant major leaguer joined the team at the same Charlottesville, Virginia, campus where he had trained with Boston in 1901. On his first day he ran into the concrete wall at Lambeth Field, but his spring sparkled after that. On Opening Day, playing shallow, Jones made a sprint to the wall and nabbed a Willie Keeler liner with a Willie Mays effort: one hand, full sprint, his back to home plate. He made three more amazing catches in the early going and by mid-May owned 55 tough errorless chances and a .156 batting average. In Philadelphia on May 1, Rube Waddell burst into Jones's hotel room, pulled him out of bed at sunrise, and introduced him to each of his Washington teammates. Jones already knew his teammates, but Waddell insisted on doing it properly.[29] He was sub-.200 most of the summer but was never benched, although he did drop from leadoff to second slot in the lineup on June 3. Two weeks after that, on

June 17, Jones managed the club for a day when Jake Stahl was sick.

On the field: intense and laconic; off the field: overly talkative and even intellectually loquacious. He could pigeonhole anyone with his explanation on just about anything. As the team gathered to leave on its first Western trip, Mal Kitteridge noticed that pitcher Case Patten was wearing orange socks. Immediately Jones was sent for. Jones studied Patten's socks and rendered a glum verdict for the club: "It is the Indian sign of crimson-beaded moccasins. The trip will be crabbed." Patten and Jones became friends, Jones providing taut retorts to Patten's eccentric musings. Once, eating steaks, Patten asked "I wonder why they call this a porterhouse?" Jones replied "So they can charge a dollar for it."

Surprisingly, the 1905 Washingtons were contenders in the early going. Rookie manager Jake Stahl, the born leader, trained the team with football calisthenics and a vegetarian diet. Six players traveled with small dogs that would eat any meat unavoidably served at any restaurants.

They held first place nine days before losing it for good on May 12. The tying run in that loss came in the sixth inning at Cleveland when Washington pitcher Beany Jacobson promised his team that his low curve couldn't miss. Charlie Carr hit a triple off the boards behind Jones that reportedly caromed back and hit Jones on the forehead. In the dugout, Jones told Jacobson "I'd hate to be playing center if you pitched one in his groove."[30]

On May 26 Jones caught a George Stone liner "off the top board of the fence with one hand," a possible first occurrence of an outfielder stealing a home run.[31] And then came quite possibly the greatest fielding play of Jones's career, on June 15. In a close game, hosting Cleveland, with one out in the top of the sixth inning, Jones sprinted for an Elmer Flick drive against the right-center-field wall. He made the catch, whirled, and fired a strike to third base to catch Harry Bay trying to tag up from second base. *Sporting Life* wrote "Had Jones been throwing at a pin he would have hit it on the head."[32] Rookie umpire Tommy Kelly called Bay safe admitting later that he didn't think such a play was possible. A booing shower followed and police had to escort the umpire off the field. Nap Lajoie called this the greatest play he had ever seen.[33] Abysmal hitting by Jones finally led to a three-game benching in late July, but that didn't help. Jones entered Labor Day 6-for-71.

A real debate began on the value of Jones. Some thought he took away so many hits that it didn't matter how he batted. Others detested his automatic-out-making and seemed to hate him on a personal level. Jones became famous for looking at third strikes and yet still told sportswriters that he was working out a batting theory. Although batter strikeouts weren't reported until 1913, Jones remains a good bet to be one of the earliest to whiff 100 times a season. The *Washington Post* wrote that Jones "exhibits fear at the bat," adding, "It's an act of charity on the part of the pitcher when Jones gets a hit." Jones finished at .208 and would likely have been released to the minors after the season but for one thing: He batted .320 after Labor Day. In October Jimmy McAleer, considered at the time by most to be the best fielding outfielder in history, said: "Charlie Jones is the greatest outfielder playing today, and is as good as any of past days. The *Washington Post* concurred: "Jones is the greatest outfielder in the world. … The ground he covers!"

At the age of 29, Jones entered his second year with Washington at a career-high 178 pounds. He batted near .500 in a spring training shortened by bad weather and the sudden death and services for Joe Cassidy, the team's 23-year-old shortstop. Theory listened to his critics and updated his hypothesis: He would now take only one strike. He started slow, enjoyed a month-long .300 stretch, but saw it end on July 12, when a small spike wound incurred in mid-June became infected. He missed 20 games, and when he came back he lost his stroke. The *Washington Times* wrote that Jones "could not hit a river if he jumped off a bridge."[34] Called out on strikes in the top of the ninth inning by Jack Sheridan on June 18, Jones unveiled his intensity. He came back out of the dugout and threw a water glass at the ump. It missed, but shattered with a bang along the boards inches from the wife of Lloyd Rickert, the secretary of the St. Louis Browns. It should have been cause for a suspension but, because Jones had such a quiet reputation, it wasn't. When Jones hit a first-pitch triple on April 17, he "discarded his theory"; when he hit a game-tying three-run home run on August 6, he "demonstrated the theory sound." "VALUE OF THEORY" headlined the *Washington Times*, followed by the subhead: "Charlie Jones, Thinker, Applies It for Homer That Won Game."[35]

Jake Stahl was relieved of leadership duties after 1906 and Joe Cantillon was hired. Cantillon, no longer a Jones adherent, assigned him to the second-class yannigan squad. When the season opened, infielder Dave Altizer was Washington's center fielder. The *Washington Times* elaborated on Jones: "He is today a substitute, although one of the most brilliant fielders in the country, because he does not hit. For some unknown reason Jones will allow perfect strikes to go over the plate, when any kind of a tap would score a run, with never a swing at the ball. This maddens the rooters, who would rather see him try and fail than stand there like a statue."[36]

In the third game of the season, Charlie Hickman turned his ankle and Jones entered the game as the left fielder. With the score tied, New York pitcher Arthur Clarkson intentionally walked Lave Cross to face Jones with one out in the bottom of the seventh. Jones took two strikes and ripped a game-breaking two-run double into left-center field. Cantillon reluctantly penciled Jones in more and more, moving him back to center and making him a full-time regular by May 9. Jones shortened his tap swing even more and had a busy first half. He made national headlines after scoring from second base on a fly ball without the benefit of an error on May 18, and three days later got two of the team's three hits off Addie Joss to raise his average to .300. On May 29 he made yet another "greatest catch ever," a sixth-inning backhanded grab of Wid Conroy's liner near the wall in right-center. "Charles," it was reported, "tore after it like he had caught sight of a man willing to listen to his theories, and the ball stuck like Federal money in the hand of a Pennsylvania contractor."[37]

Through June Jones continued putting up one thrilling article of ball. Had there been an All-Star Game in 1907 he likely would have made the squad. On June 4 he made seven putouts including three brilliant catches. Three days later he acrobatically grabbed a bad-hop single in the left-field gap and gunned out Roy Hartzell at third base in a 2–1 win. In a 2–1 win over Cleveland, he threw out Elmer Flick going for an inside-the-park home run. He scored from second base on a groundball to third in a 1-0 win on June 19. (There were two outs in the bottom of the ninth and a throwing error was made on the play.) On July 1 he pushed his average back over .300 with a three-hit game off Al Orth. Jones was first-pitch swinging. That day he also set a personal major-league-best nine-game hitting streak, and enjoyed the aforementioned "World's Greatest" headline on the cover of the *Washington Times* sports section. "A most agreeable surprise." the *Washington Post* concurred.[38]

Jones went 0-for-4 the next day, and then injured his back sliding into Boston's Jack Knight at third base on the Fourth of July. It was a terrible time to suffer his first serious injury. He missed 18 games and when he returned he batted .183 over seven weeks highlighted by pathetic attempts to bat left-handed. During that time Walter Johnson and Clyde Milan were signed up and wowed Washington fans. After Milan's first start, Jones lamented: "I have nothing on him."[39] He did play well in September, pinch-hitting for Milan when a left-handed pitcher entered the game. He hit a key double in that role off Waddell in a Labor Day win. After September 17 Jones started only against left-handed pitchers, unusual for the time, until rookie Billy Kay sprained his ankle with four days remaining. Cantillon announced that Jones would start versus left-handers in 1908, to which Jones's final theory was an unspecified critique of Cantillon's managerial skills. Cantillon told the press: "Jones lacks class," and Jones left Washington in a huff, announcing he would launch the Jones Paint and Paper Company in Denver on New Year's Day.[40]

Jones ended the season with a .265 batting average. While Cantillon was critical of him as 1907 wound down, St. Louis Browns manager Jimmy McAleer reiterated praise, saying, "He's one of the 'old boys' like Welch, Fogarty, Johnston, and myself."[41] On December 12, at the American League meeting in Chicago, McAleer offered Ollie Pickering for Jones and Cantillon accepted. McAleer promptly announced the Browns outfield the best in baseball.

In the Browns' 1908 season opener in Cleveland, Jones made yet another incredible catch. With one out in the bottom of the ninth inning, and with Nap Lajoie the potential winning run on second base, Jones grabbed a line drive by Terry Turner near the ropes in dead center while a fan jumped on his back and put him in a headlock. In the next inning Jones singled, advanced on Addie Joss's wild pitch, and scored the winning run. A second extra-inning game followed and Jones got the game winning RBI with a hit in the tenth frame. Standard practice at the time was for game-winning batters not to run to first base. Jones stood at home plate and kissed his bat. The *St. Louis Post Dispatch* wrote that Jones is "beginning to prove he is all the candy as touted."

Once again Jones had a terrific first half, although his average only peeked over .250 on occasion. He advanced from first to third on bunts and taps, threw out Ty Cobb trying to score from second base on a roller up the middle, and was even intentionally walked the only time of his career. That came April 27 at the hand of old college teammate Frank Smith. Then came disaster. For the second year in a row, Jones suffered a serious injury sliding into third base at Boston. This time a Rhody Wallace grounder cracked him on the knee. Al Schweitzer, a gimpy rookie with no range, replaced Jones for seven games and jumped into the forefront of the American League in batting. He became "The Cheese." When Jones returned to the lineup, the Browns won 15 of 18 to grab sole possession of first place on June 25 in what turned out to be one of the greatest four-team pennant races in history. With Schweitzer—dubbed the "second Ty Cobb"—on the bench, Jones went 0-for-15 while the team was winning. On June 27, against Bill Donovan, Jones popped up on a bunt attempt, struck out with a runner on third base, and struck out with runners on second and third to end the game. St. Louis lost 1–0 and its lead was reduced to a half-game. For McAleer, the fans, and the press, this game became the symbol of Jones's shortcomings.

Jones was summarily benched. Still, he worked in a few starts when Schweitzer had a lame leg and Danny Hoffman got sick, and continued to make key day-to-day contributions despite not hitting .300. In 15 games with Jones the Browns won 11 and were driving hard toward first-place Detroit. On August 4 Hoffman returned and Jones sat. From the bench he watched Hobe Ferris's grand slam on the 9th, the highlight of St. Louis's year. On August 14 Jones started in Philadelphia against Eddie Plank. He went 0-for-3 with two strikeouts. McAleer never used Jones again, not even to pinch-run. McAleer begged stiff Emmet Heidrick to come out of retirement and replace Jones. Heidrick, having played four years of Sunday pickup games in his hometown of Clarion, Pennsylvania, gamely met St. Louis in Washington. Where Jones should have returned the conquering hero, Heidrick debuted and hit a home run. McAleer rejoiced: "Moses" had returned. Jones was immediately shipped home. He finished the season at .232. "Next year," McAleer said, "all I want is a hard hitting outfielder."[42]

The St. Louis press, too, saw no value in Jones. "He could not make a hit if he was the only man at a summer resort," grumbled one.[43] Schweitzer and Heidrick turned out to be dead weight but they had McAleer's favor. In the final 56 games of 1908 the team floundered with a 26-30 record—a far cry from the 57-39 record it had when Jones was benched. Jones was spoken of as a backup outfielder to Heidrick in 1909. But on March 13 Jones was offered and accepted his dream job: as player-manager of the Denver Grizzlies, his old Western League team. He led the team on a snowy spring trip and opened the season with a 9-3 homestand that included his only 5-for-5 game, on May 4. Fans were abuzz. At different points Jones had six straight games with multiple hits, and seven straight games with extra-base hits. By July 12 Jones was batting .344. But the team's pitching was atrocious. To help, Jones himself threw a complete game (a loss) on May 26, and worked hard to keep the team over .500 until a late-August swoon dropped the Grizzlies into the second division. His repeated telegrams to ownership for a new pitcher went unheeded. Jones even put a classified ad in the *Denver Post* for a pitcher.[44]

In late December of 1909 Jones was sold to St. Paul of the American Association for $1,000. Mike Kelley had returned to manage the Saints and remembered the pep Jones added in '04. Jones added it again. He alternated with Dave Altizer for the league lead in stolen bases, performed outfield heroics, and kept his average in the .270s while St. Paul visited first place as late as July 8. Jones even managed the team in late August when Kelley went on a scouting trip. A 9-for-79 September slump at the end of the 168-game schedule brought Jones's batting average for 1910 down to a tired .247. He handled 357 outfield chances with only one muff and 12 throwing errors. St. Paul did not contend in 1911. Jones sat out 42 early-season games with an unspecified illness, then rocked in July with an extended streak of .464 batting, the last week of which he was player-manager again. First-pitch-swinging, Jones tagged Kansas City's Chick Brandom with a game-winning 11th-inning home run on July 11. A few weeks later, Kelley sold ace pitcher Marty O'Toole to Pittsburgh for $22,000. It was a signal Kelley was giving up on the year. Highlights were scarce as Jones finished the season at .262. Ginger Beaumont had been spelling Jones in center much of the second half, and he closed out the year batting .161 in his last 20 games. St. Paul beat writer J.J. Corey wrote: "Few, if any, of the old-timers will be retained … exhibiting too much of that 'tired feeling'."[45]

Still, Jones helped the team finish in the first division. A loss on the final day, October 1, could have meant a drop from fourth to seventh place. In the top of the fourth inning, with darkness approaching, Jones got into a heated 10-minute argument over strikes and balls with the umpire. Then Milwaukee's Ray Schalk told Jones to bat, Jones gave the little catcher a theory and Cracker gave Jones a shove. The game was canceled on account of darkness.

Unwanted, Jones hrld out in the spring of 1912, but no offers came. He reportedly sued for his release, and went to work as a traveling salesman for a St. Paul haberdashery. Peace of sorts came after a year. On March 1, 1913, Henry Conrad, a successful billiard-parlor owner and a wannabe baseball magnate, hired Jones to manage the new St. Paul Little Saints in the new Northern League. The quietest manager in the league, Jones was known to "seethe and hiss" while other managers just yelled.[46] The Little Saints were no-hit in their second game, but opened the season 6-3. From there it was all downhill: players jumping, a 3-16 road trip, seventh place, and Jones playing second base with a sore arm. A shadow of his old self, Rube Waddell joined the mix, being assigned to last-place Virginia in late April. Cy Young was assigned to Minneapolis but did the honorable thing and hung up his spikes. Conrad canned Jones after a June 5 loss that dropped the team to 11-27.

Sixth-place Winnipeg scooped up Jones on June 20, to be the player-manager. Jones led Winnipeg on a .714 clip for three weeks to reach the coveted .500. That gave him just enough national recognition for Kelley's St. Paul's to claim his services once again. Jones was sidelined as ineligible on July 8, as Kelley shook down Winnipeg ownership for a prospect named Jack Clothier. When Winnipeg didn't budge, Kelley ordered Jones to report to the Double-A Saints. Jones did and sat on the bench in uniform, bringing out lineup cards at the start of games. Winnipeg refused a $500 payment for Jones. Around that time, the Northern League Little Saints were considered a drain on St. Paul big Saints' enthusiasm and attendance. Kelley wanted to move the franchise to LaCrosse, Wisconsin, but Northern League owners, upset at the treatment of Jones, voted no on July 15.

The National Commission gave Jones the only ruling he won during his career, awarding him to Winnipeg on August 4. Jones debuted with Winnipeg on August 13 and led the team to a 9-6 finish over the short season's final days, and a satisfying third place. When asked if Jones would manage Winnipeg in 1914, team president A.H. Pulford said, "No. Fans will soon forget the former big leaguer."[47] Jones got his long-sought-after unconditional release on April 5, 1914, when he was no longer a baseball commodity. The *Washington Times* lamented that Jones's career as a player was never the same after someone cracked him over the head with a billiard cue.[48]

Jones's wife, Lucille, had died by the time of 1920 Census, in which Jones listed himself as "widow," living in St. Paul where he had moved his daughters, his mother-in-law, and brother-in-law. Jones, an avid fisherman, continued his work as a painter and wallpaperer. In the 1920s he moved to Lutsen, in northeastern Minnesota, where he married and divorced a second wife, the much younger Jesse Bally. He earned a reputation as an excellent sign painter in Cook County and worked as a tax collector for the Internal Revenue Service. In March 1947 he was admitted with liver trouble to what is now Lakeview Memorial Hospital in Two Harbors, Minnesota. He died on April 2 at the age of 70.

Notes

1. *Washington Times*, April 16, 1907
2. *Washington Post*, May 30, 1907
3. *Washington Times* and *Denver Post*, both of May 9, 1903
4. *Washington Times*, April 16, 1907
5. Pennsylvania census, 1880. Thanks to Pat Collins, director of the Butler County Historical Society.
6. "Mack Says He is a Live Wire," *Duluth* (Minnesota) *News-Tribune*, February 16, 1908, 4-4.
7. "Luck with Nationals," *Washington Post*, May 2, 1905, 8. Radcliffe may not have actually joined the Knights, but there is every reason to believe he did.
8. *Sporting Life*, September 3, 1898
9. *Sporting Life*, November 4, 1899
10. *Sporting Life*, September 29, 1900
11. *Sporting Life*, April 13, 1901 and October 6, 1900
12. *Sporting Life*, September 29, 1900
13. Ibid.
14. *St. Louis Republican*, March 22, 1901
15. *Sporting Life*, May 18, 1901
16. *Sporting Life*, May 11, 1901
17. *Sporting Life*, July 22, 1905
18. *Boston Globe*, May 21, 1901
19. *Denver Post*, May 22, 1901
20. *St. Paul Globe*, July 12, 1904
21. *Denver Post*, August 2, 1901
22. *Denver Post*, September 3, 1901
23. The death of his father is mentioned in the April 3 *Denver Post*.
24. *Denver Post*, September 18, 1902
25. *Sporting Life*, August 8, 1903
26. *St. Paul Globe*, May 21, 1904
27. *St. Paul Globe*, May 31, 1904
28. *St. Paul Globe*, September 10, 1904
29. *Washington Post*, May 2, 1905
30. *Chicago Eagle*, December 4, 1915
31. *Washington Post*, May 27, 1905
32. *Sporting Life*, June 17, 1905
33. *Washington Post*, August 6, 1905. Lajoie's opinion of the play was one expressed at the time.
34. *Washington Times*, April 17, 1906
35. *Washington Times*, August 7, 1906
36. *Washington Times*, April 17, 1907
37. *Washington Times*, May 30, 1907
38. *Washington Post*, June 2, 1907
39. *Washington Post*, August 29, 1907
40. *Washington Herald*, May 7, 1908, and *Washington Post*, October 13, 1907
41. *Marion Daily Mirror*, May 7, 1908
42. *St. Louis Post Dispatch*, August 13, 1908
43. *Washington Times*, August 17, 1908 quoting from an unnamed St. Louis newspaper
44. *Denver Post*, May 30, 1909, p. 1, classified section
45. *Sporting Life*, September 20, 1911
46. *Winona Republican Herald*, March 24, 1913
47. *Winona Republican Herald*, January 12, 1914
48. *Washington Times*, April 11, 1914

Win Kellum

By Bill Nowlin

IF YOU WERE going to launch a whole new baseball franchise, what better pitcher to hand the game ball to for the very first game than someone named Win? That's just what Boston Americans manager Jimmy Collins did when he asked Win Kellum to start the April 26, 1901, ballgame in Baltimore, facing Iron Man Joe McGinnity.

Win lost.

The final score was Baltimore 10, Boston 6. In the process of pitching the game, Kellum registered a number of firsts. As a pitcher, he holds the first start and the first complete game (as well as the first loss) for the Bostons. He allowed the first hit (leadoff batter John McGraw doubled to right field in the bottom of the first inning); the first run (the second batter up, Turkey Mike Donlin, followed McGraw's double with a triple to right); and the first base on balls (Kellum walked Jimmy Williams, the third batter up in the first inning). He also record the first out—being a strikeout of Cy Seymour, it was also the first K. At bat, he collected the first hit by a Boston Americans pitcher, a scratch single in the eighth, and was the first pitcher lifted for a pinch-hitter (fellow Canadian Larry McLean, in the ninth, who doubled).

It wasn't the first game Kellum had pitched in a Boston uniform. On April 11, in Charlottesville, Virginia—the team's first spring-training home—he and two others held the University of Virginia baseball team to seven hits in a 23-0 slaughter. It was the second (and last) exhibition game of the training season.

Winford Ansley Kellum was born in Waterford, Ontario, on April 11, 1876. His family had mixed American and Canadian ancestry and at the time of the 1900 United States Census, Win was living in Grant Township, Mecosta County, Michigan, with his parents, Newton H. Kellum and Catherine Kellum, and his wife, Nanette. Newton was a farmer and Winford was listed as a farmer laborer. Newton's father was Pennsylvanian and his mother was a Canadian native,

Win Kellum, 1901.

as were he, Catherine, and Win. Catherine's parents were both New Yorkers. Nanette was born in Ohio, to Ohio natives. The 1910 and 1920 censuses show that Newton continued farming; both censuses used the nickname Cassie for Mrs. Kellum. The 1910 Census showed Winford as a baseball player. He did become a United States citizen—witness his World War I draft registration form.

He'd been sued for divorce in May 1907, his wife alleging that "while traveling with the baseball teams Kellum was unfaithful."[1] By 1910, Win had a different wife, whose name was reported differently in each succeeding census, but who appears to have been Frederika Ovidia M. Anderson Kellum. She had been born in Michigan to parents who were natives of Denmark. She was a public-school teacher, and had give birth to their daughter Winifred in 1908 and son, Edward Ford Kellum, in August 1909.

Win pitched for the Montgomery Grays beginning in 1895, according to his obituary in *The Sporting News*. The first newspaper clipping we find shows Kellum playing baseball on April 23, 1896, when the left-hander started and won a game for the Grays, beating the Atlanta Crackers, 8-1. "Kellum's Curves Too Much" was the subhead in the April 24 *Atlanta Constitution*. He struck out eight and was 1-for-4 (a double) in the game. He threw a four-hitter against New Orleans on the 27th and a one-hitter on May 1 against the Mobile Blackbirds. He hit a two-base hit in each of those games, too. There weren't that many times opponents scored against him. He was 21-5 in Southern Association play, and his 1.33 earned-run average led the league. The league started to break up in midyear and Kellum finished up elsewhere. In late September, he pitched in the final game of the year for the Indianapolis Indians of Ban Johnson's Western League.

Kellum was one of three pitchers used in the no-mercy-rule 41-0 defeat of Depauw in early April 1897, as Indianapolis prepared for regular-season Western League play. He was listed as 5-feet-10 and 190 pounds. He was a switch-hitter, but a southpaw on the mound. Tracing his steps as best we can, he pitched a full season in 1898 for Ohio's Mansfield Haymakers (Inter-state League, a Class B team). The August 12 game against the visiting Springfield Governors ended due to darkness in a 1-1 tie, with Kellum going the distance for Mansfield.

In 1899 he was back with the Hoosiers, and shut out Columbus on May 2. Indianapolis won the Western League pennant by one game over Minneapolis, a bit of a thrilling race that must have pleased league president Ban Johnson. It was sometimes a wild and woolly league; the June 11 game in the Indiana capital ended in a near-riot when 2,000 fans chased umpire Manassau from the field, protesting his decision that would have given St. Paul a victory. "There were a thousand too many umpires," he said after police arrived on bicycles to quell the disturbance.[2] Kellum's record was 14-11; he

Kellum with the Cardinals, 1905.

won the third and final game of a playoff against Minneapolis in late September. It was during this Western League play that Kellum came to know Charles Comiskey. The two long enjoyed fishing together, a fact mentioned in Kellum's obituary in the *New York Times*.

In 1900, Johnson reconstituted the Western League as the American League, which played a full season. Manager Bill Watkins was at the helm again for Indianapolis, and Kellum was his left-hander, throwing a no-hitter on June 16 against the Chicago White Sox. Chicago won the pennant; the Hoosiers finished third, Kellum winning the last game of the season, 4-1, over the Kansas City Blues, a five-hitter.

As Johnson developed the new American League, truly taking on the reigning National League head-to-head, he helped teams sign up such players as they could and Win Kellum wound up with the Boston Americans. Confusion reigned, and there was a lot of jockeying. A news report on April 2 said that Boston's National League team had secured Kellum from Indianapolis; another report the same day noted his expected arrival with the Americans in Charlottesville. The next day's *Chicago Tribune* noted Kellum as one of the absentees from the Americans' camp (along with one Cy Young). He turned up in time to pitch in the above-mentioned April 12 exhibition game. By the time the club broke camp, Collins was said to be "especially pleased" with Kellum's performance.³ Hence, presumably, Collins's decision to assign him the first start. Ten runs on 11 hits and four walks did not augur well for the start of the season. Kellum's second start was worse: May Day in Philadelphia saw the Athletics pound him for 14 runs on 19 hits. But then he threw a four-hitter against Washington on May 7 and collected his first win.

Kellum started well but faded after the fifth when he faced Washington again on the 13th of the month.

On May 25, the Americans released Kellum and outfielder Charlie Jones. "We had too many players on our list," said Collins. "We decided we might as well let two men out now as later. Neither has showed up very well. I don't know what is the matter with Kellum. He is touted as a good pitcher, but the four games he pitched for us showed that he would not do in his present form."⁴

Quickly enough, within a week, Kellum was recalled on June 1 and Ben Beville released. Kellum had his next start on June 10, which he won, 7-3, over Milwaukee. His final game for Boston was on June 14, when he was knocked out of the box during a four-run fifth, Cy Young coming on and getting the 16-7 win in relief, thanks to a nine-run Boston bottom of the eighth. Win was released again. His first-year major-league record was 2-3, with a 6.38 earned in average in 48 innings of work.

Win picked up some work in Massachusetts, pitching for the Attleboro team (to batterymate Jack Slattery, who joined the Americans later in the season). His game against North Attleboro was the "finest ever seen on the local grounds," according to the July 14 *Boston Globe*. As soon as Attleboro won the season series from its rivals to the north, Kellum headed south and racked up a 10-2 record pitching for the New Orleans Pelicans. Before December was out, he'd signed up again with Bill Watkins in Indianapolis. His 25-10 season helped win the 1902 American Association flag, and he won 23 games against 10 defeats in 1903, though the team finished fourth. In early August, the Cincinnati Reds had all but completed a deal to sign Kellum for the 1904 campaign.⁵

Kellum had a very good year in 1904, with an ERA of 2.60 and 15 wins against 10 losses. The *Cincinnati Post* ran a series on what the players were doing over the winter, and noted Kellum as a bookworm, and always buried himself in a book when he was off the field - "anything from Dumas's works to *Diamond Dan, The Daring Desperado of Dead Gulch*."⁶

The Reds had three other pitchers with 15 or more wins, however, and Kellum ended up being sold to St. Louis on January 25, 1905. Word had been that he was going to Philadelphia but league president Garry Herrmann assigned his contract to the Cardinals.

Kellum didn't have that good a year in 1905, though he kept his ERA to 2.92 (better than the team's 3.59). He won three, including a 14-inning 3-2 complete game victory on May 20 in Boston, and lost three in 11 appearances (seven starts, the last coming on June 16). This left him with a major-league record of 20-16 and a 3.19 earned run average. Within the week after the 16th, the Toledo Mud Hens had purchased his contract from St. Louis, but four days later Toledo sold him to Minneapolis. He was 10-9 the rest of the year.

Where did Win go in 1906? Back to Bill Watkins in Indianapolis. He pitched two more seasons there, 16-19 and 15-16, for a last-place team the first year and a sixth-place team in 1907. Watkins himself didn't make

Kellum lapel pin souvenir button, 1904.

it through the team's poor 1906 season, however, being replaced by Charles Carr as manager. Kellum wasn't out, though, and there were those who were watching. John T. Brush of the New York Giants had his eyes on the American Association pitcher at midseason.[7] Kellum finished out both '06 and '07 with Indianapolis, and was then traded to Newark of the Eastern League on December 30, 1907, for Bill Carrick, who'd insisted on pitching for independent teams on his offdays and thus found himself unwelcome with the Newark club. It's not as though Kellum was a choir boy, either. He was under suspension at the time for "indifferent work."[8]

By the time the 1908 season began, the trade had been called off, on second thought, and instead Kellum was traded to the Nashville Vols on March 14 for "Buttons" Briggs.

The Southern League team had finished last in 1907 but was first in 1908, and Win won 15 games against nine losses. An amusing headline in the *Atlanta Constitution* highlighted one of the wins: "Kellum Heaved Like Porpoise. He Groaned and Grunted but Beat Us Out." And Kellum's ninth-inning single broke the 4-4 tie in Nashville's favor.[9] He had arm troubles in 1909, leaving the team in early August to get some rest. He finished up well enough, though, and posted an even 8-8 record, disappointing with the team just 5 1/2 games behind the Crackers for the pennant. Kellum was not invited back for 1910 and his playing days were over.

Kellum wasn't finished with baseball, though. Starting in 1911, he umpired in the Southern League, and even wrote an article in the January 13, 1913, *Atlanta Constitution* about the "toughest decision I ever made." In 1914, he made a few headlines when manager Bill Smith of the Crackers took a swipe at umpire Kellum. Smith got himself suspended. Kellum was not rehired for the 1915 season.

Farming wasn't as profitable as Kellum would have liked, and a 1925 letter from him to NL president August Herrmann in the Hall of Fame files shows Kellum asking for any recommendation Herrmann might offer, even as a college coach or scout. "I am not as young as when I pitched for you," he wrote, "but neither am I dissipated or fat." He added that he had run a club in Michigan in 1924. He'd written on the stationery of Pleasant View Farm in Big Rapids, where he was raising cattle and doing general farming. In 1930, Win was a garage serviceman working with automobiles.

In May 1951, Kellum joined 30 ballplayers from the 1901 season in 50th-anniversary celebrations in Boston, including old teammates Cy Young, Fred Mitchell, Charles Hemphill, and Harry Gleason. Three months later, he was dead, of a heart attack while fishing with his son Ford, a conservation officer. Bill Lee's *Baseball Necrology* says he was dead on arrival at Community Hospital at Big Rapids on August 10, 1951. Lee's book also says Kellum had pitched a minor-league game at the age of 55.

Sources

In addition to the sources cited in this biography, the author consulted the online SABR Encyclopedia, retrosheet.org, and Baseball-Reference.com.

Notes

1 *Cleveland Plain Dealer*, March 14, 1907.
2 *Chicago Tribune*, June 12, 1899.
3 *Washington Post*, April 23, 1901.
4 *Boston Globe*, May 26, 1901.
5 *Washington Post*, August 5, 1903.
6 *Cincinnati Post*, December 3, 1904.
7 *Washington Post*, July 11, 1906.
8 *Cleveland Plain Dealer*, December 30, 1907.
9 *Atlanta Constitution*, July 23, 1908.

Ted Lewis

by Rory Costello

WILLIAMS COLLEGE IS best known in baseball circles for two nonplaying alumni: the last independent commissioner, Fay Vincent (1960), and the blustery Boss himself, George Steinbrenner ('52). There hasn't been an Ephman in the majors since 1934, but Ted Lewis, "The Pitching Professor," was not just the finest ballplayer Williams ever produced—like Sir Thomas More, he was a man for all seasons. Educator, elocutionist, natural leader—Lewis embodied an array of talents but always retained a winning humility.

Horatio Alger could not have conjured up a life story like this, which has the power to make the most hardened cynic believe in ideals again. Edward Morgan Lewis was born on Christmas Day 1872 in Machynlleth, Wales. His parents were John C. Lewis and Jane L. (Davies) Lewis. When the boy was 8 years old, his family moved to Utica, New York, where they lived on the banks of the Erie Canal. Little Ted earned his first quarter delivering groceries for the local corner store (though he was docked if he broke a ketchup bottle), and scouted out other odd jobs, supplementing the immigrants' straitened budget.

It is an article of faith that Welshmen have wonderful voices and a love of poetry, and the Lewis family reinforced this tradition. The great American poet Robert Frost was a crony of Ted Lewis's for 20 years—even into their 60s, they played "singles" baseball or softball in the backyard whenever they got together. Frost read from Tennyson and Whitman at his friend's memorial tribute, and his address showed the profound influence of culture on character:

"He told me once—I was afraid that the story might not be left for me to tell—that he began his interest in poetry as he might have begun his interest in baseball—with the idea of victory—the 'Will to Win.'

"He was at an Eisteddfod in Utica, an American-Welsh Eisteddfod, where the contest was in poetry, and a bard had been brought in from Wales to give judgment and to pick the winner; and the bard, after announcing the

College administrator Edward Lewis, 1922.

winner and making the compliments which judges make, said he wished the unknown victor would rise and make himself known and let himself be seen. (I believe the poems were read anonymously.) The little 'Ted' Lewis sitting there beside his father looked up and saw his father rise as the victor. So poetry to him was prowess from that time on, just as baseball was prowess, as running was prowess. And it was our common ground."

Lewis worked as a bundle boy in a department store and as a surveyor's helper, studying borrowed textbooks by lamplight. With the $50 in personal savings he managed to put aside, the youth entered Marietta College in Ohio, which gave him the opportunity to meet his tuition payments by working as a letter carrier, hotel clerk, and janitor.

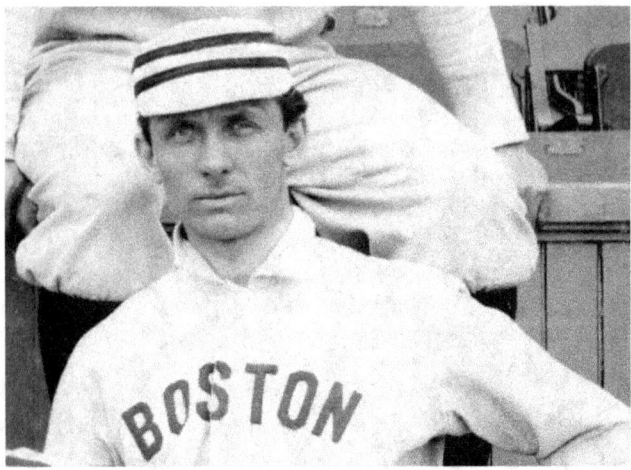

Lewis with the 1900 Boston Nationals.

In the fall of 1893 sophomore Ted Lewis transferred to Williams, the small liberal-arts school nestled in the Berkshire Hills of western Massachusetts. He made a tremendous impression on his classmates, becoming president of the elite Gargoyle Society and winning the class cup in a walkover, receiving 32 votes while no one else got more than four. Lewis's accomplishments on the mound were certainly a part of his status. In 1895 he won all eight games in the Triangular League (which then consisted of Williams, Amherst, and Dartmouth rather than Wesleyan), and he followed up with six more in his senior year.

Baseball was the most popular sport at the college in those days, and the *Williams Weekly* was full of manly exhortations to give full voice while cheering. The souvenir scorecard from the 1896 Commencement Game against Amherst is another charming curio, with Captain Ted's photo on the front cover and official yells (Osky-wow-wow, Skimmy-wow-wow, Jimmy-wow-wow, W-O-W) on the back.

Lewis faced some most intriguing opponents besides Yale and Harvard. These included the original black pro team, the Cuban Giants, whose trip to the Purple Valley bears further investigation. Another was Louis Sockalexis, then the star center fielder for Holy Cross. A year before his briefly spectacular run with Cleveland, the Penobscot Indian "played a phenomenal game, catching and batting balls, whenever and wherever he pleased."

During his college days, Lewis also won the heart of hometown girl Margaret Hallie Williams with a move that would have left Sir Walter Raleigh in the dust. At a local game in Richfield Springs, New York, he had promised her that he would meet her at the grounds and usher her in. But Margaret arrived a little late, while Ted was facing the first batter. Yet when he spied his wife-to-be, he calmly dropped the ball, walked off the hill (making the captain think Lewis had gone "bughouse"), and saw to his escort duties. The gallant then returned to a huge hand from the crowd.

Seeking money to further his studies, the graduate commenced his major-league career with the Boston Beaneaters. Frank Selee's club was the class of the National League in the 1890s, winning five pennants behind numerous Hall of Famers and near-greats. Lewis was a key part of the last two titles, especially in 1898, when he led the league in winning percentage at 26-8. He also appeared in three games in the 1897 Temple Cup series, winning one, losing one, and allowing Boston to claw back from an early blowout into a near win with a strong effort in long relief. In 1904 *Boston Globe* sportswriter and old-time player Tim Murnane remembered Lewis as "a superb pitcher, with great curves and fine speed, both of which he used with rare judgment. He was a fine batsman for a pitcher and was a willing worker for his club."

The "good guy" Beaneaters had an ongoing battle with John McGraw's Baltimore Orioles, notorious for their ruffian tactics. "Parson" Lewis prefigured the fictional Yalie Galahad Frank Merriwell and McGraw's Mr. Clean with the Giants, Christy Mathewson. A leading example of Lewis's devotion to fair play came on August 24, 1901, when he helped rescue umpire Joe Cantillon from a mob of Boston fans who stormed the field. Tim Murnane stated, "It is doubtful if good, clean sport ever had a more earnest and successful practitioner than 'Ted' Lewis." Echoing these sentiments, Damon Hall, a close friend from Williams, said: "One might have supposed in those earlier days of professional baseball that a college graduate who did not drink, who refused to play Sunday ball, who said his prayers and read his Bible daily, who even asked his teammates to go to

Friends of Ted Lewis

I first knew "Ted" Lewis twenty years ago and the first time I saw him, he was reading in public the poetry of a new poet. When a teacher, he was a teacher of literature and chiefly of poetry. He told me once—I was afraid that the story might not be left for me to tell—that he began his interest in poetry as he might have begun his interest in baseball—with the idea of victory—the "Will to Win".

He was at an Eisteddfod in Utica, an American-Welsh Eisteddfod, where the contest was in poetry, and a bard had been brought from Wales to give judgment and to pick the winner; and the bard, after announcing the winner and making the compliments which judges make, said he wished the unknown victor would rise and make himself be known and let himself be seen. (I believe the poems were read anonymously.) The little "Ted" Lewis sitting there beside his father looked up and saw his father rise as the victor. So poetry to him was prowess from that time on, just as baseball was prowess, as running was prowess. And it was our common ground. I have always thought of poetry as prowess – something to achieve, something to win or lose.

> – from a eulogy Robert Frost delivered at a memorial service for Lewis held at the University of New Hampshire on May 26, 1936.

"I never feel more at home in America than at a ball game, be it in park or in sandlot. Beyond this I know not. And dare not."

> – *Robert Frost, "A Perfect Day-A Day of Prowess,"* Sports Illustrated, *July 23, 1956.*

Courtesy Bread Loaf Writers Conference Photographs (F8 PF), Robert Frost, 1941, Special Collections & Archives, Middlebury College

prayer meetings with him, would have been esteemed somewhat of a prig by the other members of the squad. Instead, they took him to their hearts."

Indeed, Ted had seriously considered entering the ministry but decided he could reach more young people through the classroom. While with Boston he found time to coach the Harvard nine. After jumping to the new American League in 1901 and playing with the very first Red Sox team (then known as the Americans, among other early names), Lewis retired from baseball to devote his full energies to teaching. His lifetime record was 94-64, with an earned-run average of 3.53 and a batting average of .223.

A Man for All Seasons - An athlete, educator, poet and leader, Lewis (far left) with his family in front of the pergola and flower garden area at the President's House at the University of New Hampshire, ca. 1930.

The Professor had earned his master's from Williams in 1899, and from 1901 to 1903 he taught elocution at Columbia. His alma mater then lured him back to teach oratory for eight years, during which he also lectured at the Yale Divinity School. In 1910 the Welsh community of Berkshire County formed a society, acclaiming Lewis as president. For many years he would return to North Adams on St. David's Day, March 1, to address his leek-waving brethren. (The only other major leaguer born in Wales was Jimmy Austin, who was one of Lawrence Ritter's subjects in *The Glory of Their Times*.)

Also in 1910, Lewis ran for Congress as a Democrat in a staunch Republican district, and missed pulling off an upset by just 736 votes. He said, "It may be that I am starting in on this campaign in the ninth inning with the score 9 to 0 against me. But if the odds are against me I'll play the game out, for you never can tell what a score you may make in the ninth."

The next year, however, Massachusetts Agricultural College in Amherst beckoned. Lewis soon proved how capable an administrator he was, being pressed into service as acting president in 1913-14 (when he made another unsuccessful bid for Congress, supported by pioneering muckraker Ray Stannard Baker). The dean of languages and literature again stepped into the breach in 1918-19 and 1924, finally accepting the position of president officially in 1926. It was through his efforts that the modest "Aggie" school was transformed into today's University of Massachusetts. Lewis felt uncomfortable with the political pressure there, however; there was an ongoing power struggle with the state government over funding and the authority of the Board of Trustees. Thus Lewis moved to the University of New Hampshire in 1927. But before he left, Massachusetts Agricultural College surprised its outgoing president by conferring upon him the honorary degree of doctor of laws.

Under the aegis of President Lewis, UNH, in Durham, New Hampshire, established a graduate school and broadened its infrastructure considerably, building the first women's dormitory. In Durham Lewis received many of his famous friends, including Robert Frost. He had first met the then-unknown poet, a fellow MAC professor, in 1916 — and the Eisteddfod veteran delivered the first public reading of Frost's verse. Forty years later, by then a grand American institution, Frost wrote about the 1956 All-Star Game for *Sports Illustrated*, also reminiscing about his pitching lessons from Lewis.

The UNH archives also show how Lewis knew and corresponded with US Presidents William Howard Taft (then chief justice of the Supreme Court), Calvin Coolidge (as vice president), Woodrow Wilson, and Franklin D. Roosevelt. There are letters from other well-known individuals in this special collection, including another chief justice, Charles Evans Hughes; polar explorer Richard Byrd; heavyweight boxing champion

Gene Tunney; and Philadelphia Athletics manager Connie Mack.

Ted Lewis died at midnight on May 23, 1936, at the age of 63. His health had begun to fail about two years before, but even though the beloved "Prexy" was suffering greatly from liver cancer, he summoned up his old athletic reserves to climb the stairs to his office. In February he underwent an operation, and he rallied enough to make an appearance at UNH's Opening Day ballgame versus Bates—pitched and won by future major leaguer Bill Weir. The students again took heart, but Lewis relapsed shortly thereafter. He was survived by his widow, Margaret; his two sons, Edward W. Lewis and John B. Lewis; and his daughter, Gwendolyn (Mrs. Samuel W. Hoitt).

Lewis was laid to rest in the Durham Community Cemetery on May 26, with former Boston teammate Fred Tenney serving as one of the pallbearers. In a memorial tribute before the entire student body and faculty that afternoon, Robert Frost read his friend's two favorite poems, Tennyson's "In Memoriam" and Walt Whitman's "On the Beach at Night."

UNH sports teams still play today at the Lewis Fields, but this man's most fitting memorial might be the measured question he always posed to his colleagues: "Well … what can we do to better the situation?"

Quotes on Ted Lewis the ballplayer, compiled by UNH alumnus Rich Eldred for his Lewis sketch in *Nineteenth Century Stars* (SABR 1988):

"Teddy Lewis will pitch good ball for the Boston Americans no matter how many others may croak."
— Wilbert Robinson

"When at concert pitch there are few better than Lewis."
—Tim Murnane, Boston Globe

"Lewis was steady as a minister should be. … Chicago's heaviest hitters went down before his speedy deliveries like corn stalks before a gale."
—Jake Morse, Boston Herald

"Parson Lewis is closing his career in a blaze of glory."
—Boston Globe *after Lewis beat Nixey Callahan with a two-hitter in his final game*

Sources

Ted Lewis File at National Baseball Hall of Fame and Museum, Cooperstown, New York.

Ted Lewis File at Williams College Alumni Association, Williamstown, Massachusetts. (Includes a typewritten manuscript of "Edward Morgan Lewis, Early Career" by his younger relative Hobart L. Morris Jr.)

Obituary, *New York Times*, May 24, 1936.

Online census records, 1910 and 1920.

"In the Loop," News for Staff and Faculty, University of Massachusetts at Amherst, May 18, 2004.

Online records, University of New Hampshire.

Larry McLean

by Mike Lackey

AT 6-FEET-5 AND nearly 230 pounds, Larry McLean was a large presence and a sizable talent, and he did things in a big way—including getting into trouble. Owing largely to a lifelong battle with alcohol, McLean's career was punctuated by repeated suspensions, occasional brawls, and periodic scrapes with the law. Still, he spanned 15 years in the major leagues, maintained a lifetime batting average of .262, and performed with distinction in his only World Series. McLean played his best baseball for Cincinnati, for whom he batted over .285 three times. Baseball historian Lee Allen compared him to a later Reds backstop: Like Ernie Lombardi, McLean was big and slow but could hit and throw. Though he frequently drove managers to distraction, he was a favorite with writers and fans wherever he went.

Born on July 18, 1881, in Fredericton, New Brunswick, Canada, John Bannerman McLean grew up in the Boston area. His family called him Jack, but he was nicknamed Larry early in his career after someone detected a resemblance to Napoleon "Larry" Lajoie. McLean started his baseball career in 1899, playing in Canada with the Saint John Roses and Fredericton Tartars. He made his major-league debut with the Boston Americans on April 26, 1901, smacking a pinch double off Joe McGinnity in Baltimore. Boston let him go and he returned to Canada with the Halifax Resolutes. McLean had a tryout with Cleveland in 1903 before being awarded to the Chicago Cubs in a contract dispute. He played only one game for Chicago before being traded to the St. Louis Cardinals in the deal that brought Mordecai Brown to the Cubs. Years later *The Sporting News* recalled that McLean "did not lead an athletic life" in St. Louis.

There is a Bunyanesque quality to the stories about McLean. It started, perhaps, on April 18, 1906, when McLean—who had been demoted to the Pacific Coast League in 1905 after playing only 27 games for the Cardinals—survived the San Francisco Earthquake while in town with his Portland teammates. He hit .355

Larry McLean, 1913.

in 1906 and helped Portland to the PCL pennant, but already there were signs of off-the-field trouble; Portland withheld $200 of his salary against his promise to remain "sober and temperate," the first of many such clauses that would appear in McLean's contract over the years.

Toward the end of the 1906 season Portland sold McLean to the Cincinnati Reds. Larry played in a dozen games down the stretch, then returned in 1907 and spent his first full season in the majors, appearing in 113 games and batting .289. "Cincinnati has not had a more popular idol in years than Long Larry McLean," declared *The Sporting News* correspondent Charlie Zuber. While with Cincinnati McLean collared a murder suspect on the street and was said to have swum the Ohio River rather than arrive late to the ballpark. When the Reds visited Havana in 1908, admirers presented him with a silver-handled cane engraved "(T)o the greatest catcher that has ever been seen in Cuba." In 1910 Larry did a turn in vaudeville—playing himself, Zuber said, "as nearly as possible."

Schrecongost, McLean, and Criger - catchers for the 1901 Boston Americans.

Through it all, McLean strove to stay in line. In 1908 he pledged $1,000 that he wouldn't take a drink for one full year. McLean played under several managers with Cincinnati, and each tried a different way of dealing with him. John Ganzel was permissive. Clark Griffith challenged McLean with hard work and responsibility, naming him team captain and appointing him as acting manager for several days in 1909 when Griffith was ill.

Hank O'Day sat McLean down for heart-to-heart talks. Nothing worked for long. McLean's file at the National Baseball Library is rife with dunning notices, complaints about bounced checks, and a report from a private detective the Reds hired to follow him. Once, asked who would catch that afternoon, O'Day growled, "The big fellow — if he can see 'em."

McLean's association with the Reds nearly ended in 1910 when he ran afoul of training rules. Suspended indefinitely by the team and infuriated by newspaper accounts of his behavior, Larry wrote a letter of resignation. "When I take a trip through Chinatown, the 'boys' take particular delight in putting it in the papers, but when any of the other players get soused, the news is suppressed," he complained. "Can you blame me for wanting to get away from the Cincinnati Club?" McLean eventually returned to the Reds after a one-week suspension but was stripped of his captaincy and forced to sign a draconian new contract. Forty percent of his salary was held back as a season's-end sobriety bonus, the entire contract to be voided if McLean touched "a single drink." When the big catcher made his first appearance before a home crowd, he was greeted with "much applause and some kidding," which he accepted "as a matter of course."

McLean remained with Cincinnati until September 1912, when he was suspended for failing to show up for an exhibition game in Syracuse. After the season the Reds sold him to the Cardinals. Larry broke his arm in a poolroom brawl just weeks before the start of spring training. The judge let him off with a lecture after witnesses testified he had been trying to break up the fight. McLean recovered and played 48 games for St. Louis before the Cardinals traded him to the pennant-bound New York Giants on August 6, 1913. McLean hit .320 in 30 games down the stretch. When Chief Meyers hurt his hand before the second game of the World Series, McLean took over as the starting catcher. He went 6-for-12 against the formidable Philadelphia Athletics pitching staff and was one of the heroes of Game Two, the Giants' lone victory. He tagged out two runners at the plate in the ninth inning, then led off the tenth with a single against Eddie Plank to ignite a game-winning rally. After the Series, Giants manager John McGraw said, "McLean behaved like a man from the moment we got him. I found him easy to handle."

McGraw and McLean got on handsomely until June 1915, when McLean was again suspended for drinking. The Giants were at the Buckingham Hotel in St. Louis, where McLean confronted McGraw. McLean accused scout Dick Kinsella of spying on him and the club of plotting to beat him out of a $1,000 bonus. Words were exchanged, McLean lunged at McGraw, and a melee ensued. A half-dozen ballplayers jumped in, furniture was smashed, and McLean fled into the night. His major-league career was over. Larry played some semipro ball but soon drifted out of the game.

Not much is known of McLean's life after baseball, but it's a safe bet that much of it was spent in saloons. On March 24, 1921, he got into an argument in a Boston speakeasy. When he attempted to climb over the bar, the bartender drew a pistol and shot him. McLean staggered outside and died on the street. He was 39 years old. After his death, the *Reach Guide* reflected that he was "a man of great size, a convivial disposition and a bad temper when under the influence of liquor, which led him into many more or less serious rows during his baseball career."

In 2000 the New Brunswick Sports Hall of Fame recognized Larry McLean as one of the province's sports pioneers. But perhaps the highest tribute came from an anonymous sportswriter at the time of his death: "He had no enemies, even among those with whom he clashed."

Sources

The material for this article came mainly from files at the National Baseball Hall of Fame and the New Brunswick Sports Hall of Fame; newspapers including *The Sporting News*, *Sporting Life*, the *New York Times* and the *Halifax Herald*; and books including *The Bill James Historical Baseball Abstract* (Villard Books, 1986); Lee Allen's *The Cincinnati Reds* (G.P. Putnam's Sons, 1948); and Charles C. Alexander's *John McGraw* (Viking, 1988).

Fred Mitchell

By Bill Nowlin

A LIFE IN baseball is how one might best describe the life of Fred Mitchell. He pitched in the very first game ever played by the Boston Red Sox franchise (an exhibition game in Charlottesville, Virginia), and 18 years later managed the Chicago Cubs against the Red Sox in the 1918 World Series. His major-league playing career ran from 1901 to 1913; he appeared as a pitcher in 97 games and recorded a 31-49 record with a 4.10 earned run average. At the plate, he was a .210 hitter in 572 at-bats spread across 201 games. At one time or another, he played every infield position, the outfield, and even caught 62 games for the New York Highlanders in 1910. He was one of the few who played for the Red Sox, the Boston Braves, and the Yankees (albeit while the teams were known as the Americans, Braves, and Highlanders.)

Mitchell managed the Cubs for four years (1917-1920) and the Braves for the three succeeding years (1921-1923), then resumed work as baseball coach at Harvard, for which he worked until he retired in 1939. He was the manager of Harvard's team from 1926-1938.

He was born in Cambridge, Massachusetts, as Frederick Francis Yapp. Fred's granddaughter Lisa Mitchell says her great-grandmother Elizabeth's maiden name was Mitchell and Fred used the name professionally simply to make life easier. "The family tombstone in Stow (Massachusetts) is still under Yapp."[1] It's understandable that one might prefer to dodge the sort of catcalls that might come one's way with the surname Yapp—with "yap" being a slang word for mouth, we can imagine all the taunts and ribbing: "Shut your big yap" and the like. An article in the *Chicago Daily Tribune* said it was Boston Americans manager Jimmy Collins who urged Mitchell to change his name because he feared that the ribbing of the fans could drive him out of baseball.[2] His birth date is listed in the baseball record books as June 5, 1878.

Fred changed both his first and last names legally on August 20, 1943—from Frederick to Fred and from

Fred Mitchell, 1902.

Yapp to Mitchell. The same document his daughter Dorothy still has also changed the surname for her mother Mabel, and that of her brother Fred and herself. The third child in the family was already married and had assumed her husband's name, so she was not included.[3]

Fred's parents were Charles Yapp, listed in the 1880 Census as a groom in Cambridge, aged 28, having been born in England and becoming a U.S. citizen in 1871. His wife, Elizabeth, 25, was "keeping house," with three young children: William, who was 4 years old at the time, Emma (age 2), and Frederick (age 7 months). All three children are listed as born in Massachusetts. Regarding the child named Emma that is listed in the census record, the family is convinced that there was no daughter named Emma. Fred's daughter has the family Bible and a number of family records, and there is no indication, nor does she recall any mention of anyone named Emma. There was a later daughter named Mabel, who was born in October 1880. It must be noted that census information is notably unreliable; but showing Fred as seven months old could fit with his reported June 5, 1878, birthdate, if the census takers began collecting information in early 1879. The 1900 Census had Fred as born in 1887, clearly wrong — or he would have made his major-league debut at the age of 13.

Elizabeth had been born in Ireland (according to the 1880 Census) or England (as was stated in the 1900 Census). She became a naturalized American citizen in 1872. Fred was the middle of three children, his daughter Dorothy says, born between William and a sister named Mabel. Furthermore, she adds, "I'm pretty sure my grandmother and grandfather (Yapp) were not citizens of the U.S., though the census may have said so. I remember in World War II some kind of official documents had to be obtained for anybody who was not a citizen, and Grandma had to obtain one. (Grandpa was dead.)"[4]

The 1879 Cambridge city directory showed Charles Yapp as a "hostler" at the Massachusetts stables at 90 Washington, two half-blocks from this author's current residence. In 1880, the family lived at 137 North Harvard Street.

Twenty years later, when Fred was just a year away from becoming a professional baseball player for the Boston Americans, the 1900 Census had Charles Yapp working as a horse shoer and residing at 9 Appian Way in the Allston section of Boston, on the other side of the Charles River from Cambridge. His two sons were in the same trade, William working as a horse trainer, and Fred as an assistant horse shoer. Charles Yapp was apparently active in competitive horse racing in the Greater Boston area; his name turns up as a driver in trotter racing results from the early 1880s into the mid-1890s, traveling as far as Saratoga, New York, and the state of Maine. One race reported in the *Boston Globe* as late as September 1910 featured two Yapps, perhaps Charley Yapp and his son William. A feature story in the April 21, 1889, *Globe* described Charley as "a thickly-set man, standing about 5 feet 9 inches and weighs about 160 pounds in the sulky. He has the reputation of going through a field as coolly as any man who ever drove a horse and he is not particular as to the chances he takes. He drives to win and has put as many horses to the front in proportion to the number he has handled as any one." Though a profession of some danger, he had never suffered an injury of any kind. Some eight years later, however, Charles seems to have borne financial misfortune, declared insolvent as a racing track lessee and manager.[5]

The family also lived in Lawrence, Massachusetts, for a while. Fred played second base at school there, and a bit of semipro ball. In 1896, Fred's father leased a half-mile racetrack in Concord, New Hampshire, and the Yapps moved there for two years. The lease included a 30-room hotel, complete with bar, and Fred became the "all-round man clerk and bartender." He also played some semipro ball, both in Lawrence (both the *Boston Globe* and the *Harvard Crimson* say that Mitchell played for the 1897 Lawrence club in the New England League as a pitcher) and in Concord, where he pitched for a local man named Al Larsson. Unfortunately, when Charles Yapp staged a race meet at the track, the weather was bad and he "went broke" — he had to forfeit the lease and the family moved back to Boston — to Allston. Fred stayed on to play baseball, but at the end of the month, he wrote his daughter in a 1968 letter, "Larsson

During the course of his career, Fred Mitchell pitched, caught, played all four infield positions, and even played a couple of games in the outfield.

jumped town owing the players a month's salary. I was dead broke and hungry." Most of the players went back to their hometowns, but Mitchell met up with the manager of the Plymouth (New Hampshire) Fair, who came to Concord looking for the Larsson team to come play a couple of games at the fair. He had $500 to spend. Mitchell assembled a team from players around Concord, including a high-school catcher and a pitcher named Honey Annon, to whom he paid $20. "Our uniforms were of all colors, and we were a sight to look at," the letter said. The ragtag bunch was put up at the fair's expense, but they wore their spikes into the hotel and cut up the carpet and scratched the highly-polished floors, almost getting themselves thrown out.[6]

Honey Annon won the first game, and Mitchell won the second. When Fred was paid, the skeptical promoter asked if the mismatched aggregation really was the Larsson team. "There were a few fill-ins," Mitchell admitted. "Well, they looked funny, but they sure could play ball," the man replied. Fred Mitchell's first job as a manager had been a success. More than 20 years later, while Mitchell was managing the Cubs, John McGraw beckoned him into the bar at New York's Imperial Hotel and introduced him to his friend Al Larsson. "I think I've met Mr. Larsson before," Fred said. "He left me stranded in Concord, New Hampshire, and he owes me $150." "That's nothing," McGraw replied. "He left me stranded in Cuba." Larsson blamed the Concord matter on his brother.[7]

After the fair — Mitchell says Annon was the only player he paid — he joined the rest of the family in Allston. His father still had no work, but after a while Fred began to work for Austin's Livery Stable in Melrose, for $15 a week. He slept in the hayloft on a cot, taking care of 16 horses, and washed their buggies and harnesses each night. "I delivered three doctors' horses and buggies before eight o'clock each morning and hitched them to posts in front of each doctor's home." This was another day and time. After three months, Fred quit and moved back home, where his father had borrowed some money and bought a blacksmith shop on Beach Street in Brookline, next to Boston. Fred worked there for a while and played a few semipro games around town to pick up a few dollars from time to time.

As for Fred and baseball, he seems to first turn up in the Boston Globe (as Yapp), pitching and hitting cleanup for the Cambridge Athletic Association in a July 1, 1899, game won, 13-10, by the Brighton YMCA. He tripled and homered in the game, but his pitching (dubbed "a heady game," in which he struck out eight and walked one) was undercut by 10 Cambridge errors, six by shortstop Murphy.

There was a younger child in the family by the time of the 1900 Census — Mabel, born in October 1880 and working as an assistant bookkeeper; it appears that William had married a Scotswoman named Agnes and the two of them had a young daughter, Mary, born in 1898.

The book Red Sox Century, by Glenn Stout and Dick Johnson, has a photograph said to be of Mitchell with the 1900 Boston Nationals on page 7. But he never played for them that year, and his first appearance in professional baseball was as a member of the Boston Americans in 1901. It was only in 1906 that he had his first taste of minor-league ball, and it was in another country, playing for the Toronto Maple Leafs. Author Johnson surmised that the photograph was probably taken in spring training when Mitchell might have been a candidate for the team, but he didn't make the final cut.[8] Mitchell's daughter and grand-daughter both are firm that the man in the photograph is not Fred Mitchell.

Fred told his daughter how he came to become a member of the very first Boston Americans team. An "old catcher" named Harry Pope caught Fred in Allston, and he'd spent a few summers catching for a team called the Roses in St. John, New Brunswick. In the summer of 1900, he talked Fred into traveling there with him and they took the boat from Boston. "I won most of the games I pitched for the Roses, and attracted the attention of John Graham, the track coach at Harvard, who spent his summer vacation in St. John. He recommended me to Hughie Duffy when we returned to Boston." Hall of Famer Duffy was looking for players to sign up for the new American League team to be founded in Boston, and Duffy's brother-in-law, Mike Moore, signed Mitchell early in 1901 for a $50 advance against a contract of $300 per month. Another player for the Roses, Larry McLean, also signed with the new team, and both were given tickets to Charlottesville, Virginia, for the first spring training.

Charles Yapp had moved his family to the countryside by the 1910 Census. He's listed as a farmer in Stow, Massachusetts. Elizabeth was now, oddly, six years younger than her husband, rather than the three years younger she had been in 1880, and she was now listed as neither from England nor Ireland, but of Scot English heritage (the 1920 Census gives her birthplace as Scotland). Fred, age 32, is listed in 1910 as a "ball player." No others were shown in the home. Mitchell purchased the 93-acre farm in Stow for his parents in 1906, according to a July 8, 1983, article in the *Stow Villager*.

The *Chicago Tribune* article from December 19, 1916, noted that Mitch was playing for the Eastern League's Lawrence team in 1900 when the Americans purchased his contract; there's a problem with this, however: There was no Lawrence team in the Eastern League (or in organized baseball) in 1900. There had been a team in Lawrence in 1899, managed by Tim Murnane. Mitchell probably played for Lawrence in 1899 and then St. John in 1900.

The first practice of the new American League Boston franchise was held on April 1, 1901, on the grounds of the Charlottesville YMCA, the very afternoon of the day when Collins and Chick Stahl arrived in town. There were 12 players in all, Cy Young being given permission to get into shape at home. Games were planned for the weekend against the University of Virginia and other colleges in the area. By his own assessment, Mitchell wrote, "I was a little wild, but fast, and had a good curve ball. One of the older players started to rave about me to Mgr. Collins. 'Jimmy,' he said, 'this kid has got it!' Collins picked up a bat and came up to the plate. I blew a few fast ones past him and he called me over to him and said, 'Young fellow, you can work with the older pitchers from now on, and if you want a rubdown, you go up to the trainer of the University of Virginia and he'll take care of you.' I was a pretty happy kid that night. I knew I had made the Club!"[9]

The first exhibition game the Boston Americans ever played took place on the road, on April 5, 1901. The *Washington Post*'s account of the game said that all four of the Virginia team's hits were made off Kane, and that both Mitchell and Connor held them hitless, though Mitchell walked one and hit another batter. "Mitchell showed the most speed," said the *Globe*. He also showed some speed as the experienced horseman he was. Several of the players rented horses on a Sunday to ride up to visit Thomas Jefferson's home, near Charlottesville. "I thought I'd have a little fun. I put my horse into a fast trot, then a gallop, and the other horses started to follow me. You never saw such bouncing in your life. They were hanging on for dear life and hollering at me to pull up. I pulled up after a bit and most of the boys got off the horses and walked back leading their horses. Some of them couldn't walk naturally for two or three days."[10]

On April 26, it was Win Kellum who had the honor of pitching the first regular-season game for the franchise. Win lost, 10-6, to Baltimore — the franchise that moved to New York in 1903 and eventually became the Yankees. The next day, Mitchell saw some duty. Cy Young started the game, but was both wild and hittable. Boston was down 11-3 after six innings, and Collins called in Mitchell to finish the game. Baltimore manager John McGraw was coaching on the sidelines and tried to rattle Mitchell by calling out the names of each of the great hitters as they came to bat. It didn't work; he allowed just two hits and one run, and collected a hit himself in his first major-league at-bat. He struck out his second time up. The final score was 12-6.[11]

Mitchell's first start was in Chicago on June 1, and the White Sox scored five runs in the bottom of the first, the biggest blow a bases-clearing triple that followed a single, a walk, a hit batsman, and two errors. From that point on, Mitchell shut them down, allowing just one hit in the eighth and one in the ninth, while Boston

Fred Mitchell during his coaching days at Harvard.

rang up 10 runs in all. He later recounted that first day to the *Chicago Tribune*: "I was scared stiff and the first inning was awful. I was shaking with stage fright and walked two or three guys and then someone swatted one. Freddie Parent chose that time to kick a couple of grounders." Down 5-0, Mitchell was pleased to be picked up by a teammate. "There was one fellow on the club at that time who was my friend, and that was Buck Freeman. He came in from right field after the inning and I remember just what he said to Jimmy Collins. 'You're not going to take the kid out, are you, Jim?' 'Not on your life,' answered Jim. I went back and had my head with me from then on and stopped the White Sox." Mitchell went on to describe the two-run homer Freeman hit in the fourth inning and the three-run homer he hit in the eighth.[12] Mitchell (and Buck and the Boston bats) won the game, 10-5.

Mitchell won his second start as well, 7-4, in Milwaukee. His first start at the team's home field, the Huntington Avenue Grounds on June 17, saw him win the first game of a doubleheader from the White Sox, 11-1 (allowing five hits, with his "slow curves" noted in the papers) while Cy Young won the afternoon game, 10-4. The one run was unearned, due to an error by Buck Freeman.

It wasn't all good; Mitchell was pounded by Cleveland on the 24th, defeated 7-1. He was ineffective in a relief stint in July, though he'd handily beaten Baltimore on Independence Day. A couple of times he was banged out of the box early, leaving in the first inning on July 27. As the year wore on, there seemed to be more times he faltered; he wound up his first year with a 6-6 record and a 3.81 earned run average, the fourth pitcher on the team behind Cy Young (33-10, 1.62 ERA), George Winter (16-12, 2.80), and Ted Lewis (16-17, 3.53). His batting average was .159 (7-for-44, with two triples). In a postseason benefit game in Boston against the White Sox, Mitchell gamely played second base, but committed five errors. The following day, he pitched and lost in Lynn against a picked team but it was no hard-fought game; Cy Young played in right field with the aid of a bicycle. Mitchell played right field in another exhibition game, against Greenfield, and pitched and lost a 4-3 game against players from Franklin and Marlboro on October 5. (All these teams were from Massachusetts.)

Fred Mitchell was back with Boston in 1902, but he was admittedly "green" and the team had quite a few seasoned pitchers. It wasn't clear how much work he would get. He appeared in just one game before he was sent to the Philadelphia Athletics. He'd been used only in spring training and exhibition games (losing to Hoboken, 6-3, on May 11 due to costly errors). His one game for Boston was in the May 30 doubleheader against Detroit, in relief of Pep Deininger, pitching the final four innings and seeing a 5-5 tie become a 10-5 loss. The *Boston Globe* termed the pitching of both men "far below the standard of the suburban league." On June 2, as the team headed out on a road trip, Mitchell was "loaned to Connie Mack of Philadelphia."[13] As Mitchell explained it to his daughter, "Connie Mack had some trouble — losing players over in Philadelphia — and Jimmy Collins, our manager, came to me and said, 'How would you like to go to Philadelphia, over to Connie Mack?' 'Well,' I said, 'If I could get regular work, I'd like to go.'" Mack secured Rube Waddell from the Giants, and picked up some other people. "We got together and won the pennant!"[14] Waddell and Mitchell roomed together.

Had there been a World Series in 1902, Mitchell might have played in it, though Rube Waddell, Eddie Plank, and Bert Husting would have been the starters. The Athletics won the AL pennant (Boston finished third), and Mitchell was 5-7, with a 3.59 ERA. As with Boston, he walked far more men than he struck out. Despite winning the pennant, there was no one to play—it was only in 1903 that the first World Series was played—and in 1903, Mitchell was playing for the Philadelphia Phillies. Retrosheet says that before the season began he "jumped from the Philadelphia Athletics to the Philadelphia Phillies." That's the same word Mitchell used in his 1968 interview. He said he'd gone to Mack's office at the start of 1903 and asked for a raise. Mack turned him down flat. (Mitchell had been 5-8 with a 3.59 ERA; there were at least four A's pitchers much better than he.) Mitchell told Mack that since he didn't have a contract, "I'm going to shift for myself. … I'm going to jump."[15] The two Philadelphia teams met in the preseason spring series and Mitchell shut down the Athletics in the first game (1-0 against Eddie Plank) and the fourth (2-0 against Waddell.)

He won his first two starts in the regular season—against the Boston Nationals (Beaneaters) on Patriots Day, and shutting out the Brooklyn Superbas on April 24. It was a year in which he won 11 games for the seventh-place Phils, but he lost 17 games. Nonetheless, Mitchell took advantage of the time, he told his daughter: "I commenced to learn something about pitching." No Phillies starter won more than 13. He hurt his arm in 1904 and his 4-7 showing wasn't impressive enough to warrant keeping him, so a deal was made to send him to Brooklyn later in the year, where he won two and lost five. His arm was still bad, and in 1905, Mitchell was 3-7 for Brooklyn. Thus ended his major-league pitching career. Fred had filled in as a position player in 12 games in 1904—nine of them at first base. He played a smattering of games in the infield in '05, too, before being cut loose in late August. In his obituary, the *Boston Herald* cited a "chronic arm ailment" as ending his 1905 season. He next turned up in the major leagues as a catcher, for the New York Highlanders in 1910.

The 5-foot-10, 185-pound right-hander was signed by manager Ed Barrow of the Eastern League (Class A) Toronto Maple Leafs, and pitched three seasons there, from 1906 through 1908. Earned run averages weren't computed in the league at the time, but existing stats do show his most active season of all (239 innings) in 1906, under Barrow, and an 11-15 record for a last-place team. He was one of four Toronto pitchers to record 11 or more wins. In 1907, he was 6-3 in an even 100 innings of work. He was able to get in more work in 1908, throwing 166 innings with a 6-10 mark, including a no-hitter against Montreal. In the three years, his WHIP (walks and hits per inning pitched) was a very respectable 1.152. If all the runs he allowed were earned runs, which they surely were not, he'd have posted an ERA of around 3.50. The actual figure would have been substantially lower.

In 1909, none of the major-league clubs had picked Mitchell up and even though his arm seemed to be better, he still couldn't snap off an effective curveball. He decided he'd become a catcher, and told the Toronto manager, Joe Kelley, "I'm going to be a catcher or else I'm going home."[16] He was talked into sticking around, and when two of the Toronto catchers got hurt, Mitchell moved from throwing to receiving. He appeared in 109 games for the Maple Leafs as the team's first-string catcher. He came through at the plate as well, batting .295. He'd earned himself a promotion back into the American League, and caught for New York in 1910, signed in January and joining the team for spring training in Athens, Georgia, under manager George Stallings. He appeared in 68 games, almost precisely splitting playing time with Jeff Sweeney, who had 19 more at-bats. Mitchell's .230 was better than Sweeney's .200 but it was Sweeney who stuck with the Highlanders and Mitchell whose playing career was finished (save for four plate appearances with the Boston Braves in 1913—in which he singled once, executed a sacrifice, and struck out twice.) A third catcher on the 1910 New York team was Mitchell's former teammate with Boston in 1901 and 1902, Lou Criger.

Mitchell played in the postseason for the Highlanders as they fell in a city series against the Giants, Mitchell catching right to the very last game of the year. On January 3, 1911, the Highlanders sold Mitchell to Rochester in the Eastern League. He was one of three players sent to Rochester, apparently as — in effect — players to be named later in a deal that allowed New York to bring up catcher Walter Blair late in 1910. There's a story behind the sale. Mitch and Lou Criger had become suspicious that Hal Chase was throwing games ("he was a little on the crooked side"). Stallings said he wouldn't manage the team as long as Chase was on it. New York owner Farrell fired Stallings and made Chase manager! Chase heard that Mitchell had accused him in a meeting with Farrell and sold him and Jimmy Austin, and fired Criger.

Stallings had been fired in mid-September 1910, and spent 1911 and 1912 managing in Buffalo. Mitchell rejoined Stallings in Buffalo after the 1911 season (he'd hit .292 for the Rochester Bronchos in 1911.) It's a little difficult to pin down some of Mitchell's moves, but a March 19, 1912, item in the *Hartford Courant* reports that he has "been in charge of the Buffalo teams in the absence of Manager Stallings." Mitchell hit .232 for the Double-A Bisons. Stallings became manager of the Boston Braves in 1913 and acquired Mitchell ("the stocky Buffalo catcher") from Buffalo, planning to use him "as instructor and trainer of his young catchers and pitchers."[17] Mitchell even appeared in those four games for the Braves. In 1911, Fred had married Mabel Dorothy Goulding, and she came to stay at the farm on Walcott Street in Stow. In 1915, the couple had their first child, also naming her Mabel.. Her second daughter she then named Dorothy. When the third child turned out to be a boy, he was appropriately named Frederick F. III.

In early 1914, Mitchell — though "of the George Stallings aggregation" — worked coaching the baseball team at the Georgia Military College of Milledgeville.[18] Mitchell was on the Braves roster as a catcher but, the *Washington Post* reported, "he never plays, his duty being to warm up and instruct the young pitchers."[19] In effect, he was the team's pitching coach, in an era which had less formal nomenclature for coaches. These were the "Miracle Braves" of 1914, who had a losing record as late as July 31 (44-45, nine games out of first place) but went on to win the pennant by winning 27 of their last 33 games.

Looking ahead to the World Series, Stallings closed his remarks to newsmen by declaring as one of his most valuable men, "Fred Mitchell, my right eye." A Stallings-bylined article in the *Boston Globe* added, "The fans do not appreciate the work Mitchell is called upon to do. … He is the hardest worker on the team." He detailed some of Mitchell's instructional work with Paul Strand and George Davis. The three Braves aces (Bill James, 26-7; Dick Rudolph, 26-10; and Lefty Tyler, 16-13), Stallings wrote, "Mitchell, almost single-handed, is responsible for their remarkable showing this year. Mitchell has worked with the catchers with equal care and has made [Hank] Gowdy, once turned back by McGraw, one of the best backstops in the league."[20] Stallings also praised Mitchell's work coaching runners and batters during games. Braves swept the World Series from the purportedly unbeatable Philadelphia Athletics in four games. Sportswriter Frederick Lieb heaped praised on Mitchell, declaring that their success "would not have been possible with the battery coach, Fred Mitchell … one of the few men who ever played in the majors on both ends of the battery." Lieb agreed with Stallings as to the three Braves pitchers, but quoted Stallings as giving Mitchell credit for George Davis's no-hitter: "The kid never could have done it without 'Mitch' having told him how to pitch to each batter."[21]

That December, Mitchell worked training ballplayers at St. Mark's School, in Southborough, Massachusetts. He also worked as a scout for the Braves, and in mid-February was reported at Dartmouth trying to sign shortstop Fletcher Low. Later in the month, he headed for Macon for spring training, where he took on Braves coaching duties once more and carried through the full 1915 season, even added to the reserve list at the end of the year — though there were some hoops he had to jump through. When rosters had to be cut to 21 men, he had been put on waivers and was dropped from the active roster, working as a "scout" once more. When rosters expanded, he was signed again as a player and resumed coaching at third base. He actually had done some scouting, with Art Nehf perhaps his best signing.

On December 1, 1915, the *Harvard Crimson* reported that Mitchell had been appointed coach of Harvard's baseball team, but would work for the Braves as well, simply turning up later than usual for the Braves. On the 7th, the Braves officially gave him his unconditional release, allowing him to take the position with Harvard.

Working with the Harvard nine saw one early success: On April 10, 1916, the varsity team took on the Boston Red Sox, world champions both in 1915 and again in 1916, in an exhibition game at Fenway Park. Harvard shut out the Red Sox, 1-0, both teams collecting five hits. Eddie Mahan pitched for Harvard. The Crimson posted a 21-3-1 season. Because of the World War, Harvard did not field a team in 1917. When baseball resumed, Mitchell's replacement as Harvard head coach was old friend Hugh Duffy.

Mitchell while a coach with the 1916 Boston Braves.

Mitchell became acting manager of the Braves in early August, when Stallings was suspended for three days "for words addressed to Umpire Rigler" after the August 2 game. The Braves apparently decided to better lock Mitchell in, and signed him in September to a three-year contract that prevented him from continuing as head coach of the Harvard team, but he took charge of each fall's practice season for the university team. It was a "dual job" that required a little give-and-take from both sides regarding scheduling. Just two months later, word began to circulate that the Chicago Cubs were considering Mitchell as manager to take over from Joe Tinker, assuming that the Braves would let him out of their contract. Stallings said that, despite having worked with him for 10 years, "I would not stand in his way if there is an opportunity for him to better himself, but I will not give him away. He is too valuable a man, and besides, I had to pay the Buffalo club for him when I took over the management of the Braves."[22]

The Cubs may have actually wanted Stallings, but taken Mitchell instead. They traded for him, sending outfielder Joe Kelly and some cash to acquire Mitchell from the Braves, and Cubs owner Charles Weeghman signed him to a two-year contract on December 14, 1916. The next day's *Chicago Tribune* wrote that Weeghman had traveled to New York determined to secure John McGraw, George Stallings, or Fred Mitchell. "If Mitchell is good enough for the Braves, he's good enough for the Cubs," the owner declared (and saved himself a fair amount of money in the process, as Mitchell's salary going into negotiations was reportedly $5,000 compared with $20,000 for either of the other more experienced men. "I know Chicago needs rebuilding," he told the *Tribune*.

That seemed like an understatement at the time. The *Tribune* pointed out that most of the bigger-name players on the team had passed their prime, and that there were only "about half a dozen men of undisputed major league ability."[23] *The Sporting News* correspondent from Boston declared, "Good old Mitchell was handed over to the tender mercies of the bunch of restaurateurs, meat packers, chewing gum makers, and others who own the Cubs.... Mitchell knows what he is up against, but he is reconciled and even hopeful."²⁴ Within two years, the Cubs won the pennant.

Mitchell got the team off to a strong start in 1917. By May 17, they were 22-9 and Grantland Rice's column in the May 19 *Boston Globe* recalled how instrumental Mitchell had been with the Miracle Braves of 1914. Taking over the Cubs, Rice wrote, "the general dope was that he had tail-end material and faced a famine. He was given a ball club composed in the main of athletes cast adrift, and many of these were injured or dismantled or out of gear." Why were they playing so well? "Mitchell is the type of manager capable of lifting the best from each player's system." The Cubs finished in fifth place, not much different from the year before, but there was a sense that things were getting better rather than the foreboding sense under Tinker that they were sure to get worse.

Weeghman spent some money in the offseason, acquiring Grover Cleveland Alexander and Bill Killefer, and was hunting for a couple of other players as well. As William Wrigley purchased increasingly larger shares of the Cubs, and replaced Weeghman as principal owner, there was more reason for hope.

In 1918, while managing the Cubs, Mitchell may have been the first to employ what is today known as the Williams shift. When first implemented by Cleveland manager Lou Boudreau to defend against left-handed slugger Ted Williams, it was initially known as the Boudreau shift—but giving it Williams's name may have inadvertently harkened back to Mitchell's innovative stacking up of fielders on the right side of the diamond against left-handed hitter Cy Williams in 1918, his first year with the Phillies. Cy had been with the Cubs for the prior six seasons, and Mitchell would have seen him hit all year long in 1917.

The Cubs breezed through the abbreviated 1918 season, finishing up a full 10 1/2 games ahead of the second-place New York Giants. Veteran southpaw Hippo Vaughn had another excellent year, his 22-10 record leading the league in wins. His 1.74 ERA also led the league. Claude Hendrix was another 20-game winner (20-7, 2.78 ERA) and Lefty Tyler was every bit as good (19-8, 2.00). The pitching staff's ERA as a whole was a miserly 2.18, though the Red Sox staff ERA was just 2.31. The Cubs were odds-on favorites going into the September 5 start of the World Series; their team batting average also gave them an edge—.265 to Boston's .249.

Babe Ruth just barely beat Vaughn, 1-0, in the first game, but beat him Ruth did. Tyler gave the Cubs a 3-1 win in Game Two, and the battle was joined. The Red Sox won it in six games, despite Cubs pitchers collectively registering a stupendous 1.04 earned-run average across all six games, holding the Red Sox to a team batting average of .186, and despite outscoring Boston 10-9. It was almost as close a low-scoring season as one could have, and many sportswriters simply ascribed the difference to more of the breaks going Boston's way. Talking privately with his daughter, Mitchell was asked how the Red Sox had been able to beat the Cubs. He said, simply enough, "They had pretty good pitching and they had a little better hitting ballclub than mine, but the games were very close. They could have been turned either way."

Had Grover Cleveland Alexander not been taken off to war early in the 1918 season, he might well have made all the difference. Alexander had won 30 or more games three years in a row for the Phillies. He was traded to the Cubs in December 1917, but pitched in only three games before he was drafted. Mitchell told his daughter that he'd tried hard to buy Rogers Hornsby, too, and secured Wrigley's authority to offer as much as $125,000, but Branch Rickey of the Cardinals somewhat reluctantly turned him down: "We can't make that deal. We'd love to make it, but if we sold Hornsby we might as well toss in the franchise," Rickey said.²⁵ Mitchell had been the man who spotted shortstop Charlie Hollocher, playing for Portland in the Pacific Coast League. He spotted him through his careful reading of *The Sporting News*, and decided to wire the Portland president to ask how much it would take. "$5,000 and a pitcher" was the reply. Mitchell closed the deal, and Hollocher reported to the Cubs in the spring of 1918, hitting .316 in his first season in big-league baseball.

Mitchell added the position of president of the Cubs to his portfolio in December 1918, and soon hired the man who became his successor: Bill Veeck Sr., whom Mitchell plucked from a position as a sportswriter for the *Chicago American* and installed as business manager of the ballclub, offering more than double the salary the paper had provided. It was, he said, a mistake. He complained to his daughter that when Philip Wrigley promised to split any dividends from the club with both Mitchell and Veeck, the new business manager stopped spending money: "Instead of buying ballplayers, he was standing pat, and my ballclub was getting old." Mitchell asked Veeck one day where the scouting reports were, why he hadn't been seeing them. Veeck had them in his desk drawer. Veeck wasn't involved in baseball operations but had decided on his own that the players being scouted weren't worth investing in. Veeck apparently bad-mouthed Mitchell and worked the board of directors sufficiently against him that Mitchell was out after the 1920 season and Veeck was installed as the new president. In Mitchell's four years at the helm, the Cubs had won 308 games and lost 269, with the one pennant.

As soon as word got out, Mitchell received wires from the Braves, the Yankees, and one from Harry Frazee of the Red Sox. The Yanks wanted him as a coach; no, thanks. He waited on Frazee for two or three days, but the Sox owner was under the weather, and so he took up the offer from owner George Grant of the Braves, joining as field manager from 1921 to 1923, then as business manager after the Braves brought in Dave Bancroft as field manager. Mitchell's tenure was disappointing in terms of results: 168-274. The Braves finished fourth in 1921, with a marginal winning record, but lost an even 100 games in both 1922 and 1923, dead last in '22 and only a step out of the cellar in '23. Right-hander Joe Oeschger was a 20-game winner the first year, but collapsed to become a 21-game loser the second and posted a poor 5-15 record the third. His ERA had plunged, but few on the team performed as well.

After being relieved of his post on the field, Mitchell remained as business manager of the Braves and continued to work as a scout. In the meantime, he was able to work things out with Harvard in January 1924 that he could coach the Harvard batterymen—the pitchers and catchers. On taking an initial three-year position with the college team, he told the *Harvard Crimson*, "I shall be able to put in every afternoon until the middle of April," said Mitchell. "I want all the pitchers and catchers in college—both Freshman and Varsity—to report at the Locker Building this Wednesday. The routine work will begin Thursday."[26] He worked for the Braves in the mornings, and the afternoons at the university.

Mitchell finally resigned from both positions in 1938 to retire to his home in Newton Centre, outside Boston. There were times when the positions conflicted, such as in March 1925, when the Braves called him urgently to their St. Petersburg spring training camp; Mitchell promised Harvard he'd put in more time to make up for the lost time.[27] Harvard was sufficiently satisfied with his work ethic and results, and that December the college appointed him head coach of the team on a three-year contract. He was taking the place of the resigning E.W. Mahan—whom Mitch had coached as a Harvard student back in the spring of 1916.[28] One of his assistants beginning in 1926 was Fred Parent, a teammate from the 1901 and 1902 Boston Americans.

Another former Red Sox player, albeit from the time after Mitchell had left the team and it had adopted the name, was Harold Janvrin, who joined as a coach in 1930. One of the better products of Harvard at the time was Charlie Devens (Class of 1932), who pitched for a while for the Yankees. He told the *Crimson*, "Coach Mitchell's coaching, together with that of Herb Pennock and Cy Perkins of the New York Yankees, have been the chief factor in whatever pitching success I have enjoyed thus far."[29]

Prompting Mitchell's 1938 decision to resign was some of the politics within the athletics department at Harvard. For a while, the college experimented with a "noncoaching system" meant to empower the players more, with Mitchell and the other coaches more in the background. Some felt this placed too much of a burden on the team captain, who was—after all—a student.

Among those who feared losing Mitchell was captain Ulysses Lupien of the Class of 1939. Lupien wrote a letter to the *Crimson* in March 1938, reading in part, "We are especially privileged to have a man of Fred Mitchell's character and ability as our coach. We wish to express publicly our respect and confidence in him." Mitchell did resign. Lupien debuted with the Red Sox in September 1940. At Harvard, reports *The Second H Book of Harvard Athletics*, Mitchell oversaw teams compiling a record of 216-134 (with a few ties); Fred Mitchell was inducted into Harvard's Hall of Fame in 1958.

Mitchell continued to live in Greater Boston, and was feted at a number of events and anniversaries over the years. In May 1951, he was among many former players celebrating the 50th anniversary of the Boston Americans. He noted how concerned they had been as to whether the new team would catch on. "We could see both parks from the train," he recalled, as well as how pleased they were that the Americans had outdrawn the Nationals by a huge margin. Remembering some of the deceptions they'd used in the early days, he added, "I yearn for the days when we'd warm up a right-hander in front of the grandstand and then bring out a lefty who had been warming up under the grandstand. That would foul up a batting order."[30] The very next month, Mitchell was back for another ceremony, this one at Braves Field celebrating the 75th anniversary of the National League.

Fred's obituary says he left his two daughters, Mabel L. Bassett of Los Angeles and Dorothy Patti of Needham, and son Fred Mitchell Jr. of Needham. Fred Jr. passed away from cancer in 1998 at age 71, but as of late 2009, Mabel was 94 and Dorothy was 85.

Sources

The sources used for this article are identified within the text. This biography was greatly enriched by the assistance of Fred's granddaughter Lisa Mitchell. The author also consulted Retrosheet.org and Baseball-Reference.com, and Mitchell's player file from the National Baseball Hall of Fame.

Notes

1. E-mail communication July 7, 2009.
2. *Chicago Tribune*, December 15, 1916.
3. E-mail communication from Dorothy Patti, October 27, 2009.
4. E-mail communication from Dorothy Patti, October 26, 2009. Dorothy explains the listing of England as Elizabeth's place of birth as perhaps a minor fib: "The Irish were looked down on in Massachusetts and she didn't want anyone to think she was an Irish Catholic. Her older sister, my Aunt Mary Mitchell, told us this behind Grandma's back. She probably also fibbed about being six years younger than her husband, instead of three."
5. *Boston Globe*, September 10, 1897.
6. There are references in the *Chicago Tribune* of December 15, 1916, and the *Washington Post* of December 19, 1916. A considerable amount of material on Mitchell's early years comes from a letter he wrote his daughter Mabel Mitchell Bassett in 1968, following a lengthy interview she did with him on July 13, 1968.
7. Fred Mitchell 1968 letter to Mabel Mitchell Bassett.
8. Communication from Richard A. Johnson, September 14, 2009.
9. Letter to Mabel Mitchell Bassett, 1968.
10. Letter to Mabel Mitchell Bassett, 1968.
11. Mabel Mitchell Bassett interview with Fred Mitchell, July 13, 1968.
12. *Chicago Tribune*, January 9, 1917.
13. *Boston Globe*, June 3, 1902.
14. Mabel Mitchell Bassett interview with Fred Mitchell, July 13, 1968.
15. Mabel Mitchell Bassett interview with Fred Mitchell, July 13, 1968.
16. Mabel Mitchell Bassett interview with Fred Mitchell, July 13, 1968.
17. *Christian Science Monitor*, February 27, 1913.
18. *Atlanta Constitution*, March 6, 1914.
19. *Washington Post*, August 30, 1914.
20. *Boston Globe*, October 8, 1914.
21. *The Sporting News*, October 6, 1948.
22. *Los Angeles Times*, December 6, 1916.
23. *Chicago Tribune*, December 17, 1916.
24. *The Sporting News*, December 21, 1916.
25. Mabel Mitchell Bassett interview with Fred Mitchell, July 13, 1968.
26. *Harvard Crimson*, January 7, 1924.
27. *Harvard Crimson*, March 6, 1925.
28. *Harvard Crimson*, December 7, 1925.
29. *Harvard Crimson*, November 18, 1933.
30. *The Sporting News*, May 23, 1951.

Frank Morrissey

By Bill Nowlin

THE SHORTEST PITCHER in major-league history, Frank "Deacon" Morrissey threw right-handed for the 1901 Boston Americans (later the Red Sox) and the 1902 Chicago Orphans (also the Cubs). Aside from the one game with Boston and seven with Chicago, he spent 12 seasons in the minor leagues playing a wide variety of positions (every position but catcher), though he won more than 150 games on the mound. Morrissey is listed at 140 pounds and stood 5-feet-4, something apparently deemed not that remarkable at the time he played.

Morrissey was born as Michael Joseph Morrissey to Irish immigrant parents on May 3, 1876, in Baltimore. It was a difficult life for the Morrisseys, particularly Frank's mother, Mary (O'Fogarty), who came to the United States at the age of 10 and bore 10 children, but saw only four survive. At the time of the 1900 Census, she was working as a "servant" in Baltimore, living with her son the ballplayer and his sister Katie, an operator. Using the 1880 Census and even an 1873 map of Baltimore, Maurice Bouchard presents a very convincing case that Frank's father was Michael Sr., a stevedore.

Frank attended St. Patrick's Boys School but did not go on to high school. His first known appearance in organized baseball came in the Virginia State League in 1896, primarily as a pitcher (1-6) with the Petersburg Farmers—a team that transferred to Hampton on August 13 and became known as the Hampton-Newport News Clamdiggers. The club finished 39-90, in fourth place in what had begun as an eight-team league. Two of the teams disbanded in mid-August, and the league itself failed to continue in 1897. Morrissey wasn't necessarily just a good pitcher on a bad club; in an August 20 game against Norfolk, he walked nine batters. Morrissey took advantage of *Sporting Life*'s willingness to mention players seeking work, and the publication indicated in 1897 that he was "open to business with any other club."[1] *Sporting Life* reported that he was "disengaged" and provided his address in Baltimore.

Frank Morrissey, isolated image from 1902 Manchester team photograph.

There was an incorrect report that he'd signed with Wheeling (West Virginia) for 1897, but it's not clear where he may have played. In 1898 Morrissey pitched for Meadville (Pennsylvania) in the independent Iron and Coal League. It was a league comprising both black and white ballplayers, but no more successful for that. The Oil City team transferred to Dunkirk-Fredonia (New York) on June 18. The Acme Colored Giants team (based in Celeron, New York, near Jamestown) disbanded on June 5 and was replaced by a white team, the Acme Giants. Then, when the Olean, New York, club disbanded on July 14, the league folded. Not one of the six clubs covered their expenses.[2] Morrissey was Meadville's best pitcher; the club finished 23-30 but he was 10-3 according to a letter to the editor in the August 20 issue which said he'd gone on to play in the Inter-

State League for Dayton. Morrissey apparently also hooked on with Youngstown to get in a little more play before the season was over.

Occasional newspaper subheads in 1899 showed Morrissey battered around a bit in the New England League, playing both for the Newport Colts in Rhode Island (4-2) and Manchester (9-9), and Newport didn't hesitate to take advantage of him once he'd moved to the New Hampshire team — which went by the name of the Manchester Manchesters. Morrissey often played the outfield when he wasn't pitching. This was a league, under President Tim Murnane, struggling to survive as well. The Fitchburg club moved to Lawrence on May 24, and the Cambridge club moved to Lowell on May 29. Both teams disbanded on June 1. Both Brockton and Portland disbanded on August 8, at the end of the first half of the season, and the Taunton ballclub finished the season but left owing its players between two and four weeks of salary. Apparently neither Portland nor Manchester wanted Newport to win the second half of the season, so they expanded the schedule on the final day from a doubleheader to play six games in one day. Perhaps not coincidentally Manchester won all six, to top Newport, but the league threw out the results of the questionable competition.[3] Portland refused to play Newport in the finals, fearing defeat.

In 1900 Morrissey played in the newly organized Virginia League. He had been signed to Richmond but was apparently cut before the season began. In March *Sporting Life* advised readers that "Frank Morrissey, pitcher, late of Richmond, is free to sign anywhere." When the baseball season got under way, things are difficult to reconstruct today. *Sporting Life* reported in its May 26 issue that Portsmouth had signed three new pitchers, Frank being one of them, but the season was well under way at the time. Morrissey played with the Portsmouth Boers (also known as the Pirates), but the Petersburg club disbanded on June 11, then Richmond disbanded on the 13th, and soon then the whole league did — though not before Morrissey threw a 1-0 no-hitter against Norfolk on June 16, walking just two and scoring the game's only run. The August 18 issue of *Sporting Life* carried word that he "would like to finish the season with some club."

In 1901 the newly organized Virginia-North Carolina League was launched, embracing Norfolk, Portsmouth, Richmond, and three other clubs. Frank played some third base, second base, and right field but primarily pitched, for three different teams, Norfolk, Portsmouth, and Raleigh.

On July 13 he appeared in his first major-league game, with the Boston Americans. The team was in Philadelphia but the weather was threatening, the field of play was soft, and the game was delayed for a considerable period of time before play began. The Americans' Tommy Dowd singled to lead off the game, but it was the only hit Boston had off Chick Fraser over the first four innings. Boston manager Jimmy Collins started Fred Mitchell. He gave up one run in the first inning and was getting manhandled in the second, after hitting a batter and throwing a wild pitch. With two outs, Fraser singled and two more hits followed. Collins asked the newly acquired Morrissey to relieve. Though the first thing he did was uncork a wild pitch of his own (according to the game account in the *Boston Globe*, though it doesn't show in Morrissey's career stats), and he saw two more inherited runs come in on another base hit, the game account in the *Globe* said that "Morrissey made a favorable impression, and showed coolness and headwork." But "it was too late for him to save the game, as the mischief had been done." Philadelphia had a 5–0 lead and won the rain-shortened game, called in the seventh, by a score of 6–1.

Giving up just one earned run in the bottom of the fifth, and given that this was the only time he appeared for Boston, he held an earned run average of 2.08. He walked two, hit two batters, struck out one, and surrendered five hits in 4⅓ innings. He had three at-bats, but failed to get a hit. He did reach base one of those times, but was thrown out trying to score. He earned a subhead in the *Globe*, which after mentioning Mitchell wrote: "Young Morrissey Relieves Him and Does Well."[4] Morrissey stayed with the club for a while but is thought to have been released about a month later.

The Manchester team, 1902.

In 1902 Morrissey accompanied John F. "Phenomenal" Smith, who had been appointed manager of Manchester, and returned to the New England League, where he played for Manchester from 1902 through 1904 and into 1905.[5] He also returned briefly to the major leagues, though not as briefly as he had for Boston. He starred for Manchester. On May 3, he threw a three-hitter against Lawrence, a four-hitter against Fall River on August 4, and a five-hit shutout of Lowell on August 15. And there was another three-hitter (with nine K's) against Lawrence on August 20. Frank Selee of the National League's Chicago Orphans (later the Cubs) wanted to give him a tryout in September. He had helped Manchester win the pennant, 12 1/2 games ahead of the second-place Haverhill Hustlers, and had won 15 straight games. Not every game was a good one (he was pounded for 25 hits by Dover on July 12), but he finished the season with a league-leading 27 wins and lost only four games.[6]

For Chicago Morrissey first appeared on September 3, a complete-game start against the Brooklyn Trolley Dodgers. As had the *Boston Globe* the year before, the *Chicago Daily Tribune* praised his coolness. Though he'd been tagged for 13 hits, and lost the game, 4–0, he didn't walk anyone (he hit one) and struck out two, and showed that "he had good control of the ball and is possessed of plenty of nerve, accompanied by coolness."

He lost to the Boston Beaneaters on September 8, but it was a 2–1 defeat and he held Boston to just five hits, three of them in the first inning, before he settled down. He didn't allow a hit after the third inning. Morrissey pitched in five games (1-3, with a 2.25 ERA), throwing 40 innings and giving up 40 hits. He walked eight and struck out 13 — and hit two more batters.

Three days later, on September 11, Morrissey pitched against the Giants in New York and won his only game in the majors, 7–2. Chicago benefited from seven errors, including four in Chicago's four-run third inning. Morrissey gave up only four hits, and the *Tribune* reported that he "pitched the locals onto a comatose state."[7] He lost on September 21 to visiting Pittsburg, 4–1. The last game in which he appeared was a 4–4 tie on October 4 in St. Louis, called after seven innings because of the extreme cold (and perhaps the fact that only 250 people had come out to see a game that mattered not in the standings).

He also played two games at third base, and was saddled with a .600 fielding average, with two errors in five chances. While pitching, he handled 14 chances without an error. Morrissey batted .091. He never drove in a run.

In November *Sporting Life* expressed surprise that Morrissey had not been on Chicago's reserve list, as it had been understood he "was supposed to be entitled to a fair shake." Manchester gladly placed him on its reserve list at the end of the year.

Frank was back with Manchester again in 1903 and once more had a number of low-hit games. He lost a 6–1 game to Fall River on August 13, then just two days later pitched a 1–0 six-hit shutout at Manchester—and then proceeded to throw the second game that day, too. He was hit hard, giving up 15 hits, but limited Concord (New Hampshire) to just two runs. Even though he took part in a triple play, his teammates couldn't produce more than one run and so he finished the day with one win and one defeat.[8]

In January 1904 there were reports that the Haverhill (Massachusetts) team was after Morrissey, but in fact he signed for manager Smith in March and played for Manchester again (and shut out Haverhill in at least the August 16 game, 5–0). That year he played a little more in the field, appearing in 49 games and batting .275. On July 4 he threw a 1–0 five-hitter against Concord; his second-inning double put him in scoring position, and he scored on a double by his shortstop, Louis Knau. On July 7 he shut out Lawrence, 2–0.

On August 30 Morrissey beat Fall River 15–1, allowing five hits and going 4-for-5 at the plate himself. But it was still pitching that was his forte. In November *Sporting Life* said it was being "whispered" that Morrissey was going to be drafted by the Boston Americans again.

Morrissey started the 1905 season again with the Manchesters, but quit the club at some point in July. The ballclub itself moved to Lawrence, Massachusetts, on July 20. According to *Sporting Life* Morrissey had a row with new manager Win Clark and he quit. "Morrissey claims he was overworked, and when he refused to play he was fined seven days' pay and suspended 10 days additional. Morrissey is planning to join the Harrisburg team."[9] Instead, he started working for the New Bedford Whalers, among his work a 2–0 shutout of Nashua (New Hampshire) on September 7.

After the season Morrissey made another move. He married Jennie Idalia McNew in early October, and worked over the winter in a wholesale liquor store in Baltimore.[10] The couple had two daughters—Mary Catherine, who became a nun, and Margaret Cecelia, who married a William E. Merson.

In June 1906, with the New Bedford Whalers again, the Deacon was working on developing a spitball and reportedly having some good luck in mastering it.[11] By late July, he was said to be "pitching as good ball as when he led the league in pitching honors several years ago."[12]

The 1907 and 1908 seasons saw Morrissey back in the Class C Virginia League, pitching for the Roanoke Tigers—perhaps ironically under manager Win Clark for the first part of the season (before Clark left Roanoke and went to manage the Portsmouth Truckers). He was 15-10. In early 1908, Morrissey contemplated not pitching, but he came back and pitched a lot of games, particularly after the warmer weather arrived. He threw a three-hitter against Danville on May 29 and shut out Richmond on five hits on June 1, but was 18-20 for the season. He was extremely popular in Roanoke ("the idol of the Roanoke fans" in the words of *Sporting Life*) and "one of the most popular players ever to don a

Roanoke uniform"[13] He even demonstrated more versatility than previously, playing every position on the team except catcher.

Morrissey threw a two-hitter against Lynchburg on September 7. During the winter, though, Roanoke traded him to the Danville Red Sox for catcher Ray Ryan.[14] He put up a 15-14 year for Danville in 1909, throwing another two-hitter against Lynchburg on July 13. Morrissey started the 1910 season with Danville, but in late May the team sold his contract to Richmond. He was 12-11 for the full season. In 1911, his last year in Organized Baseball, he played in the Carolina Association for either Greensboro (North Carolina) or Greenville (South Carolina), or both. SABR's minor-league records show him as 16-11 for Greensboro, but other listings show him as on Greenville's suspended list at the end of the season.

After baseball Morrissey continued to live in Baltimore, where the 1920 Census has him as a paperhanger, but at the time of his death it was noted that he had become a diamond broker and self-employed jeweler. He died of a coronary thrombosis on February 22, 1939, in Baltimore. Morrissey is buried at New Cathedral Cemetery in Baltimore, which also contains the remains of four members of the National Baseball Hall of Fame (Ned Hanlon, Wilbert Robinson, Joe Kelley, and John McGraw) — the most of any cemetery.

Sources

In addition to the sources noted in this biography, the author also accessed Morrissey's player file from the National Baseball Hall of Fame, the online SABR Encyclopedia, Retrosheet.org, and Baseball-Reference.com. Thanks to Maurice Bouchard for assistance.

Notes

1 *Sporting Life*, March 20, 1897

2 *Sporting Life*, July 23, 1898. Information about minor-league team transfers and closings comes from the *Encyclopedia of Minor League Baseball, Third Edition*, edited by Lloyd Johnson and Miles Wolff (Durham, North Carolina: Baseball America, 2007)

3 *Sporting Life*, September 30, 1899

4 *Boston Globe*, July 14, 1901

5 Bevis, Charles, *The New England League*, pp. 116–117, shows that the John Smith listed is the one we know as Phenomenal Smith.

6 *Sporting Life*, November 1, 1902, and the *Encyclopedia of Minor League Baseball* both show four losses. The minor-league data on baseball-reference.com shows five.

7 *Chicago Tribune*, September 12, 1902

8 Maurice Bouchard notes that Morrissey was a teammate of Moonlight Graham with Manchester in 1903

9 *Sporting Life*, July 22, 1905

10 *Sporting Life*, March 3, 1906, and the player questionnaire at the National Baseball Hall of Fame, completed by Morrissey's daughter, Margaret Merson.

11 *Sporting Life*, June 6, 1906

12 *Sporting Life*, August 4, 1906

13 *Sporting Life*, August 1 and August 29, 1908

14 *Sporting Life*, March 20, 1909

Freddy Parent

by Dan Desrochers

SPARKPLUG SHORTSTOP FREDDY Parent, the "Flying Frenchman," led the Boston Americans with MVP-type seasons to the first modern World Series championship in 1903 and the American League pennant in 1904. An early American League star, Parent (along with teammate Buck Freeman) was its first ironman, playing in 413 consecutive games from the April 26, 1901, opener to September 25, 1903, surprising considering his aggressive playing style. Beset by injuries, including multiple beanings that hampered his play later in his career, Parent nevertheless ranked among the all-time American League leaders in several categories after its first decade, including second in games played and at-bats, fourth in hits and sacrifice hits, and sixth in total bases.

Alfred L. Parent was born on November 25, 1875, in Biddeford, a predominantly textile community in southern Maine. He was the oldest of ten children of Alfred, a fireman, and Celina (Paul) Parent, both French-Canadian immigrants. Freddy quit school at the age of 14 to labor in Biddeford's Laconia Mill harness shop for 65 cents a day. When not working, he enjoyed playing scrub ball on the city's back lots, captain of a team he helped organize. When he was 16 Parent moved to Sanford, Maine, where he worked in the Goodall Worsted Company's weave room and played amateur ball.

Parent married the former Fidelia LaFlamme in 1896 and they had one child, Fred Jr. His "proposal" to the 16 year-old Fidelia included a conditional baseball provision: "I want to marry you, but I do not want to work in the mill. Okay?" The young Fidelia, aware of his baseball desire and potential, replied "yes." Thus began a 67-year relationship.

The 5-foot-5, 148-pound (some sources say 5-foot-7) Parent's introduction to league play was a secondary role on the Sanford town team. "Everybody pretty nearly told me I was too small to play baseball and that I would never make a player anyhow." Once given the

Freddy Parent, with the 1903 Boston Americans.

opportunity to start at shortstop for the town's first team, he developed into a strong infielder. Parent stretched his playing time by playing on teams in Maine and New Hampshire over the next two years.

Parent's first professional season came in 1898 with New Haven in the Connecticut League. Boasting one of the league's top batting averages at .326, he helped New Haven to a second-place finish. In July 1899 the shorthanded St. Louis Perfectos of the National League recruited him from New Haven while they played the New York Giants. The Brooklyn Superbas had expressed an interest in Parent to replace the injured Hughie Jennings, and maintained the initial rights to him after paying New Haven $1,000 for his release. But the team changed its plans, and the Perfectos got Parent on a trial basis for the same offer.

Parent started at second base for two games, contributing to a Perfectos victory in the first game and getting two hits overall. But he suffered a sprained ankle and the Perfectos subsequently released him, stating that he needed more experience in the minors. Parent returned to New Haven and helped the team win the 1899 Connecticut League championship. He finished second in the league in batting (.349) and third in runs scored (76).

In 1900 Parent played shortstop for the champion Providence Grays in the more advanced Eastern League, batting .287 with 23 stolen bases, 21 doubles, six triples, and four home runs. In March 1901, Parent signed with the Boston Americans, where the sturdy little shortstop's solid hitting, fielding, base stealing, and hustle endeared him to the Boston fans.

A right-handed batter, Parent was a dependable hitter. He was a wrist hitter, slapping balls to all fields. He hovered over the plate with an exaggerated piece of lumber, a wagon-tongue bat of suspicious weight. Known as an excellent bunter, Parent also showed some power. In 1901 he augmented a .306 batting average with 36 extra-base hits. The following year his average dipped to .275, but he also cranked a career-best 31 doubles. Crowding the plate enhanced his bunting and opposite-field hitting, but it also exposed him to being hit by pitches. He ranked sixth in the American League in times hit by pitch in the league's first decade, including multiple blows to the head.

Parent was also a snappy infielder. An unassuming player with great range, he was a "little general" on the field. He compensated for his size with keen instincts, quickness, and dexterity covering the ground. In 1902 he led the American League with 492 assists, and also set an American League record by fielding 20 chances without an error in a 17-inning match-up against the Athletics. Recognized for his superior fielding skills, Parent at times ranked low in fielding percentages, possibly attributable to his ability to get to balls and being a risk-taker. *The Washington Post* affirmed this view when reporting the 1904 fielding statistics: "But fielding averages really do not demonstrate the value of any player, for there is Fred Parent, probably the foremost shortstop in the country occupying a position next to last."

With second baseman Hobe Ferris and first baseman Candy LaChance, Parent was part of the early Boston Americans' dynamic double-play combination. Like the famous National League keystone duo of Johnny Evers and Joe Tinker, Parent and Ferris went years without speaking to each other. While they demonstrated spontaneous and effective teamwork on the field, off-field their association was one of unspoken enmity. Fortunately, the proud and quiet Parent and the hotheaded Ferris's baseball instincts outweighed their lack of verbal discourse, and this translated into defensive brilliance.

Parent enjoyed his best seasons as a professional in 1903 and 1904, when Boston won back-to-back American League pennants. In 1903 he posted a .304 batting average, and registered career highs in triples (17, tied for fourth best in the league) and RBIs (80, eighth best

Parent holding cap, walking over third base at South Side Park III, home of the Chicago White Sox, ca. 1905.

in the circuit). In the first modern World Series, in 1903, Parent outshined the legendary Honus Wagner of the Pittsburgh Pirates, outplaying him in the field and notching a batting average nearly 60 points greater than Wagner's for the Series. A "two-way standout Parent made several sparkling plays—cutting off a half-dozen hits with great plays," and ended the eight-game series with 28 assists. He established a record for most runs scored with eight (broken by Babe Ruth 25 years later). The newborn American Leaguers, considered "soft touches" for the senior circuit stars, came back from a three-to-one deficit to win the best-of-nine series.

The next year Parent again enjoyed an outstanding season, batting .291 with 85 runs scored and six home runs, tied for fourth best in the league. But he was simply a passive observer in his most famous at-bat of the season, when 41-game-winner Jack Chesbro of the New York Highlanders unleashed a wild pitch in the ninth inning on the last day of the season to bring in the run that won the pennant for the Americans. Forgotten to most, Parent followed this most famous wild pitch with a base hit that would have scored the run anyway.

His hitting effectiveness declined considerably after the 1904 season, however, as he batted just .234 and .235 in 1905 and 1906, respectively. Parent's average rebounded to .276 in 1907, despite two beanings that year that caused him to become an early proponent of the batting helmet. During the season he began sporting a pneumatic head protector. "Those two blows which felled me had an effect of making me timid whenever I faced the pitcher, and instead of stepping into the ball I was pulling away, the result being that I did not hit up to my standard," he said. He claimed he would wear the protective gear for the rest of his career. However, while the "bombproof" headgear provided him security and reassurance, it spurred hazing and timorous, chickenhearted jousting. In the spring of 1908, Parent claimed he was no longer shy at the plate and discarded the headgear.

Parent's home in Sanford, Maine, built with the proceeds from his 1903 World Series bonus check.

Parent's salary battles with owners were epic, as he constantly challenged baseball's moguls. When he first signed with Boston he demanded an extra $300, and got it. In 1904 he demanded that Boston match an offer by Cincinnati's John Brush of $4,000 per year. He got it. In 1907 Red Sox owner John Taylor was in dire financial straits and proposed cutting Parent's reported salary of $4,250. Freddy was determined to hold out for a "fancy" salary, and did so until mid-April. This stunt cost him his starting shortstop job and precipitated his trade to the White Sox. In October the Red Sox sent Parent to Chicago in a three-way trade involving the Highlanders, who got Jake Stahl from the White Sox and sent infielder Frank LaPorte to the Red Sox. (After one season the Red Sox acquired Stahl from New York, and he managed them to victory in the 1912 World Series.)

Parent struggled mightily at the plate during the next three seasons, posting batting averages of .207, .261, and .178 from 1908 to 1910. In 1911 he staged his final battle with major-league ownership. Coming off a strong spring training, Parent tangled with Chicago owner Charles Comiskey over his pay. After playing in three games for the White Sox, Parent was sold to the Baltimore Orioles of the International League. His tenure with the Orioles gave him opportunities to extend his playing career, gain coaching experience, and influence his former team's purchase of the greatest player ever.

In 1914 Baltimore owner Jack Dunn signed 19-year-old Babe Ruth, regarded as a great pitching prospect, but one who required guidance and mentoring. Parent was proud of his work with Ruth. "I coached Babe more than anybody else at the time," he later recalled. "I remember he was pitching in the late innings of a close game and there were two outs and the bases loaded and a dangerous left-handed hitter was up. He got two strikes on him, and I ran out and told him to waste a pitch. The next pitch he threw right up the middle. Oh, gee, a triple. Babe comes in and I said, 'What happened?' He said, 'I threw one waist high, didn't I?'" Parent later noted, "I used to see him later, after he was a big star, and I'd ask him how his 'waist pitch' was. He did not like it much." (Parent's claim of having had a role in this incident is part of a historical conundrum: Two other player-coaches with the 1914 Orioles, Ben Egan and Neal Ball, also claimed to have been the one who gave Ruth the advice that led to the disastrous result.)

The Orioles, despite their star-studded lineup, faced stiff competition from the nearby Baltimore Terrapins of the newly formed Federal League. The day after his team played to an attendance low of just 17 fans, the financially stricken Dunn began a fire sale. In July 1914 he visited Red Sox owner Joe Lannin and player-manager Bill "Rough" Carrigan in Washington. Dunn took Parent along as a reference whom Carrigan would trust. Carrigan said he sought Parent's advice "as one of the Orioles master-minds at the time and I figured he could give me the dope." Parent told Carrigan that while Ruth lacked finish, "he can't miss with a little more experience." Carrigan concurred with Parent's advice, with Lannin and Dunn closing the deal.

Parent never lost his enthusiasm for baseball. After Baltimore, he played a short stint with Toronto of the International League. He was a player-manager for the Springfield, Massachusetts, Eastern League team in 1918 and Lewiston, Maine, in the New England League in 1919. From 1922 to 1924 Parent was a successful head coach at Colby College in Waterville, Maine, and later assisted former teammate Fred Mitchell as junior-varsity coach at Harvard from 1926 to 1928.

In 1936 Parent was presented a Lifetime Pass by the American and National Leagues in appreciation of long and meritorious service to the game. In 1969 he was elected to the Maine Baseball Hall of Fame. An avid outdoorsman who loved to hunt and fish, Parent spent the rest of his life in his home state. After professional ball, Parent dabbled in a few ventures, including owning and operating a boarding home and running a gasoline station for a number of years. Along with former teammate Harry Lord, he once tried to purchase a minor-league team in Portland. He also unsuccessfully ran for county sheriff.

As the last survivor of the 1903 World Series and one of the last 19th-century players, during his later years Parent was often sought out for interviews by reporters, and proved to be a strong advocate for the Deadball Era style of play. He described modern baseball as a different game, using "a rubber ball," with rosters composed of "mostly Class A ballplayers, with only three or four major leaguers on a club." Parent also described modern players and game conditions as timid in comparison to his rough-and-tumble days. "People get real excited when someone throws a paper cup or something at a player. They didn't throw those kinds of things in my days. They threw beer bottles. And they aimed at your head."

Freddy Parent died on November 2, 1972, three weeks shy of his 97th birthday, in Sanford, Maine. He was buried in Saint Ignatius Cemetery, in Sanford.

Note

This biography originally appeared in David Jones, ed., *Deadball Stars of the American League* (Washington, D.C.: Potomac Books, Inc., 2006).

Sources

Biddeford Weekly Journal (Maine)

Boston Globe

Boston Herald

Boston Post

Brooklyn Daily Eagle

Chicago Daily News

Chicago Evening American

Chicago Journal Tribune

Foster's Daily Democrat (Dover, New Hampshire)

Kennebec Journal (Maine)

New York Times

Portland Press Herald

Philadelphia Daily News

Providence Journal

Sanford News (Maine)

Sanford Tribune (Maine)

St. Louis Republic

Washington Post

Baseball Magazine

Colby College Oracle

Reach Guide

Spalding Baseball Guides

Sporting Life

The Sporting News

Anderson, Will. *Was Baseball Really Invented in Maine?* (Portland, Maine: Will Anderson Publisher, 1992).

Boyle, Frederick R. *Later Families of Sanford-Springvale Maine.* (Peter E. Randal, 1995).

Davids, L. Robert. Baseball Briefs, April 1971.

Evers, Johnny and Hugh S. Fullerton. *Touching Second.* (Chicago: The Reilly & Britton Co., 1910).

Fullerton, Hugh S. "Between Games," *The American Magazine*, 1911.

Keene, Kerry, et al. *The Babe in Red Stockings.* (Urbana, Illinois: Sagamore Publishing, 1997).

Lieb, Frederick G. *The Boston Red Sox.* (New York: G.P. Putman's Sons, 1947).

MacWilliams, Don. *Yours in Sports.* (Monmouth, Maine: Monmouth Press, 1969).

McGraw, John J. *My Thirty Years in Baseball.* (Lincoln: University of Nebraska Press, 1995).

Niss, Bob. *Faces of Maine.* (Portland: Guy Gannett Publishing Company, 1981).

Reisler, Jim. *Before They Were the Bombers.* (Jefferson, North Carolina: McFarland, 2002).

Ritter, Lawrence S. *The Glory of Their Times.* (New York: William Morrow, 1985).

Smelser, Marshall. *The Life That Ruth Built.* (Lincoln: University of Nebraska Press, 1975).

Interviews and Credits

Armand Chabot, Paul Demers, Therese Desrochers, Glenn Ledoux.

George Pepper Prentiss

By David Forrester

MANY MAJOR LEAGUERS who have died while still active have met their ends in dramatic accidents. Their careers have been cut short by cars, trucks, airplanes, boats, guns, and—in one case—the Niagara Falls. George Prentiss's death in 1902, one of the first recorded in the American League, was less sensational. Yet the 26-year-old Prentiss had packed enough drama into his brief time in the game to match some of the longest-lived ballplayers.

George Pepper Prentiss was born in Wilmington, Delaware, on June 10, 1876, the third child of five born to James and Eliza Prentiss. James had emigrated from England as a child, learned the butcher trade, and married Wilmington native Eliza Simmons. The family lived in relative prosperity—the household had two live-in servants when he was a child. As young Prentiss grew up, he became well-known locally for his athleticism and speed; he was said to be able to complete the 100-yard dash in 10 seconds. In 1896 and 1897 Prentiss made a name for himself in both baseball and football, earning the nickname Kitten in the local press. During the fall and winter, he was the star halfback of Wilmington's Warren Athletic Club team. According to author Doug Gelbert, Prentiss is considered to be the greatest football player in Delaware in the 19th century. In the spring and summer, Prentiss pitched and played multiple outfield and infield positions for a Cape May, New Jersey, semipro team and an amateur club in Wilmington. The local team's games drew press attention and large crowds after what had been a lull in baseball interest in Wilmington in prior years. Perhaps Prentiss's pitching was part of the attraction in his two seasons with Rockford. At the start of the 1898 season, during their preseason barnstorming tour, he was asked to join the National League champion Boston Beaneaters for a tryout.

On April 11, 1898, the right-handed Prentiss, 5 feet 11 inches tall and weighing 175 pounds, joined the Boston squad in a game against the Lancaster (Pennsylvania) Maroons on their home field. The locals had won the

GEORGE P. PRENTISS,
Pitcher on the staff of the Boston Americans.

George Prentiss, depicted in the *Boston Post*, 1902.

Atlantic League pennant the prior season and they gave Boston a game. With Lancaster leading 4–2 in the eighth inning, Boston manager Frank Selee gave Prentiss a chance to show what he could do. Prentiss walked the first batter, then allowed four singles in a row. Boston lost the game and Prentiss lost his chance.

The following month Prentiss signed with the Waterbury Pirates in the Connecticut League. His first regular-season professional game went about as well as his tryout with Boston. The Waterbury squad had won the first six games of the season when Prentiss took the mound on May 17 against the team from New Britain.

He gave up 11 runs in eight innings. Newspaper accounts claimed that manager Roger Connor became so frustrated that he pulled his whole team off the field in the top of the ninth. Connor had said it was to make sure the team caught their train. The next day Prentiss redeemed himself in front of a crowd of 1,000 in Danbury. In addition to recounting Prentiss's pitching a 13–3 victory, the newspapers noted that Connor had laid down new rules for his team, including a curfew. "I expect every man to go to bed no later than 11:30 every night, and if I learn that anyone stays up later than that, he'll have to explain to me," he told the *Meriden Morning Record*.[1]

Prentiss went on to have a good year pitching and often played in the outfield when not pitching. Waterbury needed a victory in the last game of the season to clinch the pennant, Prentiss was given the starting nod and he delivered, again beating Danbury. Later that month, his winning percentage was misreported in *Sporting Life*, prompting a letter from Prentiss that was printed on the front page of the October 1, 1898, issue. He wanted to make sure he was credited for 18 wins, 11 losses, and 2 ties instead of the 17 wins, 18 losses, and 2 ties that had been reported. "[A]ppreciating the value of your paper to the national game and particularly to beginners," he wrote, "I should esteem it a personal favor if you will be good enough to correct your error concerning me as a pitcher." A review of game-by-game newspaper accounts indicates that Prentiss probably had his numbers right, putting him just about in the top third of the league's pitchers that year. The switch-hitting Prentiss made no protest about his batting statistics; his .240 placed him in the middle of the league.

Waterbury opened the 1899 season at home on May 17 with a new name—the Rough Riders—and a grudge match against New Haven in front of 1,200 fans. Prentiss pitched well and gave up one run in the final inning. After winning 3–1, he undoubtedly went on to break Connor's curfew. On the evening of June 20, Prentiss was picked up by the county sheriff and brought to the courthouse. Once there, the sheriff told him that he was charged with bastardy—impregnating a woman out of wedlock—and that the fastest way out of the trouble was to marry the local woman involved: Boston Beaneaters pitcher Fred Klobedanz's 20-year-old sister, Emma. It appears from newspaper reports Emma had been a baseball fan, attending many games in the previous year, but it is unclear whether the two had met before the night of the season opener. As the *Bridgeport Herald* put it, "It was after the first game that the alleged act making her a mother took place." After consulting James Watts, a saloon keeper and co-owner of the Waterbury team, Prentiss decided to consent to the forced marriage, despite his being engaged to a woman back in Wilmington. It was after 11 p.m. when the sheriff, Emma, her attorney, and Prentiss visited the Second Congregational Church parsonage. They roused the Rev. Davenport from his bed to officiate. The husband and wife then went their separate ways: Prentiss back to his room downtown and she back to her parents' home on James Street. Emma filed divorce papers the following week.

The soap opera in Prentiss's private life doesn't seem to have adversely affected his progress as a professional player. He became the acknowledged star pitcher of the team and improved his numbers to 24 wins and 14 losses and a .279 batting average. Perhaps the addition of the tragic Louis Sockalexis to the Waterbury outfield in mid-July—and the brutal focus the newspapers took on his losing battle with alcohol—took the heat off Prentiss for the remainder of the season. Talk of Prentiss being sold to the National League was persistent and came to a head in late summer. On August 15 manager Connor met with Ned Hanlon, manager of the Brooklyn National League team to try to sell Prentiss and perhaps two other players. While Connor was visiting New York, Charlie Klobedanz, Emma's other baseball player brother, was given a trial as pitcher for the Waterbury team. Prentiss played right field as the Meriden Silverites drilled Klobedanz's slow delivery, racking up 15 runs.

At the end of that month, *Sporting Life* reported that Prentiss had pitched two games of a doubleheader against New London, one of which had gone 11 innings, and had won both games. At the end of the season he was presented with a watch by Waterbury fans in thanks for his solid work. Nevertheless, whatever deal Connor

1—T. O'Brien, 1b.   2—Simon, c. f.   3—Duffy, r. f.   4—Hess, c.   5—Tamsett, 3b.   6—Jones, p.
7—Cargo, ss.   8—J. O'Brien, 2b.   9—Rudderham, p.   10—Millerick, p.   11—Cristal, p.
12—Prentiss, p.   13—Rosson, p.   14—Bernard, l. f.   15—Baker, p.
THE ALBANY TEAM, CHAMPIONS NEW YORK LEAGUE FOR 1902.

1—Rudderham; 2—Simon; 3—Hill; 4—Millerick; 5—T. O'Brien, Mgr.; 6—Duffy; 8—J. J. O'Brien; 8—Wiltse; 9—Wilson; 10—Kennedy; 11—Tamsett; 12—Cristall; 13—Cargo; 14—Ostrander, Mascot; 15—Jones, 16—Hess; 17—Weygand
Photo by Albany Medallion Studio.
CHAMPION ALBANY BASE BALL TEAM, NEW YORK STATE LEAGUE.

Top image—George Prentiss is listed here in a photograph of the 1902 Albany team published in the *Reach Base Ball Guide*. (top row, second from the right side).

Bottom image—The *Spalding's Official Base Ball Guide* ran the same photo as the *Reach Guide*, but with a different background, and named #9 as Wilson.

and Hanlon had discussed didn't materialize. In March 1900 the *Meriden Morning Record* observed: "Connor did everything in his power to get Prentiss into the bigger leagues. ... The big managers have not asked for Prentiss and as Roger does not want to throw Prentiss on the market for all to get a try at, he will keep him for himself. So George will wear a Waterbury uniform or he will not wear any, so say the powers that be." [2]

Prentiss sought a salary increase, but Connor wasn't disposed to give him one two years in a row and held firm.[3] Prentiss stayed in Delaware and was not among the 400 fans who witnessed the spectacle of his two former brothers-in-law pitching against each other in an exhibition game on April 14—Charlie for Waterbury and Fred for the Worcester team of the Eastern League. Prentiss ended his holdout and arrived in Waterbury just in time to see the 1900 season opener against Meriden on May 10. He pitched his first game of the season on May 15 against the Derby team. The opposing pitcher was Charlie Klobedanz—recently dropped by Waterbury and picked up by Derby. Waterbury won the game, 1–0, and Prentiss pitched another 11 games before July 4, for a total of eight wins and four losses. His batting had improved to .280, but he never picked up another bat that season.

Just after the Fourth, Prentiss sat out a game with a sore throat. The following week he was admitted to Waterbury Hospital, housed in a Victorian mansion overlooking the city. Tonsillitis was mentioned in some news reports and at some point he was operated on, perhaps more than once. In early August he was transferred to New York City's Manhattan Hospital to be seen by specialists, as blood poisoning had now set in and his condition was described as "critical." The season ended and by the end of September Prentiss was still in the hospital, but his condition had improved to the point that his recovery was expected. He was on Waterbury's reserve list for the 1901 season.

In early March 1901 Waterbury sent contracts to Prentiss and the rest of the team from the prior year. Later in the month Connor told reporters that most of the players wanted more money, which he said they would not get since there were many players out of work and willing to play for less. A few days later Prentiss returned his contract and the note that was sent with it, without a word of comment and without signing the contract. Newspaper stories interpreted this as a personal insult to Connor since they felt Prentiss had been well treated during his illness. In late April the *Waterbury Democrat* said, "George Prentiss will be watched closely by the local management. He of all others was least grateful for what had been done for him and if he attempts to play with any team under the National league rules, he will be taught a lesson he will not soon forget."[4] At the time of that statement, Prentiss had already been signed to the Albany Senators of the New York State League under the pseudonym Wilson.

Despite being a hunted man and in recovery from a serious illness, Prentiss's pitching performance followed a similar arc to those of prior years. His first outing with Albany, on May 9, was not auspicious: he was wild and hit a batter in a home game against Rome. But it wasn't a catastrophe either; he lost just 4–3. And as in other years, Prentiss's performance improved as the season progressed, to a final tally of 18 wins and 10 losses, the victories including shutouts in two of his last three appearances of the season. Though his hitting did decline (.220), his pitching was heralded by newspapers in August as "a wonder" and "the best in the league."

Prentiss's disguise had not lasted past the end of June, when *The Sporting News* reported that officials of the Connecticut State League were making inquiries about him. According to newspaper reports, the new Waterbury manager, George Harrington, traveled to Albany to bring back the "star pitcher of the New York State League" or get paid for his services. It appears that neither happened. At the end of the season, Prentiss joined the Boston team of the new American League for a tryout.

On September 23 Prentiss, still using the Wilson alias, was sent in to relieve Boston's Ted Lewis in the seventh inning of the second game of a doubleheader with Detroit in front of nearly 5,000 spectators at Boston's Huntington Avenue Grounds. When he stepped to the mound, Boston was behind 7–2. Detroit gained two more runs under Wilson's watch and the game was called in the eighth inning because of darkness. Four days later Prentiss pitched a full game for Boston against Milwaukee and gave up only one hit in the first five innings. He won the game 7–2. *Boston Journal* correspondent W.S. Barnes, Jr. called it a "hands down" win and "a very favorable performance." After the game, Prentiss went home to Wilmington.

In mid-October, when the reserve list for 1902 was printed, Prentiss appeared twice: as Prentiss reserved by Waterbury and as Wilson reserved by Albany. Later that month, at one of the first meetings held by the newly formed National Association of Professional Baseball Leagues (the minor leagues), Secretary John Farrell was "ordered to rigidly investigate" Waterbury's claim on Prentiss. At the end of November Albany's owner, William Quinlan, provided *The Sporting News* with a letter from Prentiss in which he claimed that he had signed to play for Waterbury for three years, 1898–1900, and that he had never received a contract from Waterbury in 1901. "As for my treatment when I was sick in Waterbury," he wrote, "the way I was used when out of shape was enough to make me give that town a wide berth, and I will never go there again, no matter what turns up."[5]

The contents of the letter, which he signed "George P. Wilson," are at odds with news accounts from 1900 and 1901. These discrepancies and the lack of any explanation for adopting a new last name, make it difficult to interpret Prentiss's note as anything other than an attempt to lie his way out of a difficult situation. Albany was certainly a better-financed team than Waterbury and it had the benefit of no Klobedanz family members playing in the league or living nearby. In mid-March of 1902, Farrell's investigation came to a conclusion. After reviewing the case—including a notarized affidavit from Roger Connor—the National Association awarded Prentiss's services to Waterbury. Since the American League had not yet joined in a cooperative agreement with the National League and the minors, if Boston were to release him, Prentiss would have to either join another American League team or revert back to Waterbury if he wanted to play in Organized Baseball.

A few days later, on March 23, Prentiss arrived by train in Augusta, Georgia, with Boston manager Jimmy Collins and 14 other Boston players for spring training. The weather was rainy, but the team got to work.

Sometime during the next couple of days manager Harrington of the Waterbury team appeared in Augusta and met with Prentiss. He received a signature on a new contract and a promise that he would play for Waterbury as soon as the new season opened in May. News accounts of Boston's spring training reveal Collins trying to decide if Prentiss would get the last of the five pitching slots he wanted filled. On the night of April 4, during an exhibition night game of indoor baseball at the local armory, Prentiss let his bat slip and it injured a woman in the audience. The mishap was covered by newspapers across the country, probably because the woman, whose teeth were broken, was Ruth Randall, the daughter of James Randall, author of the Confederate anthem (and now Maryland's state song) "Maryland, My Maryland" and the right-hand man for Georgia Congressman William Fleming.[6] That wasn't the kind of impact Collins was likely looking to leave with Augusta during the team's first visit south. The interest in the events subsided after a few days and Prentiss joined the team as it headed north for the season.

On April 18 Prentiss pitched in the Boston's last preseason exhibition game, against the Worcester Hustlers. He must have been relieved to find that Fred Klobedanz had left Worcester during the offseason to join the Lawrence, Massachusetts, team. Prentiss pitched the full nine innings and Boston won, 5–4.

On May 2 Prentiss played his first major-league game under his real name when he relieved Cy Young in the second inning of a home game against Baltimore. Young had given up six runs before Prentiss was put in. Although Prentiss's pitching was good, the team's hitting and fielding were poor and Boston lost, 14–6. Prentiss didn't play again until June 4, when he pitched a complete game in Cleveland. The crowd was large, estimated by some at as high as 10,000, to see Nap Lajoie's debut in a Cleveland uniform.[7] Less than a year before, Lajoie's legal case against the Phillies had been used by a newspaper columnist to try to defend Prentiss's jump from Waterbury. Prentiss held Cleveland to six hits, but lost the game, 4–3.

On June 6 Prentiss relieved George Winter in the fifth inning with bases loaded, no outs, and Boston down by one run. Thanks in part to fielding errors and some wild pitches, Prentiss made matters much worse. The final score was 14–3, but the loss went to Winter. On June 13 in Chicago, fresh from celebrating his 26th birthday, Prentiss provided better relief to Bill Dinneen. After the White Sox had hammered Dinneen in the fifth and sixth innings, Prentiss relieved and held Chicago to a single run in the ninth inning. It didn't make much difference in Boston's 9–0 loss. Five days later Prentiss pitched nine innings at home for an 8–3 win over Cleveland. According to the *Boston Globe*, the win was attributable to good fielding because Prentiss's pitching was comparable to Cleveland's and he was "hit freely." On June 22 Prentiss won a 7–5 victory at Detroit. The local fans attempted to attack the umpire because of some bad calls against the Tigers, but the players of both teams protected him.

On July 8 Prentiss started in a home game against Philadelphia and gave up two runs in the first inning and another in the second, before Young relieved him. Boston went on to lose the game, 22–9. When Collins and the team headed to Philadelphia for a series two days later, Prentiss was left behind. On July 18 he was "turned over" to Baltimore to help shore up the Orioles.[8] Baltimore was in a shambles after manager John McGraw jumped to the New York Giants in midseason and then pulled his best players with him. On July 22 Prentiss put in a terrible performance against Detroit in a 7–5 loss. He gave up 10 hits in six innings and walked five men before being relieved by Charlie Shields. Seven days later, he was put in again in a game against Cleveland. Now clearly not in good health, Prentiss gave up two singles and a triple in the first inning and started the second inning by giving up two singles before being relieved by Shields. Prentiss was released by Baltimore that day and went to Wilmington to recuperate from what was later diagnosed as typhoid fever.[9] Prentiss had appeared in 11 major-league games with a 3-3 record and a 5.31 earned run average.

After a couple of weeks of recuperating in early August, Prentiss joined the Wilmington semipro team for two games, since he was now ineligible to play in the minor leagues due to his now unquestionably broken contract with Waterbury. The August 17 edition of the *Wilmington Sunday Morning Star* recounted Wilmington's game with the Chester, Maryland, team. Prentiss had led the team to victory, striking out four without a walk and hitting a home run deep over the left-field fence. It was his last game. On page one of that edition of the *Star*, there was a discussion of the high number of deaths from typhoid fever in the town. That day—or soon after—Prentiss had a relapse and visited his mother's summer cottage at Rehoboth Beach to regain his strength. But his condition worsened, and he was brought back to the family home on Franklin Street in Wilmington after a few days. He died there on September 8, 1902, possibly from peritonitis caused by the typhoid fever infection. He was buried in the Wilmington and Brandywine Cemetery in Wilmington. Prentiss was one of 41 Wilmington residents the disease killed that year. Tens of thousands of people across the US succumbed to the bacterial infection each year in that time before antibiotics, water chlorination, and effective health codes.

In March 1903 the *Waterbury American* recalled George Prentiss: "About this time last year, the papers were full of an episode which took place in Augusta, Ga., linking the name of George Prentiss and a prominent Augusta society belle. The young woman, it will be remembered, was struck on the head with a bat, which slipped out of the hands of Prentiss. The sequel, it was said, was to be a marriage. The sequel in reality was a death. Now poor George Prentiss is forgotten, even by those with whom he was most intimately associated. There is a lesson, or rather two or three lessons here." There is no evidence that Prentiss ever met Ruth Randall after delivering flowers and an apology in the days after the accident. Perhaps the writer was conflating Randall with Klobedanz—intentionally or not.

When Prentiss's former teammate Dan Manley joined the Waterbury team in April 1903, the *Bridgeport Herald* took the opportunity to recall the heroics of the 1898 pennant year and Prentiss's later career. Its last word on Prentiss: "He is with one of the minor league teams this year." [10]

Sources

In addition to the sources cited in the text, the author consulted US Census records, birth, marriage, and divorce records via Ancestry.com. Also consulted: *Typhoid Fever* by Prentiss Chandler Whipple; *The Great Delaware Sports Book* by Doug Gelbert; *Reach's 1902 Baseball Guide*; and statistical data from Baseball-Reference.com and Baseball-Almanac.com. The author read contemporaneous reports from the following publications: *Augusta Chronicle, Boston Globe, Boston Journal, Bridgeport Herald, Hartford Courant, Kansas City Star, Meriden Daily Journal, Meriden Morning Record, New York Times, Sporting Life, The Day (New London), The Sporting News,* and *Wilmington Sunday Morning Star*.

Notes

1. *Meriden Morning Record*, May 18, 1899.
2. Ibid., March 17, 1900.
3. *New Haven Register*, March 28, 1900.
4. *Waterbury Democrat*, quoted in the April 25, 1901, issue of the *Meriden Daily Journal*.
5. *The Sporting News*, November 30, 1901.
6. See, for instance, *Sporting Life*, April 12, 1902.
7. The *Boston Globe* reported attendance at 9,827, which was more than the other three American League games put together.
8. The phrase comes from the July 21, 1902, *Washington Post* which says Prentiss "has been turned over by Collins to the Baltimore team." It was, perhaps, a move orchestrated by the league, a not-uncommon thing in the first decade of the AL.
9. The *Baltimore Sun* of July 30, 1902, reported, "He has not been well for some time," and later notices in newspapers about Prentiss's death indicate that he took ill in Baltimore. The incubation period for typhoid fever is 10 to 20 days depending on several factors.
10. *Bridgeport Herald*, April 26, 1903.

Osee Schrecongost

By Bill Nowlin

IF EVER THERE were a battery that was bound together in life and in death, it was probably pitcher Rube Waddell and catcher Osee Schrecongost. They were both born in small communities in western Pennsylvania, on opposite sides of the Allegheny National Forest, and a little less than 100 miles from each other. They both broke into the majors with the same team on the same day. For four seasons (1902 through 1905), they both served for the Philadelphia Athletics as teammates, batterymates, and roommates. They both ended their professional careers in the same year, 1910, and they both died within a little more than three months of each other—neither of them having reached the age of 40.

Waddell was a star pitcher, and has been a member of the National Baseball Hall of Fame since 1946. "Schreck"—as he was typically called—was often a team's backup catcher, both in the minor leagues and the majors, but he got in a fair amount of work and was both a good hitter and an excellent defender.

Osee Freeman Schrecongost is an unusual name, though his surname was not uncommon, particularly in Pennsylvania in his day. With a brother two years older named Harry and a sister two years younger named Annie, one might wonder today where the Osee came from. There have been numerous spellings of his name, both first and last, and the spellings differ on some records of the day. He was born on April 11, 1875, in New Bethlehem, Pennsylvania, a Clarion County borough about 60 miles northeast of Pittsburgh. Two years later he was baptized in Mt. Lebanon (under 10 miles from Pittsburgh in a southwesterly direction) and is listed in the baptismal records of the Mt. Lebanon United Presbyterian Church as Osie Freeman Schreckengost.

His family appears in the 1880 United States census living in Redbank Township, Clarion County, Pennsylvania, not to be confused with another Red Bank about 200 miles further east. His parents were

Osee Schrecongost with the 1901 Boston Americans.

listed as Naman Shrecongost, a miner, age 29, and his wife, Sarah C. Shrecongost, 26. Their three children were Harry H., Osee F., and Annie I. They also had three boarders in their household at the time, all three of whom were miners: Adam and John Huffman and Emet Murphy. The area was one of coal mines and most of the people in their neighborhood were miners. Listed only a couple of residences away was another Naman Shrecongost and his wife, Sadie, both a few years younger but without children. Newspapers of the day did refer to Osee's father as "Big Norman."

On our man's gravestone in nearby Kittaning Cemetery, the marker—not infallible itself—presents his name as Osee F. Schrecongost. SABR member Dan O'Brien interviewed grandson Charles Dundas and family genealogist Christine Crawford-Oppenheimer and concluded that the correct rendition of his name is F. Osee Schrecongost, that his father's name was spelled Naaman and that mother Sarah was born Sarah Caroline Protzman. The Schrecongost name was German. Osee was pronounced "Oh-See."[1]

What we're most interested in, of course, is his life in baseball. Josh Walzak, a writer for the New Bethlehem newspaper, the *Leader-Vindicator*, wrote a lengthy feature on Schreck in its September 8, 1999, issue. He says the family lived in Fairmount City, less than two miles from New Bethlehem, and that the young man attended school there until about the age of 10, when the family moved to an apartment on Broad Street in New Bethlehem. Osee went to work in the mines as a teenager, but played baseball too, and was a standout with the town teams of 1893 and 1894. The newspaper at the time spelled his name Ossee Schreckengost.

In 1895 Osee struck out on his own, moving to Williamsport to play semipro ball for a team sponsored by the Domestic Sewing Machine Co. He wound up playing for the Demorest Base Ball Club of Williamsport, which became the championship team in Central Pennsylvania League ball that year. The *Philadelphia Inquirer* carried him in box scores as Schrecongost, though more often in the lineups as "Schr'st" and "Sch'st," and the like. Virtually the whole Demorest team was signed again for 1896.[2] Schreck started 1896 by hitting a home run on Opening Day, May 16. While no league statistics could be located, *Sporting Life* did note at year end, in its December 2, 1896, issue, that the "Demorest Manufacturing Company will put one of the strongest ball teams in the field next year that has ever represented the city of Williamsport on the local diamond. If the Central Pa. League is not reorganized again the team will play independent ball, and will probably travel in a private car and make trips through the South and West, and will rival the Page Fence Giants. [The Giants were one of the best black teams of the 1890s.] The Demorest team will be composed of a set of gentlemanly players, and will contain some of last year's players." Among them, it was noted, was F. O. Schrecongost, the young and coming player, [who] will cover first bag and act as change catcher."

Schrecongost had an active year in 1897 and it's a little difficult to track just where he played and when. His record shows him playing for Augusta in the Maine State League, possibly as early as the latter part of 1896.[3] He'd been on a Brockton (Massachusetts) contract, somehow, but was released to Augusta on a temporary contract on May 6.[4] He was returned to Brockton and then released by Brockton on July 6.[5] He next turned up with Fall River, Massachusetts, in the New England League, playing on July 10 but appearing in only four games for the Indians, hitting .353. A few weeks later the *Boston Herald* noted that he was now playing for the Shamokin club in the Central Pennsylvania League.[6] The Coal Heavers folded, though, "owing to lack of patronage," on September 7.[7] The paper noted that Osee had received offers from both Louisville and Philadelphia. Indeed, the very next day—September 8—he shows up catching for Louisville (presented as Sch't in the box score).

That was the day Schrecongost first played in the major leagues, debuting with the National League's Louisville Colonels on September 8, 1897. He was 0-for-3 in the game, his only one that year. He was charged with a passed ball. Pitcher Rube Waddell made his big-league debut in the same game, Baltimore beating Louisville, 5–1. The syndicated news report from Baltimore described it as "a dull and uninteresting game." Waddell, it was written, "pitched a good game, but worked against some very hard luck."[8] How good it was could be debatable, given the four bases on balls Rube doled out and the 11 hits he surrendered. Waddell also hit a batter. He struck out two.

The *Baltimore Sun* noted, "Catcher Schrecongost was merely given a trial by Louisville yesterday, and while he caught a good game he did not show any extraordinary talent, and his batting was rather weak. President Pulliam refused to buy him, and Schrecongost left for home, in Fall River, last night. Mr. Pulliam said, 'He caught well, but we have two catchers already who are just as good, if not better, and we did not need him.'" The *Sun* said that Pulliam did like Waddell and would keep him. "He has much to learn, but shows promise...."[9]

The *Sun* also reported that a Chicago paper had sent a telegram to Pulliam asking, "Is that catcher's name on the level?" It was only one of a number Pulliam received when sports editors at various newspapers saw the full name Schrecongost.

That this first meeting between Schrecongost and Waddell ultimately led to a lifelong, intertwined relationship is remarkable in that they'd only been in the same place at the same time for about 24 hours, and, as noted in the newspaper, neither of them knew the other and hardly had had anyone else known who they were. The *Washington Evening Star* reprinted a story from Baltimore:

"That was a peculiar state of affairs in the Louisville team on Wednesday; in which the pitcher did not know his catcher's name, the catcher was ignorant of the pitcher's name, and the members of the team, including the manager himself, were unacquainted with the names of either of the young men composing the club's battery for the day. Waddell only joined the team in Washington and Schrecongost joined the team only a short time before the game, having come here on trial. This all-around ignorance of names was shown when some spectators in the grand stand asked the catcher who was pitching. 'I don't know; I never saw him before,' was Schrecongost's reply. Presently Waddell came to the bench and some one asked him who the catcher was, and he replied, 'Couldn't tell you—first time I ever saw him.'"

" 'Who will be in the points today,' was asked of Manager Clarke before the game by the *Sun* reporter. 'This man will pitch,' he replied, pointing to the name 'Weddel' in the score card, and that tall fellow over there will catch. I don't know what his name is.' But he called to Schrecongost and got that young man to spell his name out for the newspaper man, regardless of how long it delayed the game.

"When asked if 'Weddel' was the correct name, Manager Clarke replied, 'Don't know; you will have to ask him.'"[10]

Some listings also show Schreck as having been with both Williamsport and the Sunbury Pirates (both of the Central Pennsylvania League) at one point or another, in addition to Shamokin. There were quite a few shifts in teams within the league that year. Once again, in a postseason (November 6) issue, *Sporting Life* anticipated him playing for Williamsport in 1898.

It had been quite a year. "My minor league experience was a nightmare," he said. "I played with four different minor leagues in one season. The manager of the Augusta club of the Maine State league owed me $70. When I asked him for it he told me that I had been fined that amount, and I didn't get a cent. When I hooked up with the Williamsport team the manager soon owed me $50, and he just tacked a fine that took all that was coming to me. I have no growl coming about my experience in Youngstown."[11]

Schreck played for three teams in 1898. He began the season with Cedar Rapids (Iowa) in the Western Association, but Cedar Rapids disbanded on June 9 and the whole league followed suit on the 26th. Between the two June dates, Schrecongost caught for the team in Ottumwa, Iowa. After the league folded, he played the rest of the time with the last-place Youngstown (Ohio) Puddlers in the Inter-State League. Baseball-Reference.com has him hitting .280 in 78 games for Youngstown, but the October 8 *Sporting Life* said he had led the team with a .310 average. He hit a couple of homers, on July 5 and September 14. As it happened, the very next day, Stanley Robison, owner of the NL franchise in Cleveland, came to look over both him and pitcher Knepper.

Schreck was described as "the premier backstop of the league" and was sold to the Spiders for $300 in a deal announced on September 27, getting into ten games for them and hitting .314 with ten RBIs.[12] Cleveland manager Patsy Tebeau was high on him: "We will use Schrecongost in almost every game next year ... for his hitting ability. He is an Indian at the bat, biting at everything, high, low, out or in, and very often making doubles and triples off wild pitches. It is next to impossible for a twirler to get 'Schreck' in a hole, for all pitching looks alike to him."[13]

In 1899, Schrecongost trained with Tebeau's team in Hot Springs, Arkansas, but shuttled back and forth from Cleveland to St. Louis during the year. Tebeau continued to boost him in the springtime and it was written that even as they arrived for training, "[w]hen Tebeau introduced Schrecongost to the people at the

Another 1901 photo of Schrecongost with Boston.

depot he added after each hand shake: 'Here is the little boy who is to lead our team in batting this year.' Patsy hopes to make a change first baseman out of Schreck, and to use him in nearly every game."[14] Schreck wasn't all that little; at 5-feet-10 he stood two inches taller than Tebeau, and at 180 (a weight he admittedly may not have yet attained) he had nearly 20 pounds on his manager.

Early on, on March 28, 1899, the entire Cleveland ballclub was transferred to St. Louis after the league expelled the earlier St. Louis owners and installed a new group in its place. Schrecongost was one of 16 Spiders—including Tebeau—so assigned. It's a story we'll not go into here, but brothers Frank DeHaas Robison and Stanley Robison each owned shares in both ballclubs in 1899. Frank had founded the Cleveland club, and he and Stanley were part of a group that purchased the bankrupt St. Louis Browns, and then moved most of the better players to St. Louis, loading up the team they dubbed the Perfectos but leaving Cleveland with a team that finished 12th with a record (the worst in major-league history) of 20-134.

In the early going, Osee appeared in six 1899 games for St. Louis without a hit. On June 5 he and Frank Bates were assigned to Cleveland. There were "Rumors of a Rumpus" between Tebeau and McKean which led to the trade. In any event, once he joined the Spiders in New York, in time to get into the June 7 game, it was soon reported that "Schrecongost made an instantaneous hit here. Like Tebeau, Schreck plays ball all the time."[15] The trade came in time for him to get his photograph published in Base Ball magazine over the caption: "Ossee Schrecongost, The Rising Young Catcher of the Cleveland Club."[16] He had "fought his way into popularity here [Cleveland] by the desperately earnest manner in which he plunges into every game. He is a second Pat Tebeau in this respect, forgetting everything else when he is playing ball, but the desire to win."[17] The Cleveland club was sometimes given the nickname the Exiles in the national press, and the Washington Post called the catcher the "Ghost."[18] Schreck even beat St. Louis, winning one of those 20 games for the Exiles, with three hits—including a triple—in a 3–1 win over the Perfectos on June 25 in St. Louis.

But then, on July 31, Osee was back with St. Louis, having arrived that morning. Though indeed both clubs were owned by Robisons, it was reported that "Tebeau 'purchased' him yesterday from President Stanley Robison of the Cleveland Club."[19] Schrecongost played the rest of the '99 season for St. Louis, and is listed as—overall—hitting .313 in his time with Cleveland and .286 for St. Louis, with two homers but otherwise not that much power—though on August 28 he hit a double and a triple in the same game, a 14–12 loss to Washington. He played a mixture of first base and catcher, sometimes playing first when Lou Criger was catching.

And there was some passion in Schreck's play. He even got into a fight with teammate Mike Donlin at the Grand Central depot in Cincinnati on August 7 just before the train pulled out for Pittsburgh. Schreck was upset that two of Donlin's "rifle-shot throws to the plate" had been low and struck Scheck in the shins. He said something to Donlin, three years his junior, at the station and "quick as a flash the Californian turned and whipped his right across the catcher's jaw, who went down in a heap. When he regained his feet he started for Donlin, who again felled him like a log. Schrecongost again got up and an exchange of vicious blows followed, but Donlin was getting the best of it when Schrecongost stopped to pick up a coupling pin." Several players and some bystanders stepped in at that point to disarm Schreck.[20]

In 1900 Schrecongost played for Buffalo, in the one year that Ban Johnson's Western League was named the American League but considered a minor league. In 1901 Johnson founded a different American League, the first year of the AL, which has lasted into the 21st century. The 25-year-old Schrecongost had been farmed out to the Buffalo Bisons by St. Louis before the season began in May. He played in 125 games, batting .282, catching more than 75 percent of the games and playing first base the rest of the time.[21]

Schreck joined that new American League in 1901, signing on early with the Boston Americans (manager Jimmy Collins, a Buffalo-area native, knew of his work), but destined from the start to be backup catcher behind Lou Criger. On March 4 it was reported that he would break his contract with St. Louis and jump to the new league to play for Boston.[22] Acknowledging that he was a hitting catcher, the April 14 *Boston Journal* ran a trick photograph showing two overlapping images of Schrecongost both batting and catching at the same time.

In fact, he performed admirably, appearing in 86 games—ten more than Criger—and hitting for a .304 average, exceptional for a catcher in those days and well above the .278 team average. Criger was surer on defense, however, and—no small consideration—was Cy Young's favorite catcher. Cy Young was 33-10 that year, and if he wanted a personal catcher, that was fine with manager Jimmy Collins. All three—Schreck, Criger, and Young—had been on the Perfectos in 1899, and the latter two played for St. Louis in 1900 while Schreck was in Buffalo. Charlie Hemphill was the fourth St. Louis player to jump leagues and come to Boston.

Scheck did take part in the first triple play in franchise history, on August 7, 1901, at Baltimore, a 1-5-2-6-1 affair.

The day before the season ended, owner Charles Somers re-signed Criger and Young for 1902, but not Schrecongost, Hemphill, or Tommy Dowd. Schreck played for Cleveland (an American League city from the start), and then the Philadelphia Athletics in 1902. Exactly why Somers didn't want to retain Schrecongost, we don't know, but a *Boston Herald* report a year later—enthusing over his 1902 season—said that Schreck had "proved a most unreliable man for Boston last season."[23] In any event, Boston traded him to Cleveland on November 16 for Candy LaChance, who became the first baseman for the Bostons for the next few years. Cleveland fully intended to use Schreck at first base, rather than as a catcher.

Schrecongost picked up a little extra work in the preseason of 1902, coaching the batteries and the hitters for the University of Virginia baseball team in Charlottesville.[24]

Though he was hitting .338 for Cleveland after 18 games, playing first base exclusively, Schrecongost was released on May 13. It's a bit of a mystery why, but as it worked out Cleveland added Charlie Hickman a few weeks later and Hickman wound up batting .378.[25] Schreck signed as a free agent with the Philadelphia Athletics on May 22, and appeared in 79 games for them (71 as catcher), batting .324.[26] For a catcher, who presumably had a good eye for the strike zone, he didn't walk that much, just 102 times in 3,501 career plate appearances. His career batting average was .271 and his on-base percentage .297.

Athletics manager Connie Mack had tried to get Schreck the year before, according to a few April 1901 newspaper stories.[27] Now, in 1902, Mack had his man. In the first few years of building the American League, there were transactions and transitions that occurred for reasons that are opaque to us today.

A few weeks after he joined Philadelphia, Schreck became reunited with Rube Waddell, who joined the Athletics on June 19. One of their most productive pairings on the field in 1902 came against Boston on July 9 when Bill Dinneen and Waddell each pitched all 17 innings in Boston, a game that went to Waddell, 4–2. Schreck was 4-for-6 and was involved in couple of the runs. He drove in the first Athletics run and then tripled in the top of the 17th and came in on Rube's

Schrecongost with the 1906 Philadelphia Athletics.

long fly for the fourth run of the game. His two-out double (some papers had it as a triple) in the ninth won another game for Waddell on July 18 against the White Sox. He was literally carried off the field on the shoulders of the crowd.[28] And on the 21st, his single in the ninth gave Waddell another "W."

Philadelphia won the 1902 pennant and Waddell was 24-7, with a 2.05 ERA, both being the best marks on the club — all those victories coming in two-thirds of a season, given that he'd only arrived a little after mid-June. Waddell was a pretty good hitter, too, batting .286 in 1902. Winning the pennant didn't take the team to the World Series. It was only the following year, in 1903, when Boston and Pittsburgh squared off in the postseason that the modern "World's Series" began. Shreck and Rube had become roommates and began to have associations away from the Athletics, too. The two picked up a little more cash playing a pair of late September and early October games for the Camden, New Jersey, ballclub.

Newspapers had generally dropped "Schrecongost" a year or two earlier and adopted "Schreck" or a mangled "Schreckengost" in their stories. Baseball researchers need to hunt for all three names. One of Osee's nicknames was "Rocking Horse," which began when Williamsport teammate Humphries had called him that, in mispronouncing his name, wrote the *Philadelphia Inquirer* in explaining why cartoonist Charles Bell always showed Schreck on a rocking horse.[29]

Boston won the pennant and the World Series in 1903; the Athletics finished second, but 14 1/2 games behind. Schreck fell off sharply in his batting, dropping from .324 to .255. He played in 13 more games than in 1902, but drove in 30 percent fewer runs (30 instead of 43) and scored 42 percent fewer runs (26, down from 45). And in 1904, he played in 95 games and saw his production drop yet further: hitting just .186, driving in 21 and scoring 23. He improved his defensive work behind home plate, however, climbing in fielding percentage from .960 to .975 and .979. Schreck had an unusual style of catching one-handed, and somehow managed to deal quite well with Waddell's unpredictable pitches. The eccentric pitcher didn't always throw the ball as signaled. Teammate Harry Davis wrote of Schreck after Waddell and the catcher had died, "There are very few catchers today who can catch one ball if they are crossed in this manner, particularly with the gloved hand alone, as Schreck invariably did."[30]

Schreck was also noted for his success in throwing out would-be basestealers. There was even one time that injuries to the other catchers forced him to play despite a broken finger on his throwing hand, and he managed to throw out a St. Louis batter attempting to steal second on him. Davis recalled opposing manager Jimmy McAleer exclaiming, "What is the use, they can beat us with a one-armed catcher."[31]

Waddell was clearly a great pitcher, accurate but also deceptive. Schreck had been known to say that "on days when Rube's fast ball was right all the batsmen would hit so far under it that he could see an inch or two of daylight when the bat and the ball as the latter shot by."[32]

Waddell was fortunate to be able to pitch at all in 1903. During spring training in Jacksonville, he and Schreck were sitting on a pier watching the waves, when Waddell suddenly said, "Ossie, I believe I will jump in here and commit suicide." Schreck said, "Go ahead, it will be a good thing." He jumped, fully dressed, and narrowly missed several piles sticking out of the water which had long spikes on them. "When he came up he walked out on the beach and, taking a soggy baseball, proceeded to amuse the spectators by splitting a board with terrific drives from his arm." He then went out on the pier and plunged off it again.[33]

In July Rube suddenly left the Athletics and started playing for a team of college players in Atlantic City. He said Schreck was going to join him.[34] Cooler heads prevailed, and Waddell got married instead and spent Sunday, July 12, with Mr. and Mrs. Schrecongost and a volunteer fireman from Atlantic City named William Stephany.[35] He threw a 2–0 shutout against the White Sox on the 14th.

They were roommates, but the notion that they were inseparable was decried by Athletics first baseman Harry Davis: "This was not so. 'Rube' seldom went anywhere with any of the ball players. He preferred to travel with the many friends he had who were in no way connected with the game. Schreck only went along when Waddell was asked to bring his catcher with him, and that might not happen more than once or twice in a season."[36]

They were both eccentric, though, and the most widely circulated story regarding them as roommates (sharing a double bed, as baseball roommates often did in those days) is that Waddell refused to sign an Athletics contract one year unless manager Mack agreed to prohibit Schreck from eating animal crackers in bed. Another version had Schreck voicing that complaint about the Rube.[37]

There's another tale that had Schreck getting a very tough steak at a hotel restaurant in Cleveland. He sent it back, and the same steak came back again, presented differently. After the third visit of the steak proved equally difficult to cut, he asked the waiter, "Say, can you get me a hammer and some nails?" He then took the steak, and the hammer and nails, into the hotel lobby and nailed the steak to the wall.[38]

Schreck sold cigars during the winter after the 1902 and 1903 seasons.[39] His application for a liquor license was rejected in April 1904.[40] And the cigar business was said to be why his last name became truncated: "Owing to the limits of the building in which he does a cigar business, the Athletic backstop sawed his sign name down to O. Schreck."[41]

The year, 1904, had been a true down year, with Schreck hitting that .186, and three of the outs he made came early in the season, on May 5, when he, Waddell and the other Athletics were victims of Cy Young, who pitched a perfect game in Boston.

Osee's 1905 season got off to a halting start. He missed most of spring training, with his father dying and then, not long after he returned to camp, his sister, Annie, died and he had to go back home once more.[42]

Things turned around in 1905. Schreck hit .271, drove in 45 runs, improved his fielding percentage to .984 in 123 games, and helped roommate Waddell post a 27-10 record with an ERA of 1.48 (leading the league in wins and ERA), and helping boost the Athletics from 1904's fifth place to the pennant. He set a record, catching 29 innings in one day, on July 4, 1905, in Boston. This year was his worst one, though, for working bases on balls. He came to the plate 429 times and walked just three times.

Schreck caught the first three games of the 1905 World Series against the New York Giants, hitting .222. Waddell missed the last month of the season and the Series, and the Giants won it in five games. Alcohol played a factor in things falling apart near the end of Waddell's season. Connie Mack was reported to have felt compelled to hire a bodyguard for Waddell "to keep the Rube straight as possible, and now the latter's catcher, Ossie Schreckengost, has also fallen from grace."[43] He had been "breaking the temperance clause in his contract."[44] Schreck's .222 in the Series may not seem impressive, but was second only to Topsy Hartsel's .235 on an Athletics team that hit only .155. The Athletics scored just three runs in the five games, all in Game Two, and all the runs were unearned (Schreck scored two of them); they were shut out three times by Christy Mathewson.

Despite not being present over the final weeks, save for starting in a loss on October 7, Waddell had nonetheless won 27 games, his fourth year in a row as a 20-game winner. There was discussion that winter of Rube and Schreck performing in a vaudeville show called *The Battery*.[45] It's not clear if the show was ever staged.

The Athletics finished fourth in 1906, 12 games out of first place. Schreck had hit for a better average, .284, and been more productive in the games he played, but he appeared in 98 games, down 25 from 1905. And there were some suggestions that he hurt the team significantly. Sportswriter Francis C. Richter, writing from Philadelphia, told *Sporting Life*: "Mack sent catcher Schreck home from St. Louis because he remained out all night on September 21 without the knowledge or consent of the manager. The latter made no bones of saying that Schreck had misconducted himself frequently during the second half of the season; that his conduct was

one of the chief causes of the breakdown, and that Schreck stood suspended for balance of season."[46] Schreck said he had done no drinking, but merely stayed overnight with some "old-time German friends." One suspects the discipline was not the result of just one infraction. A month earlier, Richter had written, "Schreck appears to have let down all round."[47]

Whatever other issues may have obtained, perhaps Schreck had simply passed his peak in terms of play on the field. The stats he put up in 1907 were comparable to 1906: .272 instead of .284, three fewer RBIs, one more run scored, and he improved on defense to a .985 fielding percentage, remarkably high for a catcher.[48] He did suffer what at first, seemed to be a broken thumb on July 13, but it turned out to be just one which was "mashed"; he still played in 101 games.

In 71 games in 1908, Schreck hit .222 for the Athletics, with only 16 RBIs. Near the end of the season, he was ready to leave Philadelphia "and had outlived his welcome with the fans of that city," so Mr. Mack placed him on waivers.[49] One wonders what else was going on with the team; an August 1 story in *Sporting Life* said, "[h]alf a dozen of the Athletics have shaved their heads to stall off baldness. Schreck mowed a four-inch swathe along the middle of his scalp." There were indeed recurring notes in his last few years that made it clear Schreck had a problem with alcohol.

Only one team claimed him off waivers—the White Sox. He played in six games for them at the tail end of 1908 and had three singles in 16 at-bats, suffering a true broken finger in the bottom of the eighth inning on October 2. A spitball from Big Ed Walsh was the culprit. Walsh was a 40-game winner in 1908, but lost this one to Addie Joss, who threw a perfect game. Schreck was on the losing end of another perfecto, and out for the season. It proved to be his last game in the major leagues.

On January 25, 1909, Chicago's owner Charles Comiskey traded Schreck to the Columbus Senators. He hit a far from impressive .203 in 60 games. Sold on April 19, 1910, Schreck began the season with Louisville and hit .207 in 71 games before he was traded for Emmet Reilly—sent all the way down to Class D ball, reporting on August 29 to play for the Marion Diggers in the Ohio State League. There Schreck hit .275 in 29 games, and left Organized Baseball. His arm had "gone back on him completely," according to a June 20, 1911, story in the *Washington Evening Star* that had him playing with an independent team in Ford City, Pennsylvania. He also did some scouting for Connie Mack—and, along with scout Al Maul, is credited with signing Shoeless Joe Jackson to the Athletics in 1908.[50] According to the story, Schreck started traveling north with Jackson to bring him to Philadelphia, but when they got as far north as Charlotte, Jackson was getting homesick and jumped off the train, hiding from Schreck.

Schreck did sign to play for York in February 1913 and may have played some for teams not in Organized Baseball. It's not clear if he ever played for York.

Just as Schreck's father and sister had died one not long after the other in 1905, so it was for Rube Waddell and Osee Schrecongost in 1914. It appears that both neglected their health. Waddell died of tuberculosis in San Antonio on April 1, 1914. When he learned of the pitcher's death, Schreck is reported to have said, "The Rube is gone and I am all in. I might as well join him."[51]

One hundred days later, on July 9, 1914, Osee Schrecongost died "of a complication of diseases" at Northwestern General Hospital in Philadelphia—the same hospital where Doc Power, the other main catcher on the Athletics during Schreck's years, had died in 1909, at age 38. Schreck was 39.

He had collapsed around noon the day before in a local café. His constitution had been undermined. The City of Philadelphia death certificate indicates heart disease and Bright's disease, a kidney disease. Uremia was noted in newspaper accounts at the time. The death certificate notes that he was divorced. He is buried in Kittaning Cemetery. His mother survived him, and lived until 1927.

After the loss of Rube and Schreck within such a short time span, *Sporting Life* averred: "Waddell and Schreck, when they were working right were almost unbeatable. Shreck's most notable trait was that he was the only catcher who could make Waddell pitch his best. If their habits had been on a par with their professional skill, Rube and Shreck would probably be alive and playing ball today."[52]

Sources

In addition to the sources noted in this biography, the author also accessed Schrecongost's player file from the National Baseball Hall of Fame, the *Encyclopedia of Minor League Baseball*, Retrosheet.org, and Baseball-Reference.com.

Notes

1. Dan O'Brien, "F. Osee Schrecongost," in David Jones, ed., *Deadball Stars of the American League* (Dulles, Virginia: Potomac Books, 2006), 600. Presented in the book is Schrecongost's signature, and that is the way he signed his name.
2. *Sporting Life*, December 21, 1895.
3. The *Bethlehem Leader-Vindicator* reports that he had gone to Augusta later in 1896, though—and more likely—*Sporting Life* that December had him as up-and-coming still with Williamsport.
4. *Sporting Life*, May 1 and May 15, 1897.
5. *Boston Herald*, July 8, 1897.
6. *Boston Herald*, August 5, 1897.
7. *Philadelphia Inquirer*, September 8, 1897.
8. See, for instance, the *Cleveland Leader* of September 9, 1897.
9. *Baltimore Sun*, September 9, 1897.
10. *Washington Evening Star*, September 10, 1897.
11. *Boston Herald*, May 19, 1899.
12. The quotation comes from *Sporting Life*, September 24, 1898. The date of the release comes from the May 7 *Boston Herald*.
13. *Sporting Life*, December 17, 1898.
14. *Sporting Life*, March 18, 1899.
15. *Sporting Life*, June 17, 1899.
16. *Base Ball*, July 8, 1899.
17. *Sporting Life*, July 15, 1899.
18. *Washington Post*, August 13, 1899. The "Ghost" nickname seems not to have stuck.
19. *Sporting Life*, August 5, 1899.
20. *Cleveland Leader*, August 8, 1899. Over a year later, Donlin offered a whole different take on what happened, saying the row had been in Philadelphia, between Burkett and Schreck, and resulted in those two becoming fast friends, though he did admit to punching Schreck in Pittsburgh. See *Sporting Life*, November 17, 1900.
21. The May 5, 1900, *Boston Herald* characterized Schreck's assignment to Buffalo as having been farmed out by St. Louis, as had other papers such as the *Rockford Republic* of April 27. He also played eight games in the outfield and one at third base.
22. *Boston Herald*, March 5, 1901.
23. *Boston Herald*, September 29, 1902.
24. *Washington Post*, February 5, 1902.
25. His release was reported in the May 14 *Cincinnati Post*.
26. There was a moment when it appeared Schreck was going to play for Worcester instead of Philadelphia; the May 20 *Cleveland Leader* reported that he'd accepted terms with Worcester, but it wasn't to be.
27. See, for instance, the *Pawtucket Times* and the *Boston Herald* of April 26, 1901.

28 *Sporting Life*, July 26, 1902.

29 *Philadelphia Inquirer*, August 29, 1904.

30 *Springfield Republican*, August 2, 1914.

31 Ibid.

32 *Sporting Life*, April 11, 1914.

33 *Denver Post*, May 15, 1903.

34 *Cincinnati Post*, July 10, 1903.

35 *Philadelphia Inquirer*, July 14, 1903.

36 *Washington Post*, August 23, 1914.

37 Norman Macht, *Connie Mack and the Early Years of Baseball* (Lincoln: University of Nebraska Press, 2007), 337.

38 *Bethlehem Leader-Vindicator*, September 8, 1999. Walzak likely got the story from the unidentified November 7, 1929, clipping found in Schrecongost's player file at the Hall of Fame.

39 *Washington Evening Star*, October 13, 1903.

40 *Philadelphia Inquirer*, April 19, 1904.

41 Whether true or not, we are unsure, because the source of the story was reportedly Charles Dryden of the *Philadelphia North American*, a sportswriter frequently given to wild flights of fanciful fiction. See *Sporting Life*, June 4, 1904.

42 Norman Macht, *Connie Mack and the Early Years of Baseball*, 339.

43 *Denver Post*, September 25, 1905.

44 Ibid.

45 *Washington Post*, November 5, 1905, and *Sporting Life*, November 11, 1905.

46 *Sporting Life*, September 29, 1906.

47 *Sporting Life*, August 25, 1906.

48 Shrecongost had almost 200 more chances than the second-place catcher in this category. This is almost exclusively due to Philadelphia pitchers striking out almost 200 more batters than the next best pitching staff. Since it is very difficult for a catcher to make an error on a strikeout, Schreck's outstanding fielding percentage is largely the due to his battery mates.

49 *Sporting Life*, October 31, 1908.

50 *Sporting Life*, July 25 and August 1, 1908, and the *New Orleans Times-Picayune*, August 18, 1912.

51 *Bethlehem Leader-Vindicator*, September 8, 1999.

52 *Sporting Life*, July 18, 1914.

Jack Slattery

By Bill Nowlin

JACK SLATTERY WAS the only man on the 1901 Boston Americans who was born in Boston (and, as of 2010, one of only 16 natives of the city to play for Boston's American League team.) Slattery just barely qualified, only getting into a game on the very last day of the franchise's first season. In the first game of a doubleheader against the Milwaukee Brewers, catching George Winter, Jack got up to bat three times and got one hit, driving in Freddy Parent for a run with a third-inning single. He drew a walk in another plate appearance and scored a run later in the game. He handled five chances without an error, three putouts (strikeouts by Winter) and two assists. A foul tip split his thumb in the eighth inning and he was forced to leave the game, Osee Schrecongost taking his place and catching the second game as well. Boston won both games of the doubleheader, 8-3 and 10-9. The team finished in second place.

John Thomas "Jack" Slattery came out of South Boston, where he was born on January 6, 1878. One could say he lived a life devoted to horsehide and leather. His father, John, a merchant tailor in men's clothing, had come to the New World from Ireland. His mother, Ellen, was from Foxboro, Massachusetts. Jack had four brothers and two sisters. Brother Robert worked for a while as a stage manager at a Boston-area theater, Frank worked as a commercial traveler dealing in hay and grain, Mary worked for a while as a tailor, and Marcella was a public school teacher; the others went into the leather business.

Slattery played ball around Boston, and for Boston College in 1896-1898, playing first base and catching. One local area match after school got out was interesting. On June 11, 1898, he led off and collected three hits, stole a base, and scored twice for the South Boston AA team in a 17-6 win over the Bankers and Brokers at the Locust Street grounds. The Bankers and Brokers pitcher was Jack Dooley, father of Lib Dooley. Both Jack and Lib had a long history with Red Sox baseball stretching into the 21st century.[1] Slattery graduated from college with a degree in dentistry that he'd begun at Fordham.

Jack Slattery played in one game for the 1901 Bostons.

That's where he caught the eye of several scouts which catching for the Fordham nine in 1899 and 1900. He may have also caught the eye of a Boston scout while catching for Attleboro in the summer of 1901. His batterymate for the July 6 game was Win Kellum, who just a little more than two months earlier had been the starting pitcher in the first game ever played by the 1901 Boston Americans. Kellum's game against North Attleboro was the "finest ever seen on the local grounds," according to the July 14 *Boston Globe*.

Before December was out, Slattery signed again for the 1902 Americans, and started the season with the team but never saw any action. Collins decided to go with Lou Criger and John Warner behind the plate, so Slattery was available for play in the New York State League and was signed to Gloversville in late June.[2]

In 1902, Slattery was catching in the New York State League, working under manager (and 1901 Boston teammate) Tommy Dowd for the unwieldy-named Amsterdam-Gloversville-Johnstown Jags. The Jags wound up in last place. Slattery and William Stroh shared backstop duties, with Jack hitting .342 in 257 at-bats over the course of 62 games. He started the 1903 season with the Columbus Senators of the American Association, and was called up to Cleveland in early May. He hardly saw any work—11 at-bats without a hit in four games—and was released on May 29, to keep the roster down to 15 men. A few days later, Charles Comiskey of the White Sox signed Jack up for fill-in duties with Chicago when backup catcher Billy Sullivan underwent an operation for appendicitis. Ed McFarland was the other catcher on the team, but a month later the *Chicago Tribune* wrote, "Young Slattery has been doing the better work of the two, all things considered."[3] Then McFarland became ill, so Comiskey and manager Nixey Sullivan had to add another backup, named Felton, to stand behind Slattery. For the 1903 White Sox, Slattery hit .218 in 63 games. He played first base in a handful of games.

Right at the end of spring training in 1904, on April 13, the White Sox sold Slattery to the Milwaukee Brewers and he spent the season in the American Association. He played a pretty full season of 125 games, batting .263, and had his first three home runs as a pro. In 1905, Slattery doesn't show up in the record books at all, though a July 13 story in the *Washington Post* said that Clark Griffith had signed him to be ready in a backup role with the Senators. It was to be a two-week rental at $1,000 a week.[4] Both stories proved premature. Slattery never came to Chicago. Griffith reportedly went to Milwaukee himself to try to straighten matters out but "found the player so badly enmeshed in a baseball tangle that he decided he did not want to shoulder the trouble."[5] Slattery had simply chosen to stay out of Organized Ball rather than report to Milwaukee after the Brewers proffered him a contract that cut his pay from $1,800 to $1,000 a year, and played with the Coatesville ballclub in the outlaw Tri-State League. The National Commission ruled that Slattery was still property of the Milwaukee club, so the Brewers reserved him and the St. Louis Cardinals claimed him in the draft. Once more, the National Commission commented, this time saying the Cardinals had clear title to him. Then the Commission decided Slattery himself needed to apply for reinstatement to Organized Baseball.[6]

Another report said that Slattery was with the New York Americans "for about two days last summer."[7] More than three months later, he'd still not heard from the Cardinals, according to the *Boston Globe*.

Slattery worked things out and appeared in all of three games, in May, for the Cardinals, but spent most of 1906 with Toronto and Kansas City, not excelling in either location. The 1907 season was split between the Johnstown Johnnies (.203) and the Sioux City Packers (.326 despite being Class A instead of Class B ball). Slattery spent 1908 on the West Coast, playing in the Pacific Coast League for the Oakland Oaks and getting in a full season's work, some 99 games, hitting a sturdy .331. There he primarily played first base, since an arm injury had hampered his throwing to some extent. After the 1908 season, he came back home, playing in 1909 in the New England League for most of the summer—for the Lawrence Colts and the New Bedford Whalers (under Tommy Dowd again).

Joe Cantillon managed Washington in 1909 and gave Jack his last shot at the major leagues. In mid-August he was looking for a catcher and Germany Schaefer told him Slattery was playing well and working out every day in the Boston area, so Cantillon wired him and never heard back—until a day or two later when Slattery turned up unannounced.[8] He hit .214 in 56 at-bats. In November, he was told that Washington wouldn't be sending him a contract for 1910.

It was north of the border to Toronto in 1910 and Slattery played in an even 100 Eastern League games, hitting .310. He hit .343 in 15 games for the Maple Leafs in 1911. Why he didn't play more hasn't yet been discerned. He didn't play ball at all, unless it was in one of the outlaw leagues, until 1916 and 1917 when he caught for the Montreal Royals. There was some wild and woolly baseball, and he wrote up a couple of stories—including one where the umpire was thrown in the showers after a game in Williamsport.[9] At the time of the column, Slattery had put in his application

Slattery in 1903.

to manage the Brockton club. He officially retired from the game that year.

Instead of taking up his intended trade of dental work, Slattery coached baseball at Tufts (hired in January 1914 through 1917), spurning offers from Dartmouth and Princeton and building the Jumbos into a team to be reckoned with. Though he still had a couple of years to run on his contract with Tufts, the university let him leave to take a position coaching and scouting for the Boston Braves starting in 1918. That lasted two years, after which Slattery took over from Hugh Duffy as baseball coach at Harvard from 1920 to 1924. During the summers, when college was over, he continued to be a "seasonal scout" for the Braves. In June 1924, he accepted a position to coach Boston College baseball, which he did from 1925 to 1927, when the Braves beckoned again. On November 2, 1927, after Dave Bancroft resigned, Jack Slattery was named manager of the Boston Braves, given a one-year contract—and Hugh Duffy took his place at BC.

Slattery's managerial tenure with the Braves didn't last long. One of the things he did before the season got under way was to name Rogers Hornsby, recently traded over from the New York Giants, to captain the team, and he announced that the two would room together when the team was on the road.[10] Strangely, Slattery was called back to Boston just before spring training ended, the first time anyone could recall a manager being summoned back to the team offices at such a juncture. The Braves' owner, Judge Emil Fuchs, said it was to discuss some trades and denied it was because he was replacing his manager before the season began. Hornsby was made interim manager. Everyone denied there was friction between the two, and the season got under way. But on May 23, Slattery resigned and Hornsby was named the new manager. Fuchs said he hoped Slattery would stay with the team. The Braves had gotten off to a bad start, and there was worry that Boston fans were shifting in droves to the Red Sox. When Fuchs hired Slattery, it was before he knew that the more colorful "draw" Hornsby might be available. It was an awkward situation, and Slattery had a lot of support from people around Boston who felt he'd been treated shabbily. It was likely no coincidence that Boston College decided to play its football games at Fenway Park rather than Braves Field.[11] For his part, Jack and his brother William took a cruise to Europe (Jack was being paid his contract without needing to work). After the 1928 season was over, Fuchs traded Hornsby to the Cubs for five players—and announced that he himself would manage the team in 1929. That didn't happen, but that's another story. His first act as manager was to invite youth from the area to attend a baseball school that the Braves were sponsoring, which would be run by … Jack Slattery.[12]

Slattery then spent 20 years working with his brothers William and Robert at the Slattery Brothers leather firm in Boston. They had one sister who married, and another, Mary, who did not and with whom Jack lived in Jamaica Plain until the time of his passing.

Slattery died of pulmonary edema at Boston City Hospital on July 17, 1949. He had been suffering from atherosclerosis (hardening of the arteries) and both chronic bronchitis and emphysema. He never married. The particulars on the death certificate were supplied by his brother Robert.

Sources

In addition to the sources cited in this biography, the author consulted Jack Slattery's player file at the National Baseball Hall of Fame, the online SABR Encyclopedia, retrosheet.org, and Baseball-Reference.com.

Notes

1 *Boston Globe*, June 12, 1898. For more on the Dooleys, see this author's *Red Sox Threads*.
2 *Boston Globe*, June 21, 1902.
3 *Chicago Tribune*, August 2, 1903.
4 *Chicago Tribune*, July 15, 1902.
5 *Washington Post*, July 19, 1905.
6 Unattributed April 21, 1906, clipping found in Slattery's Hall of Fame player file.
7 *Atlanta Constitution*, December 3, 1905.
8 *Washington Post*, August 15, 1909.
9 *Boston Globe*, February 7, 1913.
10 *New York Times*, February 22, 1928.
11 *Washington Post*, October 19, 1928.
12 *Atlanta Constitution*, November 9, 1928.

Chick Stahl

by Dennis Auger

Before committing suicide under mysterious circumstances in the spring of 1907, Chick Stahl forged a reputation as one of the best center fielders in the game over the course of a 10-year major-league career. A lifetime .305 batter, the left-handed Stahl could also hit with power, and often ranked among the league leaders in extra-base hits. Among his teammates, the popular Stahl "possessed a pleasing personality that endeared him to all that came in contact with him." When the 34-year-old ballplayer killed himself on March 28, 1907, his Boston teammates were overcome with grief. "Stahl was a king among men," said catcher Lou Criger. "He was the squarest man I ever knew. He had only one fault—he was too generous. I never saw him go back on a friend or a deserving acquaintance. In fact, he was often bunkoed because he believed in the goodness of all mankind."

Charles Sylvester Stahl was born on January 10, 1873, in Avilla, Indiana, the sixth child of Reuben and Barbara (Stadtmiller) Stahl, Catholics of German descent. During his early childhood, his father supported the growing Stahl clan as a peddler, but in 1885 the family moved to Fort Wayne, where Reuben found work as a carpenter. In an 1898 interview, Charles reported that he had 23 siblings. "We had just enough in our family to make a couple nines—eighteen boys and half a dozen girls."

Young Charles attended Catholic school and developed his skills as a left-handed pitcher and outfielder on Fort Wayne's vacant lots and diamonds south of the railroads. After playing for Brunswick, a local amateur team, in 1889 the teenager pitched for the Pilsener club in the City League. Between 1889 and 1894, he also pitched for semiprofessional teams in Paducah, Kentucky; Decatur, Illinois; and Kalamazoo and Battle Creek, Michigan. He also worked in his father's carpentry business. His father wanted him "to tend store at Fort Wayne and give up baseball. But I took an inventory of the soft soap sale and the output of pickles to our customers, and I couldn't figure how I could turn out

Chick Stahl with the Boston Beaneaters before coming over to the American League, circa 1897.

the revenue in the grocery business that came to me in baseball."

In 1895, Stahl signed a professional contract with Roanoke of the Virginia League. At his own insistence, he became a full-time outfielder, and excelled at his new position, playing brilliantly in the field, posting a .311 batting average, and leading the league with 13 triples. His performance attracted the attention of the Buffalo team of the Eastern League, which drafted the young outfielder after the season. In 1896 Stahl continued to show improvement with his new team, finishing the year with a .340 average, 34 stolen bases, 52 extra-base hits, a league-leading 23 triples, and 130 runs scored. Based on Stahl's "splendid hitting and excellent fielding," Jimmy Collins, the star third baseman of the Boston Beaneaters, and Sam Wise, a former Beaneaters player, advised Beaneaters manager Frank Selee to draft him, and Selee did so.

Selee planned to use Stahl in a utility role, but the 24-year old quickly became the club's starting right fielder. In 1897 he emerged "as the game's most outstanding frosh hitter." Not only did he lead all rookies in 11 hitting categories, he also paced Boston with a .354 average, a mark that remains the franchise record for rookies. Stahl also topped the Beaneaters with a .499 slugging percentage, helping the Boston offense score more than 1,000 runs and capture the National League pennant. Another crown awaited Boston in 1898, and even though Stahl's average declined to .308, his fielding talents were highlighted in the sports pages. In one descriptive account, the *Washington Post* wrote "the soubrette fancier from Fort Wayne retrieved Tommy Leahy's fly in the eighth with the speed and celerity of a hound retrieving a jack rabbit." The Beaneaters fell from first in 1899 but the Husky Hoosier (one of Stahl's nicknames), hit .351, produced career highs in hits (202), triples (19), home runs (7), total bases (284), walks (72), on-base percentage (.426), stolen bases (33), and runs scored (122). On May 31 he went 6-for-6 in a nine-inning game against Cleveland, "five of which [were] very long drives."

Boston's fortunes tumbled in 1900 but Stahl still knocked in 82 runs, his second highest career total, and led National League outfielders with a .968 fielding percentage. In 1901 his teammate and best friend, Jimmy Collins, signed with the American League's Boston entry to become that squad's player-manager. Because of religious tension on the Beaneaters, the third baseman targeted talented Roman Catholic ball players to join the upstart club. Considered a devout Catholic as well as one of the National League's best outfielders, Chick fulfilled the criteria. Moving to center field, the intracity jumper became one of the Americans' main offensive threats while helping the squad to a second-place finish (.303 batting average, 105 runs scored, 72 RBIs). As for the character of 5-foot-10-inch, 160-pound athlete, it was demonstrated in a late August contest. After rookie umpire Joe Cantillon made a call that went against the home team, furious Boston fans assaulted him. Stahl and teammate Ted Lewis intervened, protecting Cantillon and escorting him off the field.

Stahl coached Notre Dame's college baseball team from January to April of 1900—leading them to a 15-2 record—he spent his offseasons primarily in Fort Wayne. On the evening of January 26, 1902, while he was walking with a friend in his hometown, Louise "Lulu" Ortmann, a 22-year-old stenographer, approached him. Described as "a very handsome girl," she reached for a revolver concealed in the folds of her dress, with the intent of killing him. The local police superintendent, who had been tipped off that the infuriated woman was stalking Stahl, arrived just in time to disarm and arrest her. In accounting for her actions, Ortmann said she felt jilted by her "recreant lover." "Mr. Stahl, on the other hand, had nothing to say" and dropped any charges. This episode did not affect his 1902 season, as Stahl batted .323 with 92 runs scored and the Americans finished in third place.

In April 1903 Stahl injured his leg while sliding, and was limited to 77 games and a .274 average. Nevertheless, the Americans easily won the pennant. In the World Series against Pittsburgh, which Boston won in eight

Chick Stahl at the 1903 World Series with Boston's Royal Rooters encroaching on the roof over the players' bench.

Chick Stahl.

games, he was the only Boston player to hit .300, as he banged out 10 hits, including three triples, in 33 at-bats.

Stahl's health improved in 1904 and the outfielder returned to his old form with a .290 batting average, 27 doubles, and a league-leading 19 triples, as the Americans captured a second consecutive pennant. Stahl also showcased his glove during Cy Young's perfect game on May 5 against Philadelphia. After the game Young expressed his gratitude for Stahl's play on a sinking line drive off the bat of Ollie Pickering "that Chick caught around his knees after a long run from center."

Along with many of his teammates, Stahl's play declined precipitously in 1905. He finished the year with a .258 batting average—by far the lowest of his career—and only 21 extra-base hits. The next season he improved to .286 with four home runs and 51 RBI, while leading American League outfielders in putouts and double plays. The Americans, however, won just 49 games, and Stahl became the acting manager in late August after the suspension of the increasingly disenchanted Jimmy Collins. One scribe wrote that Stahl was "the only man on the team who played his real game this season." In what turned out to be his last major-league at-bat, he hit a home run off Tom Hughes of the New York Highlanders.

On November 14, 1906, Stahl married Julia Harmon at St. Francis de Sales Church in the Roxbury section of Boston. They had met at a church function and she was described as "a pretty little brunette" and accomplished musician. Their honeymoon took them to Arkansas' Hot Springs and ended as guests of Jimmy Collins in Buffalo. The other significant event during this month was that Stahl, at the urging of owner John Taylor and with the approval of his closest friend Collins, accepted the manager's position for the coming season.

In 1907 the Chicks, as the team was nicknamed in deference to their manager (they wouldn't become the Red Sox until 1908), reported to Little Rock, Arkansas, for spring training. It soon became evident that Stahl's personality and the duties required of a manager were incompatible. On March 25, with the team in Louisville, Stahl abruptly resigned. Explaining his decision, he said, "This handling of a baseball team both on and off the field is not what it is cracked up to be. Releasing players grated on my nerves and they come so frequently at this time of the year that it made me sick at heart." On March 27 the team arrived at West Baden Springs, Indiana, where they were to play the next day. Having agreed to serve as acting manager until a replacement could be found, Stahl said in a telegram to his wife that night, "Cheer up little girl and be happy. I am all right now and able to play the game of my life."

The next morning Stahl ate breakfast, checked the condition of the field, and returned to the hotel room to put on his uniform. Jimmy Collins, who shared the suite, saw Stahl go into the next room for a moment, then stumble back toward Collins and fall onto his bed. He had swallowed four ounces of carbolic acid, which had been prescribed for a sore on his foot. There are a number of variations, but Stahl's last words were, "I couldn't help it. I did it, Jim. It was killing me and I couldn't stand it, Jim." In another version Stahl simply said cryptically, "It drove me to it." Medical help arrived, but to no avail. Stahl suffered excruciating pain, dying in 15 minutes from poisoning. Since the death was ruled a suicide, a Catholic burial was denied. On March 31 the funeral rite, conducted by the Benevolent Order of Elks and the Fraternal Order of Eagles, took place at Stahl's mother's residence. The emotional state of the two women he had loved most "were pathetic in the extreme," according to one newspaper account. "The young bride of a few months was almost prostrated and the grief of the aged mother of the deceased was pitiful to behold." Five former teammates—Criger, Buck Freeman, Bill Dinneen, Freddy Parent, and Jake Stahl (no relation)—attended, but Collins was too distraught to be present. Stahl's body was conveyed to Lindenwood Cemetery "in one of the largest funeral corteges ever seen in Fort Wayne." Thousands marched to the burial place, where Congressman James Robinson gave the eulogy.

Why did Stahl commit suicide? Initially, baseball-related stress was given as the reason, but soon other theories began to surface. Frederick P. O'Connell, the baseball editor of the *Boston Post*, contended that a nonbaseball factor had led to his suicide. He wrote, "a great trouble was generally admitted" which was known to many. The truth was never known, as O'Connell developed pneumonia while in West Baden covering Stahl's funeral, and died there on April 21. Glenn Stout, a baseball historian who has written about the Red Sox, wrote that the "trouble" referred to a brief affair that Stahl had with a woman in Chicago in 1906 and its aftermath. In March 1907 the woman, claiming she was carrying Stahl's child, threatened to blackmail him unless he married her. Unable to deal with the pressure and scandal, he ended his life. Stout cited another historian, Harold Seymour, who wrote, "There is reason to believe that a woman who asserted she was his pregnant wife hounded Chick Stahl into committing suicide." Seymour provided no documentation. Stout also cited David Voigt, another baseball historian, who accepted the theory, referring to a 1959 quote from Al Stump, similar in content and with no identifiable source. In short, all of the historians provided an inconclusive theory based on questionable allegations.

From *Boston Herald* newspaper caption, March 6, 1907: Boston Americans Leaving Their Hotel at Little Rock Bound for the Game. In the left in the immediate foreground is seen the massive figure of Hobe Farris, with Nuf Ced McGreevy next in line. Beyond, on the same side, are Sullivan, Al Shaw and Hoey. To the right the first profile is that of Jimmy Barrett, and looking further down the line, sitting together may be seen in order, Bob Unglaub, Manager Stahl and Jimmy Collins. Way up in the right hand corner, looking down the car, is old Cy Young.

The most significant contribution in examining Stahl's suicide came from baseball researcher Dick Thompson, who uncovered a crucial story in the *Fort Wayne Journal-Gazette* of March 30, 1907. In an article that ran with the headlines "MEDITATED SELF-SLAYING, CHICK STAHL HAD OFTEN TALKED ABOUT SUICIDE," and "BASE BALL PLAYER HAD ENTERTAINED DANGEROUS IDEAS ABOUT SELF-DESTRUCTION," the paper wrote that Stahl had suffered from depression and suicidal ideation since 1889. The paper quoted close friends "who were not surprised at his suicide." Statements ranging from "Chick talked about killing himself several times" to "sometimes the slightest disappointment would sink him into almost a stupor of depression" appear to confirm that he suffered from clinical depression.

This glimpse into Stahl's psyche helps us to understand his behavior. If his reputation as a womanizer was true, clinically, it is not unusual for a depressed person to self-medicate emotional pain through unbridled sexual activity. Also, since baseball was an integral dimension to Stahl's identity, his perceived failing as a manager could have intensified his depression. There is yet another element to the story. On March 30, 1907, a syndicated newspaper article related that David Murphy, an engineer in Fort Wayne, had committed suicide by swallowing carbolic acid. Stahl was described as "an intimate friend of Murphy," and the latter left a note that read, "Bury me beside Chick." From a psychological perspective, this language and behavior strongly indicates that the relationship was not merely a platonic one. Was Murphy delusional, resulting in an unreciprocated sexual obsession? Or, if it was mutual, was this Stahl's "dark secret"?

Chick Stahl a strong Catholic faith. As one newspaper report after his death said, "Stahl never forgot his religious duties during the baseball season. Only a week ago last Sunday, Stahl did his Easter duty in Little Rock. He never missed mass if it was possible for him to attend." To understand his behavior, it is important to realize that Jansenism, typically known for its ultra-rigid moral outlook and emphasis upon human nature as being corrupt, heavily influenced the nature of the Catholic Church during Stahl's lifetime. As a result, Stahl would have been exposed to teachings about God's love and forgiveness, countered by sermons regarding sins of the flesh and the fires of hell, with suicide being the ultimate sin. The unresolved conflict between his beliefs and behavior could have increased his inner turmoil and consequently his chronic depression. The healthy and unhealthy components of his persona were expressed during the last week of his earthly life, when he both fulfilled his Easter duty and committed suicide. As Thompson wrote, "I think O'Connell [the *Boston Post* writer] did know the truth, but the truth was not that Stahl was responding to a blackmail threat. It was that he was responding to his own haunted emotions."

Speaking to his teammates after the ballplayer's death, Cy Young—named temporary manager in Stahl's absence—said, "It is mighty tough, boys. I never dreamed such a thing could happen. In fact, none of us could imagine Stahl doing away with himself. Players may come and go, but there are few Chick Stahls."

Note

This biography originally appeared in David Jones, ed., *Deadball Stars of the American League* (Washington, D.C.: Potomac Books, Inc., 2006).

Sources

Boston Globe

Boston Post

Chicago Tribune

Evening Times (Pawtucket)

Journal-Gazette (Fort Wayne)

Los Angeles Times

New York Times

Washington Post

Browning, Reed. *Cy Young: A Baseball Life*. (Amherst, University of Massachusetts Press, 2000).

Carroll, Charles. *Drugs in Modern Society*. (Dubuque, Iowa: William C. Brown. 1989).

Carter, Craig ed. *The Sporting News Complete Baseball Record Book*. (St. Louis: Sporting News, 2001).

Christensen, Chris. "Chick Stahl: A Baseball Suicide," *Elysian Fields*, vol. 20, n. 2, 20-32, 2003.

DeValeria, Dennis, and Jeanne DeValeria. *Honus Wagner*. (Pittsburgh: University of Pittsburgh Press, 1998).

Gentile, Derek. *Baseball's Best 1000*. (New York: Black Dog & Leventhal Publishers, 2004).

James, Bill. *All-Time Major League Handbook*. 2nd ed. (Morton Grove, Illinois: STATS, Inc., 2002).

James, Bill. *The New Bill James Historical Baseball Abstract*. (New York: Free Press, 2001).

Kinney, Jean, and Gwen Leaton. *Understanding Alcohol*. (New York: Mosby, 1982).

Masur, Louis. *Autumn Glory: Baseball's First World Series*. (New York: Hill & Wang, 2003).

Neft, David, Richard Cohen, and Michael Neft, editors. *The Sports Encyclopedia: Baseball 1999*. New York, 1999.

Nemec, David, and David Zeman. *The Baseball Rookies Encyclopedia*. (Washington: Potomac Books, 2004).

Palmer, Pete, and Gary Gillette. *The Baseball Encyclopedia.* (New York: Barnes & Noble, 2004).

Reichler, Joseph. *The Baseball Encyclopedia.* 6th ed. (New York: Macmillan, 1985).

Reichler, Joseph. *The Great All-Time Baseball Record Book.* (New York: Macmillan, 1981).

Seymour, Harold. *Baseball—The Golden Age.* (New York: Oxford University Press, 1989).

Stout, Glenn, ed. *Impossible Dreams.* (Boston: Houghton Mifflin, 2003).

Stout, Glenn. "The Manager's End Game", *Sports in Massachusetts: Historical Essays*, 121-136. (Westfield, Massachusetts: Institute for Massachusetts Studies, 1991).

Stout, Glenn, and Richard Johnson. *Red Sox Century.* (Boston: Houghton Mifflin, 2000.)

Thompson, Dick. "In Name Only," in *The National Pastime*, n. 20 (2000), 54-57.

Thompson, Dick. "Stahl's Suicide," in *Baseball Research Journal*, n. 28 (1999), 7.

Thorn, John, Pete Palmer, and Michael Gershman. *Total Baseball.* 6th ed. (New York: Total Sports, 1999).

Wesson, Donald. *Detoxification from Alcohol and Other Drugs.* (Rockville, Maryland: U.S. Department of Health and Human Services, 1998).

Zoss, Joel, and John Bowman. *Diamonds in the Rough.* (Lincoln: Bison Books, 2004).

Heritage Quest

Chick Stahl's file from the Baseball Hall of Fame

Jake Volz

by Bill Nowlin

WITH A FOURTH-GRADE education from the Marshall Street school in San Antonio, Jake Volz did his family proud. Born in the city of San Antonio on April 4, 1878 to parents who had immigrated from Germany a little over 10 years earlier, Jacob Phillip Volz took up baseball as a youth and broke in professionally in 1898 for the Texas League's San Antonio Missionaries.

His parents are Michael (1836-1906) and Margretta (Hemes) Volz (1837-1914), both of whom immigrated from Prussia. Michael was a painter. Jacob was the youngest of seven children on the 1880 US census; there were five boys and two girls. The oldest two children were born in Prussia.[1]

In 1899, when the league was reorganized, Volz became "the first pitcher to sign with the new Texas League."[2] San Antonio's team was the Bronchos; Volz appeared in 26 games, showing some versatility. He pitched in 13 games, played outfield in 12, and second base in one game. Batting was not his forte; he hit .176. On the mound, Volz was 7-6 in 111 innings. He struck out 43 and walked 39. Earned runs were not compiled, but he'd allowed 74 runs with a WHIP (walks and hits per inning pitched) of 1.351, thanks in good part to all those walks. Twelve of his 13 pitching appearances were complete games.

Volz also turned up in one game that year for the Austin Senators, also in the Class C Texas League, starting and winning a complete game, allowing four runs on 10 hits (and four bases on balls.) He was a right-hander, listed as 5-feet-10 and 175 pounds. And someplace along the way, he picked up the nickname "Silent Jake."

What he did in 1900 is not clear; he wasn't in organized baseball. The 1900 census lists him living in Quincy, Gadsden County, Florida. He is listed as an engineer and is a boarder in the home of newspaper editor Thomas Scott. Two other men living in the home are

Jake Volz, with Manchester in 1902.

listed as baseball players but they do not appear to be in SABR's minor-league database.

Volz came to New England in 1901, playing for three teams during the baseball season. He began with the Portsmouth Browns in the Virginia-North Carolina League (Class C), but only briefly, listed as an infielder; SABR's minor league database is not able to offer a statistical record, though *Sporting Life* reflects his pitching a nice three-hitter against Norfolk on May 14. He spent most of the year pitching in 19 games for the Manchester, New Hampshire team in the New England League. We don't know how many he won, but he showed well enough that the Boston Americans signed him on August 16, asking him to report when Manchester's season was over.

Jake Volz's major-league debut came on September 28, 1901. It was the last game of the year, the second game of a doubleheader at Boston's Huntington Avenue

Grounds. Boston had won five games in a row, including an 8-3 victory in the first game. Game two was shortened by the onset of darkness, stopped after seven innings. In those seven innings, Volz had surrendered seven earned runs and two unearned ones. He'd only given up six hits, but he'd walked nine — and two of the hits were home runs. He struck out five of the 35 batters he faced. The *Boston Globe* spelled his name phonetically: "Voltz, the Manchester pitcher, was given a trial in the second game and proved very wild, giving nine bases on balls. He had a 'sweet william' delivery, that was taught him by some scientific man, but the conditions were not right and his kite was continually snapping off its tail." The paper pointed out that after Milwaukee had scored five runs in the top of the first inning, by rights they should have won the game. But their own pitcher, Bill Reidy, was hit even harder - the seven-run fifth inning giving Boston the edge. Chick Stahl's two-run bases-loaded single and a three-run homer by Jimmy Collins, one of two homers that Boston's player/manager hit in the game.

The *Globe* also called Volz (getting the spelling right a few paragraphs later) a "slow-going 'old' youngster." He walked three of the first four batters he faced, and gave up a single to the other one. Wid Conroy's triple made it 4-0; Conroy scored on an error by Parent at shortstop. In the second inning, Davy Jones hit "the longest hit ever made on the grounds" for the first of Milwaukee's two home runs.

Despite his 9.00 ERA, and nine runs allowed, Volz won the game, since his teammates had scored 10 times. Volz hadn't helped offensively; he was 0-for-4 at the plate. As a fielder, he had two chances and flubbed them both. Nonetheless, he pocketed the win, and was 1-0 as a big leaguer. The doubleheader had drawn 5,388 fans. Boston's record was 79-57, finishing in second place, four games behind the league-leading Chicago White Sox.

Manchester welcomed Jake back to Varick Park in 1902, and he put up a 19-7 record for manager John A. "Phenomenal" Smith (Volz's obituary in *The Sporting News* says his record was 26-8, though the same obituary claims his major-league record in 1905 was 0-3, rather than the 0-2 in the record books. *Sporting Life* reports his record as 21-10.)[3] The team finished first in the New England League, now a Class B league, and led the league in strikeouts with 220. He hit a home run himself, but overall was .147 as a batter. Volz joined in a shutout in the May 13 game and, despite five walks, threw another shutout against Lawrence 10 days later. He had a two-hitter against Lawrence in August and closed the season with a four-hit 2-1 win over Concord. Despite his wins total, there was a reputation which seemed to have attached to him: early in the year, sportswriter Tim Murnane dubbed him "'base on balls' Volts."[4] Murnane, in addition to being the principal reporter covering baseball for the *Boston Globe*, was also the president of the New England League.

In December, Volz was signed for the 1903 season by the St. Paul Saints. He jumped his contract with Manchester, but they said no effort would be made to reclaim him. The Saints won the American Association pennant, but Volz was not with the team for long. St. Paul was reported to have released him to Duluth in mid-May, that he might return to Manchester, but later on it was reported that he had been farmed out to Winnipeg in early August.[5] It doesn't appear that he ever played for any of the three teams. On August 18, it was announced that his contract was assigned to the Indianapolis Indians, back in the American Association.

In 1904, he was released by Indianapolis in April and he returned to Manchester. Records are sketchy. Though he appeared in 36 games, batting an even .200, we don't know how he fared on the mound, though there were some spectacular games such as the July 28 two-hit 2-0 shutout he spun against Fall River, striking out 15, and his 5-0 win over Concord on August 6 with nine K's. Five days later, he shut out Lawrence on four hits with eight strikeouts, a 10-inning, 1-0 win. On August 17, he shut down New Bedford, 9-0, all the shutouts occurring in front of the home crowd at Manchester. By September, the Boston Beaneaters had taken on his contract for 1904. The October 1 *Sporting Life* called him "easily the most effective pitcher of the [New England] league"

1, Mullaney; 2, Hopkins; 3, Volz; 4, Munson; 5, Chandler; 6, Murdock; 7, Otey; 8, Fox; 9, W. W. Clark, Mgr.; 10, Temple; 11, Bonner; 12, Jackson; 13, Busch; 14, Seitz.
NORFOLK TEAM—VIRGINIA LEAGUE.

Volz, #3, with the 1901 Norfolk Tars.

and said he'd led the league in strikeouts. He was "a mighty promising young man."

It was an opportunity to return to the big leagues. Playing in the National League, Volz was given two starts but neither turned out well; he lost to the Giants, 16-3, on May 3 and 11-1 to the Pirates on May 24. He appeared in two other games in relief, finishing 0-2 with a 10.38 ERA. He was 5-5 with Manchester and Lawrence (the franchise moved to Lawrence, Massachusetts on July 20) in 1905, and spent some time with the Sioux City Packers (1-4) in the Western League.

There was a little controversy in that he continued to pitch for Lawrence for some time after his trade in August for Gerry Wilson. Volz filed a claim of some sort against Sioux City, but his claim was denied in early 1907. In 1906 and 1907 Volz returned to New England, playing in the Connecticut State League for Holyoke, Hartford, and Bridgeport (14-19 for the Holyoke (Massachusetts) Paperweights the first year, and with a combined 12-12 mark for the Paperweights, Senators, and Orators in 1907.) One of Holyoke's three managers in 1906 was Jake's teammate from the 1901 Americans, Tommy Dowd.

There was a third return to the major leagues in 1908. Why, might be a good question, since he was 9-19 for the Columbia (South Carolina) Gamecocks in the South Atlantic League before joining the Cincinnati Reds in mid-August after throwing a couple of two-hitters on July 6 and 11. In 22 2/3 innings, he started four games for the Reds and appeared in three more (1-2, with a 3.57 ERA.) It was with Cincinnati that he collected his one and only big-league hit, a single, and drove in his only run. The hit came on August 16 in Cincinnati off George Bell of the Brooklyn Superbas. Volz started and won the game, his only National League win. He gave up five hits, three bases on balls, and struck out three in the 5-1 victory. He was 1-for-10 in the majors. Given two more chances in the field, he converted both successfully, so wound up with a lifetime .500 fielding percentage. He was released back to Columbia, returning back home to San Antonio after a couple of weeks.

He'd begun the 1909 season with Charleston (South Carolina) but was released before the season began. He signed on with the Norfolk Tars and after a 14-12 season with the Class C Virginia League team, he moved to Canton in the Ohio-Pennsylvania League. In March 1910, he pitched some for San Antonio, but his baseball career seemed to peter out at this point.

On his Hall of Fame questionnaire, Volz reported that he had worked 42 years for the Judson Candy Company, retiring from that firm. He married twice, first in November 1909 to Annie Zuercher, but 18 months later she had died. On October 28, 1916, Volz married Elsie Boehm, both of whose parents had also emigrated from Germany. They had one son, Jacob Junior, born in 1917, but their son predeceased his parents. On his WWI draft registration card, Volz states his occupation as Fireman, for what appears to be a manufacturing company, though the name of the company is very difficult to decipher.

The 1920 United States census reported that Jake's occupation was "none" while Elsie is listed as a tinsmith. It's likely the enumerator inadvertently transposed the occupations on the census form. Furthermore, the occupation of the person listed two lines above Jake is "Engineer—Candy Factory"—which jibes with the 1900 census for Volz. On the 1930 census, Jacob is listed as a Machinist in a Candy Co. (the family name is indexed as Voltz). Elsie, Jake Jr, William and Louisa are all still there, but Jake Sr. is the only one working. Living with the couple at the time were Jake's brother William, a Pullman porter, and his sister Louisa, a laundress.

Volz required the amputation of both legs in 1957 and was bedridden for two years until former minor league ballplayer Lou Barbour moved from Chicago home to his native San Antonio and learned of Jake's condition. Barbour had worked as traveling secretary for the White Sox for many years, and made arrangements with the Association of Professional Ball Players of America to provide a wheelchair and a monthly pension. It may have helped that the secretary of the APBPA at the time was infielder Win Clark, who'd been active with Volz on at least four different teams: San Antonio in 1899, a few seasons in Manchester, and in Columbia (1908) and Norfolk (1909.) The obituary in *The Sporting News* noted that Clark was manager in Manchester, in 1905. Their travels were clearly intertwined; he also managed Volz in Columbia in 1908 and Norfolk in 1909. There may also have been additional empathy for Jake's cause in that Clark was himself a double amputee.[6]

Volz was survived by his wife Elsie when he died at home on August 11, 1962.

Sources

In addition to the sources cited within this biography, the author consulted the subject's player file and questionnaire at the National Baseball Hall of Fame, the online SABR Encyclopedia, Retrosheet.org, Baseball-Reference.com, and the *Encyclopedia of Minor League Baseball*.

Notes

1. Thanks to Maurice Bouchard for essential genealogical research.
2. *Sporting Life*, January 14, 1899
3. *Sporting Life*, November 1, 1902. Some sources show Smith's middle name as Francis.
4. *Boston Globe*, May 14, 1902.
5. *Sporting Life*, May 16, May 23, and August 8, 1903
6. *The Sporting News*, August 25, 1962

George Winter

By Tom Simon

BACK IN THE Deadball Era, when sassafrass was the primary ingredient used to flavor root beer, just as ginger provided the flavoring for ginger ale, a baseball player who displayed "sassafrass" or "ginger" was a lively player who put forth extraordinary effort, sometimes compensating for a perceived lack of natural ability. Several players have been nicknamed Ginger, but George Winter is the only player in the history of professional baseball with the nickname Sassafrass. Another of his nicknames was Spec, probably because he stood only 5-feet-8 1/2-inches tall and weighed only 133 pounds at the time of his entrance into the American League.

Winter's nicknames give us clues about how he was perceived by his contemporaries. A right-handed pitcher who fielded his position exceptionally well, and also had great running speed, Winter worked hard and overcame the prejudice that a small man could not pitch successfully in the majors. He topped the 200-inning mark five times and averaged more than 10 wins per season over the course of his eight-year career in the American League.

George Lovington Winter was born on April 27, 1878, on a farm near New Providence, Pennsylvania, a tiny village in the Pennsylvania Dutch Country of Lancaster County. He is not listed in the 1880 census, and the 1890 census records were destroyed by fire, but census records from 1900 indicate that George, whose occupation was listed as "teacher," was still living in New Providence, albeit with his stepfather and mother, Harry and Ada Paes, and their six children.

After winning 38 out of 43 games during the summer of 1900 for teams from nearby Myerstown and Manheim, George enrolled in the Preparatory Department of Gettysburg College, where one of his classmates was future Hall of Famer Eddie Plank. For the rest of their careers both Winter and Plank would be mentioned in articles about college-educated major leaguers, but neither actually attended college, and in Winter's case he "prepped" for only one year.

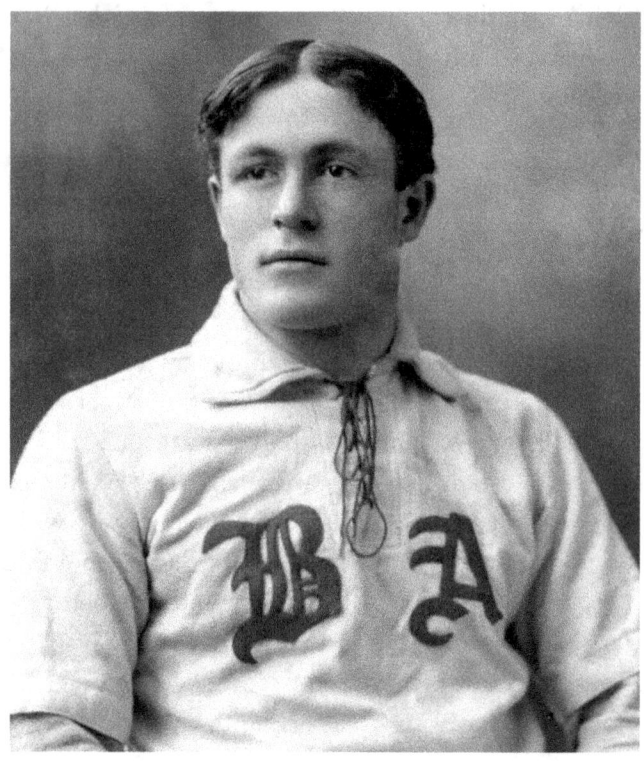

Winter, with the 1902 Boston Americans.

Under the rules of the era, however, both were eligible for Gettysburg College's varsity baseball team, and for most of the season the 23-year-old Winter and the 25-year-old Plank alternated between pitcher and right field and batted third and fourth, respectively, in the batting order. "Plank, the reliable southpaw of last year, and Winter, a new man, have already showed remarkable ability and seem almost unhittable," reported *The Gettysburgian* on April 24, 1901. Though Plank and Winter both moved on to the American League before Gettysburg completed its 1901 schedule, the Orange and Blue compiled a 12-3-1 record, which the yearbook reported "has never been surpassed in the history of the college."

Plank was the first to sign, joining the Philadelphia Athletics in mid-May. At the time he recommended his undersized teammate to Connie Mack, but the Tall Tactitian, according to *The Sporting News*, "turned thumbs down on Winter because of his size." After making his professional debut with the A's on May 13, Plank returned to pitch one last game for Gettysburg two days later. In that game Winter, playing right field, collided with Gettysburg's center fielder and missed the next contest, but he returned to action on May 24. With "one eye partly closed, the knee and ankle on his right locomotor dangerously weak, the result of injuries received over a week ago," Winter closed out his college career by pitching Gettysburg to victories over Washington & Jefferson and Bucknell.

"Gettysburg lost her other veteran ball tosser last week when George Winter left to sign with the Boston American League team," reported *The Gettysburgian* on June 12. "Fortunately for Gettysburg the call came at a more desirable time than Plank's, for the Varsity schedule was nearing completion and hence the loss, although it will be felt in the coming years, was not so disastrous for this season's work."

Making his professional debut with Boston on June 15, 1901, Winter won his first six starting assignments in the majors. Plank, meanwhile, had won six of his first seven, and on July 11 the ex-teammates squared off against each other for the first time at the Huntington Avenue Grounds. In a game that was shortened to six innings by rain, Winter prevailed, 4-1, but in Philadelphia four days later Plank turned the tables with a 6-1 victory over Winter. *The Sporting News* later reported that Winter "became a thorn in the side of Connie Mack and Plank, winning nearly every meeting with his former teammate," which was only a slight exaggeration: Winter was 6-3 in the nine games he started against Plank over the course of his career.

Winter claimed success against another future Hall of Famer, Napoleon "Larry" Lajoie, who was in the midst of a .426 season in 1901. "The first time I ever pitched against the Cleveland Club was at Boston," he told a reporter from *Sporting Life* in 1909. "Now I'd always noticed in my college ball games that when a big fellow came up to the plate and stood straight up with his feet together, he had difficulty in hitting a curve ball that broke around his knees. I didn't know what the other fellows had been throwing to Larry, but he seemed to demand the prescription, though the catcher didn't signal it. Larry missed the first two and rolled the third one over to [manager/third-baseman Jimmy] Collins. 'My goodness, Spec,' Collins said when I came in after the inning was over, 'don't ever hand that big fellow a low ball again. He murders it. Just shut your eyes, say a little prayer and shoot one up, fast and high.' 'But I got him, didn't I?' 'Yes, but you were mighty lucky.' Well, to cut a long story short, I pitched two games of one series against Cleveland and won both of them. Lajoie didn't get a single safe hit, and, inside of two weeks, all the pitchers on the other teams were pitching him the same thing. He hits it once in a while and, now and then, somebody tries to fool him with something else, but usually wishes he hadn't."

George Winter

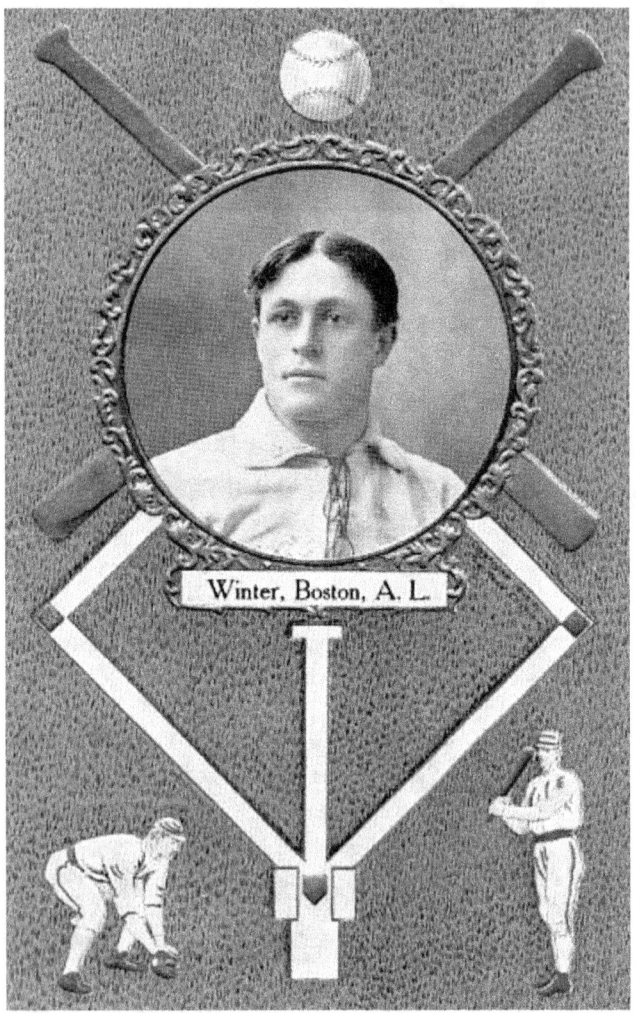

Circa 1908 The Rose Company Postcard of Winter.

After setting career highs for games started (28) and wins (16) during his rookie year, Winter got off to a strong start in 1902, but during a mid-July road trip to St. Louis he contracted typhoid fever, a contagious and, in the Deadball Era, sometimes fatal bacterial infection. (Winter was known to experiment with a spitball, and one may speculate that he contracted the disease by licking his fingers after handling a contaminated baseball.) He spent the rest of the season confined to his room at Boston City Hospital, where he met Mabel Willis, a graduate nurse from Burlington, Vermont, whom he married on October 19, 1905.

The couple made their offseason home in Burlington, where George became a partner in the city's leading men's store. He kept in shape during the winter by exercising each morning at the YMCA,, just down the street from his haberdashery, and training in the cage with the University of Vermont baseball team. It was as a result of those preseason workouts that Winter made perhaps his greatest contribution to Boston, recognizing the talents of UVM classmates Larry Gardner and Ray Collins, future Red Sox whom he recommended to his employer.

Winter defeated Philadelphia's Rube Waddell on Opening Day 1903 and was the winning pitcher in Boston's pennant-clincher over Washington on September 9, but during that year's World Series he participated only as a ticket-taker when Collins relied on his "big three," Cy Young, Big Bill Dinneen, and Long Tom Hughes. The undersized pitcher suffered a similar fate the following season, starting a career-low 16 games despite a glittering 8-4 record and 2.32 ERA, which nonetheless was the highest ERA among the team's five hurlers. That offseason several sources reported that Winter would be dealt to Washington in a trade that would return Long Tom Hughes to Boston, but the Senators eventually refused the exchange and Winter came back to Boston for a fifth season.

After a year in which he reportedly "was not in good health and pitched very little ball," Winter arrived at spring training in 1905 "in far better shape" and rebounded to post his best season since his rookie year. In his first start, at Washington on April 18, he pitched the finest game of his major-league career, a one-hitter that he lost, 1-0, when the Senators scored a run in the first inning on a two-base error, a sacrifice bunt, and a sacrifice fly. Pitching frequently to Art McGovern, who became a sort of personal catcher, Winter tied his career best with 16 wins and set career highs in innings (264⅓) and strikeouts (119). "Not even the great Cy himself has done more consistent work in the box this season than George Winter," reported *Sporting Life*. "Strange, indeed, that that brace of former Gettysburg pitchers — Eddie Plank and George Winter — should be the mainstays of their respective clubs this season, and two of the finest pitchers in the country. Less doubt as to Winter's fortune, next spring, I guess, than there was a year ago about the spring to come."

Reminiscent of Winter's bout with typhoid fever in 1902 after his successful rookie season, a "bad stomach" forced him to return to his farm in New Providence in July 1906 and miss nearly six weeks of the season. When he did pitch he was ineffective, compiling a 6-18 record and a career-high 4.12 ERA. Once again he rebounded, however, posting a 2.07 ERA over 256⅔ innings in 1907, his last full season in Boston. After reporting late to spring training due to the birth of his first child, Winter began the 1908 season pitching in hard luck—the Red Sox failed to score in his 36 innings up to May 2—and on July 26 Boston placed him on waivers. That six American League teams passed on him was not surprising, given his 4-14 record and 3.05 ERA. The surprise was that the first-place Detroit Tigers claimed him. Perhaps Hughie Jennings could not resist adding Winter to a pitching staff whose ace was Ed Summers. "Spring and Fall have yet to come to terms," quipped *Sporting Life*.

Winter continued his hard-luck pitching with Detroit, losing five of his six starts despite a stellar 1.60 ERA, but the Tigers held on to win the American League pennant. After failing to appear in the 1903 World Series, Winter must have been thrilled when Jennings inserted him as a pinch-runner in Game One of the World Series ("George Winter can leg it around the bases about as fast as any man on the team," *Sporting Life* had reported in 1904), and when he pitched a scoreless ninth inning in relief of Summers in Game Four.

That appearance proved to be Winter's last in the major leagues. When Detroit offered him less money for 1909 than he had made the previous season in Boston, he held out and the Tigers ended up selling him to the Montreal Royals of the Eastern League, where he went 15-12 in 253 innings. After Winter went 2-10 in 175 innings in 1910, Montreal traded him to the Toronto Maple Leafs, whose star-studded roster included player-manager Joe Kelley, veteran major leaguers such as Wee Willie Keeler, Bill Bradley, Tim Jordan, Ed Killian, and Johnny Lush, and future standouts like Jeff Tesreau and Dick Rudolph. Winter reported to spring training with his new team but refused to sign a contract when Toronto insisted on cutting his salary.

Before the Eastern League's 1911 season opened, Winter returned to Burlington to coach the University of Vermont team. Kelley granted him a leave of absence until June 16, when the college season ended, and on June 15 Winter wrote a letter to Garry Herrmann, head of the National Commission, explaining his predicament and requesting advice: "I don't want to bring this case to the National Commission, as I've never in the ten (10) years I've played had any trouble with magnate, umpire or players, never been put out of a game or been fined." Herrmann forwarded the letter to American League President Ban Johnson, who confirmed that Winter "is a splendid young man and was always faithful in the performance of his duty. It seems to me the Commission should inquire how great a reduction in

Winter on the right at a train station in 1908 with Tigers teammates Sam Crawford (L) and Ed Summers..

salary the Toronto Club wanted to impose upon this player."

In response to Herrmann's letter requesting that information, Winter wrote on June 28 from St. Johns, New Brunswick, where he was serving as player-manager of an independent team: "Toronto Club sent a contract of $325.00 per month but later offered me $350.00 per month. When I was traded to them I was getting $400.00 per month from Montreal which they must have known. In Montreal my season's salary was $2,133.33⅓. I offered to stay with the Toronto Club for $2,000.00 allowing them to cut me $133.33⅓ on the season, which they refused." When that information was passed on to him, National League President T.J. Lynch wrote: "I have looked over the case of Player GEORGE L. WINTER, and my opinion is the Toronto Club has acted fair regarding the salary offered this player. The cut from his Montreal salary was so small that I think the player was at fault in not accepting it and save himself from suspension. I for one cannot see where the Commission can help him, except to suggest to him to join the Toronto Club." In his own hand Herrmann scribbled a note to his secretary on Lynch's letter: "Send to J [Johnson]. Tell him I agree with Lynch." That same week Johnson wrote back to Herrmann: "I am in receipt of the letter sent you by George L. Winter. I think the Toronto Club made him an exceedingly generous offer when they agreed to give him a contract calling for Three Hundred Fifty ($350.00) Dollars per month. I believe it would be well to write the player to that effect."

George Winter never did join the Toronto Maple Leafs, though he did play for Binghamton, Scranton, and Troy before retiring from professional baseball in 1914. He also coached the baseball teams at the University of Vermont and Princeton University. In 1916 Winter moved to New Castle, Delaware, and opened a sporting-goods store in nearby Wilmington. There he played with various semipro teams and also did some umpiring.

Mabel Winter died following an operation in New Haven, Connecticut, on January 28, 1937. After a lingering illness, George Winter died of a heart attack at the age of 73 on May 26, 1951, at Mrs. Dathe's Convalescent Home in Franklin Lakes, New Jersey, the town where his daughter formerly resided. He was buried in Wilmington's Riverview Cemetery. His survivors included a son, George W. Winter of Mississippi; a daughter, Betty Sulloway of Portland, Oregon; and four grandchildren.

Sources

The author relied extensively on Winter's file from the National Baseball Library and several sources found online, including census records, the Gettysburg College student newspaper and yearbook, *Sporting Life*, *The Sporting News*, and Retrosheet. Thanks to Peter Morris for his assistance.

Cy Young

by David Southwick

Along with that of Napoleon Lajoie, Cy Young's defection to the American League in 1901 generated instant credibility for the upstart circuit, as the league gained one of the game's greatest pitchers. The winner of 286 games in his first 11 seasons, Young had established himself as a model of consistency and excellence, pitching more than 300 innings every year from 1891 to 1900, and ranking among the National League's top five in earned-run average six times during that span. Still, cracks were starting to show in the great pitcher's façade. At 34 years of age, Young had already entered the phase of his career when most pitchers start to break down. Indeed, in 1900, Young suffered through one of his worst seasons to that point, failing to win 20 games for the first time since his rookie season, and pitching fewer innings than he had in any previous full season. Opposing batters attested that Young was more hittable than ever, and newspaper reporters began routinely affixing the adjective Old in front of his name. By all appearances, then, when the Boston Americans signed Young to a $3,500 salary, the acquisition represented more a public-relations coup than a legitimate pitching upgrade.

As it turned out, Boston, not to mention the rest of the American League, got much more than it ever could have expected. During his eight years with the Americans (later renamed the Red Sox), Young won 192 games, becoming the first pitcher in baseball history to pitch effectively into his 40s. In 1901, his first season with the Americans, he led the league in victories, strikeouts and earned-run average in 1901, a feat now called pitching's Triple Crown, and tossed the first perfect game in American League history. The many photos of Young that survive from this period portray a man advancing in years and gaining in weight. But as his girth expanded, his control sharpened; five times after 1900 he led the league in fewest walks per nine innings. And though his fastball lost some of its effectiveness, the wily Young more than made up for it with a pair of curveballs, one thrown overhand with a

Cy Young was 28-9 with Boston in 1901.

sharp break, the other thrown sidearm with a sweeping arc. Both pitches were delivered from a variety of arm angles; occasionally Young even threw submarine-style to upset the batter's timing. In his continued mastery of opposing batters in the face of declining strength and advancing age, Young raised pitching to an art form, and earned his place in baseball's pantheon of all-time greats. "If I were asked who was the greatest pitcher the game ever knew, I would say Cy Young," sportswriter Francis Richter wrote in 1910, when Young was 43 years old. "Cy is now pitching as good ball today as he did twenty years ago."

Denton True Young was born on March 29, 1867, in Gilmore, Ohio, the oldest of five children of McKinzie Young, Jr. and Nancy (Miller) Young. Gilmore was a small farming community about 100 miles south of Cleveland, and the Young family was raised on a farm owned by McKinzie's father, McKinzie Sr. Cy's education stopped at the sixth grade so he could help his parents with farming chores, but it was also at this time that he discovered the game of baseball. Encouraged by their father, the Young boys played baseball every chance they got. Developing into a better pitcher than hitter, Denton practiced throwing during lunch breaks from farm work. Besides practicing and playing in recreational games, he organized his own team in Gilmore, then in the summer of 1884 he played on semipro teams in Newcomerstown, Cadiz, and Uhrichsville, Ohio.

Having to make a living after his marriage to Robba Miller, and believing he could make money playing baseball, Young signed with Canton, Ohio, of the Tri-States League in 1890. After he compiled a 15-15 record in his rookie season, the right-hander's contract was sold to the National League's Cleveland Spiders for $500. Young's quick ascendancy to the majors was the result of the emergence of the ill-fated Players League, which forced National League teams to dig deep into the minor leagues for any available talent.

Young pitched with the Spiders through the 1898 season, winning 30 games or more three times, and capturing the 1892 ERA title with a 1.93 mark. The following year, the pitcher's mound was moved back five feet to its present distance of 60 feet 6 inches, and Young responded well, finishing the year with a 34-16 record and a 3.36 ERA, third best in the league. He was able to compensate for the increased distance with his terrific fastball. It had been the pitch that reportedly gave rise to his nickname, Cyclone (or Cy for short). Honus Wagner, who regularly faced Young in the National League toward the end of the decade, thought it the greatest fastball he had ever seen. "Walter Johnson was fast, but no faster than Rusie," Wagner observed. "And Rusie was no faster than Johnson. But Young was faster than both of 'em!" Another contemporary, Cap Anson, observed that when the 6-foot-2, 210-pound Young unleashed his speed, it seemed as if "the ball was shooting down from the hands of a giant."

When the syndicate of owners that controlled both the Cleveland and St. Louis franchises shifted Young to St. Louis in 1899, the pitcher's overpowering fastball began to lose some of its steam. He collected 26 wins that year, but only 19 in 1900, as a bruised rib suffered in a collision with the New York Giants' Ed Doheny caused him to miss significant playing time for the first time in his career. Additionally, as the summer progressed and Young suffered his share of tough losses, the normally quiet and reserved star uncharacteristically vented his frustration, charging into the stands on August 20 to confront a heckler who had accused him of quitting on the team. Young finished the year with a lackluster 19-19 record, and the Perfectos slumped into fifth place, ten games below .500.

After the season ended, several St. Louis players de-

Young warming up in 1908, the year the Boston Americans first became the Red Sox.

fected to the American League, including catcher Lou Criger, Young's batterymate, who signed with Boston. Though he was hounded by Boston's owner, Charles Somers, for several weeks, the cautious Young did not sign with the Americans until the March 19, 1901. St. Louis owner Frank Robison had declined to match Boston's offer of $3,500, insisting that Young, about to turn 34, was just about "all washed up."

Cy Young, 1905.

Young soon demonstrated otherwise. Though, like Napoleon Lajoie, he had the advantage of facing competition watered down by the sudden addition of eight new major-league teams, Young enjoyed one of the greatest pitching seasons in baseball history. He led the league in victories (33), ERA (1.62), strikeouts (158), and shutouts (5). In 371⅓ innings, he walked just 37 batters. Asked to explain his success, Young said, "I have almost perfect control of the ball this year, and I try to keep it bumping over the plate. If two or three men get on bases, I put on a little more steam and shoot 'em over as fast as I can—but I try all the time to keep 'em over."

Over the next three seasons, the American League's talent pool expanded vastly as more players made the jump to the junior circuit, but Young remained unfazed by the new arrivals, leading the league in victories in 1902 and 1903, and finishing second in 1904. Though he began to rely more exclusively on his assortment of breaking pitches, Young's control remained as sharp as ever: In 1904 he walked just 29 in 380 innings. His success helped the Americans win back-to-back pennants in 1903 and 1904, and though teammate Bill Dineen stole the spotlight in Boston's eight-game victory over Pittsburgh in the first modern World Series (1903), Young aided the cause with a 2-1 record and 1.85 ERA in the inaugural fall classic.

Young's greatest achievement, however, may have come on May 5, 1904, when at the age of 37 he pitched the first perfect game in American League history—just the third in major-league baseball and the first from the 60-foot-6-inch pitching distance—against Rube Waddell and the Philadelphia Athletics. Before the game Waddell, who had defeated Young in their previous encounter a weak earlier, taunted the old pitcher, promising to beat him again. After Young pitched his masterpiece and Boston won, 3-0, Cy uncharacteristically returned fire, shouting to Waddell, "How did you like that one, you hayseed?" It was his second career no-hitter (his first came in 1897); he would pitch a third in 1908, against New York.

Young's perfection against the Athletics came in the midst of a major-league record 24 consecutive innings in which the pitcher did not allow a single hit, as well as a scoreless innings streak that stretched to a then-record 45 innings. "And they said Uncle Cy was all in, did they?" observed Boston catcher Duke Farrell of his 37-year-old teammate. "He fooled them, didn't he?" Down the stretch, Young continued to impress, pitching shutouts in each of his last three starts to help the Americans to their narrow pennant victory over the New York Highlanders.

In the wake of Young's historic accomplishments, much of the baseball world began to acknowledge his unparalleled place in the pantheon of great pitchers. "Rusies have come and gone, in their turn, by Cy Young still pitches on," observed the *Detroit Tribune*. "Perhaps no ballplayer ever lived who paid stricter attention to business and who came out of a long series of honors showered on him with lesser opinion of himself and with such strict attention to temperate habits." For his part, Young placed no special emphasis on his remarkable durability and longevity. He downplayed the significance of his offseason conditioning program, which consisted mostly of splitting wood at his Peoli, Ohio, farmhouse. "It isn't any secret," Young said, "just outdoor life, moderation, and a naturally good arm. I don't know that I take any better care of myself than any other pitcher does, it just happens, this thing of my lasting. It isn't the result of any system."

In an era when ballplayers were often regarded as dissolute, inveterate slackers, Young won praise for his clean living and moderate temperament. He prided himself on his work ethic, and reacted with indignation when accused of easing up with a big lead. "When you see me let any club make runs off my pitching on purpose," he snarled, "come around and I'll give you a brand new hundred dollar bill." Easing up, he declared, placed the game "on the level with lawn tennis, tiddle-de-winks, or some other schoolgirl frivolity." Later in life Young articulated a personal philosophy for playing the game the right way by enumerating five rules of conduct: 1) Be moderate in all things; 2) Don't abuse yourself; 3) Don't bait umpires; 4) Play hard; and 5) Render faithful service to your employer. Adhering to this creed, Young continued to enjoy success long after other pitchers had left the game. Thus, his unbreakable career records (511 victories, 7,354⅔ innings, 749 complete games) were the product not just of exceptional talent and good fortune, they were also the result of his own exacting standards.

As Young approached and then passed his 40th birthday, he continued to rank among the game's best pitchers, thanks in large part to the wide assortment of breaking pitches and arm deliveries he employed to fool opposing batters. "If a right-hander crowded my plate," Young said after retiring as a player, "I sidearmed him with a curve, and then, when he stepped back, I'd throw an overhand fastball low and outside. I was fortunate in having good speed from overhand, three-quarter, or sidearm. I had a variety of curves—threw a so-called screwball or indrop, too—and I used whatever delivery seemed best. And I never had but one sore arm." After enduring the worst season of his career in 1906, when he finished the year 13-21 for the woeful (49-105) Americans with a terrible 3.19 ERA, Young came back strong in 1907 and 1908, winning 21 games in each season and posting ERAs of 1.99 and 1.26, respectively.

In February 1909 Young, then 42, was traded by Boston to the Cleveland Naps for Charlie Chech, Jack Ryan, and $12,500 cash. Back in the city where he had started his big-league career 19 years before, Young enjoyed one more solid season, going 19-15 with a 2.26 ERA. The following year, he started only 20 games, finishing with a 7-10 record. Still, he resisted calls for him to retire from the game. "Quit the game, well, I guess not," he told a Cleveland reporter. "I'd be awfully lonesome, and you know this is a healthy game. I'll not quit until I have to."

Cy Young, 1905.

Young was a 21-game winner in both 1907 and, as shown here, in 1908.

In 1911 the 44-year-old Young fared even worse, going 3-4 with a 3.88 ERA in seven starts before drawing his release on August 15. He was quickly picked up by the Boston Braves of the National League, who wanted him, according to one writer, "just to draw the crowd." Young started 11 games for Boston down the stretch, going 4-5 with a 3.71 ERA. Despite much speculation that he would retire, Young attempted to hang on with the Braves for the 1912 season, remaining with the team through spring training and warming the bench for the first month of the campaign. But a chronically sore arm prevented him from ever taking the field; when he attempted to do so, on May 23, he gave up after a brief warm-up session, declaring, "It's no use. I'm not going on. These poor fellows have lost too many games already." Finally, at the age of 45, Young's major-league career was officially over.

In retirement, Cy returned to his home in Peoli, where he lived out a quiet retirement on his farm, growing potatoes and tending to his sheep, hogs, and chickens. He and his wife, Robba, did not raise any children; their only offspring, a daughter, died a few hours after her birth in 1907, leaving, in the words of Young biographer Reed Browning, "an almost inexpungeable hole" in their lives. When Robba died in 1934, a grieving Young sold his farm. "Somehow, after she died I didn't want to live there any more," he said. Elected to the Hall of Fame in 1937, Young was formally inducted with the Hall's first class at the museum's opening in 1939. Despite his frugal habits and status as a baseball legend, however, Young was beset by financial problems late in life. In 1935 he traveled to Augusta, Georgia where he joined a group of baseball veterans looking to make some money during the Great Depression by playing exhibition games. When this venture failed, Young returned to Ohio, where he found work as a clerk in a retail store and lived with a local couple, John and Ruth Benedum. He was still living with the Benedums when he died of a coronary occlusion on November 4, 1955, at the age of 88. He was buried in Peoli Cemetery. The next year, baseball instituted the pitching award that bears his name.

Note

This biography originally appeared in David Jones, ed., *Deadball Stars of the American League* (Washington, D.C.: Potomac Books, Inc., 2006).

Sources

Browning, Reed. *Cy Young: A Baseball Life.* (Amherst, Massachusetts: University of Massachusetts Press, 2003).

Ivor-Campbell, Fred, editor. *Baseball's First Stars.* (Cleveland: SABR, 1996).

Masur, Louis P. *Autumn Glory: Baseball's First World Series.* (New York: Hill & Wang, 2003).

Boston Globe

Boston Post

New York Times

The Sporting News

Washington Post

Baseball-reference.com

Baseballhalloffame.org

Retrosheet.org

Hi Hi Dixwell

By Joanne Hulbert

Crank: a baseball fan in the late 19th century. "The real, simon-pure baseball crank ... thinks baseball, talks baseball, dreams baseball and, does all but play it. It is generally a fact that the real baseball crank cannot play right-field in even a 'scrub nine.'"

Milwaukee Sentinel, *October 12, 1884.*

THEY WERE THERE in all the cities; all the teams had at least a couple of them. New York had several, some of them from the theatrical crowd. There was De Wolf Hopper of "Casey at the Bat" fame, and his friend, fellow actor Digby Bell. The comedian Henry Dixey, born in Boston, strongly believed that life was a game, while baseball was very serious. Actress Helen Dauvray, creator of the Dauvray Cup in 1887, was so smitten with baseball that she married John Montgomery Ward, proving that not only had she a passionate love of the New York Giants, but she also kept a player for herself—for a while anyway, until their divorce in 1893.

But there was one baseball crank in America whom baseball writer Hugh Fullerton in 1915 called the greatest of them all, a man who preceded the Royal Rooters and Nuf Ced McGreevey and all the others in Boston's sports history, and set the bar high for his 20th-century successors. His name was Arthur Dixwell. He left his mark on baseball history, even if he is not easily recalled today. Besides being considered the greatest baseball crank of them all, he was a director of Boston's Players League club in 1890. He showered his favorite players with gifts of cigars for all when the team won, diamond scarf pins, recliner chairs, loans that often were never paid back, and even an invitation of a European tour to catcher Morgan Murphy. His Dixwell trophy was awarded to the New England League pennant winner. He turned over the ceremonial first shovel of dirt for construction of the Huntington Avenue Grounds when the American League settled into Boston as the new team, threw out the first ball at the first game played there on May 8, 1901, and sent Ban Johnson $100 for season tickets that first year. After the 1903 World's

Isolated image of Arthur Dixwell from the photograph of the groundbreaking for the Huntington Avenue Grounds.

Series win, he presented the Boston club with a lavishly designed pennant flag. And then he virtually disappeared.

Few remember Arthur Dixwell today. His name crops up only fleetingly; a mere mention of his name is all there is in most books about Boston sports. He never occupied a position on any baseball team, yet his impact left an indelible mark on the city's sports history during the 1890s. Born on August 6, 1853, into a prominent Boston family, he was the son of John James Dixwell, a banker who died when Arthur was a young man, leaving him with a comfortable trust fund—$10,000 annually, and an additional $10,000 if he maintained any sort of useful employment.[1] He was the grandson of Nathaniel Bowditch, famed author of *The New American Practical Navigator*, considered the best treatise on navigation ever written. Arthur was a cousin of Fanny Dixwell, wife of Supreme Court Justice Oliver

GEN DIXWELL MARKING DOWN BOSTON'S RUNS ON HIS SCORE CARD.

Arthur Dixwell keeping score.

Wendell Holmes, Jr. His upper-class connections served him well when he navigated Boston's Brahmin society.

In an 1889 interview with the *San Francisco Examiner*, Dixwell explained, "I never played a game of ball in my life. Once they put me out in right field on the Common. You know in those days if you couldn't play they put you in right field. There was one ball knocked out my way in the first part of the game, and I disgraced myself by running away from it. That settled my career as a ball player. But I've been a crank for many years. Last season I missed but one championship game played by the Bostons."[2]

That settled Arthur into a permanent position in the grandstand. There he found fame, fortune, and notoriety for his signature yell, "Hi! Hi!" That was his way, he explained, of expressing his appreciation of a good play. He did not consider it too noisy, not half as bad, he maintained, as some other cranks had in giving expression to their feelings. Dixwell was celebrated in 1890 with a song and chorus dedicated to him and the Players League, words by Charles Sleeper and music by J.W. Wheeler, titled "Hi! Hi!" and published in the *Boston Globe*.

Dixwell honored his father's wish that he in some way earn a living to supplement his trust-fund allowance. Dixwell's Art Furniture Store, 4 Park Street [a/k/a Arthur Dixwell's Art Parlor], opened after his father's death in 1876, but the enterprise went bust in 1884. He reopened at 175 Tremont Street as the agent for Marks' Adjustable Chair, an early version of a recliner, and it became a gift he often gave to baseball players.

By 1889 Dixwell abandoned forever all his business interests and devoted himself full-time to baseball. He could be found at every game, scorecard in hand and punctuating the air whenever a good play was made with a shrill chorus of "Hi Hi's!" He traveled with the team during spring training and to all the league games as far away as Chicago. When out of town, he had the results of all the league games cabled to him. He always kept score and was never so distracted that he failed to record a play. Scoring became his field of expertise. He kept impeccable records of the players, including height, age, average ability, color, race (nationality), and "previous condition of baseball servitude of every professional player"[3]—information he found useful as a director of the Boston Players League team. He was a sabrmetrician long before there was such a thing.

He became known as "Hi Hi" Dixwell, and eventually assumed the title "General," although he never served in the military. The title was bestowed on Dixwell for the General Petition, a request for season tickets that he sent to Boston's National League owners—a request they declined. Perhaps it was the controversy over the season-ticket issue or an opportunity he could not pass up, but when the Brotherhood of Base Ball Players was organized, General Hi Hi Dixwell was at the front of the line to support the new Players League league team in Boston with "Hi Hi's" and his bankroll. Elected a director, he set out to attract the best players his money could buy. He offered John Clarkson $6,000 to join the Brotherhood in Boston, but Clarkson told him that was not enough money and negotiations ceased.[4]

At a game in Buffalo in 1890, Dixwell's hi-hi-ing got him into trouble when a police officer demanded, "You'll have to stop that noise here or else go out on the bleaching boards."

"Well, I've made the noise 130 times before this year and I don't believe I'll stop it now," the General replied with a scornful smile, and asked whether his cheering was likely to keep the policeman awake on his beat. Several fans in the crowd sympathized with the General and started up a solid defense with a chorus of "hi hi's" that sent the defeated officer away.[5]

The Brotherhood and the Players League were gone in 1891. Dixwell stood by the players and had been persuaded to invest a large sum of money which he expected to lose. He had also invested in Boston's American Association club, but the only return he would foresee from that would be a few good games to exercise his "hi-hi's." The Boston Reds won the AA pennant in 1891, the Association considered a major league of the day. With regret Dixwell returned to the games at the South End Grounds, but it wasn't the same. He was seen less often at the ball grounds and Hugh Fullerton reported that Dixwell's devotion to the National League team was damaged by feeling he had been insulted by some of the players.

He pursued other interests—was founder and president of the Boston Bowling Club, started a bowling team that sported fashionable gray uniforms with close-fitting caps, and kept bowling records as meticulous as his baseball scorecards. The Dixwell team included ex-Commodore Charles F. Morrill of the South Boston Yacht Club and George L. Whitney, an African-American waiter whom Dixwell was acquainted with by way of the private clubs he frequented. He was also highly devoted to the theater and attended all 160 performances of the play *Peggy from Paris*, and was disappointed when he was unable to see all 200 performances of *Yankee Consul*. He always purchased two tickets, attended all engagements alone, and reserved the second seat for his hat. He prevailed upon the orchestra to move the bassoonist to the other end of the pit, far away from his seat in the front row as the noise, ironically, highly displeased him.

In September 1899 Dixwell endured an embarrassing lawsuit filed by the wife of George L. Whitney, his waiter friend. She accused Dixwell of alienating the affections of her husband. The Boston newspapers kept the story subdued on a back page in the Friday evening edition, and requests for more information by probing reporters were turned down. "You wouldn't publish it if you knew all the facts, and I won't give them to you," declared Mrs. Whitney's lawyer.[6] She wanted $10,000 in damages, but the lawsuit was eventually dropped. Mr. Whitney simply wanted a divorce.

The only known photograph of Dixwell was taken at the March 7, 1901, ceremonial turning of the first shovelful of dirt for the new Huntington Avenue Grounds for Boston's new American League team. He was a diminutive figure, surrounded by much taller Royal Rooters, and standing next to 6-foot-2-inch former pitcher and State Senator Michael J. Sullivan. Other clues about Dixwell's physical attributes can be gleaned from his 1872 passport application, which described him as 5-feet-4 1/2-inches tall, with a high forehead, gray eyes, regular nose, medium mouth, round chin, brown hair, light complexion, and oval face. In other accounts, he was described as having "victorious blue eyes, a flood of wavy golden whiskers, attired in fancy-colored vests and looking like a Merovingian prince,

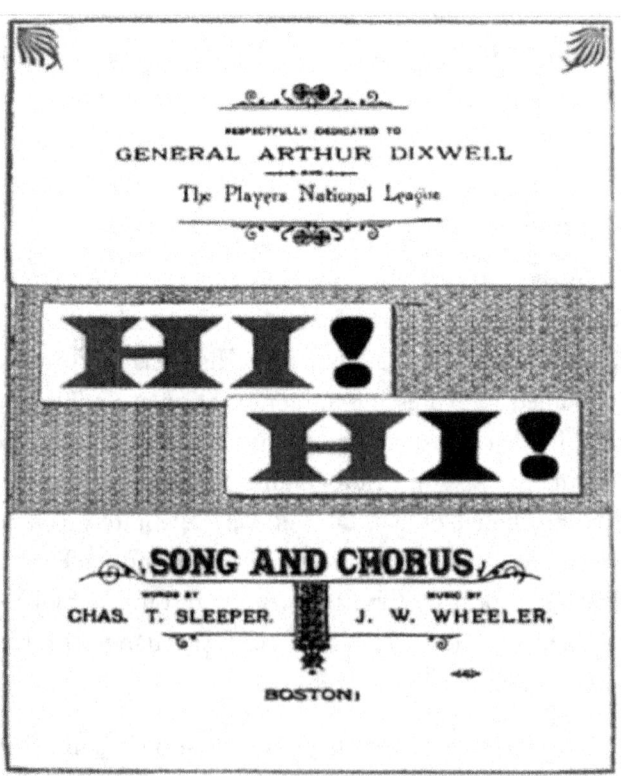

Sheet music dedicated to Hi Hi Dixwell.

too magnificent to be ill-natured and enjoying the most agreeable relationship with himself."[7]

But the Prince of Cranks no longer graced the sports pages after the 1903 season. The Royal Rooters dominated the scene from then on and General Hi Hi Dixwell faded away. Although he was reported to be dead in *Everybody's Magazine* in 1907, that was a Hi Hi-ly premature declaration. Dixwell survived until September 16, 1924, and died in virtual obscurity in his apartment at the Copley Square Hotel. Boston has had its share of cranks, rooters and fanaticals, but they would not ever see again another like General "Hi Hi" Dixwell. He's buried at Mount Auburn Cemetery among his siblings, his parents, and many of his distinguished ancestors.

Sources

Hugh Fullerton, "Fans Formerly Were Noisy Lot," *Muskegon* (Michigan) *Chronicle*, January 26, 1915.

"All Sorts of Sport," *Chicago Daily Inter Ocean*, November 16, 1890.

"Players," *Chicago InterOcean*, June 28, 1890.

"Baseball Brevities," *Haverhill* (Massachusetts) *Bulletin*, July 21, 1891.

"Goes Away Satisfied," *Boston Herald*, January 24, 1901.

"Dixwell's Ultimatum: Team Must Win or Buy Their Own Cigars," *Boston Daily Globe*, June 27, 1890.

"Boston and the Brotherhood," *Boston Herald*, October 26, 1889.

"General Dixwell Speaks," from *San Francisco Examiner*, *Boston Daily Globe*, December 30, 1889.

W.I. Harris, "Baseball Cranks," *Wichita* (Kansas) *Daily Eagle*, June 13, 1891.

"Ball Player Clarkson Explains," *The Patriot* (Harrisburg, Pennsylvania), January 16, 1890.

"Pop Ups," *Chicago Daily Inter Ocean*, October 3, 1890.

"HI HI Dixwell," *Morning Herald* (Baltimore, Maryland), September 25, 1891.

"Highest Salary Scorer, General Dixwell Earns $10,000 Per Annum as a Statistician," *Philadelphia Inquirer*, January 26, 1899.

"King of Theater Goers," *Boston Journal*, November 1, 1903.

James A. Hart, "The Story of 'General Hi Hi Dixwell,'" *Saturday Evening Post*, April 26, 1902.

"'Gen.' Dixwell Sued for $10,000," *Boston Traveler*, September 8, 1899.

"Husband's Love Alienated," *Boston Post*, September 8, 1899.

"That Prince of Rooters," *Sporting Life*, January 20, 1900.

"Work Commenced on New Grounds," *Pawtucket* (Rhode Island) *Times*, March 8, 1901.

Passport Application—Arthur Dixwell, May 13, 1872, www.Ancestry.com.

"Arthur Dixwell, An Old Fan, Gives This Most Unique Present To Collins' Team," *Pawtucket Times*, March 18, 1904.

Allan Sangree, "Psychology of the Fan," *New York Herald*, October 4, 1911.

"Famous 'Rooters,'" *Berea* (Ohio) *Advertiser*, November 1, 1907.

"'Hi Hi' Dixwell Is Called By Death," *Boston Daily Globe*, September 17, 1924.

Notes

1. Dixwell's gravestone shows his year of birth as 1854 but City of Boston birth records and a couple of his passport applications agree on the year as 1853.
2. "General Dixwell Speaks," from *San Francisco Examiner*, *Boston Daily Globe*, December 30, 1889.
3. "Baseball Brevities," *Haverhill Bulletin*, July 21, 1891, 4.
4. "Ball Player Clarkson explains," *The Patriot* (Harrisburg, Pennsylvania), January 16, 1890, 1.
5. "Pop Ups," *Chicago Daily InterOcean*, October 3, 1890, 3.
6. "Husband's Love Alienated," *Boston Post*, September 8, 1899, 2
7. "Players," *Chicago Daily InterOcean*, June 28, 1890, 2.

Michael T. "Nuf-Ced" McGreevy

By Peter J. Nash

IF YOU TAKE a close look at some of the iconic Boston baseball photographs created at the turn of the 20th century by Elmer Chickering, you might see him. He's the mustached chap in the bowler cap holding his Brownie camera with Hi-Hi Dixwell at the groundbreaking for the Huntington Avenue Grounds; he's the guy in his skivvies being pulled out of icy winter waters after swimming polar-bear style at the L Street Baths; he's the head peeking over a Pittsburgh Pirate's shoulder in a first-base-line team portrait taken during the first World Series; and he's the Royal Rooter posing with a platoon of the Red Sox faithful holding a fistful of dollar bills and a megaphone in front of Boston's South Station upon his arrival from Pittsburgh after singing "Tessie" at Game Seven of the 1903 World Series. "Nuf-Ced" McGreevy was his name. Base ball was his game.

Michael T. McGreevy was born in Roxbury, Massachusetts, on June 16, 1865. He was the first child of Margaret (Glinnon) McGreevy and Michael McGreevy, Irish immigrants living at 11 Vernon Street in Roxbury, then an independent city neighboring Boston. In 1869 his parents gave young Michael a baby brother. His father, Michael McGreevy, worked as a day laborer in the building trade until his death on January 6, 1872, a victim of tuberculosis. Margaret and her two sons moved in with relatives at 7 Smith Street in the same neighborhood.[1]

Without a father, the young and competitive McGreevy grew up on the streets of Roxbury, played sandlot baseball and developed skills as an expert handball player. From an early age he was a dyed-in-the-wool baseball crank idolizing the Irish ballplayers who played for the hometown Boston baseball clubs at the old Walpole Street, Congress Street, and South End Grounds. His first idols on the diamond were characters like King Kelly, Old Hoss Radbourn, John Morrill, and Billy Nash, and by the time those players had reached their prime, McGreevy had moved out of the family

Michael McGreevy, saloon owner, student of the game and leader of the Royal Rooters, a vocal and colorful fanbase of the Boston Americans, ca. 1903.

home and taken a room at 29 Station Street in 1887, employed as a clerk at 1153 Tremont St.[2]

On October 8, 1890, McGreevy married Annie L. Downes. The couple moved into a house at 122 Vernon Street and started their own family when daughter Alice arrived about 11 months later. It's not clear how he got into the spirits trade, but after being listed in city directories for several years as a clerk, McGreevy found his calling and opened his first saloon, on the corner of Cabot and Linden Park Streets in his Roxbury neighborhood. In the only surviving photograph of the exterior of that first saloon, McGreevy is seen leaning against the doorway entrance near a large hand-painted sign sponsored by a local brewer that read: "M.T.

McGreevy & Co. Ales Wines and Liquors — A.J Houghton Co.'s Celebrated Lager."

As a gregarious and popular barkeep, McGreevy quickly carved a niche for himself as a leader and organizer of many of his patrons who were fellow members of the Boston Elks Lodge and who shared his love for sport, particularly baseball. Boston, along with New York, Baltimore, and Philadelphia, had significant contingents of dedicated fans with close ties to the game's early days, including Boston's Arthur "Hi-Hi" Dixwell and New York's Frank "Well-Well" Wood, who both gained notoriety as the sport's most devout and vocal fans. In the 1880s New York City establishments like Nick Engel's Home Plate steakhouse and saloon incorporated baseball themes and decorations and embraced ballplayers and the characters associated with the game. A rabid fan of the New York Giants, Engel organized a group of fans known as the High and Mighty Order of Baseball Cranks of Gotham, and also led a contingent of 160 New York fans by train to Baltimore for Opening Day in 1894.

When McGreevy opened his saloon the same year, he was following in the footsteps of Engel who was already exhibiting assorted cabinet photographs of players on the walls of the "Home Plate" and incorporating personal souvenirs from players like a telegram he'd once received from King Kelly, who also owned a New York City saloon with ex-umpire Honest John Kelly called the Two Kell's. Famous for his tenderloin dinners, Engel regularly entertained the greats of the game including John Ward and Buck Ewing and when he died in 1897 at the age of 52, the members of Boston Elks Lodge No. 10, likely including McGreevy, traveled to his funeral service in New York City to pay their respects to one of the game's greatest fans.

Perhaps influenced by Engel's Home Plate, McGreevy took the concept of a baseball-themed saloon to a new level and gradually transformed his establishment into a gallery of baseball photographs and lithographs that immortalized his customers' favorite players. Operating in a politically charged era when Irish politicians, including Mayor Pat Collins and Congressman John F. "Honey Fitz" Fitzgerald, were consolidating their ethnic

Nuf-Ced standing in the doorway of his liquor store M.T. McGreevy & Co. Ales Wines and Liquors – A.J Houghton Co.'s Celebrated Lager, the precursor to his famed 3rd Base Saloon.

Tossing the game's first pitch at the Huntington Avenue Grounds is Boston Mayor John F. Fitzgerald, who also served as a United States Congressman. A longtime member of the Royal Rooters, "Honey Fitz" formed an alliance with Nuf-Ced McGreevy and was instrumental in organizing the Rooters and participated in fan trips to opposing sites. Fitzgerald's daughter Rose is to the right looking up at her father. Rose would marry Joseph P. Kennedy Sr. and become matriarch of an American political dynasty.

base in Roxbury and the neighborhoods beyond, McGreevy emerged as an organizer and leader in a community that was consumed by baseball. McGreevy and his customers mimicked the pubs from the old country that served both as watering holes and clubhouses for soccer teams and other athletic organizations. In Roxbury McGreevy and his fellow cranks were devoted to the hometown Beaneater baseball clubs managed by Frank Selee that featured native New England stars like Hugh Duffy, Fred Tenney, Marty Bergen, and a third baseman from Buffalo named Jimmy Collins.

The affinity McGreevy and his followers had for the Boston club culminated in a frenzy of fanatic devotion in September of 1897, when McGreevy organized an army of Boston fans to travel via rail to Baltimore and root for the Beaneaters in what would be the deciding games for the National League pennant. Wearing badges incorporating beanpot themes created by the *Boston Globe* and *Boston Herald* identifying themselves as the "Boston Rooters," the group of nearly 200 fans toured the streets of Baltimore with a hired marching band. Led by Congressman Fitzgerald, the group ended at the Baltimore grounds behind the Boston dugout where McGreevy and the entire Boston contingent rooted on their boys "with horns, rattles and a specially arranged battle-cry."[3] *Sporting Life* also reported that after the Rooters posed for a photograph with the Boston team on the steps of Baltimore's Eutaw Hotel, a superstitious Sliding Billy Hamilton blamed a loss in that series on posing with the Rooters. However, before the road trip was over Boston clinched the pennant and McGreevy and his Roxbury Rooters had returned home victorious, "enthusiastic beyond measure with their reception and treatment, and (would) never forget the trip."[4] As one cohesive cheering unit, McGreevy and his cohorts had successfully transformed themselves into baseball's original "tenth man."

The trip of 1897 laid the groundwork for McGreevy's more formalized contingent that would later become known famously as the Royal Rooters, a group dedicated to traveling and rooting for Ban Johnson's newly organized American League club in Boston that snatched Jimmy Collins and other stars away from the longstanding fan favorite Beaneaters. As noted by *Boston Globe* scribe Tim Murnane, a Royal Rooter sat atop the world of fandom, distinguishing himself as a cut above the lower classes of baseball fans for his willingness to travel on his own dime to root for his club in enemy territory. McGreevy and his men revolutionized the concept.

By 1900 McGreevy had moved his Linden Park saloon to a larger space in a standalone structure at 940 Columbus Avenue in Roxbury, located equidistant from the South End Grounds and the site of the Huntington Avenue Grounds, which was built the following year. In 1901 McGreevy, Tim Murnane, and 19th-century fan extraordinaire Hi-Hi Dixwell appeared with a large contingent of Boston Rooters to break ground for the new ballpark on Huntington. McGreevy placed a photograph of the groundbreaking ceremony in a display window at his new location, the first of many in his collection that would embrace the new American League franchise that swayed Roxbury loyalties from the National League. By the time the new American League club played its first game in Boston, in 1901, McGreevy's bar was known as the 3rd Base Saloon, nicknamed as such because it was said to be any fan's "last stop before home."[5] However, the name appears to have also been in part a tribute to local hero and third baseman Jimmy Collins, upon whose shoulders the success of the fledgling American League franchise rested. With Collins already in the American League camp, it only took cheaper ticket prices to secure the full devotion of McGreevy's Rooters for Boston's entry in Ban Johnson's competing big league.

By 1901 McGreevy was already being identified by the nickname Nuf-Ced, a term he was said to have coined after he pounded his fist down on his oak bar. One of his bartenders, Tom Kenny, experienced Nuf-Ced in action and said his boss:

"got his tag from a short terse statement he'd make whenever a customer from the Midwest might become a little over-enthusiastic over Bill Bradley's third-basing talents, as compared to Jimmy Collins, the idol of the Boston fans. … When the argument started to heat up, Mr. McGreevy would say 'Nuf Ced,' which meant the agifiers would have to pipe down or be ejected. And he always had a big strong bouncer on the payroll to see that the peace prevailed."[6]

As the Boston Americans drew crowds to the new Huntington Avenue ballpark, McGreevy's saloon kept its own bouncers busy and became a drawing card itself, before, during, and after games. Taking advantage of the business opportunity, McGreevy enhanced his own developing celebrity in town by placing ads on the covers of the Boston scorecards and programs that read: "McGreevy on the Avenue … Nuf Ced." In the coming seasons he would even buy ad space on the ballpark's left-field wall so fans could read: "What's the last stop before home? Third Base — Nuf Ced."

McGreevy's saloon became the headquarters for the baseball community during the season and extended well into the Hot Stove League during the winter. Season after season, the establishment gradually was transformed into what would become baseball's first true museum, with nearly every square inch of wall space dedicated to small and large mounted pictures of former Boston teams and massive individual portraits of stars dating back to King Kelly and the heroes of McGreevy's youth. Game-used equipment, including gloves and balls, was hung behind the bar and McGreevy went so far as to fashion the game-used war clubs of star players like Cy Young, Nap Lajoie, and Freddie Parent into lighting fixtures that hung from the high ceilings of the saloon. At the end of the bat barrels were affixed frosted glass domes transformed into baseballs with hand painted laces.[7] Players and fans commiserated and drank among McGreevy's collected relics of the

The Rooters in their special on field seats adjacent to the Boston Americans' dugout along the third-base line at the Huntington Avenue Grounds during the 1903 World Series.

Sounds from the drum fill the air and rallying the Boston faithful, thanks to the Royal Rooters drummer positioned on the dugout roof. According to Peter J. Nash in his book *Boston's Royal Rooters*, the Rooters traveled with this large brass drum to provide additional rhythmic accomplishment for their war cries, with their success and popularity influencing future baseball bands.

game with characters who were also notorious oddsmakers and gamblers like Joseph "Sport" Sullivan, who would later be implicated in the scheme to fix the 1919 World Series. It was likely at McGreevy's that Sullivan first became friendly with Eddie Cicotte a decade before the scheme was hatched at the nearby Buckminster Hotel. At McGreevy's 3rd Base Saloon, baseball and betting went hand-in-hand and McGreevy was the arbiter of all baseball arguments and skirmishes. With so many visiting baseball writers, players, and executives frequenting his establishment, Nuf-Ced began to cultivate a national reputation as baseball's most devoted fan, one who also had the inside dope on the diamond at his disposal.

Without question it was at the World Series in 1903 that McGreevy and his Royal Rooters solidified and expanded upon their legend as living good-luck charms who could invariably root their beloved Boston teams to victory. Traveling back and forth between Pittsburgh and Boston, McGreevy and his henchmen Charlie Lavis and Louis Watson adopted the popular song "Tessie" as the Boston fight cry and taunted the opposition with slurs and chants to distract them from the task at hand. In Lawrence Ritter's *The Glory of Their Times*, Pirates third baseman Tommy Leach recalled McGreevy's antics in Games Four and Five and how he and the Rooters sang, "Honus, you hit so badly" in place of "Tessie, you make me feel so badly" from their reserved seats in Section J whenever the great Wagner came to the plate. Leach's first-hand account is perhaps the greatest testament to McGreevy's legacy as the ultimate fan as he recalled:

"I think those Boston fans actually won that series for the Red Sox. We beat them three out of the first four games, and then they started singing that damn 'Tessie' song, the Red Sox fans did. They called themselves the Royal Rooters and their leader was some Boston character named Mike McGreevey. He was known as "Nuf-Sed" McGreevey, because any time there was an argument about anything to do with baseball he was the ultimate authority. Once McGreevey gave his opinion that ended the argument: nuf sed!"[8]

When McGreevy returned to Boston on the same train as Cy Young and the team after the "Tessie"-fueled victory, he was unaware that some fellow Rooters had dressed up the exterior of his saloon with patriotic bunting and a painted sign hailing the Boston club as soon-to-be World champs. The *Boston Globe* reported how upon his return McGreevy, "one of the prime movers of the Pittsburg trip," would be surprised to see 3rd Base decked-out in his honor.[9] Atop the entrance of the 3rd Base Saloon the life-size mannequin known as McGreevy's "Baseball Man" was dressed in a flannel Boston uniform doing his best impersonation of King Kelly and looking down upon the horse-drawn buggies and carriages that made their way down Columbus Avenue towards the ballpark. Riding the momentum of the notoriety he received during that first World Series, McGreevy was further embraced by the baseball press and transformed into a local celebrity with his exploits (just like those of the players) rendered in cartoons drawn by Wallace Goldsmith and Sid Green for the Boston daily newspapers.

When the Giants refused to play Boston after the 1904 season, McGreevy and the Rooters settled on an American League pennant and channeled some hero-worship towards the team manager, Jimmy Collins. The third baseman was honored by McGreevy and Charlie Lavis with a massive silver loving cup paid for by contributions made by the rooters and Boston fans to the *Boston Journal* newspaper. McGreevy sent in his own $6 contribution towards the cup he hoped would bring good luck and the pennant to Boston. In a note to the *Journal* he referred to the honor they were bestowing upon Captain Collins as a "Crack-a-Jack."[10]

Collins and his men faced Jack Chesbro and the New York Highlanders at season's end in a dead heat. McGreevy and Louis Watson paraded on top of the visitors' dugout at Hilltop Park in Upper Manhattan with megaphones leading organized chants and renditions of "Tessie" that were said to have rattled the New York nine. Chesbro, who won 41 games that season, threw a wild pitch to blow the pennant in the ninth inning and McGreevy and his boys went wild. They marched victoriously down 165th Street with a 20-foot banner identifying the posse as the "Boston Rooters" and they posed for a group portrait that was destined for the walls of the 3rd Base Saloon picturing McGreevy and the Rooters savoring their victory over New York. By the time the 1904 season had ended, McGreevy had revolutionized the culture of the fan as the first rooter documented in a photograph who displayed his own signs at the ballpark. At Hilltop Park McGreevy had held a sign that read, "Boston Wants These Games — Nuf-Ced" and another directed at the New York Giants owner who declined to play in a World Series, which read: "Mr. Brush We're on Plush, where

Front side of an advertisement card for McGreevy's 3rd Base Saloon, distributed during the 1903 World Series. The reverse side of the Rooters souvenir captured the lyrics to the Boston Americans' rallying songs, including "Tessie."

are you? Don't be Vain, Give us a Game. One or Two. Do. Do. My Huckleberry Do!"[11]

As much as Michael T. McGreevy was devoted to the Boston baseball teams, he was just as much in love with the game itself. When his beloved team failed to make it into the postseason in 1906, he still traveled to Chicago for the first intracity World Series, between the White Sox and the Cubs, and was recognized in the national baseball press for his acquisitions of several large photographs of the 1906 Series."[12]

In January 1906, the New Year's resolutions of baseball notables were published in the sporting papers, including Cy Young's desire to "pitch a few more no-hitters" and Ban Johnson's vow to call Charles Comiskey a "good fellow." After the Series of 1906, Nuf-Ced made good on his published resolution: "To get a few more souvenirs for his champion collection."[13] It was in 1907, however, that Nuf-Ced made his greatest acquisition to date after learning that a gold medal presented to King Kelly as the Champion Base Runner of the Boston team in 1887 had been deposited in a New York City pawnshop window looking "tarnished, dusty and forgotten."[14] Knowing how much he wanted it, his fellow Rooters purchased the medal for $200 and presented it to McGreevy at the 3rd Base Saloon, where the 33rd-degree rooter polished it and placed it in a display case for all fans to see.

By 1906 McGreevy's baseball museum was a well-known destination for fans and players alike, a spectacle for any baseball enthusiast of that era. As historian John Thorn has said, "McGreevy's saloon looked like Cheers after a Victorian interior decorator had got a hold of it."[15] The saloon resembled the salons of Europe where Rembrandts and Vermeers were assembled to cover entire walls, except that McGreevy's masterpieces were the works of Hy Sandham, Prang, Hastings, Horner, and Chickering. The importance of having your picture up on the walls of McGreevy's baseball shrine was described by Nuf-Ced himself in a broken-English poem he published on the cover of the Boston Americans scorecard sold at the ballpark in 1906:

"Kum, Kum, pla bal & get your piktur up at 3rd Base. The bst koleksion in the Kuntry,

A histry uv the game in pikturs, The tok uv the base bal world.

Have u seen them?

& 2 qot Kaptain Fred Clark (Pitts)

"Kum, Kum b alyv, b alyv, Get in the game." Nuf Ced M.T. McGreevy 940 Columbus Av.

While McGreevy was a rabid collector, he was also a ballplayer at heart, and known as a skilled amateur from accounts of the day that reported both his play and financial support for his own semiprofessional teams. He ate, drank, and slept baseball and extended his devotion to the local sandlots in Roxbury, sponsoring some of the earliest youth and junior baseball clubs dressed in uniforms with "Nuf-Ced's" emblazoned on their chest. It was reported that McGreevy had "organized the youngest uniformed team in Massachusetts" and that the youth team readily challenged "any nine or ten year old players in the state."[16]

McGreevy and his clan also liked to play against the old pros and after each season would gather at O'Brien's

"Boston, Pittsburg, Who are we? We are the rooters for 19-3. We will win, Go tell your pa, We Beaneaters, Beaneaters, Rah! Rah! Rah!" - With his back to the camera raising his megaphone is Nuf-Ced McGreevy, leading the die-hard Royal Rooters in call to battle cries including the popular "Tessie" and other lyrics designed to taunt the Pittsburgh players and fans, such as the one above.
To McGreevy's left standing holding a bowler hat is Rooters' Jerry Watson, a founding member. Below are Boston Americans outfielder Chick Stahl (l) and pitcher Bill Dinneen chatting with the police officer, with neither seeming to share quite the same excitement as the fans. This image was probably taken during Game Six of the 1903 World Series in Pittsburg, when Pirates fans showered the field with paper while Dinneen pitched. The Americans won the Game and eventually the World Series.

A baseball shrine - McGreevy's Third Base Saloon adorned with patriotic bunting during the 1903 World Series between the Boston Americans and Pittsburg Pirates. The Saloon was decorated for the triumphant return of the team and of the Boston Royal Rooters from Pittsburg, where Boston took a lead in the first World Series. The Saloon was located at 940 Columbus Avenue in the Roxbury Crossing neighborhood. BPL

Sunset Farm in rural Holliston, Massachusetts, to play a pickup game followed by a lively smoker that usually honored one of the greats of the game. In McGreevy's presence were old-time greats like the Heavenly Twins Hugh Duffy and Tommy McCarthy, Rooters Jack Dooley and Charlie Lavis, sportswriters including Paul Shannon and Tim Murnane, and current stars of the game like Hughie Jennings, who was honored with his own Winter League event in 1913.[17]

But baseball didn't end in Holliston for McGreevy and the Rooters, who also saw fit to make annual trips at their own expense to Hot Springs, Arkansas, to follow the club. Each season the Boston contingent including McGreevy and fellow Rooters like Mike Regan, "Uncle Bill" Cahill and C. F. Madden, "The Roxbury Kid," would flee the frigid temperatures of Boston and travel by rail with the players to spring training, where they were treated like celebrities. Upon his arrival at the Eastman Hotel in 1908, McGreevy was described in a Hot Springs newspaper as "a fan known all over the country."[18]

According to the *Boston Post*, as early as the spring of 1905, McGreevy was proving himself as a "bit of a player" against the big leaguers. The *Post* quoted Cy Young as saying that he could get McGreevy signed by a team in the South if he ever agreed to cut off his mustache.[19] McGreevy regularly suited up in his own Boston uniform and played so well in exhibition games in 1908 that the manager of the Natchez club of the Cotton States League saw him playing in Hot Springs and actually inquired if he was available for purchase. Playing the manager for a fool, Red Sox owner John I. Taylor fielded a first offer of $200 and promptly upped the price to $300, which was accepted. Upon learning that he was sold, McGreevy said to the Natchez manager, "I guess you've been handed a good sized lemon." Realizing he'd been had, the Natchez man first drew for his gun, but realizing the prank was good-natured and the joke was on him, calmed down when the Boston men bought a few rounds for his men.[20] Thus grew the legend of McGreevy, who was described in the *Arkansas Gazette* as a "wonder" discovered by

President Taylor and "in all probability a member of the Boston team for the upcoming season."[21] It was also reported that Hugh Duffy had attempted to buy him for the Providence club and Barney Dreyfuss for the Pittsburgh Pirates. One spring Nuf-Ced even jokingly signed an official contract with the Boston club.

McGreevy was also famous for showering the real players with gifts and awards and at spring training in 1908 he offered a diamond ring to the Boston player who could steal the most bases during the coming season. It was said that his offer would "increase the number of those who try to steal 'Third Base' on the way home."[22] Making good on his word at Hot Springs in 1909, McGreevy proffered a "nice speech" and presented winner Amby McConnell with an impressive $250 diamond ring.

For McGreevy and the Rooters who accompanied him, the spring ritual was all fun and games, as evidenced at a "cakewalk" given by the "colored waiters" in the Arlington Hotel's skating rink. The local press reported that McGreevy and New York Giant mascot Charles "Victory" Faust had agreed to referee the event and that they even sought out hotel guest and multimillionaire Andrew Carnegie to join them.[23] In his day McGreevy rubbed elbows with the rich, the notorious, and the poor with relative ease and by 1911 he was accompanying the Red Sox owners on the "Red Sox Special" train headed to spring training in California, where the *Los Angeles Express* described him as the "Oldest Baseball Rooter" and the game's greatest fan, coast to coast.[24]

Aside from baseball, Michael T. McGreevy was also known locally in Boston as "one of the best all-around athletes of his age" and was similarly accomplished as a champion handball player known to enter local and regional competitions as well as promoting matches that were wagered upon heavily.[25] He once arranged a $100 match at the L Street Baths between New Yorker Parkie Donegan and Boston's Dick Fitzpatrick in which "considerable money changed hands on the result."[26] Similar challenges were presided over by McGreevy at the candlepin bowling alley in the basement of his 3rd Base Saloon. In 1910 McGreevy was famously challenged to a bowling match by Boston Doves manager Fred Lake and succumbed to Lake by ten pins at the neutral site of Joyce's Lanes in Boston. Losing the challenge, McGreevy took Lake and his friends out to dinner to make good on the wager.[27]

The popular rallying song "Tessie" captured on a handout distributed during the 1903 World Series. It was originally from the Broadway show "The Silver Slipper".

But McGreevy garnered even more notoriety for his athletic activities in the dead of winter at the L Street Baths. It was on the frozen waters of Boston Harbor that McGreevy exhibited his ice-skating skills dressed in nothing but bathing trunks for a motion-picture camera in the winter of 1906. Afterwards, with the film reels in hand, McGreevy took the Boston Americans to a "local picture house" where his antics on skates made a "big hit with the players as well as with the rest of the audience."[28] In February of 1910, McGreevy was also profiled in a feature article in *Baseball Magazine* inspired by his other winter skill, "Swimming in Ice Water," which was also captured on the 1906 motion picture. McGreevy and several of his rooter pals had for decades swum polar-bear style in the icy waters after playing some vigorous games of handball. When asked by *Baseball* why he and his fellow L Street

Mike McGreevy, king of the Royal Rooters, often visited the Boston team during spring training. Shown here in Hot Springs, Arkansas resting after a hike with McGreevy are members of the 1912 Red Sox club, left to right: Bill Carrigan, Fred Anderson, Clyde Engle, McGreevy, Jake Stahl, and Charley Hall.

Brownies ventured into the treacherously icy waters, McGreevy said that he and his pals enjoyed their swims so much during the summer and through October that "someone suggested that we stick it out all Winter." McGreevy added, "The idea made a hit and it was carried by a unanimous vote. It was easy. We grew used to the gradual change in the weather and never minded it a bit."[29] Each winter, McGreevy appeared on the pages of virtually every Boston newspaper in underwear and his ice skates. He told the *Boston Post*, "I have gone out swimming every day this winter, and look at me. I never felt better in my life." The *Post* added, "His eyes sparkled. He is patiently waiting for the baseball season to begin and is pining for another World's Series next fall."[30]

It was in the year of 1912, in the newly constructed Fenway Park, that Nuf-Ced McGreevy and his Royal Rooters reached the apex of their careers in baseball fandom. They rooted Jake Stahl's Red Sox all the way to the American League pennant in the newly christened ballpark, and the rooting alliance between McGreevy and John F. "Honey Fitz" Fitzgerald reached new heights. McGreevy attended every World Series and in 1911 sat in a section reserved for official scorers and the press at the Polo Grounds in New York and at Shibe Park in Philadelphia. In 1912 the Royal Rooters returned to October form, led by McGreevy and Fitzgerald, who by then was the well-established and powerful mayor of Boston. Challenged by the Giants of John J. McGraw and Christy Mathewson, McGreevy and Fitzgerald organized the largest-ever contingent of Royal Rooters to travel to New York City; the mayor secured 300 tickets from the Giants, although there was an army of 1,000 Rooters who wanted to make the trip.

Upon their arrival in New York, the Rooters "caused quite a stir" as they paraded down Broadway in automobiles raucously taunting Gothamites with megaphones and noisemakers singing "Tessie" and a new number called "Knock Wood," penned by McGreevy in tribute to Red Sox pitching ace Smoky Joe Wood.[31] The words to the songs were printed on cards McGreevy produced for the trip depicting a cartoon of him and the "Roxbury Rooters" that read: "At Baltimore in '97, Pittsburg in '03, New York '04, with the odds against us in the enemy's battlefield we cheered them on to victory and brought home the flag. Now for New York 1912 – "NUF CED."

McGreevy and Fitzgerald led the Rooters in organized songs and chants at the Polo Grounds and marched with the Boston Elks band around the perimeter of Fenway Park when the Series returned to Boston. But McGreevy and the Royal Rooters would experience some unexpected drama at Fenway for Game Seven after they realized Red Sox management had sold off their left-field reserved seats to other fans, causing a ruckus by Duffy's Cliff as the Rooters had to be restrained by mounted police. Irate at Red Sox executive Robert McRoy for selling their seats, McGreevy and the Rooters announced that they would be boycotting Game Eight (Game Two ended in a tie), also at Fenway, despite the fact that Red Sox management found space for them in standing room among the other 32,000 fans at Fenway that day.³²

McGreevy's fellow Rooter, the bandleader Johnny Keenan, said, "We are through with the Red Sox, so far as the rooting goes, and we will not attend the final game tomorrow as a body."³³ Lots of fans followed suit and only 17,034 showed up at Fenway for the deciding game of the World Series. However, the Rooters' stand may have had more to do with McGreevy and the boys having inside dope that the Series wasn't on the level and, perhaps, may have known that the Red Sox would win the deciding game as rumors swirled that players were disgruntled with management. Notwithstanding, McGreevy and the Rooters jumped back on the bandwagon quickly as the Red Sox took Game Eight from the Giants and the world championship returned to Boston.

McGreevy and Fitzgerald joined automobiles transporting the players and led a victory parade from Kenmore Square to Faneuil Hall, where the champions were tendered a grand reception compliments of the mayor and the Royal Rooters. Honey Fitz called it the greatest reception he had ever witnessed in Faneuil Hall and McGreevy led his platoon of marching Rooters through the streets like a conductor at Symphony Hall. The outpouring of support McGreevy and the Rooters showered on the players cemented the feeling that they had no axe to grind with the players and with an apology in hand from Sox president and owner Jimmy McAleer, the local press reported that the entire ticket debacle would "probably be largely forgotten before the winter was over."³⁴

With Boston's return to baseball prominence and another world championship under McGreevy's belt, the Rooters continued their support of both the Red Sox and Boston Braves franchises. In 1914 McGreevy organized another road trip to the World Series in Philadelphia to support George Stallings' Miracle Braves against Connie Mack's Athletics. Nuf-Ced produced specially printed song cards and badges for the Royal Rooter, contingent, which included Mayor Fitzgerald, his newlywed daughter, Rose, and her husband, Joe Kennedy. Both newlyweds sported "Royal Rooter" badges made especially for the Series by McGreevy and Fitzgerald. However, Nuf-Ced would miss the Braves' victory after receiving the tragic news of his brother's death in Maine via telegram at the Series.

Under McGreevy's continued leadership the fraternity of fans made road trips to Philadelphia, Brooklyn, and Chicago and experienced additional World Series triumphs for the Red Sox in 1915, 1916, and 1918. In 1915, with Fenway Park less than strategically positioned near McGreevy's 3rd Base Saloon on Columbus Avenue, the barkeep decided to move his business and baseball museum to a corner property at Tremont and Ruggles Streets. McGreevy's saloon continued to flourish at its third location until the Volstead Act and Prohibition closed its doors in 1920, just six days before Babe Ruth was sold to the New York Yankees. While Prohibition was a death blow for McGreevy and the Rooters, it was the sale of Ruth that signified the nails in the coffin for golden age of the Royal Rooters. Upon learning of the Babe's sale to Jacob Ruppert, Nuf-Ced told reporters

Good to his promise - McGreevy in the white Boston jersey with diamond ring winner Amby McConnell, surrounded by players, writers, and visitors on March 2, 1909 at Boston's spring training site in Hot Springs, Arkansas. With the Red Sox finishing last in the American League in stolen bases in 1907, McGreevy promised a diamond ring to the Red Sox player with the most stolen bases in 1908. Sox rookie second baseman McConnell was the winner with 38 steals, beating Harry Lord by nine steals. The Sox team stole 31 additional bases that year.

prophetically, "Every real Boston fan will regret his departing."³⁵

As for Prohibition, McGreevy chalked it up as the result of "bad conditions brought about by intoxicating liquors" but he also predicted in a *Boston Post* "Prohibition Forum" that the old days would soon return in a modified form when the powers that be realized "the bad conditions under Prohibition." Nuf-Ced was quoted as saying, "Light beer and wine will solve the problem," and added this parting shot: "With cheap whiskey on the increase and no beer, surely there are trying times ahead."³⁶ With his beer taps dry and his back bar devoid of the Ky. Taylor's Whiskey that had occupied the shelves for decades, McGreevy's baseball museum stood frozen in time until 1923, when Nuf-Ced leased the space to the Boston Public Library to create an annex for the Roxbury neighborhood that had at once been home (along with Jamaica Plain) to at least 24 breweries.³⁷ Upon its closing, the *Boston Traveler* published a nostalgic farewell to the former Boston landmark and what the writer called the "ghost of McGreevy's cellar," the stuffed and mummified "Baseball Man" dummy that used to sit atop the entrance of the once famous watering hole that was also known as "The Baseball Place." The *Traveler* reported, "The room that once resounded with wholehearted laughter, where stories of Boston's baseball victories were the all-absorbing theme of history and fiction, where the ringing strains of 'Tessie,' the old Boston baseball war song made the rafters tremble, that room is now strangely silent—almost deathlike."³⁸

McGreevy himself reminisced about his old bar and his baseball souvenir collection, which included not only a comprehensive lineup of pictures of the diamond stars but game-used bats, balls, and gloves used by legends like Kelly, Anson, Duffy, Speaker, and Ruth. McGreevy decided that the best fate for his collection was to donate it to the Print Department at the Boston Public Library so that future generations could experience Boston baseball's glory days through his pictures. The library's director, Charles Belden, recognized the significance of McGreevy's collection and welcomed the donation that constituted what he viewed as an "accumulation of photographs showing the evolution of our great national game over a period of fifty years."³⁹

The vast collection included everything from an 1872 image of Harry Wright's Boston club in front of a primitive wooden grandstand featuring a "Refreshments" sign to a 1904 shot of heavyweight champ John L. Sullivan in the Boston dugout with Jimmy Collins. The library staff at the main branch in Copley Square took roughly 200 rare photographs out of the original frames that once hung on the walls of the 3rd Base Saloon and stamped them with the identification mark, "M.T. McGreevey Collection." Books replaced the bottles at the former bar location and the show window that used to exhibit daily baseball scores and statistics was reconfigured with suggestions of literature available at the annex for Roxbury residents. The Red Sox were replaced by Shakespeare with a transition from the "dispensation of lager" to the "distribution of letters." No longer would Nuf-Ced's old grandfather clock, which incorporated a bat for a pendulum and a ball for a weight, "impatiently count off the seconds from game to game." It was the end of an era.⁴⁰

After his collection was deposited at the library, Nuf-Ced and the Royal Rooters vanished further from the baseball scene with each passing season. In 1926 the Red Sox named old Rooter favorite Bill Carrigan as manager and McGreevy called for a short-lived

In for a refreshing dip on Boston's frigid shore in 1906 is Nuf-Ced, in his skivvies being pulled out of icy water. For decades, McGreevy and his Rooters pals took the plunge. A larger version of this photo once hung above a cash register in McGreevy's bar.

McGreevy's spirited leadership continued when the team moved to a new park in 1912. Led by "Nuf-Ced" the Royal Rooters above are parading along the outfield fencing at Fenway Park to their seats in left field. The Boston Lodge of Elks Band leads the tunes with chants with the likes of "Tessie" and the 1912 "Oh, You Red Sox".

resurrection of the original Royal Rooters. Nuf-Ced told reporters, "Carrigan's return is just what the Boston fans have been waiting for." Although the over-the-hill McGreevy thought that Carrigan was "a born fighter who command(ed) the respect of the players," the return of the rooters never took flight and the Sox remained in the American League cellar.[41]

In 1930 McGreevy and some former fellow Rooters made it out to Braves Field to honor and support retired Red Sox catcher Lou Criger in an old timer's game to benefit the disabled veteran. McGreevy couldn't control his glee as he told the *Boston Post*, "What a kick, what a thrill. I felt 25 years younger when I saw the old-time stars coming to bat and showing their old-time stuff." McGreevy got to commiserate once again with Red Sox legends Jimmy Collins, Candy LaChance, and Freddy Parent and contributed $25 to the cause for Criger. McGreevy made a point to tell the organizers of the event, "Distribute tickets among some poor kids or disabled veterans that they may enjoy the same thrills that I am going to get."[42]

In 1939, to celebrate baseball's mythical centennial, the Boston Public Library exhibited choice selections from the McGreevey Collection in a store-front window at Filene's department store in downtown Boston, including one of the oval portraits of Nuf-Ced that once hung above the back bar in his Roxbury watering hole. In that store window the portraits of Fred Tenney, Hughie Duffy, and King Kelly joined large team portraits of almost every prominent Boston nine of the 19th and early 20th centuries. McGreevy was so far removed from the modern baseball scene that a writer from the *Boston Transcript* commented on the Filene's display and referred to Nuf-Ced in the past tense.[43] But McGreevy was still alive and kicking and after the Filene's display returned to the library he was able to witness the naming of a Boston street after him, a portion of Longwood Avenue in Roxbury renamed McGreevy Way.[44]

At the age of 74, Michael McGreevy expressed his hope that the baseball trinkets and souvenirs he'd retained would make a nice exhibit at the 1939 World's Fair in New York, but aside from an article in the *Globe* in 1938 picturing him showing off his prized possession, the King Kelly gold medal, his plans never came to fruition.[45]

On February 2, 1943, Michael T. "Nuf-Ced" McGreevy, the acclaimed "King of the Rooters," died at the age of 77, a victim of heart failure. A few weeks after his burial at Mount Calvary Cemetery in Roslindale, his 13-year-old granddaughter, Alice Ann Thompson, strolled into the offices of the *Boston Globe* and handed over his King Kelly medal to sportswriter Melville Webb. McGreevy's last wish was that his most prized artifact be returned to the *Globe* and then donated to the Baseball Hall of Fame in Cooperstown, New York. Webb ran a story with a headline: " 'Nuf-Ced' Wills Medal to Globe: Asks That Baseball Prize Be Sent to Hall of Fame." Even in death, Nuf-Ced figured out a way to get his mug in the Boston papers.[46] Even *The Sporting News* covered his passing and noted that the Royal Rooters originator "hit the front pages as far back as 1897."[47]

After his death McGreevy's legend was kept alive by fellow rooters like Jack Dooley, who recounted the stories of the old days for a new generation of fans, and by his old employees like Fenway Park attaché Tom Kenney, who recalled bartending at 3rd Base in the good old days when the likes of Jimmy Collins and Babe Ruth would drop by the bar "to do a little fanning with Nuf-Ced."[48] McGreevy gave Kenney a job shortly after he came to Boston from Galway, Ireland, and he never forgot the generosity of the man who always "had a nice free lunch at the end of the bar and a fellow to wait on the trade." Kenney recalled, "You might say a lot of fellows got as far as third base, but sometimes it took them a long time to get home."[49]

A testament to McGreevy's legacy as baseball's greatest fan was also offered up by his baseball fan wife, Annie, in 1955 at a time when Ted Williams wasn't sure if he'd re-sign with the Red Sox. Blind and on her deathbed, the 87-year-old widow was receiving Holy Communion from a visiting priest when she said, "Tell me, Father, has Ted Williams signed up yet? I'm saying prayers that he does." Considering her own condition, the priest was surprised she wasn't saying prayers for herself as she was clearly in her last days. *Boston American* reporter Alan Frazer wrote, "Mrs. McGreevy had just time enough to get to Heaven" and "rejoined 'Nuf-Ced,' the most loyal fan the Red Sox ever had, when Ted announced he was coming back." Frazer added, "Good night, Mrs. McGreevy, I know where you are." Annie McGreevy passed away on May 8, 1955, a few days after a *Boston American* headline read: "Ted's Return Answered Dying Woman's Prayers." Nuf-Ced.[50]

While Nuf-Ced McGreevy was mentioned every now and then in the Boston newspapers in the 1960s and 1970s, baseball's greatest fan and Boston's Royal Rooters faded away into relative obscurity. In 1970 historian Harold Seymour and his wife, Dorothy, utilized Nuf-Ced's collection for *Baseball: The Golden Age*, but it wasn't until 1979, when authors Daniel Okrent and Harris Lewine published *The Ultimate Baseball Book*, a coffee-table tome that featured numerous selections credited specifically to the Boston Public Library's "M.T. McGreevey Baseball Picture Collection." It was

This pin featuring McGreevy's nickname "Nuf-Ced" was produced by McGreevy likely around the time of the 1903 World Series to be worn by the Boston Royal Rooters during games.

the first time in years that the general public got a peek at a large portion of the images that once graced the walls of the nation's first and foremost sports bar, and it sparked the interest of other baseball authors who sought out rare and captivating baseball photography from the turn of the century.

In 1986 author Glenn Stout was employed at the Boston Public Library and essentially rediscovered Nuf-Ced and his remarkable collection in the library's Print Department, along with McGreevy's personal scrapbooks and papers. Stout was the first to research and write about the man and his career and reintroduced McGreevy to Boston fans in several articles, including one which was published in *Sox Fan News* in August 1986 under the title, "The Grand Exalted Ruler of Rooters Row." With Stout's promotion of the man and his collection, McGreevy's photographic treasures became even more popular with authors including *Sports Illustrated*'s Frank Deford, who used the McGreevey Collection to write a 1988 article, "Huge Commotion in Mudville," that included a profile of Nuf-Ced.[51]

In the early 1990s filmmaker Ken Burns worked with the McGreevey Collection and in 1994 Nuf-Ced was reintroduced to a national audience in the award-winning documentary film series *Baseball*, which featured a full segment under the title "Nuf-Ced" and utilized the library's images of the 3rd Base Saloon, McGreevy, and the Rooters.

In 2000 Stout and co-author Richard Johnson began their definitive Red Sox history, *Red Sox Century*, with a scene from McGreevy's 3rd Base Saloon and incorporated many of Nuf-Ced's images throughout the book, as did the 2005 book *Boston's Royal Rooters* and the 2007 documentary film *Rooters: Birth of Red Sox Nation*, both written by this writer. When *Rooters* aired on the cable channel NESN, Red Sox fans witnessed for the first time the original 1906 motion pictures of Nuf-Ced frolicking in the flesh with the rooters and "brownies" at the L Street Baths.

In 2004 Nuf-Ced was immortalized in song by the Boston punk rock band the Dropkick Murphys, who reworked the turn-of-the-century Red Sox fight song "Tessie" with the help of *Boston Herald* baseball writer Jeff Horrigan and backup vocals by Red Sox players Johnny Damon, Bronson Arroyo, and Lenny DiNardo. The Dropkicks evoked the spirit of McGreevy as they sang:

Tessie, Nuf Ced McGreevey shouted
We're not here to mess around
Boston, you know we love you madly
Hear the crowd roar to your sound
Don't blame us if we ever doubt you
You know we couldn't live without you
Tessie, you are the only only only

The Rooters gave the other team a dreadful fright
Boston's tenth man could not be wrong
Up from "Third Base" to Huntington
They'd sing another victory song [52]

Whether it was sheer luck or the ghost of Nuf-Ced McGreevy assisting the band, each time the Dropkicks played "Tessie" live at Fenway Park during the 2004 playoff run, the Red Sox won as they brought home the first World Series championship to Boston since Nuf-Ced and the Rooters traveled to Chicago singing "Tessie" in 1918. They repeated the feat for the postseason of 2007.

In 2008 Dropkick Murphys frontman Ken Casey and this writer reopened McGreevy's 3rd Base Saloon at 911 Boylston Street in Boston in a faithful replica of the original bar with reproduction and original pictures from McGreevy's original location, including the original painted glass portrait of Nuf-Ced that hung behind the original back bar in Roxbury.

Sadly, in the decade before Glenn Stout's rediscovery and promotion of the McGreevey Collection, close to one-third of the photographic images that were originally donated to the library in 1923 were wrongfully removed from the Copley Square branch, the victims of a large-scale heist that was perpetrated sometime in the mid- to late 1970s. Amazingly, nearly half of the photographs that were documented as part of the 1939 Filene's store window display were absent from the Print Department's holdings. Luckily, library staff had photographed many of images before they were stolen and over the years several of those McGreevy treasures have been recovered. After several items from the collection appeared for sale at local baseball-card conventions and in advertisements published in *Sports Collectors Digest* in 1983, SABR member Bob Richardson and the Boston Public Library's keeper of prints, Sinclair Hitchings, conducted an independent investigation and recovery effort that yielded several returns of Nuf-Ced's stolen treasures.[53]

In the past few years, other McGreevy gems have appeared for sale on sites ranging from eBay to Sotheby's, and thanks to additional recovery efforts spearheaded by McGreevy's 3rd Base Saloon, some of those rare and historic images have been returned to the institution Nuf-Ced originally donated them to. The most notable recovery was that of the 1904 photograph of John L. Sullivan and Jimmy Collins in the Red Sox dugout. The Boston Public Library stamp on the photograph had been defaced and obscured to conceal its McGreevy provenance but was still visible when it was sold as part of New York Yankees partner Barry Halper's collection at Sotheby's in 1999. In 2008 the *Boston Globe* reported the recovery of the iconic photograph after it was offered for sale online by a dealer in Maine and purchased by the reconstituted

McGreevy's 3rd Base Saloon. In the article headlined "A Home Run for the BPL," library official Aaron Schmidt, who had been instrumental in assisting the recovery effort, said, "Every time we get one of these back it's like a homecoming. Of all the ones that we're missing this is No. 1 in terms of importance."[54] The photograph was put on display in the museum showcase at the revived McGreevy's 3rd Base Saloon on Boylston Street.

Note: Over the years there have been several spellings used for both Nuf-Ced's last name and his nickname (Nuff-Said, Nuf Sed, etc.). Authors Glenn Stout and Don Hubbard have commented on the spelling issue in their books *Fenway 1912* and *The Red Sox Before the Babe*, respectively. Stout chose "McGreevey" based upon several bits of evidence including the 1903 photograph of the 3rd Base Saloon which read: "M.T. McGreevey & Co." and several listings in the Boston directories and U.S. census records that identified Nuf-Ced as "McGreevey." Stout was also influenced by the well-established use of "McGreevey" in relation to the Boston Public Library's collection, which now designates the official name of the collection as the "M.T. McGreevey Collection of Baseball Pictures" in bibliographic records. While Stout also noted that it was common for Irish surnames to have alternate spellings or misspellings, he said, "Irish spellings are often so fluid anyway going from Gaelic to English, but the best part is the whole notion just opens up a little window to another time."[55]

When I had to decide what spelling to use for the reconstituted 3rd Base Saloon at 911 Boylston Street, I considered all of Stout's information as well as additional information available at the Boston Public Library, the Suffolk County Courthouse, and in the U.S. census and Boston directory records. I found that although Nuf-Ced's birth was recorded with the surname "McGreevey" in the official Roxbury ledgers in 1865, he signed his last will and testament, in 1938, as well as other documents including the lease of his bar property to the library in 1920, as "M.T. McGreevy." The only surviving photograph of Nuf-Ced in front of his first bar location at 17 Linden Park (circa 1894) shows the name "McGreevy" hanpainted on the business sign. In addition, the vast majority of Nuf-Ced's baseball advertisements printed on scorecards and programs sold at the Huntington Avenue Grounds bear the "McGreevy" name, including the advertisement for the bar on the cover of the program sold at the first World Series in 1903.

Nuf-Ced may have come into this world in 1865 as a "McGreevey," but by the time he checked out the flourish from his own pen read: "McGreevy." As Glenn Stout has said, "Others are free to disagree (after all, in regard to Nuf-Ced, some kind of argument seems wholly appropriate)."[56]

So, with that being said, both camps have now pounded their fists upon the bar and shouted, "Nuf-Ced."

Sources

In addition to the sources noted in this biography, the author also utilized the following Sources

M.T. McGreevey Collection of Baseball Pictures, Print Department, Boston Public Library

The McGreevey Scrapbooks, M.T. McGreevey Collection of Baseball Pictures, Print Department, Boston Public Library

McGreevey Timeline, Glenn Stout, compiler, Print Department, Boston Public Library

Don Hubbard, *The Red Sox Before the Babe* (Jefferson North Carolina: McFarland, 2009)

Peter J. Nash, *Boston's Royal Rooters* (Charleston, South Carolina: Arcadia, 2005)

Bill Nowlin, *Day by Day With the Boston Red Sox* (Cambridge, Massachusetts: Rounder Books, 2006)

Glenn Stout and Richard Johnson, *Red Sox Century* (Boston: Houghton Mifflin, 2000)

Probate Records of Michael T. McGreevey, Suffolk County Courthouse, Boston.

Glenn Stout, "The Grand Exalted Ruler of Rooter's Row," *Sox Fan News*, August 1986

Don Jensen, "They All Went to Nick's: High and Low Life in Manhattan's First Sports Bar," *Base Ball: A Journal of the Early Game*, Spring 2009

Author interview with Alice Thompson, 2006

Author interview with Fran Canario, 2006

Author interview with Glenn Stout for *Rooters: The Birth of Red Sox Nation* (Cooperstown Monument Co./Killswitch Productions, 2007)

Author interview with John Thorn for *Rooters: The Birth of Red Sox Nation* (Cooperstown Monument Co./Killswitch Productions, 2007)

Notes

1. *McGreevey Timeline* by Glenn Stout, M.T. McGreevey Collection, Boston Public Library.
2. *Boston Directory*, 1887.
3. *Boston Globe*, clipping undated.
4. *Sporting Life*, October 2, 1897.
5. "Nuf Ced's Bar Fond Memory To Sox Attache," *Boston Traveler*, undated clipping. Author's collection.
6. John Drohan, *"Nuf Ced's Bar Fond Memory To Sox Attache," Boston Traveler*, undated clipping. Author's collection.
7. *Boston Traveler*, April 23, 1923.
8. Lawrence Ritter, *The Glory of Their Times* (New York: Macmillan, 1966).
9. *Boston Globe*, October 12, 1903.

10 *Boston Journal*, October, 1904. Clipping otherwise undated. McGreevey scrapbook.
11 *Boston Herald*, October, 1904. Clipping otherwise undated. McGreevey scrapbook.
12 *McGreevey Scrapbooks*, Boston Public Library.
13 *McGreevey Scrapbooks*, Boston Public Library.
14 *McGreevey Scrapbooks*, Boston Public Library.
15 *Rooters: Birth of Red Sox Nation* (Cooperstown Monument Co./Killswitch Productions, 2007).
16 *McGreevey Scrapbooks*, Boston Public Library.
17 *Boston Sunday Post*, January 19, 1913.
18 *McGreevey Scrapbooks*, Boston Public Library.
19 *Boston Post*, February 1906. Clipping otherwise undated. McGreevey scrapbook.
20 *Arkansas Gazette* 1906. Clipping otherwise undated. McGreevey scrapbook.
21 Ibid.
22 *McGreevey Scrapbooks*, Boston Public Library.
23 *Arkansas Gazette*, 1906. Clipping otherwise undated. McGreevey scrapbook.
24 *Los Angeles Express*, February 28, 1911.
25 *McGreevey Scrapbooks,* Boston Public Library.
26 *McGreevey Scrapbooks,* Boston Public Library.
27 *Boston Globe,* January 28, 1910.
28 *McGreevey Scrapbooks*, Boston Public Library.
29 *Baseball Magazine*, February 1910.
30 *Boston Post*, undated clipping in McGreevey scrapbook.
31 *McGreevey Scrapbooks*, Boston Public Library.
32 Peter J. Nash, *Boston's Royal Rooters* (Charleston, South Carolina: Arcadia, 2005).
33 *McGreevey Scrapbooks*, Boston Public Library.
34 *McGreevey Scrapbooks*, Boston Public Library.
35 *McGreevey Scrapbooks,* Boston Public Library.
36 *Boston Post (undated clipping) McGreevey Scrapbooks*, Boston Public Library.
37 Michael Reiskind and Peter O'Brien, "*Boston's Lost Breweries*," Jamaica Plain Historical Society. March 25, 2006. Transcription posted on the Society's website.
38 *Boston Traveler*, April 28, 1923.
39 Letter from Charles Belden to Michael T. McGreevy, May 3, 1923, McGreevey Papers, Boston Public Library.
40 *Boston Evening Transcript*, April 24, 1923.
41 *Boston Post*, December 3, 1926.
42 *Boston Post*, August 21, 1930.
43 *Boston Evening Transcript*, 1939. Clipping otherwise undated, author's collection.
44 Glenn Stout, *McGreevey Timeline*, Boston Public Library.
45 *Boston Globe*, June 3, 1938.
46 *Boston Globe*, February 18, 1943.
47 *The Sporting News*, February 11, 1943.
48 "Nuf Ced's Bar Fond Memory To Sox Attache," *Boston Traveler*, undated clipping. Author's collection.
49 Ibid.
50 *Boston American*, May, 1955. Clipping otherwise undated.
51 Author interview with Glenn Stout via e-mail January 2013.
52 "Tessie," Dropkick Murphys, 2004.
53 Author Interview with Sinclair Hitchings, 2009.
54 *Boston Globe*, December 31, 2008.
55 Glenn Stout, *Fenway 1912* (Boston: Houghton Mifflin, 2012).
56 Ibid.

1901 Timeline

How It All Began — The First Season

January 4 — Team owner Charles Somers returned to Boston, staying under an assumed name. Baseball entrepreneur Arthur Irwin had leased the land at Charles River Park and was hoping to make a deal to offer it to a second ballclub in Boston, but Ban Johnson favored Somers and turned down Irwin, who thus preferred to see a National Association team come to Boston rather than one from the new American League.

It was clear that a number of the players were looking with interest on the new league. Tim Murnane of the *Boston Globe* quoted Hugh Jennings as saying, "I would rather sign for $1,200 with the American league and give it a chance to build up than accept $2,000 from the National league and be a slave in every sense of the word. If a break to the American league is necessary I hope the ballplayers will look at things the way I do. If the National league insists on ignoring us we have got to do something. A baseball war is preferable to playing further under the conditions that have made the protective association a necessity. We know that the American league is backed by men of brains, fairness and considerable money. …. I would rather see the National league grant us our demands and have next season begin harmoniously, but I have it on the best of authority that the league men never had any idea of granting what we ask and will not give us another hearing." Jennings added, "If a fight comes, we wish the public to understand that the league magnates brought it on by their bull-headedness and double dealing."

Murnane himself opined, perhaps a bit naïvely, "There is no intention on the part of the American Leaguers to grab the players of the National league, but they are working so that if it should come to a game of grab, the American league would be in a position to do the most business."

January 5 — It appeared that the National Association and the American League might be squaring off to do battle, and that the National League owners would not be saddened to see the two of them duke it out, as they watched the two from the sidelines.

January 6 — Somers had reported on his Boston trip to Ban Johnson and a story filed this day said that it looked as though the two had determined to place a franchise in Boston, though they still lacked the land. Either Buffalo or Indianapolis would have to be dropped from their plans, should they add Boston and go head-to-head with the Beaneaters. Johnson said he would "poo-hoo" the notion that the National League would try to revive the American Association to counter the American League. Somers had also visited Philadelphia and Baltimore on his trip and reinforced the commitment of John McGraw to the American League. McGraw had reportedly been offered management of the New York Giants franchise by owner Andrew Freedman in a fruitless effort to keep him with the National League, and — on the same day — also reported to have been offered the Baltimore franchise in the National Association. He reportedly wrote to Ban Johnson reaffirming his loyalty.

January 10 — Ban Johnson said that if the vaunted Charles River Park site could not be obtained, he would try to secure a parcel of land on Huntington Avenue, but that he truly intended to place a team in Boston. In Philadelphia, Connie Mack continued to talk with Arthur Irwin about the Charles River Park land. President Soden of the NL believed that the signatures of club owners to the National Agreement meant they could be enjoined against playing any games in Chicago against an American League team placed there, and that they could be enjoined if they attempted to do so.

January 12 — Connie Mack came to Boston and had a long talk with Hugh Duffy about Duffy coming over to the American League. Duffy had captained the National League team in 1900. The January 13 *Globe* suggested that perhaps the AL would not be coming to town, in part because no one from the league was coming to terms with Arthur Irwin and his partner, Hart. Boston's NL owners "smile at the idea of Johnson locating a club here," said the paper. They didn't think that another ballclub in Philadelphia was going to happen, either, and that the legal situation in Chicago was so ironclad that it would scare away anyone trying to place a second team there.

January 14—Duffy said he was looking for new worlds to conquer. He knew the Nationals were looking for someone else to captain the team. Connie Mack had been coming to Boston daily from his home in West Brookfield, looking over the "baseball situation," wrote the *Globe*.

January 15—President Soden of Boston's National League baseball club denied he'd given his permission for an American Association club to be placed in Boston. In fact, he was likely hostile to the idea, according to the *Boston Post* correspondent, telling him, "In general my opinion is that no two clubs in a city can prosper, because there is a division of interest and patronage. ... I hold, as a principle, that if two clubs are located in one city it will be a case of the survival of the fittest."

January 16—Ban Johnson talked about expanding to the Hub: "Boston is a good city. It is only a question of time, and unless our plans fail, we will have a club there this year." - *Globe*

January 17—GETS A FOOTING. American League Leases Baseball Grounds. Secures "Shoots the Chutes" Space from Elevated Railway Company. (*Boston Globe*) On behalf of the Boston club, Connie Mack signed a five-year lease for a parcel of land on Huntington Avenue that had previously been used by a "shoot the chute" outfit, whose summer patrons would slide down a chute into water. The location was as easy to get to as the South End Grounds, and a larger one.

January 18—RIVAL BASEBALL NINE FOR BOSTON. Since Messrs. Irwin and Hart were still seeking to place an American Association team in the Charles River Park area, there was a possibility of *three* major professional teams competing in Boston for the loyalties of local fans. It was said that Hugh Jennings would manage the team. Opening Day would be less than four months away, but it was clear that there had been some planning—Mack turned up with Hugh Duffy at the building commissioner's office with plans in hand for a grandstand similar to the one at Philadelphia's park. The new club said it would charge 25 cents admission (half the price the Boston Nationals had been charging), with an extra quarter for grandstand seats. The owners were prepared to lose money in their first year. Mack said that the new league would also field teams in Milwaukee, Detroit, Chicago, Cleveland, Washington, Baltimore, and Philadelphia.

January 19—TO PLAY RIVAL AGAINST RIVAL. Soden's Team Will Use One Newcomer to Fight Another. The announcement on the 17th that Ban Johnson's league would place a team in Boston prompted a reaction on the 18th that Soden et al. would consent to the American Association coming to town, under the national agreement. Better to have another team playing under the guidelines he and the other magnates had promulgated and to use them as competition to the American League team. Would the NL help fund the AA? Billings laughed that they were "in no position to give anything more than its moral support and the privileges which the national agreement guarantees." He declared that even with the NL contracting from 12 teams in 1899 to eight teams in 1900, only Pittsburgh made any money. He said he couldn't understand why someone who appeared to have such business acumen as he heard Somers had would want to proceed. "Baseball is not the attractive investment it was. Those in it stay largely on account of the fascination," he said, and continued, "We are going to be at the South End grounds ... giving the best baseball to be had. The other leagues can't compete with us in this respect. At the league meeting in New York, we looked over the American League players, when it was apparent that Johnson was to withdraw from the agreement, and we found none desirable. Most of them were players cast adrift by the National League, or young men whose worth was yet to be proved. We give the best salaries and can command the best talent. ... The new-comers will have to surrender. The old Brotherhood had everything, the best players and grounds, but we crushed it in twelve months." Soden's confidence would soon be undermined. Would he ever come down to 25-cent baseball? "Never."

The American Association (not to be confused with the American League) announced plans to place teams in Washington, Baltimore, Philadelphia, Boston, Detroit, Milwaukee, Louisville, and Indianapolis. The next day's paper assessed that this league's moves were frankly meant to be a "buffer" to Ban Johnson's. The January 22 *Post* couldn't have been clearer: "The magnates of the National League became bitterly disposed toward Ban Johnson and in order to kill off his plan, they helped to organize the Association circuit." The Association leaders wrapped up their meeting in New York, signing the national agreement.

January 20—The *Boston Sunday Post* reported that Johnson and Somers were visiting cities where they had placed teams. They were asked why Boston, instead of (as thought to have been intended) Buffalo, and he said it was in response to the hostility of the National League. In other words, he was prodded to do battle. New York Giants owner Andrew Freedman's attempt to lure John McGraw back into the fold was cited by the paper; McGraw had been offered some real inducements, but elected to stick to his word and stay with Johnson, and Johnson was most appreciative of his loyalty.

January 22—BAD FOR BASEBALL. Unless War Ends Disaster for Owners Must Result. BOSTON A STORM CENTER. Philadelphia also faced three teams under the three leagues planned, two of which were brand-new. Arthur Irwin's American Association team had the Charles River Park land leased and it would be easy to prepare for baseball. The land on Huntington Avenue previously leased by the Chutes Company had a lake (into which the chutes dumped their patrons) that had to be filled, "the plank walks removed, the sideshows transplanted and the ground leveled. After this, grandstand and bleachers must be built, all at extra expense." It was quite a challenge facing the American League team, to in effect take an amusement park and translate it into a major-league ballpark in more or less three months.

Ban Johnson and Charles Somers arrived in Boston on the 22nd, visited the land they'd leased and looked over plans for the park itself. Staying at Young's Hotel, Johnson said they hadn't sought local investors, and that the financing was all taken care of before they'd committed to Boston. He said they had settled on a manager, but weren't prepared to name him yet. He did not declare open war. "We are not here to trample on anyone, nor to indulge in any cut-throat policy," he said. "If possible, the schedule shall be arranged so that there won't be any conflicting dates. In making this move, we are trying to build up the game, not tear it down." In Philadelphia, Mack secured a ten-year lease on grounds there. Boston wasn't the only team building a new ballpark in a hurry.

January 23—Johnson and Somers returned to the Chutes grounds and settled on the exact placement of the diamond and grandstand. An architect was working on the plans. Attorney M.J. Moore learned that there had been an effort at City Hall to withhold a license to play baseball on the Huntington Avenue grounds. "From what source the opposition arose could not be learned." One could hazard a guess. The matter was resolved.

January 26—Arthur Irwin was able to get Soden's consent in writing; the NL team owner had no objection to the Association fielding a team in Boston. He said he and Soden had talked about the two teams playing a preseason series of games against each other.

January 27—Hugh Duffy was in Chicago for a meeting of the American League and announced that he would become the manager of the Milwaukee team. He said his attorney had told him he had completed his contract with Soden's club in Boston, and that the reserve clause didn't apply to him since he was leaving the National League. He volunteered his opinion that "Boston is ripe for a second team and I predict success for the club there" (meaning, of course, the new American League club).

January 28 — Had things worked out otherwise, Duffy might have been the first manager of the team that became the Red Sox. He told the *Boston Herald* on this day, "I would prefer managing the new club in Boston, but I can't go back on my agreement with Milwaukee."

January 29 — In Cleveland, President Charles Zimmer of the Players' Protective Association issued the statement: "If the National League does not grant us our request we may go over to the American League in a body. That league has given us what we want without any demands on our part and has shown a disposition to be entirely fair with us. The National League seems to be afraid of us; they distrust us. The National League will learn that we are not to be trifled with."

January 30 — Echoing efforts to lure John McGraw away from the American League, Hugh Duffy reported that he had been made a big offer by the planned Milwaukee team of the American Association if he would only jump his American League contract. It was $1,000 more than he'd been offered to run the AL franchise in Milwaukee, but — like McGraw — he declined the offer.

January 31 — The plans for the new ballpark were completed. Bids would be put out in the coming week for construction. There were hints that Soden might seek an injunction to prevent Duffy from working for the AL team in Milwaukee.

February

February 1 — The American League was trying to adopt a more player-friendly stance. "The Ban Johnson organization has shown the players the greatest consideration, has recognized their body [the Players' Protective Association] and acceded to their demands so that the respect the players have for the Johnsonian band is something akin to affection."

The word had been out for two or three days that the Boston Nationals had a "brilliant star in tow" for the season, and speculation ran from Sheckard to Honus Wagner to Jesse Tannehill.

February 2 — The Players Association issued a statement instructing its members not to sign any contracts with the National League, the American Association, or the Eastern League. The National League indicated it as simply going to promulgate its own schedule, without regard to any other league.

February 3 — The day's *Boston Post* ran a drawing of the new ballpark for the Americans, approved, and going out for bids. The capacious outfields would do away with what the paper called "fake" home runs. The bleachers were to have a canvas roof. The home team's quarters were said to be roomy, with a dressing room, lockers, and shower baths. There was even a room with lockers provided for the sports reporters, an innovation that couldn't hurt coverage.

Veteran sports editor Horace S. Fogel of the *Philadelphia Ledger* was blunt about the strategy of creating a third league: "The proposed new American Association is to be organized for one purpose only, to block, annoy, harass, and fight the American League. In other words, not as a sporting organization for sport's sake, but merely to be used by the National League merely as a club to be beat off and kill all opposition to the big baseball trust."

February 8 — Word was both that Napoleon Lajoie had signed with the American League and that Jimmy Collins had visited Connie Mack in Philadelphia, and either signed or accepted terms.

February 10 — The *Post* ran a lengthy interview with Hugh Jennings. He talked about the "awful management" of the magnates and the "arrogant and highhanded manner" in which they ran the game, which had "disgusted and driven away thousands of supporters and enthusiasts," and went on to say: "The American League looks strong. There is no question that the men connected with it, and especially those in official capacity, are men of executive ability, resourceful and conservative. … I do not say that the American League is sufficiently strong to defeat the National League in a baseball war, but I do say that the American League stands better with the public and therefore would have the support of the people."

The *Boston Globe* pointed out that the planned AL team in Boston still had no manager, and the park had yet to be built. It was no small thing to place a team in Boston, the paper averred with a touch of superiority: "A first class team must be picked up, for only the real thing will go in Boston. What might do in Milwaukee will not satisfy the 'fan' here."

Some of the NL magnates were starting to get worried, reported the *Washington Post*, writing that the new American League no longer seemed like the joke it had a month or two earlier. Responding to rumors that Nap Lajoie, Jimmy Collins, and others might be signing with the new league, the Phillies owner, Colonel John I. Rogers, sniffed with a bit of bravado, his man Lajoie in mind, "You cannot tell when a man may go crazy. He may have lost his mind and gone over to the American League. I would not insult Mr. Lajoie's intelligence by approaching him on such an absurd question."

February 11—COLLINS LEAVES NATIONAL LEAGUE. Readers of the morning *Post* saw a story on page 3 saying that Collins had agreed to manage (and play third base for) the Boston Americans. "By securing Collins the American League has undoubtedly dealt the Boston National League club a powerful blow. Outside of Herman Long, there is no player in the ranks of the Boston team whose claims as a drawing card are so great, nor one who has ever stirred thousands by his brilliant work so often." It was clearly a smart strategic move.

February 12—Compromise with the American League was now impossible, said the NL. "Don't want one," said Ban Johnson, in effect. And Tim Murnane said there really were plenty of players to go around. Of those reportedly signing with the AL, he wrote, "No doubt the players are looking for the biggest bundle of long greens with the proper safety valves attached."

February 14—Charles Somers visited Boston, to sign the contract for building the ballpark "and to advise about the multitude of details incident to establishing a club here." The contracts were apparently not quite ready so Somers continued making his rounds of the cities of the league, and left Philadelphia on the 19th to return to Boston for another go at the contracts. Somers did say that local investors were not forthcoming, but he was prepared to finance the ballclub entirely by himself.

February 16—Construction was under way for the new parks in Philadelphia and Baltimore. There was some design modification for the one in Boston. And the team had still not announced who the manager would be. "The manager has been signed … but his name will not be given out at present," stated Somers. Negotiations were still under way with the Players Association and it might be impolitic to announce any signings before some of the details of the relationship of the association to the new league were worked out. The *Philadelphia Public Ledger* declared, "It is not yet too late to stop this war, effect a compromise and proclaim peace before the time for the season to open comes around in April. A few reasonable concessions on the part of the National league will bring about this much desired result. If these concessions are not made—and they would bring money into the treasury of every National league club, instead of taking the coin out of the pockets of the magnates—the latter are bound to pay dearly for their stubbornness, even if in the end they should succeed in vanquishing the American league."

February 21—The contracts for construction of the park and the grading of the grounds were executed in Boston, and Somers returned to Philadelphia. The deal called for completion on May 1—building a major-league baseball park from scratch in 78 days. Somers still had not confirmed the signing of Jimmy Collins, or for that matter anyone else. No park, no players—with about two months to go? Somers said that most of the team had already been signed but nonetheless he declined to name any names.

February 25—The National League met two weeks earlier than usual, alarmed as the owners were by the challenge from the American League.

February 26—PLAYERS WILL WAR ON AMERICAN LEAGUE. Early word out of the meetings was that the NL magnates had agreed to almost everything demanded by the Players Association, but that the price paid was that the players agreed not to sign contracts with organizations not under the national agreement. "This, it is claimed, will be almost a death blow to the American League," even though the AL had agreed to the same terms months earlier. (See March 9, however.)

February 27—Feeling his team had secured the upper hand, thanks to the deal with the Players Association, President Soden said he wanted to arrange the schedule so that both Boston teams would play on the same dates and go head to head. He was angry that the American League had signed players he felt were under obligation to the NL and was now ready for outright war.

February 28—KILLED BY MAGNATES. American Association Dies from A Foul Blow. Broken Promises of Support. Such was the *Washington Post* headline announcing the apparent end of the league thought to have been a stalking horse for the National League.

March

With the Association gone, Tim Murnane talked about the prospects for two-team baseball in Boston. "Star Players Flirting for High Salaries" was the subhead of his column, and he began suggesting that both Philadelphia and Chicago could support two teams if the quality of ball was good enough. "The most interesting fight will be right here in Boston, where the new comer will offer a good thing for popular prices. ... If the American league succeeds in securing a first-class team and has the attractions, it will no doubt do good business. To get these men it will have to pay large salaries, larger than the old league paid, and in this way better the condition of the player, for a time at least, that is the star players that are enticed away from the big league." Almost predicting the moves in the offing, he added, "Here in Boston players of the Collins, Criger, Stahl, and Dinneen stamp would be a guarantee of fast ball. The public is ever ready to support a good fast winning ball team."

Should the Nationals lose some players, it might actually prove salutary. "The South End grounds will have the best talent to be had for money and can be depended upon to play the finest kind of ball. The loss of some of last year's players will really help matters, as the public was anxious for a change of faces. The big league is bound to have at least three-fourths of the best players in the business and or that reason will naturally play the best all round ball. ... Taking players like Collins and Dinneen out of the league club, the chances for a winner are reduced, unless other clubs should suffer in the same way."

Of course, even a player as popular as Collins had to perform. "Should Collins and DInneen change their base of operations, Collins in particular, it is not a sure thing that the move would be a popular one for the game in this city. Should Collins make a bad showing with the team it would be a trying time for him. ..."

If both teams won, things would be wonderful, but Murnane recalled that just a decade earlier, both the Boston Beaneaters and the Boston Reds won their respective pennants, but neither made money—even though their game dates never conflicted. Murnane noted that the American League had won the early public-relations battle; they had "posed as the champion of the players' cause, and in this way won the sympathy of the public." (*Boston Globe*, March 3, 1901)

March 1—COLLINS IS FIRM. Catcher Bill Clarke, who'd hit .315 for the Beaneaters in 1900, left the league to take a position of team captain in Washington. He'd been the main man promoting the American Association team planned for Baltimore and when the NL dumped those plans, he was far from pleased. The Nationals were said prepared to go all out to entice Jimmy Collins back, realizing that at least a couple of his teammates would probably go with him, and maybe as many as three or four of them. Collins stuck to his guns, conferring in Cleveland with Somers. Clarke suggested that the players may have "played a very clever hocus pocus" on the National League magnates, getting them to agree to all their demands while promising to suspend players who signed with the American League. He predicted, "If the players sign with the American League, they will be suspended, but not expelled and at the next meeting of the association they will all be reinstated." (*Boston* Globe) (Also see March 9.)

J.B. Billings, one of the Boston Nationals' triumvirs, said that he and manager Selee had spent a full day with Collins in Buffalo and that he'd be returning to the team. "That you can depend on." Collins had reportedly told him he's signed nothing.

March 2 — Somers contradicted Billings on Collins, making what was deemed "the official announcement" that Collins had signed with his team as player and manager, and that Hugh Duffy would manage Milwaukee.

Ned Hanlon of the Brooklyn team said the league would seek to enjoin any players from signing with American League clubs. The *Boston Globe* referred to "the apparent stampede of players to the American League."

March 3 — Manager Frank Selee said he still didn't believe Collins would desert him. He added, "It seems to me any players is acting rashly and imperiling his future, if he has any, by signing with any league which is lowering the price of baseball. There is no occasion for 25-cent ball in Boston."

March 4 — Collins announced that he had indeed signed with the Americans. Chick Stahl was said to have signed as well. He would, he declared, "have a team that will be first-class in every particular. Boston is an ideal baseball town, and I know that the American league will make a complete success."

March 5 — Word came out of Cleveland that Charles Hemphill had signed with the Boston Americans. A good part of the team was now listed, though not fixed in stone:
Collins, 3B
Ferris, SS
Parent, 2B
Freeman, 1B
Dinneen, P
Schrecongost, C

with Stahl, Hemphill, Dolan seen as the outfielders.

March 7 — About a hundred people turned out for the official groundbreaking, a little after noon, each one presented with a miniature American flag. Photographs were taken of noted Boston baseball booster, Gen. Arthur "Hi Hi" Dixwell, who had placed his order for season tickets and was given a ceremonial shovel to turn the sod. With Dixwell were Somers' attorney, M.J. Moore, and former Representative M. J. Sullivan. As soon as the ground was turned, a round of firecrackers was fired off and the flag was raised over the entrance to the grounds. At this point "the party repaired to the little house on the grounds where luncheon was served" along with a toast proposed by Sullivan to the health of the American League. After lunch, Moore showed the guests around the grounds, pointing out how the diamond would be positioned. The stakes were already in the ground showing the location of the grandstand.

March 8 — Collins had been expected in Boston, but did not show, his absence said to be because of a pitcher he was visiting and hoping to sign for the team. The *Boston Herald*, however, ran an article in which he described his decision to sign with the Americans and predicted that many other former National Leaguers would feel the same way, even if they weren't paid any more than they had been in 1900. "The National league's threat to reduce salaries to $2000 had a bad effect upon the men." He also added that he was going to "take the team to Charlottesville, Va., for spring practice, and will expect to have the men in prime condition for the first-call of the umpire."[1]

> **YOUNG TO PLAY HERE.**
>
> Boston Americans Get the Famous Pitcher.

March 9 — Former St. Louis pitcher Cy Young was said to have signed with Boston.

Perhaps the Players' Protective Association was backtracking, and more than a little, saying that the deal President Charles Zimmer had reached with the National League was just to suspend players who signed with the American League, and that the suspension was a temporary one. In a statement that the attorney for the association and the dissembling Zimmer both signed, they said Zimmer really had no authority to bind the association. Asked when the association would next meet, he said it would not be until after the season.

March 11 — Collins was in town at Brigham's Hotel and let it be known that he'd placed an order with the Wright & Ditson sporting-goods firm, and that his team's uniforms would be white with black stockings at home and gray with blue stockings on the road. (The *Post* on the 13th said the home stocking would be dark blue.) Collins said that Lou Criger was on the team, too, and that he expected the team would land Young. He added, regarding his own decision, "I don't believe there is any rule or law to prevent a man from bettering his condition, if he had the opportunity." He'd had a visit from Hugh Duffy, then went with Duffy to Cleveland to meet Somers, and became a believer. With no intended edge, he said of the triumvirs, "They've been treated as fairly as they treated me." Somers said from Cleveland that he'd talked with Cy Young but that they were still just talking. President Soden of the Boston Nationals was buoyed at a report from Philadelphia that Colonel Rogers, the owner there, had received a written opinion that the option clause in the NL contracts would hold up in court.

March 12 — The Board of Aldermen had granted a permit to give "exhibitions of the national game" at the Huntington Avenue grounds. In the *Boston Herald*, Jimmy Collins explained why he thought the new park would be a better venue: "You will see better ball this summer than was ever seen in Boston, for the reason that there will be more room, and the outfielders will be able to do better work." The next day's *Post* reported that Cy Young had indeed signed with Boston.

March 13 — Somers sold his stock in the Cleveland club, the better to devote more time to Boston. There was a delay in Boston, however, with the *Globe* reporting, "The grounds at Huntington av are in such wretched shape that the contractors refuse to start work, and the only change since the club came into possession has been the taking away of the hemlock trees and old boards that were strewn over the grounds."

In Cambridge, Ted Lewis announced that he was retiring from baseball and expected to pursue a career in teaching. He said he was inclined to sympathize with the American League and added, "I suppose the reason why the National League does not enjoy great popularity is the same which applies to the case of a trust. People don't like to see one organization have a monopoly of the game." It wasn't long before Lewis returned to baseball—with the Boston Americans.

March 14 — The Americans signed John B. "Larry" McLean, at 6-feet-5 reportedly the tallest *p*layer to date in Organized Ball. At the Huntington Avenue Grounds, the removal of the Chutes enterprise was well under way: "All of the board walks have been torn up. The cemented walk encircling the artificial lake is to be removed."

March 15 — The *Globe*'s Baseball Notes remarked, "The old league must be losing its hustling powers judging from the way the American League is taking players from under their noses."

March 16 — Fred Parent signed with the Americans. The real angling for his commitment was between Providence and the new Boston team. President Soden "didn't think he would quite do" for Boston's Nationals.

SOMERS' PURSE was the headline on Murnane's column in the *Globe*. He indicated a couple of techniques the AL had employed. One was Somers' offering a large bonus for players to sign: "At one time it looked as if Somers' bank roll had no bottom, and he would keep on giving out the necessary $1000 bonus, which was proving a good bait, and landing the fish in fine shape." He also said that the Ban "Johnsonites" had often announced players had signed, when they really had not, thus sowing confusion in the NL ranks.

March 17 — The foundations for the grandstand were being set and the grounds were being leveled.

March 20 — The American League announced its schedule for Opening Day, April 24, and what the matchups would be on Memorial Day and the Fourth of July. Neither the Boston nor Washington park was expected to be ready, so Washington would open in Philadelphia and Boston in Baltimore.

March 21 — The full AL schedule was released at the league meeting in Philadelphia, and there were 24 dates when both the Americans and Nationals would be in Boston on the same day. The Americans added George Cuppy to their pitching staff; Cuppy had worked with Lou Criger in St. Louis in 1899 but had pitched in Boston for the Nationals in 1900. The steel pillars for the ballpark were on the grounds, ready to be worked into place.

March 22 — After the American League meeting several came to Boston for a meeting that included Somers, business manager Joe Gavin, architect Frank Wells, and others. Somers said the first schedule had 29 conflicts, and he was glad to have reduced the number. He was disappointed that Dolan would not be working the outfield, since he had signed with Chicago. Soden complained that it looked as though they were trying to arrange conflicts; Somers said on the 23rd that he would rather have no conflicts at all, but the Nationals had planned home games for the entire month of May and the last third of June, and that the Americans' grounds wouldn't be ready any earlier than May 8. Sixteen of the 24 conflicts were in May and June. It is not known whether the National League had planned the schedule hoping to disadvantage the new American League club in getting established in Boston.

March 23 — Brooklyn's Hanlon said that the NL clubs realized they were going to lose money in 1901 and had set aside funds to raid the AL clubs and try to entice back some of the better players who had signed with the junior league.

March 25 — DINNEEN FLOP NO. 2. An intriguing, perhaps ambiguous headline regarding the 20-game winner for Boston's NL club in 1900. He'd been among the first to sign with Somers, but now had signed with Soden, a two-year contract with a bonus as well. (Despite the two-year pact, Dinneen pitched for the Americans in 1902.)

March 27 — Joseph W. Callahan was appointed assistant business manager of Somers' Boston team. He had business experience but was also known as being "numbered among Boston's well-known singers."

Work on constructing the actual grandstand began on this day.

March 28 — Neither Collins nor Cy Young had anything good to say about Dinneen. Collins said sarcastically, "I don't wish him any harm. I only told him that I hoped his arm would drop off the first ball he pitched. It won't affect the playing strength of our team. We will get another good man. Where will he come from? I will not say just now, but one thing is sure, he won't be a contract jumper." At least Cy Young was solid. He had this to say: "Please pay no attention to any reports about my jumping contract. I have signed with the Boston American League club for 1901, and I will play in that city or nowhere. I have no respect for a contract jumper. When I have given my word to a man or a club the deal is closed." He added, "I am pleased to see that the press and the public are practically solid for the American. I can't understand how a man with any sense of honor can sign with the new league and then jump back into the National, where he claims to have been only a slave."

March 29—The Americans signed two more players—veteran outfielder Tommy Dowd of Holyoke, Massachusetts (he'd played with the Boston Brotherhood team back in 1990), and a left-handed pitcher named Win Kellum. The pitcher wasn't well known to Boston sportswriters or typographers—the *Post* called him "Keelum" and the *Globe* had him as "Killum."

March 30—Hugh Duffy was quite amused to receive a telegram in Milwaukee from President Soden ordering him to report to the Boston Nationals in Worcester on April 15.

The *Herald* printed a special dispatch from Chicago claiming that the three owners of Boston's National League club—Soden, Conant, and Billings—had offered Charles Somers the sum of $150,000 and the promise of a franchise in the National League in 1902 if he would desert the American League. Had the offer succeeded, it would have severely wounded the launch of the new league. A confident Ban Johnson was quoted as saying, "The National people could not get Somers away from us for $1,000,000."

Both teams left Boston in the evening to head for their respective spring-training quarters. Ted Lewis came over from Cambridge to see the Nationals off, heading as they were by the 6:00 P.M. boat train to Fall River, while the Americans left half an hour later by rail via Stonington, Connecticut. Oddly, both teams knew they would be meeting at Jersey City and be on the same train from there to Washington before separating once again, to Norfolk and to Charlottesville.

April

April 1—With the season approaching and the new American League looking like a threat that wasn't going away, even wild rumors received some credence. The *Boston Post* ran a story on April 1 denying another paper's report that the triumvirs had offered Somers $150,000 and the award of a National League franchise in another city if he would desert the American League. Treasurer Billings of the Boston Nationals said, "Why, we wouldn't give so much as a dime. There's to be no compromise." He reported that he had spent a day in Syracuse with Dinneen and Dinneen's lawyer, and persuaded them not to abrogate the club's claim on him, signing him for 1901. They were determined to press their case against Jimmy Collins and Chick Stahl.

The Nationals were based in Norfolk, Virginia. The Americans were in Charlottesville. Why Charlottesville? Back on January 22, Selee had said that his team would begin its spring work in Charlottesville. Plans changed, and it was the Americans who trained there, while Selee's squad went to Norfolk.

It wasn't the first time a Boston club had held spring training in Norfolk. In 1890 the Boston Reds of the Players League had trained there; the Boston Beaneaters had held ten days of practice in 1892 and manager Frank Selee took the team there in 1896 as well, for another ten days. Jimmy Collins had been with the 1896 team, but arrived a little late since both he and Bill Yerrick had failed to make connections at Jersey City. They were able to use the YMCA grounds and the facilities of the University of Virginia, and play against their team, too. In 1896 they played against visiting Lehigh College as well.

There was another reason, too, explained in the March 24 *Boston Globe*: "The U. of V. team was the only outside team that would play against the Boston Brotherhood team in '90, and the boys may do so again, as they play pretty fast ball." Besides, "they can find no clubs to play since they are outside the national agreement." The idea of playing other AL teams had either not occurred to them, or it just was not something they wished to do.

SPRING TRAINING 1901 — a quick glance

1901 — Charlottesville, Virginia: 2-0 with one intrasquad game
April 5 at Charlottesville: Boston 13, University of Virginia 0
April 11 at Charlottesville: Boston 23, University of Virginia 0
April 12 at Charlottesville: Regulars 25, Subs 6 (12 innings — though there was no tie. They just played a few extra innings to get some extra work in.)

These days, baseball's regular season begins more or less around the first of April. Before the introduction of the 162-game schedule in 1961, teams typically played 154 games a year — but in 1901 the schedule was being set for the very first time. And even Opening Day was fluid. It was basically a 138-game schedule for the league's first three years, then it was expanded to 154 beginning in 1904 (though with tie games and postponed or canceled games that were not made up, the first season in which the team played precisely 154 games did not come until 1912).

April 26 was the opening date for the Boston Americans, and the first game in franchise history was played in Baltimore against the Orioles, the team that in 1903 moved to New York as the Highlanders, and eventually became the New York Yankees. The first home game, at Boston's Huntington Avenue Grounds, was played on May 8, 1901.

The league's first game had been played two days before the Boston-Baltimore game, in Chicago on April 24, with the White Sox beating the Cleveland Blues, 8-2.

The team's major competition for local sports dollars was, of course, the National League's Boston Beaneaters. Their season began at home on Patriots Day, April 19, with the team playing one game and then going on the road (their games on the 20th and 22nd in New York were both rained out, bracketing the day of rest on Sunday the 21st) before opening a 19-game homestand that ran from May 3 through a doubleheader on May 30. Far from orchestrating their schedules so that there was only one team home on any given day, beginning with the Americans' first home game, on May 8, there were eight head-to-head matchups in May.

The results of the head-to-head play on those eight dates could have hurt the Americans, since they lost five in a row after winning the first two. But the Nationals didn't fare much better; they also won their first two, then lost four of the next six. Each of the eight dates matched exactly. May 12 was a Sunday, so neither team played that day. Local blue laws prohibited playing baseball on Sundays. And while both Philadelphia teams were in Boston on Friday, May 10, rain prevented either contest from being held.

Attendance for those 16 games? See below.

But let's back up and go to spring training with the Americans.

SPRING TRAINING

April 1 — Wearing crimson sweaters, the first 12 members of the Boston Americans showed up on April 1 to begin the first spring training of the franchise, and held a light two-hour workout on the grounds of the local YMCA. Some students and others from the town turned out to observe. Four more players arrived the following day and that constituted the full contingent, as the plan was to field 14 players on the roster. Cy Young was given special permission to arrive only when the team broke camp to head north. The plan was to play three games against the University of Virginia, which had its own schedule to play as well. The *Post* wrote, "Collins will try to arrange some games with other nines than the local team, but it is his purpose to keep his boys here until it is time to open the championship season." In other words, no road trips. But there were to be two workouts a day, from 10:00 A.M. to noon and from 2:00 to 3:30 P.M. They booked into the Clermont Hotel, which had housed the Boston

Brotherhood team in 1890, the Boston Reds of the Players League.

On the rails heading south, Collins and those of the team who traveled with him rather than making their own way to Charlottesville found they had some other traveling companions: manager Frank Selee and his Boston Beaneaters National League team. "There was considerable good-natured 'kidding' between the two organizations," according to the *Post*. It was the owners—the magnates, in the parlance of the day—who were at bitter odds, but not the players themselves.

Though the term "racially diverse" would not be used at the time, there were both black and white spectators at some of the early workouts, though Boston's American League team would not field an acknowledged player of African ancestry until 1959.

April 2—An "incessant drizzle" (*Washington Post*) prevented practice. Even though the gym at the Y was open, Collins was not feeling any urgency and more or less gave his men the day off. The *Globe* informed its readers, "Collins is not a believer in indoor work for a ball player." The newspaper's Tim Murnane felt he was "too easy with his boys."

Criger, Cuppy, Ferris, and Parent all arrived in town. The University of Pennsylvania baseball team put up at the Clermont, too, scheduled to play Virginia on April 3. There was indeed a strong Cleveland component to Boston's new team—from owner Charles Somers to the aforementioned Criger and Cuppy, Cy Young, Tommy Dowd, Osee Schrecongost, Charlie Hemphill, and a pitcher named McKenna.

Cuppy said he'd be glad to have a better catcher: "I will have a catcher in Criger this year who will not keep telling Selee that I have crossed him in signs every time he has a passed ball." (*Globe*)

The citizens of Charlottesville hadn't been following baseball news as closely as those in major-league cities. "Where is Long, Tenney, and Lowe?" the Americans were asked on a number of occasions "and it keeps one busy explaining the situation." The locals knew of three names connected with the Boston team in 1900, and hadn't realized there were now *two* Boston teams, and that the three men named were with the Nationals.

April 3—PRACTICE IN THE MUD. The headline was the *Globe*'s. The day was clear, at first, and Collins had the men out and practicing at 10 A.M., but it started raining almost immediately. It was a field with a "skin diamond" and there was "deep mud and puddles" all over the field, but Collins still had the men persevere at batting practice (there was no point trying to field given the condition of the grounds). Collins called off the afternoon practice, and the Penn-Virginia game was called off, too. Collins was going to umpire the college game.

April 4—A clear, crisp day and the team got in two good practice sessions, one in the morning and one from 2 to 4 in the afternoon. It was McLean who earned rave notices from the *Globe*'s Murnane: "I have never seen his exhibition for throwing equaled. His hitting was about as marvelous as his throwing, and the American club had a wonder in this young man, who is just of age." The *Herald* said that Arthur Irwin had called him a "second Lajoie." Collins said of his men, "There isn't a shirker in the lot."

April 5—The first game the new organization ever played took place at Charlottesville and saw Boston defeat the University of Virginia nine, 13-0. The Boston infield was said to already be in midseason form, despite this being their first competitive game; no one made an error for Boston. Kane, Connor, and Mitchell shared the pitching, a few innings apiece, and no Virginia batter got a hit after the third inning. Chick Stahl served as the umpire, while Charlie Jones played center field and collected three hits. Hemphill and Criger each hit a pair, one of Criger's

COLLINS TRIES COLTS.

Kane, Mitchell and Connor Take Turns Pitching.

The Team Beats Virginia University, 13 to 0.

being a triple. Boston scored three runs in the first inning, five in the second, and three in the third. Virginia pitcher Carcraft was charged with five wild pitches. The one hour, 50-minute game lasted just 7 1/2 innings, Boston being dubbed the home team. The Virginia nine had been playing games since its March 13 opener.

April 6—Heavy rain prevented play. The sun broke out about noon, but then another downpour came shortly afterward.

April 7—Another day lost to rain and wet grounds. The *Boston Post* raved about Larry McLean of Cambridge, Massachusetts, about whom Providence manager Billy Murray was raving—a big 6-foot-5 catcher who could also play first base.

April 8—Given the glacial pace at which some construction projects seem to progress, it may be remarkable that a full week into April, the building of Boston's new ballpark was still under way. "The larger part of the grading has already been finished, but the leveling remains to be done. As soon as the weather permits, a larger force of men will be employed, and then the rolling will begin. All of the steel standards of the three sections of the stand are in place, and the floor work is partially completed. The bleachers on both sides of the field are practically finished, and now that the frames of the pavilions are in place, some idea of the large seating capacity of the grounds is obtainable. The old fence that bordered the grounds on the Huntington avenue side is to be removed, and a higher and more substantial one will be erected."

The Boston Nationals played Portsmouth in Portsmouth, and lost their first spring game, 2-1. The Americans enjoyed a Sunday that was warmer and had a couple of "brisk and gingery" workouts to limber up, one in the morning and one in the afternoon.

April 10—Rain and unusually high winds kept the team off the practice field all morning and most of the afternoon. In terms of getting in shape one would think that the pitchers would have the easiest time working out in the gymnasium, but they "have not as yet been able to let themselves out." McKenna—whose home was in Lynchburg, not all that far away - still hadn't shown up, though he'd received his advance money. Schrecongost was umpiring Virginia's games against various colleges.

April 11—The second (and last) of the games against opponents was an even more lopsided 23-0 win for Boston over the university team, the Americans scoring ten more runs than in the game six days earlier. The scoring by inning was 2-5-7-3-2-2-0-2. Cuppy, Kellum, and the finally-arrived McKenna each got in some work. Collins and Ferris each homered. Dowd had four hits. Parent and Ferris both had three. Boston suffered three hit batsmen.

April 12—The missing McKenna finally turned up, and got right into the intrasquad game, in which the Regulars easily subdued the Subs, by scores variously reported as 25-6, 28-6, and 20-6. It was 15-2 after the first nine innings but—no mercy rule here—the two teams just kept on competing. Chick Stahl hit two home runs his first two times up. A lot of the work was on hit-and-run plays and double steals, and Schreck of the Subs didn't even bother attempting throws to put out "the purloiners." Fred Mitchell made a brilliant one-handed catch and there was good glovework from a few other men, too.

April 13—Tim Murnane ventured to compare the two Boston teams. "In training a ball team, Jimmy Collins is proving a success. To start with, he outgeneraled Frank Selee in picking out a good training place. Selee had been warned against going to Norfolk for training purposes as the wind is usually strong and cold in the spring at that place. But then the comforts of a good hotel were too much for the league manager to resist. Capt. Collins picked the poorest hotel, with all the best of it in other ways, and the latter's judgment will tell most in the long run.

"It is too early to compare the two Boston teams, although I saw the boys at work at their training quarters. I would not hesitate to place Collins' team ahead of Selee's men in their respective leagues."

Murnane also felt that the advent of the American League had already inspired a new interest in baseball and that, overall, attendance could as much as double in 1901 in the cities where two teams were competing.

April 14—This day and the next saw more rain plague the players.

April 15—The day's *Post* said that the pitching staff had really rounded into shape, and had Dinneen not re-bolted back to the Nationals, the staff would be a really strong one. Freddy Parent and Hobe Ferris were both looking good, too. The team went for an invigorating 15-mile run over rough terrain around the countryside. They were looking good, the reporter averred, "and will make the Baltimores, hailed as the best in the American League, hustle for the bunting." The paper entered a note regarding Sunday ball: "The American League schedule provides for an innovation in Boston baseball affairs, as Collins' team is booked for several Sunday games in the Western cities of the circuit. The Soden, Billings, and Conant triumvirate has refrained from having their team indulge in Sunday ball, either at home or abroad."

April 16—It was a fine day and the pitchers really let loose. In particular, "General" Cuppy had "worked off much surplus flesh and is now close to playing weight. He has the best assortment of curves and speed at command." Kellum was predicted to be one of the best pitchers in the league—"heady" and "cool as a cucumber… [with] plenty of speed. His delivery is easy and effective." Kane was ranked as a real standout in the *Globe*.

April 17—COLLINS'S TEAM HUSTLING. There was meant to be a third game against Virginia, but it was "canceled by the collegians." The team was thus again divided into two squads for a 2:15 game. Everyone was rounding into form, both the more veteran players (Collins, Stahl, Dowd, Freeman, and Criger) and the "young bloods" like Ferris, Parent, and Charlie Jones. The two middle infielders were clicking around the keystone sack. Collins was as reliable as ever at the hot corner, and Dowd is "rejuvenated … capering in the outer garden like a colt." Collins himself said, "It was glorious practice this morning."

April 18—GINGER IN SOMERS'S TEAM. Another intrasquad game was "especially lively. The outfield played a fast game. Dowd, Stahl, and Hemphill gave a brilliant exhibition, killing long drives that looked good for extra bases. Their fielding of ground hits was swift and sure and throwing was excellent." Parent and Ferris executed four double plays.

Readers of the *Boston Globe* learned a little more about the field where the Americans were practicing. "A number of tennis nets, high and low, are at the foot of the college campus on which the practice is held. Many high flies and long low hits go over these nets. Today Dowd, Stahl, and Hemphill gave an exhibition of going around these obstacles and pulling down drives that looked good for extra bases."

Criger and Schrecongost took time out to help coach Virginia students before their forthcoming game against North Carolina for the championship of the South.

On this day, the Americans received more good word in the pitching department. Ted Lewis had pitched for the Boston Nationals from 1896 through 1900 (leading the National League in winning percentage in 1898 with a record of 26-8), and then retired. He had only turned 28 on Christmas Day of 1900. Lewis let it be known that he would come out of retirement to play for Jimmy Collins and the Americans, and more than adequately filled the hole left when Dinneen had reneged and returned to Selee's Nationals. "Parson" Lewis was a highly respected player of some stature among ballplayers. He explained that there had been some things standing in the way of his return to baseball but that they had been cleared up and that he was especially pleased to be able to resume playing with Collins. "There isn't a man in baseball who I should prefer to succeed more than he," Lewis said.

The April 19 *Herald* reported an item of interest from this day - the first time the Boston Americans played some racially-mixed ball: "After the game a colored battery came on the field, calling themselves the

'Invincibles.' They could not be touched, they thought, but the boys tackled them and three out of the first four up put the ball out of the lot."

April 19—The Boston Nationals opened their season, beating the New York Giants, 7-0, in front of 6,500 Boston fans at the South End Grounds. In Charlottesville there was rain and a biting wind so no play, but Collins took the men on a 15-mile "jaunt across country" which was rough but good for keeping them in shape. Word came from Baltimore that Cy Young was awaiting them there and in better shape than he'd been in for years.

April 20—COLLINS'S MEN SEE SOUTHERN GAME. Heavy rain again prevented practice, and now the whole area was too water-logged to even go for a cross-country run. But the University of North Carolina team played the University of Virginia nonetheless, for "the championship of the South." The red mud field was in "miserable condition" but they got in a game, with Collins and his men among the spectators. Virginia won, 9-2, with six of the runs driven in by the right fielder, Walker, who had a single and two home runs over the center-field fence.

The Nationals played just the one game before going on a road trip, so anticipation focused on the May 8 home opener for the Americans. Construction was, if anything, ahead of schedule. "What appeared to be the herculean task of getting these new grounds in shape for the initial game has progressed so far that were it necessary to complete them by May 1 the contractors would be equal to the task. ... Already the new park has caught the favor of the public eye, if what is heard of all sides be taken as a criterion." The weather had cooperated in the preceding week and the field of play had been leveled. "The three sections of the grand stand are up, and the timber work completed, so that now the plasterers are free to apply their brushes to produce the cement effect intended. When all completed the grounds will be among the best in the country, and with reference to location second to none." The *Post* added, in the days before home runs were everything: "One feature that will be particularly valuable is the enormous area of the outfield, which will allow some great fielding, and make the batsmen earn their home runs and other long hits, instead of being aided by friendly fences." Grandstand capacity was 2,400 and that in the bleachers 10,000.

The lengthy article continued by discussing pricing, noting that 50-cent ticket prices were charged only by Boston, New York, and Pittsburg, because those three cities had enjoyed a monopoly, whereas Chicago and Philadelphia—with teams competing there—had 25-cent seats. It was also pointed out that the Beaneaters had lost 12 of their final 14 decisions at the end of the 1900 season. Left unsaid was that with so many of the better players enticed to the American League team, the Nationals might not be expected to play the best brand of baseball.

April 21—Again, no morning practice due to rains, but they did get in a cross-country run.

April 22—Heavy rain once more, but at least the men were said to be down to playing weight. The players themselves were said to believe they'd finish the season among the top three teams in the league.

April 23—There was a 2 1/2 hour practice in the morning, though the diamond was "heavy and slippery" (*Herald*.) They nonetheless got in some good work. The team then departed for Baltimore, ready for the first game on April 24. Everybody was down to playing weight and anxious to get the season under way. The team had never left its Charlottesville spring-training base. There were a few intrasquad "regs vs. subs" games and a lot of bad weather. The April 18 *Boston Globe* reported that manager "Collins is disappointed with the south as a training ground," a sentiment reiterated (almost verbatim) in the *Post* on the 23rd. In addition, the *Globe* remarked that the team was "unfortunate in not having any strong team in this section against whom they can play." As we've seen, Collins never intended road travel, and there had been no provision for teams to play preseason games against each other. The only two games the club played against opponents were both shutouts of the university, so Boston concluded its first spring training with an aggregate score of 36-0.

On arrival in Baltimore at 11:30 PM on the 23rd, Collins said, "We have a good team; it is evenly balanced and strong all-around, infield and outfield. The bad weather has kept us back, but when we get going I believe we will be around the top." McGraw seemed to underplay the chances of the Orioles, who had not truly had a spring training, saying, "Our men have very little outdoor practice and are not by any means themselves. They are going up against a strong team in the Bostons, who have had several weeks' practice in the South, and in that particular have much the best of us." Cy Young had come to the city, traveling with President Somers from Cleveland.

April 24 — BALTIMORE SAD. Baltimore had lost its NL Orioles after the 1899 season, so the fans there were ready for big-league ball to return, and they'd added John McGraw as manager, a forceful personality now back in his hometown. A major city celebration was planned, with a parade of ten carriages for state and city officials alone, including Governor Smith and Mayor Hawes. The game never happened. It was postponed because of rain. Chicago beat Cleveland, 8-2, but the other three AL games were also rained out.

April 25 — BIG SLICE OF EARNINGS LOST. Relentless Rain Severe Blow to Baseball Magnates. Back-to-back postponements in Baltimore and Washington pushed the full launch of the new league back even further. The Boston team "has had to while away the hours since their return from the Southern training grounds in hotel corridors, thereby regaining the softness which had been shaken off while in practice."

April 26 — The headline in the *Post* probably gladdened the National League owners: COLLINS'S MEN LOSE; SELEE'S TEAM WINS. A closer look at the attendance figures might have soured that first impression. There were 10,371 paying customers in Baltimore, where the Orioles beat Collins and company, 10-6, while the Boston Nationals drew only 779 fans in Philadelphia. The Beaneaters won, 4-3, but the American League won the day since the Philadelphia Athletics hosted the Washington Senators and drew 10,057. There had indeed been a parade in Baltimore and Ban Johnson threw out the first pitch. Baltimore scored three runs in the first inning against Win Kellum and never lost the lead, adding one in the third. After Boston scored one in the fourth, the Orioles added two more in the sixth. The Bostons finished with a late flourish, two in the eighth and three in the top of the ninth, but Baltimore had inserted four more runs in the eighth. Win Kellum did not win; he lost. Iron Man McGinnity was far from his best, but he won the game.

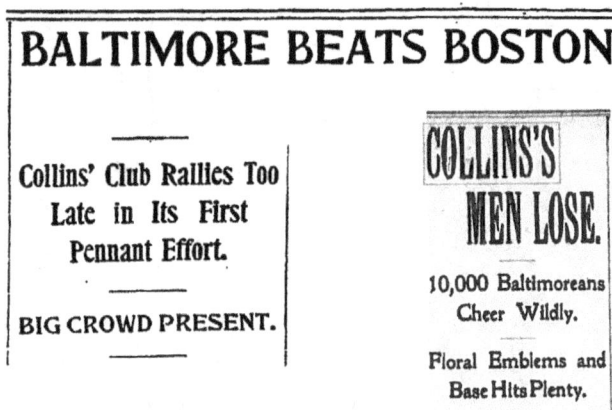

April 27 — COLLINS AND MEN NEVER HAD A SHOW. Were Easy Victims for McGraw's Merciless Sluggers. Cy Young was far from invincible, an easy mark giving up three runs in the first, three runs in the third, two more runs in the fourth, and three more in the sixth — 11 runs in all. Fred Mitchell replaced Young in the sixth. It was never close. The final score was 12-6, Baltimore winning — and Boston still waiting for a win.

April 28 — Rather than take a day off, the Americans went to Weehawken, New Jersey, and played an exhibition game there against a team from West New York (winning 5-2), and then returned to Philadelphia. The *Globe* suggested that Charles Somers — though he was also the principal backer for the Philadelphia Athletics — would be rooting more for the Bostons. Ban Johnson and Somers consulted with their legal team in Philadelphia, and then Johnson headed west.

April 29 – SELEE MEN WIN IN 10TH — COLLINS LOSES; THE AMERICAN NINE OUTCLASSED. Three games into the first season of the franchise, the

The Huntington Avenue Grounds

At the risk of some redundancy, let us reprint here a description of the team's ballpark from the book *Red Sox Threads*.

The first home of the Boston Americans (from 1908, the Red Sox) was the Huntington Avenue Grounds. Many ballparks of the era were simply known as "league park" or the "National League grounds," but the ballpark where the Red Sox first began was the Huntington Avenue American League Base Ball Grounds. It was constructed very quickly, on the former Huntington Carnival Lot, with groundbreaking on March 7, 1901. "Hi Hi" Dixwell turned the first shovelful of dirt. The first home game for Boston was played on May 8, just two months later. Dixwell threw out the first pitch.

Boston already had a major league team—the National League's Boston Beaneaters. The competition between the Americans and the Nationals was accentuated by the proximity of the two parks. It was approximately 600 feet as the crow flies from home plate at the South End Grounds to home plate of the Huntington Avenue Grounds. It was even closer between the outside perimeters of the two parks. In between lay the tracks of the New York, New Haven and Hartford Railroad and a couple of repair sheds used to service the trains.

When the Red Sox later moved to Fenway Park in 1912, they moved less than half a mile away from the Huntington Avenue Grounds, effectively just across the Muddy River and the Fens.

The architect of the American League, Ban Johnson, had a willing financier in a Cleveland magnate named Charles Somers, who not only provided initial funding for the Cleveland Indians but the Boston Americans as well. Somers was active in shipping on the Great Lakes, in coal, and in lumber. Frederick Lieb writes that Somers also advanced $10,000 to Charles Comiskey to help him finance the Chicago White Sox and "was Connie Mack's original backer" in the Philadelphia Athletics. So Somers had his financial fingers in *four* of the eight original American League clubs. Connie Mack, owner of the Athletics, was involved with the Boston Americans, too; he headed the small group selected to find a suitable site for the AL's Boston franchise. They visited possible locations in Cambridge, Charlestown, and Boston, but finally settled on a site not far from the National League park, the South End Grounds.

The site was owned by Durand Associates and leased to the Boston Elevated Railway Company. Mack's committee (which comprised Hugh Duffy and Tommy McCarthy) asked John Dooley to speak with his partner in the J.R. Prendergast Company, a cotton brokerage. Daniel Prendergast was also a director of Boston Elevated Railway, and Dooley recalls an "old newspaperman" named Peter Kelley (the *Journal*'s Peter F. Kelley) coming to his office on behalf of team owner Charles Somers to ask that Prendergast help convince the railway company to accept a ballpark on the site. Dooley says he prevailed upon Prendergast to have the Elevated accept the offer of $5,000 for the rights to use the land. It was Connie Mack who signed the lease on the Huntington Avenue land.

John Dooley was involved in many Boston baseball booster organizations, from the Royal Rooters to the Winter League to the Half Century Club and, finally, the Bosox Club. He was father to loyal and longtime devoted Red Sox fan Lib Dooley. More about the Dooleys appears elsewhere in this book.

To say the site was unimproved was an understatement. It was, in the words of Ed Walton, "no more than an expansive wasteland made up of heavily weeded bumps and lumps." It had been used as a circus lot—even the temporary home to Buffalo Bill's traveling Wild West Circus—when a show would come to town. There was a fairly large pond on the property that children would splash into during summer months from a number of chutes they would slide down, as a water slide. In the winter, of course, people could ice skate there, but this was no high society skating pond. The area was largely bounded by rail yards, a huge Boston Storage Warehouse behind the length of the left-field bleachers, some stables, breweries, and a pickle factory. The United Drug Company was situated near enough to the park that one could often smell the chemicals at work. One thing there was not, was a baked bean cannery in the vicinity. [See the story of Baseball and Baked Beans in Boston elsewhere in this volume.] Oddly enough, though, the opera house was across the street.

The park had a very large footprint. It seated around 9,000 fans at first; more seating was added in later years. On the busiest days, several thousand more simply watched from the field itself, standing behind ropes, necessitating a change in ground rules for the day. Typically, a fair ball hit into the crowd was ruled a double, but the rules did vary some from day to day. It was 350 feet to the left field corner, 440 feet in left-center field, and some 530 feet to straightaway center. Right field was close, though, just 280 feet down the line. An expansion in 1908 pushed the right-field fence out to 320 feet, but took center field out to a staggering 635 feet. After terming it "the most mis-shapen of all the big league ballparks," Michael Gershman further emphasized the unusual center field as "the most challenging in major league history, since it featured hip-high weeds and was dotted with slippery patches of sand left over from the circus. In addition to being vast, center field sloped uphill and was made even more treacherous by the presence of a sizable tool shed in deep center." The shed was in play, though by the time any ball might have traveled that far, the batter would surely have himself an inside-the-park home run.[2]

A statue of Cy Young is positioned today on the Northeastern University campus on the very spot understood to be where the pitcher's rubber had been, facing toward home plate some 60 feet, six inches away.

The field was indeed a rough one, and Philip Lowry's *Green Cathedrals* also noted the "large patches of sand in the outfield where grass would not grow." The facility itself was striking, "built with expanded metal and roughcast cement, with a light grey tone. The roof rested on columns 28 feet in the air, hipped on all four sides," in the words of Alan E. Foulds, who quoted the Boston Globe as saying the structure was "covered with granite felting, toned to a soft crimson." The interior was all of pine. There were three sections of grandstands arranged in a semi-circle, each seating nearly 800 people, and large bleachers at each end. A brand new facility, the park lured patrons away from the less-attractive South End Grounds.

There were limitations, though. Gershman quotes an Associated Press article which said the "wooden seats were rickety, soot from trains in neighboring yards filled the area, and the saloon next door was a beacon for bored players—during the games."

It worked, though, and from the very first day, fans flocked to the Huntington Avenue Grounds rather than its older neighbor, the South End Grounds. It didn't hurt that the American League franchise priced its tickets at half-price (25 cents instead of 50 cents), and that Jimmy Collins and several of the National League stars had been lured to the new league.

Boston Americans still hadn't won a game. They had wrapped things up in Baltimore and moved on to Philadelphia where Connie Mack's Athletics had also lost their first two games. Boston scored first, one run in the top of the first, and held a 3-0 lead when the Athletics came to bat in the bottom of the second. By the bottom of the third, the game was tied. Though Boston added another run in the fourth, Philadelphia put three across in the sixth and two more in the seventh. It was all in the timing; Philadelphia had one more hit, and committed four errors to Boston's three, but two of the errors were Dowd's in left field and they were costly. The Mackmen won, 8-5.

April 30—COLLINS NINE WINS ITS FIRST GAME. The headline tells the story. The score was 7-6. The win wasn't easy. And with the score 6-2 after the first three innings, it looked as though Cy Young (in his second start of the season) was still struggling. Rookie Billy Milligan was pitching for Philadelphia, and had apparently just gotten over a severe illness. One run each in the sixth and seventh closed the gap a bit, but it was still 6-4. Chick Stahl walked in the top of the ninth, but there were two outs. Buck Freeman was 0-for-4 but he hammered a "vicious high drive over the right-field fence ... when last seen, the ball was on the way south in the clutches of an urchin." The game tied, Boston scored twice again in the top of the tenth. Ferris led off with a double and Criger walked. Young tried to sacrifice but popped up to the pitcher, Milligan. Dowd singled to right field, but Hayden's throw was strong to the plate and Ferris held at third. Bases loaded with one out. Hemphill's single scored Ferris, and then Stahl hit a deep fly to center field. Young kept the gate closed; Philadelphia hadn't scored since the third. He got his first win. Milligan took the loss, the first of a career that ended in 1902 with him never having won a big-league game.

THE BOSTON HERALD—WEDNESDAY, MAY 1, 1901.
YOUNG LANDS A WINNER IN 10 INNINGS.

YOUNG LANDS A WINNER

Boston Americans Beat Athletics in a Fast and Loose Game.

COLLINS' FIRST WIN.

Eleven Thousand See Collins' Team Beat the Athletics, 12 to 4.

AUSPICIOUS OPENING

Music and Tally-Hos and a Fine Old Slugging Game—Cy Young Pitches.

STAHL BREAKS A RIB.

Won't Be Able to Play Again for Ten Days—Cy Young Pitches a Strong Game.

MAY

May 1—COLLINS TEAM TROUNCED. "Trounced" might even have been too mild a word. The score was 14-1. Win Kellum pitched the entire game and gave up 19 hits (everyone in the Athletics lineup got at least one), but walked only one. He did hit a man and committed an error—but the five other errors committed behind him were far from helpful. His own wild pitch let the 14th run score. It could have been worse; center fielder Chick Stahl threw out two runners at home plate. The 14 runs were the most Boston allowed in any game all year long.

May 2—10 RUNS FOR BOSTON IN SINGLE INNING. The franchise won its second game, by a big margin, and with relative ease after scoring ten runs in the top of the third. The *Post* began its account thus: "Of all the lurid exhibitions of baseball ever given in this town, the one witnessed today at the American League grounds surpassed anything that ever happened." Athletics starter Pete Loos pitched his first (and last) big-league game, making it through the first inning but opening the second with a stretch of 16 consecutive pitches missing the strike zone. Boston's big third inning included four singles, three triples, two doubles, a base on balls, and a batter reaching on an error. Boston pitcher Ted Lewis was hammered for 12 runs, but was left in for the complete game, a 23-12 win for Boston. The 23 runs were the most Boston scored in any game all year long.

May 3 — COLLINS'S MEN HAD NO CHANCE. Actually if one discounted the four runs Washington scored in the bottom of the first, the game was fairly even. The trouble was: Those runs counted, too. Moving on to Washington, Collins asked veteran left-hander Frank Foreman to start for Boston. He'd been pitching since 1884, but this was the only game he'd ever pitch for Boston, though he saw it through to the end, a 9-4 defeat.

May 4 — CYRUS YOUNG & CO. SWAMP SENATORS. Boston scored three times in the third and three in the fourth and had a 7-0 lead before Cy Young let Washington score the first of their two runs. Buck Freeman tripled twice and singled once. Young struck out seven.

May 5 — Sunday. No baseball in the Nation's Capital.

May 6 — AMERICANS WON BY SPRIGHTLINESS. Lewis pitched again and improved to 2-0, though the Senators outhit Boston, 11-9. The score in the game was 9-5, with Boston scoring twice in the first and four times in the second, the early scoring perhaps enough to put Washington off its game. The contrast in play was considerable: "Boston played a lively game throughout, giving Lewis fine support. Lewis showed great head work in the box, keeping the hits well-scattered and fielding his position in great style. The Senators played remarkably ragged, and completely lacked anything like team work."

May 7 — COLLINS HAPPY. The team reached the .500 mark for the first time in franchise history. It was a cold and gloomy day and the circus was in town, so the turnout was less than 1,000 — though those present made up for it in boisterousness. Win Kellum allowed only four hits (a double, two triples, and a homer), and never walked a batter, though he did hit a man. Boston won, 7-3, leaving by train for Boston after the game, ready to play its first game in the Hub.

May 8 — The first home game in what became the Boston Red Sox franchise was a success in all respects. A parade had initially been planned to welcome them, but with the train scheduled to arrive at 2:00 P.M. and the game set for 3:30, there was time only for carriages to collect them at Back Bay Station and bring them directly to the grounds on Huntington Avenue. The park was ready for play; though there was no turf yet in the outfield, it had been "rolled so thoroughly that the fielders will suffer very little handicap," proclaimed the *Post*. The Boston Cadet Band's pregame musical program was as follows:

Sousa's "March / Hail to the Spirit of Liberty" followed (this would seem bizarre today) by a waltz, "Welcome." A medley of popular airs, a two-step, a selection from the 1899 musical *The Rounders* by Austrian-born composer Ludwig Englander, a caprice named "Cocoanut Dance," and a march named "Old Friends" completed the program.

It was head-to-head competition with the National League's Boston Beaneaters, who were hosting the Brooklyn Superbas that day (and won a thrilling 7-6 game in 12 innings). The American League draw was greater, with 11,500 coming to see the first game and only 5,500 going to the South End Grounds on the other side of the railroad tracks to watch the Nationals. The *Boston Post* noted, "The cheering incidental to the game between Brooklyn and Boston on the neighboring grounds was plainly heard, and vice versa."

It was a capacity crowd at Huntington Avenue, the crowd beginning to enter shortly after 1:00 P.M. and filling the bleachers entirely and flowing onto the field behind ropes stretched to confine them. There was an air of good humor throughout, and "if the peanut man dropped all the peanuts in throwing a bag to a customer, the latter simply laughed and flung down his nickel." Cheers to welcome the most popular players were said to exceed those accorded national heroes. A four- to five-foot-high horseshoe of cut flowers, primarily yellow jonquils, was presented Captain Jimmy Collins, and "from every quarter came remarks as to the beauty of the new park. … The superiority of the new park could be taken in with one sweep of the eye." The *Globe* was equally effusive: "Everything inside the high fence was as new as this spring's tulip. The diamond shone in the sun like a great canvas of freshly spread green paint, the uniforms of the home team were as spotless as a just-from-the-wrapper ball, and the great crowd seethed with good nature." The *Globe*'s sports page cartoon showed the peanut vendor at work.

The train had arrived on time, but the team had no time to eat before the game. There wasn't even enough time to bring the team's bats from the train to the park, so they played with a new set which had awaited them. Number One fan Arthur Dixwell threw out the first pitch.

The new bats didn't appear to present a problem, as Boston battered the ball around from the start, scoring four times in the bottom of the first and producing 21 hits and 34 total bases. Before each batter approached the plate, the *Boston Globe* explained, "A new feature in baseball was the megaphone man, who announced the change of players and other interesting facts."

The quality of play by the visiting Athletics was disappointing, "one of the poorest ever played in this city by the visiting team. … The work of the Quakers was worth about 3 cents on the dollar," said the *Globe*. Matters were so bad that it was the home crowd which loudly cried to have Philadelphia starter Bill Bernhard replaced. The final score was 12-4, but the three runs scored off Cy Young in the bottom of the eighth were said to be facilitated by him laying off his curve and simply throwing nothing but fastballs, the better to spare his arm.

The outfield was a little soft and the outfielders sometimes lost their footing. This may have contributed to Chick Stahl having to come out of the game, replaced by Charlie Jones, after wrenching his side at one point.

The first-inning scoring had begun when leadoff man Tommy Dowd singled to left field. Charlie Hemphill bunted toward third base to try to advance him, but both runners were safe as Lave Cross committed the first of Philadelphia's nine errors. Chick Stahl sacrificed, moving both runners up, and Collins singled, giving the team its first run. Buck Freeman hit a hard liner to deep center field which went for an inside-the-park home run. For its first eight years, center field at the Huntington Avenue Grounds was measured at 530 feet.

It was 12-0 before Connie Mack's Athletics managed even their first run, in the top of the seventh, and easy coasting for Cy Young. The time of game was 1:48. The win gave them a record of 6-5, the first time the team had been over .500.

THE BOSTON HERALD—THURSDAY, MAY 9, 1901.
A HOME VICTORY AT THE NEW GROUNDS.

May 9 — Baseball fans of the day liked close, well-played games most of all. The 9-3 win was good for the home team, but the game itself disappointed. Philadelphia captain Larry Lajoie was ejected from the game in the top of the first inning, before he got to bat or play the field, for arguing too strenuously (even using "non-Emersonian language") as to whether the Athletics' second batter up had been safe at first base or not. Dowd was 3-for-5 and scored all three times. The winning pitcher was Cuppy.

May 10 — Weather prevented there being a third game against Philadelphia and Mack's nine took the 7 o'clock train to Baltimore.

May 11 — "Parson Teddy" Lewis struggled with control and walked the bases full in the top of the first, then put one over and Senators second baseman Joe Quinn hit a bases-clearing double. Boston never gave up another run, but scored only twice — once in the second and once in the fifth. During the second inning, Freeman was so angered by being called out on a close play that he "ran at the umpire and grabbed him by the two shoulders." (*Globe*) McLean took his place at first base. He made a couple of superb fielding plays, but was 0-for-3 at the plate, each one hit straight to the shortstop. The final score was a 3-2 loss for the Collins crew. Frank Foreman coached at third base and his antics — noted in several Boston papers — got the crowd going.

May 12 — Sunday. No baseball.

May 13 — Boston held a 1-0 lead through five, and Washington hadn't been able to get a man past first base, but Kellum weakened and surrendered two in the top of the sixth. In the first, second, and fifth innings Boston had a runner on third with just one out, and was unable to bring him home. Three double plays were part of a game in which Hobe Ferris recorded ten putouts at second base and six assists, but even with all those outs, there were five runs allowed in the sixth through the eighth, and the Senators came out on top, 5-2.

May 14 — LACK OF GINGER. The *Globe* headline suggested the story as the Americans lost their third game in a row, another 3-2 game in which the Senators scored all their runs early (this time in the top of the second, off Cy Young), and Boston couldn't quite even things up. Poor baserunning in the bottom of the fourth saw Boston score just once, despite Collins's double, followed by three successive singles. In the bottom of the ninth, Schrecongost tripled over the bag at third base — but umpire Haskell ruled it foul. Schreck then grounded out to the pitcher, and Haskell had to push through an unpleasant crowd of patrons who inhibited his passage to the dressing room.

May 15 — AMERICANS BLANKED. The Senators left Boston a happy crew, having swept the four-game set against Boston with a 4-0 finale over Cuppy. Boston managed only four hits, all singles, and the only man who reached as far as second base was Collins, in the first inning. The highlight of the game for Boston was probably the six putouts by left fielder Dowd, four of them ranked sensational.

May 16 — COLLINS MEN MAKE GREAT FINISH, BUT LOSE. It was quite a thrilling finish. Boston was down 7-2 at the end of the eighth inning, and Ted Lewis was having a bad day, including his own error that let in two of the runs. They'd had the bases loaded with nobody out in the third and failed to score. Then the Orioles scored an eighth run in the top of the ninth. But the Boston players hadn't given up yet, and finally got to Iron Man McGinnity. McLean pinch-hit for Lewis and singled. Dowd reached on a ball trapped in the outfield. With one out, Collins tripled to drive in McLean and Dowd. A single brought in Collins, but then a second out was recorded. Three singles in succession brought in two more runs — and the tying run would have scored but for third baseman John McGraw getting in the way of Fred Parent, who otherwise could have rounded the bag and scored. A long argument ensued, with Collins arguing that McGraw should be charged with interference and Parent should be waved home with the run that would have led to a tie in the game. The argument was prolonged but in vain, stopping when umpire Haskell threatened to forfeit the game. Pinch-hitter Schrecongost popped up to second and the game was lost anyhow. The *Boston Globe* account lacked the sympathy for Collins's argument, saying that Parent really hadn't tried to score on the play.

Frank Foreman was released by the Americans, signing with Baltimore several weeks later.

May 17 — After a five-game losing streak, the Americans wrapped up the eight-game homestand with a 7-2 win over Baltimore; though each team had ten hits, the only O's runs scored in the first inning and Cy Young put up goose eggs from that point on — and got the win.

The game drew 4,209 — more than double the National League attendance of 1,700. The Americans had proved they could outdraw their more established rivals. Not once did the NL team match them; it was not even close.

	Americans	Nationals
May 8	11,500	5,500
May 9	3,000	2,000
May 11	7,261	2,500
May 13	2,354	1,200
May 14	3,552	1,400
May 15	3,285	1,500
May 16	4,279	1,000
May 17	4,209	1,700
TOTAL =	39,440	16,800

All figures, rounded or precise, per *Boston Globe*

In fact, only twice did the Americans fall short of doubling the Nationals in attendance.

Because rain and wet grounds wiped out the rest of the scheduled games, the first homestand at the Huntington Avenue Grounds was complete, a 3-5 record in the eight games. Collins was quoted a couple of days later as saying that two of the games against Washington could well have gone the other way, and probably would have had Chick Stahl been able to play. Speaking of his replacement in center, Charlie Jones, he said, "Jones appears to be sick, at least he isn't showing the form he displayed when in training in the South."

May 18—Game postponed due to rain.

May 19—It was Sunday, and thus there was no baseball scheduled in the East.

May 20—The grounds were in such "wretched condition" after two days of heavy rain that there was no chance of playing ball. The team left Boston at 6:19 P.M. for Detroit on the start of a road trip to last until June 7. Economizing, they left pitcher Win Kellum behind, as well as Larry McLean and Charlie Jones. Stahl's ribs were feeling better.

May 21—Rain resulted in postponement of the first game in Detroit.

May 22—COLLINS AND STAHL BAT OUT A VICTORY. It was the first visit of the franchise to "the West" as Detroit was considered in baseball circles in 1901. The *Boston Globe* pontificated, leading its game story thus: "Eastern culture and skill, as against Western dash and luck, proved itself life "the effectual, fervent prayer of the righteous man," which the book says "availeth much." Huh? The second paragraph was more to the point: "As a matter of fact, the visitors outplayed the home team at every point. They excelled in clean, sharp fielding, proved themselves superior in consistent, consecutive batting, and in general team work were the leaders." It was the first time since 1888 that a Boston team and a Detroit team had faced each other in championship play. This time, Boston came out on top, 9-5, behind the pitching of Lewis. As the *Post* headline indicated, Collins and Stahl—with three hits apiece—both led the offense, Collins doubling and tripling in three runs while Chick drove in two.

May 23—Cy Young allowed six hits and didn't walk a man, though there were four errors behind him to complicate matters. In his 4-2 win, Young singled in the second run and scored the third as Boston pulled ahead in the fifth inning.

May 24—Free admission for ladies doubled the paid admission of 2,000 and those present saw their Tigers whitewash Jimmy Collins' crew, 3-0. Ben Beville pitched for Boston and allowed only seven hits, but he hit one batter and walked five others. Only one run was earned, the other two coming on errors.

May 25—There was a shutout at League Park, but it was Boston 5-0 over the Clevelanders, both teams playing through a little drizzle and some light snow but still drawing a most respectable 2,000 fans. It was a six-hitter for Ted Lewis. And it was a bit of a homecoming for some, since Dowd, Hemphill, and Schrecongost had all played for Cleveland's National League teams in years gone by. "In fact," observed the *Globe*, "the whole team was treated in a brotherly fashion, probably because they were Charles Somers' players." Parent's triple in the second led to one run when he was singled home by Schreck, and the Bostons put up four more runs in the third on successive singles by Dowd, Hemphill, Stahl, Collins, and Freeman.

May 26—No game was scheduled. Kellum, Jones, and McLean had all been released.

May 27—Wet grounds. No game

May 28—Steady and unrelenting rain prevented the Tuesday game as well. Collins regretted the enforced downtime because the team had begun to play well and it meant more doubleheaders further down the line, but he took advantage of the time to scoot over to his home in Buffalo. The Buffalo Express caught up with him and he said the American League seemed to be more than holding its own over the first month of league play. "We have all the best of it so far. …

Whenever we have encountered the National league the support of the public has been with our side."

May 29 — Cold and rainy weather resulted in the third game in a row lost to weather conditions, and a financial blow to the Cleveland club in particular because "the Bostons are no doubt the premier attractions of the American league, and big crowds would have been present each day." (Globe) The team took the train to Chicago.

May 30 — TWICE BEATEN. It was the first doubleheader in team history, and Boston dropped both to the first-place White Sox at South Side Park on Decoration Day, losing 8-3 behind Beville and 5-3 behind Young. Once again, Beville walked a bunch — four or five batters this time (the box scores said five) — and was pulled in the second inning of the morning game, being charged with four runs. Cuppy took over. In the third, Cuppy walked two himself and saw three errors committed and two more runs score.

The afternoon game drew as many as 13,000 people, spilling over onto the field. Boston scored the first three runs and it seemed that Cy Young might hold back the Chicago bats, but four runs in the fourth inning sank those hopes. It was nonetheless a game that went to the ninth with the threat of Boston tying the game or going ahead — but it was not to be.

May 31 — UMPIRE AND WEATHER MAN HELPED BOSTON'S OPPONENTS. To be fair, that was the subhead in the *Post*. The headline read more neutrally: BOSTON LOSES TO CHICAGO. Reading the game account, however, it seemed the bigger fault might be Boston's failure to take more advantage of John Skopec's poor pitching. The game was lost 10-5, and one surely has to look to Ted Lewis for explanations. He allowed the White Sox ten hits and walked four Boston batters. But Skopec had donated nine bases on balls to Boston, and eight hits. A five-run White Sox third gave them a 7-2 edge they never lost. Ferris was apparently quite ill, but there was only pitcher Fred Mitchell available to substitute, and Collins said he was reluctant to play him out of position. Ferris did commit two of Boston's four errors, and Lewis another one. Two close calls went in favor of the White Sox, one at second base and one at the plate. And the game was halted for half an hour at one point, then called for good with one out in the top of the eighth, but it's a little hard to fault the weather for one side scoring only half as many runs as the other.

The month of May ended with Chicago atop the AL standings, 3 1/2 games ahead of the second-place Tigers, and Boston in fifth place, with an 11-14 record and nine games out of first.

June 1 — SOMERSITES HAD IT ALL THEIR OWN WAY. Indeed, the scores from the preceding day flipped and the final score was Boston 10, Chicago 5. Fred Mitchell was given his first start and it was a disaster in the first inning, as the White Sox took full advantage of an error and a misjudged fly ball to left, scoring five runs and looking to be on the way to a rout. But Mitchell buckled down and never yielded another run. White Sox pitcher Harvey had the opposite experience, giving up just one hit through the first five frames (though it was a two-run homer to Buck Freeman). After a six-run sixth, however, Harvey was pulled. The fatal sixth included another Freeman homer, both of them fully out of the park and over the right-field fence. Stahl reached base five times, though twice were after he was hit by pitches and once on an error. The final two runs scored off reliever Jack Katoll. The *Post* admitted that one big call, while wrong, went Boston's way.

Kellum, who had been released one week earlier, was recalled and was told to meet the team when it came back home after the road trip concluded with four scheduled games in Milwaukee.

June 2 — VICTORY BATTED OUT IN NINTH. The Brewers were in last place, and Boston hoped to take some advantage since the teams were to play eight games in a row — four there and four at home. The first game was a close one, 4-2 through eight innings. And Boston was playing without both Collins and Freeman, when both were ejected in the fifth. A big part of their argument was that umpire Haskell was standing ten feet behind the pitcher, and not behind home plate, and therefore unable to accurately call balls and strikes.

Pitcher Cuppy was sent to play left field, Dowd came in from left to play third, and Beville played first.

Cy Young surrendered only six hits in the game and the two runs, and the Brewers' Bill Reidy was pounded for nine runs in the top of the ninth — after getting the first two men out — and left in to take the beating. Beville started in with a double, and Parent homered. Beville doubled later in the inning as well. In all, there were four singles, five doubles, and the home run. Nary a walk in the ninth. One of the singles was Cy Young's, a ball that struck umpire Haskell and skittered into left field. Dowd was 4-for-4, walked once, and was hit once. This was the first time that Boston had played ball on a Sunday, there being no blue laws in effect in Milwaukee. The final score was 13-2. Both teams protested to league president Ban Johnson regarding Haskell's refusal to stand behind the plate while umpiring.

Young Has the Brewers Groggy—Thirteen Runs to Two.

A PANICKY FINISH.

NINE RUNS IN LAST INNING.
Bostons Have a Ragtime Finish—Freeman Benched Along with Collins.

June 3 — Losing 4-2, with Lewis allowing just six hits but doling out seven bases on balls. Milwaukee's Tully Sparks permitted just three singles. The umpire was behind home plate, ordered there by President Johnson, and there was no complaint about his calls. A three-run third gave the Brewers the lead; Boston scored its only two runs in the top of the ninth on one hit, two walks, and three errors.

June 4 — It seemed like a replay of the previous day's game in some respects. This time, it was a 5-0 lead heading into the ninth. Again Boston averted a shutout by scoring two runs in the top of the ninth. Again, the Brewers won. Cuppy was the losing pitcher.

June 5 — AMERICANS WON A HARD GAME. It was a back-and-forth game, with Milwaukee taking the lead, losing it, taking it again, then falling behind 5-4 after the top of the sixth. Fred Mitchell went the distance for Boston. Two insurance runs in the top of the ninth led to a 7-4 win. A hard game it may have been, but a win is a win. Both teams took the train to Boston, to resume the battle there.

June 6 — Travel day; no game. After the 5-6 road trip, Collins and crew returned home. With the Beaneaters on the road, the June 7 date would be the first home game the Americans had without a competing game being played almost literally next door.

June 7 — AMERICANS WHIP MILWAUKEE AT HOME. The headline made it seem as though it was a blowout. It was instead a game that it seemed Boston might well lose, with Milwaukee taking an early one-run lead and then re-establishing it a few innings later after Boston had tied it up. In the bottom of the eighth with two outs and nobody aboard, Freeman swung and hit a nubber in front of the plate. He would have been out but for an errant throw. A single and a poor decision on a fielder's choice saw Freeman score and runners on first and second. Two more singles brought both baserunners home, before Cy Young grounded out. Cy held Duffy's Brewers scoreless in the ninth and Boston won, 4-2.

June 8 — DUFFY'S MEN PLAY ROWDY BALL AND LOSE. In the early days of baseball, players were a little rowdier than today. As noted, Buck Freeman grabbed the shoulders of an umpire in the game on May 11, and in this game Milwaukee second baseman Billy Gilbert, who was hectoring the umpire from the third-base coaching box while the Brewers were at bat, was thrown out of the game, then went out to his position to retrieve his glove and "transgressed the rules of baseball etiquette as to deliberately walk up to Umpire

[Al] Manassau and without the slightest warning to the latter to viciously stamp upon Manassau's foot with his spiked heel." Manassau moved to strike him but then pulled back his fist and decided to let further punishment suffice. The *Boston Globe* stated, "It was without question the most uncalled-for attack on a baseball official in this city, and the player should be severely punished if the American league lives up to its precepts."

In an unrelated incident, right fielder Irv Waldron had been tossed "for speaking impertinently" to the ump, which the *Globe* felt was an unnecessarily hasty move by Manassau. Boston scored once in the first. In the fourth its leadoff man was hit by a pitch, and then followed this sequence: hit, error, walk, another error, another walk, two more hits, and two more errors. By the time the inning was over, it was eight runs scored on three hits. Lewis won the game, 11-4.

A curious superstition was noted in the *Globe*: "It was reported around the ground before the game, that several loads of hay had been seen passing the grounds in the morning. This was a tip for the superstitious that Boston was to win. … There is no record of a ball team losing after taking a good look at a load of hay, especially after each player has received a wisp of the dried grass."

June 9 — Sunday. No game scheduled.

June 10 — Beating the Brewers this day put Boston a game over .500. It looked like a loss for most of the game, Milwaukee holding Boston scoreless for the first five innings while rolling up a 4-0 lead, then allowing just one run in the sixth. But another big inning turned the tide, as Boston scored six times in the seventh in a fusillade that included six singles and a double. A 7-4 win for Kellum, who'd been on the brink of being released but pitched a good game, only one of the four runs being earned.

June 11 — BOSTONS STILL KEEP WINNING. Five errors by Milwaukee and no errors by Boston. Eight runs and 13 hits for Boston, with four runs and seven hits off Cuppy for the Brewers. Rare was there a game with even one home run (the team as a whole hit 37 homers in 1901), but this game featured homers by Freeman, Ferris, and Hemphill. Hugh Duffy's Brewers limped out of town having dropped all four games.

June 12 — BOSTONS WIN FROM DETROIT. Boston won its sixth game in a row. It was another error-free game for the home team; the Tigers committed three. Cy Young walked just one man and allowed six hits … or maybe eight, depending on which newspaper's box score you read. Fred Parent hit a home run. It was a 4-2 victory.

June 13 — BOSTON'S GAME TILL SEVENTH. A loss, 11-6, which in retrospect stood out as the only L in what would have otherwise been a string of 16 consecutive W's. Boston scored four runs in the first inning and was leading 5-2 until the Tigers teed off on Lewis in the top of the seventh. To be fair, the first three runs of the inning scored on Boston throwing errors. Five runs gave Detroit the edge, and the Boston crowd was yelling two words still heard at games over a hundred years later: "Do something!" The hoped-for rally never came. Lewis lost.

June 14 — BOSTON BATTING WON THE GAME. Cy Young was not at his best, giving up ten hits and seven runs to Detroit. There were two homers, both hit by Tigers. But there was a *lot* of batting by Boston, and it made all the difference in the end. Four Detroit runs in the fifth saw the game tied, and it remained 7-7 after seven. Cy Young — who'd pitched on the 12th — came on in relief of Kellum, starting in the sixth.

Detroit was held scoreless in the eighth, but Boston batters scored nine times. Oddly, there was only one double hit in the entire game (by Dowd), but there were seven triples — five of them by Boston and, it seems, three of them in consecutive at-bats by Ferris, Schreck, and Young. That's when Dowd doubled. He was followed by Stahl, who hit yet another triple. How many Boston hits there were in the game again depends on which box score one reads; the *Post* reported 19 and the *Globe* reported 20.

Buck Freeman was thrown out of the game by Umpire Manassau for disputing an out call after he overran third base earlier in the game. It was a close call, but the *Globe* chastised Freeman for being childish in arguing the call. It was Ladies Day, and one could bring *two* ladies to the game and get them both in free.

June 15—DETROITS LOST HEART AND GAME. It's not surprising they lost heart after Boston scored one run in the first, six runs in the second (three of them on Freeman's triple), and four runs in the third. The beneficiary of the barrage was George Winter, throwing a complete-game 12-4 win in his major-league debut. He'd been brought on board, signed from the YMCA baseball team in York, Pennsylvania, according to the *Boston Post*. Tom Simon's biography of Winter has him signed out of Gettysburg College.

June 16—Another Sunday at home. A day of rest. No baseball. The team had climbed into third place.

June 17—TWO GAMES FOR COLLINS & CO. The first game of a Bunker Hill Day twin bill started at 10:30 A.M. and the second at 2:30 P.M. Boston won them both, handily, 11-1 and 10-4, to the delight of more than 15,000 patrons. Fred Mitchell's first home start was an easy win, Boston scoring early and often while holding the first-place White Sox to five singles. Ferris was ejected from the second game for poking Umpire Manassau's inflated chest protector. Cy Young was the winner of the second game.

June 18—BOSTON HAD CLOSE CALL. No lopsided contest this, a 4-3 win that was almost lost when Chicago scored two runs in the top of the ninth. The White Sox scored one run in the top of the first, and Boston matched it in the fourth. Lewis kept the score close, and then Parent tripled in two in the sixth, subsequently scoring on a fly ball. Boston's 4-1 lead held until the pair of runs on a single, a triple, and a single before Lewis tightened up and induced a game-ending shortstop-to-second double play.

Seeing themselves beaten at the box office, Boston Nationals owner Soden announced that his team would drop prices to 25 cents, matching the American League pricing.

June 19—AMERICANS IN SECOND PLACE. Winning 12 of their last 13 games propelled the Americans into second place, just one game behind the White Sox. Winter—still being called "Winters" in the papers—held Chicago to three runs on six hits. A four-run sixth inning, kicked off by a long home run to center field by Parent, helped Boston to a 5-3 victory.

June 20—BOSTON AMERICANS AT TOP OF LEAGUE. Sweeping five games from the American League leaders had bumped up Boston from where it was when the homestand began—five games behind—into the lead, by 12 percentage points, .605 to .592, dethroning the White Sox for the time being. Boston had won 13 of its last 14 games, this day's game being win number 13, a thrilling 4-3 walkoff win.

At the end of eight innings, Cy Young had pitched well against Zaza Harvey, but the score stood 3-2 Chicago, and it looked as though the Sox from Chicago (the only Sox in the game) would salvage a win in the five games. Boston had the bases loaded with one out in the sixth, but Young—one of the better hitters on the club—grounded into one of the four double plays that had repeatedly hammered Boston's hopes of overcoming the 3-0 lead the White Sox built in the early innings. In the bottom of the ninth Schreck hit one down the line in left for a single and Young worked a walk through "ludicrous gyrations of his big form at the plate" (which leaves a lot to the imagination). Tommy Dowd singled to left field, scoring Schreck to tie to game. Young held at second base. There were two on, nobody out, and first place in the standings lay in the balance. Chick Stahl bunted to advance the runners, but Harvey fielded the ball and threw out Young at third base. Jimmy Collins walked and loaded the bases. The White Sox had no choice but to pull the infield in, to try to for a sure double play or at least a play at the plate. Comiskey also had to bring the outfield in, to prevent a fly ball from resulting in the runner tagging and scoring the winning run. Boston's biggest slugger was at the plate, and Buck Freeman delivered, with a hit well over Fielder

Jones's head in left. Jones knew there was no hope and rather than run back to retrieve the ball joined his teammates by simply running in and letting the ball roll all the way to the fence. Freeman was given a single, and had won the game.

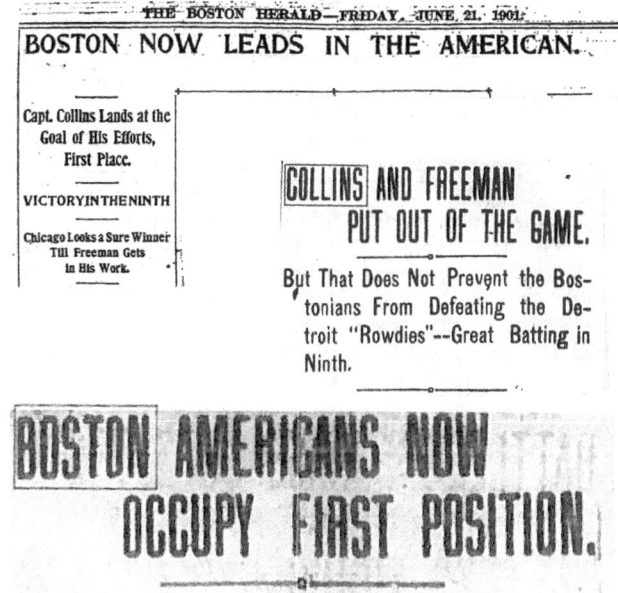

June 21 — AMERICANS HAD NO EASY TASK. The Cleveland Blues came to town for four games, and Boston kept winning. Parson Lewis pitched for Boston, and though he was staked to early leads of 1-0 and 4-1, the Blues kept up the pressure, adding single runs in the fifth and the sixth on home runs by pitcher Pete Dowling and second baseman Erve Beck. Three of Cleveland's four errors occurred in the third inning, helping Boston score three runs.

June 22 — WINTERS (sic) HAD FINE SUPPORT. It was a crisp one hour-and-24 minute game, scoreless for the first four and 1-0 in Boston's favor after the fifth. Reflecting the esteem in which fielding was held in the day, the biggest cheer came when second baseman Hobe Ferris saved two runs in the third inning by snaring a hard-hit ball batted over second base. In the later innings, Boston scored two in the sixth, three in the seventh, and two more in the eighth. All five extra-base hits were Boston's. George Winter allowed just one run on seven hits. 8-1. The team had won nine games in a row, which proved to be its longest winning streak of the season.

June 23 — Sunday.

June 24 — BOSTONS VERY KIND TO GUESTS. Fred Mitchell was no mystery, and Cleveland scored twice in the first and twice in the third, ultimately costing Mitchell his first defeat, 7-1, and snapping the nine-game Boston winning streak. Boston batters collected just five hits and scored just the one time, in the fourth, on a walk and two singles, but were as generous to the visitors as could be, committing five errors, walking five, and allowing 11 base hits. Chicago won its game and recaptured first place. The White Sox, in fact, had embarked on a ten-game winning streak of their own.

June 25 — CLOSE SERIES WITH VICTORY. Winning three out of four is good, and Boston closed out Cleveland's visit and a 15-2 homestand with a 4-2 victory. Cy Young was touched for eight hits, including two triples and a double.

June 26 — MIX-UP CAUSE OF NO GAME. The American League schedule was tangled and confused, resulting in the Boston team arriving in Philadelphia for a game. Umpire Manassau also reported to Philadelphia, expecting to umpire the game with Boston. But the Athletics were in Washington, playing the Washington Senators. Jimmy Collins said his team was in Philadelphia, the umpire was there, and the game should be forfeited to Boston if the Athletics didn't take the field. Apparently *both* Washington and Chicago were scheduled to play in Baltimore, yet (including Boston) none of the three teams that *might* have played against the Orioles ever did. Washington hosted and played against the Athletics.

June 27 — BOSTON LOST ERRORLESS GAME. It was also a scoreless game, for Boston batters. Seven scattered hits, three by Dowd, produced zero runs. Lewis let the Senators score one run in the fourth and one run in the eighth, while Senators southpaw Wyatt Lee won his third game of the year against Boston. It was actually the fifth game in a row the Boston

> **The day the team showed up in the wrong city**
>
> June 26, 1901, was the day that Boston didn't play a game, because the team showed up in the wrong city.
>
> Every time you set up a new league, you're bound to have a few problems. The first year of the American League ran very smoothly considering that it was a new enterprise, but there were a few first-year kinks.
>
> Jimmy Collins and his Boston team showed up at Columbia Park in Philadelphia, in uniform and ready to play the Athletics. Umpire Alfred Manassau turned up, too. The problem was—there was no team to play. The Philadelphia Athletics weren't there. They were in Washington, playing the Senators at American League Park. Because the umpire was in Philadelphia, no umpire showed up in Washington—so one catcher from each team was drafted to umpire in that game: Mike Grady of the Senators (who came from Philadelphia) and ex-Senator Tom Leahy of the Athletics (who came from New Haven) umpired the game. "Their work was excellent," wrote the *Philadelphia Inquirer* correspondent. The *Washington Star* added, "Their decisions were unusually accurate and satisfactory." The Athletics may have wished they had stayed at home; they were leading 4-1 when Washington scored four times in the ninth to win the game, the final run scoring on a very close play at home plate as Washington's John Farrell slid in with the winning run, ruled safe by umpire-for-the-day Leahy of the Philadelphia team.
>
> Meanwhile, in yet another city—Baltimore—the Orioles sat idle. They were waiting for the Bostons to arrive. Then the Chicago White Sox showed up instead! Baltimore manager John McGraw refused to play Chicago, since it said on his schedule that his team was supposed to host Boston. So Baltimore waited for Boston, Boston was in Philadelphia, and the White Sox had pulled into Baltimore but the Orioles wouldn't play them.
>
> Detroit had just left Baltimore and was on its way home to host Milwaukee. Milwaukee, for its part, played a game against Cleveland as it prepared to head on to Detroit. Cleveland had left Boston and was on its way to Chicago, but paused at home for the game with Milwaukee.
>
> How did this mix-up come about? Three home games in Baltimore had been rained out—those against Boston on April 24 and 25 and the June 15 game against Chicago. Chicago was nearby, having played Philadelphia the day before, on June 25. Boston had a game to make up against Philadelphia and that was scheduled for July 31. The original schedule had Boston at Baltimore on July 3. Then someone in the league office realized that Boston already had a morning game set on the Fourth of July; train schedules being what they were, the Boston team couldn't get back home in time if they'd played an afternoon game in Baltimore on July 3. So league President Ban Johnson rescheduled Boston to play in Baltimore earlier, on June 26. The problem was that Johnson apparently forgot to tell either Boston or umpire Manassau about the change. Boston (and the umpire) followed the original schedule and showed up at an empty ballpark in Philadelphia. Johnson also forgot to tell Chicago that plans had changed, so the White Sox kept to their original schedule, too, and traveled to Baltimore. At least there was another team there, but as Johnson had told Baltimore to expect Boston, when Chicago turned up instead McGraw would not play them.
>
> Somehow the *Boston Herald* had it right; the *Sunday Herald* told readers that Boston was going to play in Baltimore on the 26th, but apparently nobody on the team read the *Herald* or didn't believe everything they read in the papers.
>
> The newspaper boasted a bit, under a story headlined THE HERALD HAD IT RIGHT: "The failure of the Boston American team to appear in Baltimore yesterday can be ascribed to no other cause than downright stupidity. In last Sunday's *Herald* it was announced that the team was scheduled to play in Baltimore on Wednesday, yet, marvelous to say, President Somers, Business Manager Gavin and Jimmy Collins were not aware of that fact. It does look as if it would pay the busy representatives of the local club to read *The Herald* carefully before they go on another trip. It would save them lots of trouble and expense, and enable them to know exactly where they are expected to play."
>
> This was nothing that a cellphone couldn't have fixed.
>
> -adapted from the book *Red Sox Threads*

Americans had lost to Washington. And the game was indeed remarkable in that neither team committed an error, unusual in this time of relatively rudimentary gloves and fields that weren't always in prime shape.

June 28—WINTERS (sic) WINS ANOTHER GAME. In Washington, the home team took a 3-0 lead in the bottom of the second, each of the three consecutive batters Winter had walked scoring on singles. Boston got one in the top of the sixth and another one in the top of the seventh, pulling them tantalizingly close, to within one run. But then Washington scored a pair, making it 5-2 and deflating some of the hopes of Collins and his men. Things became heated, with the umpire even calling the police to escort Buck Freeman from the grounds. It was a game the *Post* said "was remarkable for the mixture of good and bad ball." In the top of the eighth, Hemphill drove in Collins and then Fred Parent hit a three-run homer over the left-field fence, giving Boston a 6-5 lead. Which Winter (now 4-0) held.

June 29—A 7-2 win was the last game Boston played in the month of June, which they finished in second place, 2 1/2 games behind the White Sox, who had re-established control of first place with their ten-game win streak. Cy Young won the day's game in Washington, a six-hitter. Freeman was back, and hit two doubles, but Young himself had a three-hit game with a single, double, and triple. Jimmy Collins hit a home run.

June 30 — Sunday. No game.

July 1 — Finally back in Baltimore, where they began the year and where they should have been on June 26. Cuppy was asked to pitch — and was given a 5-0 lead in the first inning. Boston took advantage of four hits and two walks and "gave an exhibition of successful base running that made the crowd turn green with envy." (*Boston Globe*) The Orioles got two runs in the bottom of the first. Four more runs for the Birds in the sixth gave them a lead, and Collins called in Lewis to replace Cuppy. Boston had a chance to score at least a couple of runs in the seventh, but what looked to be at least a Ferris triple was hauled in with an all-out running, over-the-head, leaping catch by right fielder Cy Seymour, ending the threat.

July 2 — BOSTONS BROKE BALTIMORE LOCK. The Orioles had won 11 games in a row, and were headed toward number 12 when they scored three times in the first off Winter and stockpiled a couple more in the second. But Boston didn't give up and O's pitcher Iron Man McGinnity became "a tin man, easily dented" — the phrase ascribed to a "facetious lad on the bleacher" by the *Boston Globe*. Collins walked in the third inning, and both Freeman and Parent singled. Then Hemphill doubled them all in. Freeman was on base in the sixth when Hemphill homered, giving him five runs batted in. Baltimore had added a run in the fourth, however, so Boston was still down by one. Two singles, an out (a botched sacrifice resulting in an out at third base), and an error loaded the bases. Then Stahl singled to right field, driving in two, and after Collins struck out, Freeman singled to left, driving in two more runs. The 10-8 final wasn't pretty, but it was a win and Winters went to 5-0. After the game, both teams spent the evening in Baltimore and then took the midnight train to Boston, where they had four games to play.

July 3 — ORIOLES HAD NO CHANCE TO WIN. As the game progressed, any opportunity the Orioles might have had slipped further away. Cy Young allowed seven singles and a double, but Boston racked up 16 hits, including four triples and a double. Young was the only Boston batter who didn't have a hit (0-for-4, despite leading the team in batting with a .368 average just a couple of days earlier). The only run he let in came on an error. Parent drove in two in Boston's first, and the team scored twice more in the fourth, once in the fifth, once again in the sixth, and then three times in the eighth on a Stahl triple, a Collins double, and a Buck Freeman homer.

July 4 — CROWD GOES WILD. GREATEST DEMONSTRATION EVER SEEN AT A BALL GAME. The *Globe* enthused about the passion shown during the Fourth of July doubleheader, which saw Boston win the 10:30 morning game behind Fred Mitchell, 10-2, the game ending at then minutes after noontime, then take the 3:00 P.M. game for Parson Lewis, 8-3, over at ten minutes before 5:00.

It was a festive crowd for the Fourth, and patrons behaved in ways that could get one a lengthy prison sentence today. Consider the situation in the bottom of the seventh in the second game. Baltimore was leading 3-2 and Frank Foreman was pitching for the Orioles — the same Foreman who'd been released by Boston earlier in the season was perhaps getting a little payback. With one out, Chick Stahl slashed a grounder to shortstop and reached when the ball gobbled up Dunn. Collins then hit an inside-the-park home run down the right-field line, and Tim Murnane wrote in the *Globe* that the "crowd cheered and yelled. Cannon crackers [firecrackers] were thrown out on the field and spectators discharged revolvers until the place reminded one of a war scene at a wild west show." (*Globe*)

The firing of weapons at games in Boston was not considered particularly unusual at the time, and numerous accounts of holiday games both describe and depict (in sports page cartoons) celebratory guns being shot in the air. A hit batsman and a triple followed Collins's homer, and Freeman scored on the same triple when the throw back in went wild. "The applause was more furious than ever," continued the *Globe* story. "Parent hit for three bases and the gun chorus was resumed with a vengeance." Hobe Ferris drove a deep hit to right-center for another inside-the-park home run, and "it seemed as if every spectator at the game had a gun and was firing 20 shots a second and yelling like wild Indians."

The *Boston Post* wrote, "Big firecrackers were thrown onto the field. A hundred revolvers belched, horns tooted, and those without artificial noise producers stood up and yelled. It was the most pronounced demonstration of the season, and it was fully two minutes before it subsided."

For the record, the current-day Boston Red Sox no longer permit spectators to bring loaded revolvers to baseball games and discharge them when the home team takes the lead.

On Independence Day 1901, however, Baltimore had scored first, in the first inning of the first game. Boston matched it with one run in the bottom of the inning. The Orioles scored once again in the second, but Boston banged out seven runs in the third inning and the game was effectively over from that point forward. Mitchell had allowed only six hits.

More than 10,000 people came out for the afternoon game, more than doubling the morning crowd. The morning game had one Boston error; there were none in the second game. Baltimore's winning streak was a memory; they'd dropped four straight to Boston. Boston was just one game behind Chicago in the standings. The Orioles and Tigers were tied, 6 1/2 games behind.

For more on guns being fired at Boston baseball games, see Bill Nowlin's *Red Sox Threads*.

July 5—WINTERS (sic) SET A RAPID PACE. The *Globe*'s headline was two words, also meriting a "sic": WINTERS AGAIN. He became 6-0 with a 2-1 win against the visiting Senators from Washington. The only error was Winter's. Dowd hit a couple of doubles, and the team made 11 hits, but scored only twice—which was one more than they needed. After the Senators walked off with a sweep in their first visit to the Huntington Avenue Grounds, it was good to get a win over them.

July 6—BOSTONS AGAIN IN FIRST PLACE. The Tigers beat the White Sox in an 11-inning game, while Cy Young shut out the Senators, 7-0, in Boston. Cy apparently enjoyed himself with a little showmanship on the mound, even throwing "an underhand ball at ice wagon pace [which] seemed to afford Young a good deal of amusement, especially when [team captain Bill] Clarke was the victim." Stahl homered in the first inning and tripled during Boston's five-run second inning.

July 7—Sunday. A day of rest. Freeman's .358 average now led the team, with Young second at .333.

July 8—BOSTON TOOK WHOLE SERIES. Washington had come to town for three games and scored just two runs, losing all three games, this one by 3-1. The two fourth-inning runs came in on an error, after Umpire Connolly called a ball on what appeared to the *Globe* writer to be an unambiguous third strike to Hemphill. The Senators erred two, or three, times, while Boston was again error-free in a game that was "as full of fine plays as a ripe watermelon is full of black seeds."

July 9—Game postponed due to wet grounds.

July 10—QUAKERS FOUND BOSTONS EASY. WEIRD PITCHING AND DROWSY PLAYING COST LOCALS GAME. After winning seven in a row, perhaps a loss was inevitable. Connie Mack's

Athletics were in town and they scored three quick runs off Lewis in the first inning, but Boston matched that. Philadelphia scored one more in the third, and Boston matched that. Philadelphia scored a fifth run in the fourth, and Boston matched that. This could have gone on forever, in theory, but when the Quakers scored four times in the top of the sixth and the home team scored none, the die was cast. McLean pinch-hit for Lewis but was out. Mitchell relieved. The final score was 13-6.

July 11—PLAYED IN STEADY RAIN. In a game called after five innings and 55 minutes, but which had still drawn 3,800 fans, Boston prevailed, 5-1, and it went in the books as another win for George Winter. The rain had arrived in the fourth and never let up. Fultz singled to start the sixth, but then the rain came down even more heavily and forced the umpire to call it. Despite the conditions, neither team made an error. Buck Freeman was—again—thrown out of a game, this time for "saying distasteful things to Umpire Connolly."

July 12—CY ON THE SLAB. The *Globe* headline highlighted the fact that Cy Young had won his 11th straight game for Boston, a 5-3 win with just one walk and seven hits for Philadelphia. The Athletics had taken a 2-0 lead in the first, and it looked as if Cy might falter, but he buckled down and Boston scored in the second, third, and fourth and rolled up a 5-2 lead. After the game, both teams entrained for Philadelphia to play a series there. The homestand had been a tremendous success financially, with several gates over 4,000, and quite a few over 5,000. They'd been 15-2 on the long homestand. The Americans weren't due back in Boston until August 8, scheduled to play 24 games on the road before coming back to the Hub. They were in first place; the National League's Beaneaters were in sixth place.

July 13—FAIL TO HIT. The *Globe* headline referred to Boston, which hit safely five times and scored but once, in the sixth. Weather threatened before the game, and then interrupted it, bringing it to an end after seven runs. The Athletics had already driven Fred Mitchell from the mound by then, with Frank Morrissey appearing in what would be the only American League game of his career (he appeared in seven Cubs games in 1902). The four runs Philadelphia scored in the bottom of the second gave them a 5-0 lead.

July 14—No game, because it was Sunday, and if any city had stricter blue laws than Boston, it was Philadelphia.

July 15—COLLINS'S MEN DROP A NOTCH. It had to happen sooner or later; Winter lost a game. He was matched up against fellow Gettysburg College alumnus Eddie Plank. On July 11 Winter had come out on top in a similar matchup, but this time Plank allowed just seven hits while Winter was relieved by Cuppy in the seventh and the Athletics got 14 hits (and, more importantly, six runs to Boston's one). The three runs Philadelphia got in the first inning were enough for Plank to get the win, and for Winter to drop to 7-1.

July 16—TRIED TO MOB THE UMPIRE. The game started on a friendly enough note; as in the May 25 game, the Cleveland crowd welcomed all the ex-Clevelanders on Boston's club, including starter Cy Young. And when the Blues scored once in the first and three times in the second, that made the fans feel all the better. But the tide turned, and Boston took a 5-4 lead in the eighth, then added five more runs in the top of the ninth. Cleveland battled back with four of their own, but fell short, 10-8. There were calls that bothered both teams, but one of the more egregious ones was in the eighth when even the Boston papers agreed Ferris had been struck out—but Umpire Manassau called it a ball, and the next pitch was a wild pitch on which two runs scored. The crowd was still livid after the game, and "surged onto the field and intimidated Manassau. Cushions were flying at Manassau's head, while others were crying to mob him. The crowd lacked a leader, and all they did was to knock Manassau's hat off and forced him to beat a hasty retreat to the clubhouse." The *Globe* declared that only the intervention of the Cleveland players prevented matters from truly getting out of hand.

July 17—COLLINS'S MEN ON TOP AGAIN. The White Sox beat Baltimore in their game, but the

Boston Americans won two games against Cleveland (9-3 and 10-2) and that edged them into first place. Both games were convincing wins; starters Lewis and Cuppy each threw a six-hitter—though the *Post* said that they were both hit hard, in a way that wouldn't show in the box score. Cuppy did carry a shutout into the ninth, so his pitching couldn't have been too bad. Through five innings in the first game, Cleveland led, 3-2, but the runs piled up in the late innings for Boston beginning with a two-run homer by Freeman.

July 18—BOSTON LOST BY ONE POINT. The 6-5 loss to Cleveland was ascribed to Winter, but almost all the runs were unearned runs. In the fifth inning the Blues scored three runs on errors by Collins and Ferris. Winter walked only one batter, and he contributed a two-run homer (the only one he ever hit in 223 big-league games). While Boston lost, the White Sox regained the lead. The league's leading home-run hitter, Buck Freeman, turned his foot while running to first base in the third inning, dislocated his big toe, and was expected to be out for a week to ten days. He was carried off the field by five Cleveland players. Lou Criger took his place at first base, and committed an error that let in two runs.

July 19—The Friday afternoon game was a makeup game for one of the games lost in late May. Cy Young had won 12 games in a row, but lost this one in the bottom of the tenth inning. Cleveland scored first, in the first inning, when center fielder Ollie Pickering laid down a bunt and made it all the way around to third base when Collins threw wildly to first. There was no more scoring until the top of the ninth when Collins beat out an infield hit to the pitcher, stole second after one out, and took third on an error by the shortstop. Ferris hit a fly ball to Pickering, whose throw home beat Collins—but catcher Bob Wood dropped the ball. Both teams had five hits, but two of Cleveland's came in the tenth. Third baseman Bill Bradley doubled, and then came home when Wood lifted a hit over Criger's head and into shallow right field. After the game, the Boston team took a boat to Detroit.

July 20—DETROIT WINS CLOSE GAME. Both teams scored two runs in the first, and the game was tied 3-3 after three. Boston scored once in the fifth, but the Tigers scored five times off Lewis in the bottom of the fifth. As the *Globe* put it: "then came disaster to the Athenians." (The city of Boston liked to call itself the "Athens of America.") Boston accounted for all three of the doubles in the game, but the home run and the bases-clearing triple followed by a run-scoring fly were all Detroit's. The final score was 8-6.

July 21—Sunday. But there was a game—because the Boston club was playing in "the West"—Detroit. "Collins Plays Superb Game" read the *Post*'s headline. "His Men Did Well, Too" continued the subhead. After the first two batters were retired in the top of the first, Collins singled and so did Freeman. Parent doubled, and so did Ferris, and there were three earned runs across. The paper said, "The work of Collins at third base was superb, and he easily carried off the fielding honors. In almost every inning the Boston captain made a brilliant stop, and only once did a hit get past him." This wasn't as easy as it might have been, because the infield was said to be "worse than sand lot diamonds on which scrub teams play." Collins and Winter were the only two with two hits. The Tigers got three runs of their own in the fifth, tying the game. In the top of the eighth, a walk to Stahl, a fielder's choice, a single, and then a wild pitch gave Boston the go-ahead run. Winter won, 4-3.

It was an odd feature of the 1901 and 1902 seasons, in that Detroit's Sunday home games were played at Burns Park, not Bennett Park, which hosted all the other games. This was the only game Boston played at Burns Park in 1901.

A story in several morning newspapers reported that the arrival of the American League was presenting financial problems for some of the National League clubs, and particularly in Boston. In information obtained in the NL office, Boston and Chicago were singled out as losing money. The two clubs "in years past have generally been among the regular and consistent money-makers of the league." Later in the article, a hint at the magnitude was reflected in the words "heavy financial losses." The *Boston Globe* and *Washington Post* were among the papers that carried the story.

Seven of Boston's players were hitting over .300: Collins, Freeman, Stahl, Schreck (listed this way in newspaper statistics), Parent, Young, and Hemphill.

July 22—BOSTONS LOST GAME IN 12TH. YOUNG PITCHED GREAT GAME, BUT WASN'T PROPERLY AIDED. It didn't help when Cy's teammates committed three errors in the fourth inning, letting three runs score on just two hits. Boston had 13 hits to Detroit's 12, and was outdone in errors, by the Tigers' six to their three. It was all a matter of timing. It was 4-4 after. Boston scored once in the tenth; so did Detroit. In the bottom of the 12th, with one out, Barrett singled, then stole second on Young, advanced to third base on Boston's fourth error (Schreck's wild throw trying to catch him stealing), and then scored the run that give the Tigers a 4-3 win when Gleason singled to center field.

July 23—BOSTONS WON FROM BREWERS. Visiting Milwaukee for the second time, Cuppy started but he didn't last long. He gave up one run in the second and two in the third. Boston tied it in the top of the fourth, thanks to the first of three errors by third baseman Bill Friel. When the first Milwaukee batter in the bottom of the fourth singled, Collins decided he'd seen enough of Cuppy and brought in Fred Mitchell. And then Boston scored four more times in the fifth, with the pitcher, Mitchell, leading off with a triple. By the time the game was over, it was 9-7.

July 24—HEMPHILL'S MUFF COST THE GAME. Lewis allowed one run in the first and one in the second, and the Brewers were threatening in the third, with two on and two outs. A long fly to right field looked like the third out, but Hemphill muffed the ball and both baserunners scored, giving Milwaukee four runs in all. Criger had to leave the game after being hit in the head by a pitch. Boston pulled off a double steal, with the runner at third scoring on the play—but could put across only three runs.

July 25—BOSTONS PLAYED ROCKY BALL. You can't commit six errors and hope to win. Winter did give up 11 hits, all singles save one double. Neither pitcher walked anyone. Milwaukee won, 6-2.

July 26—HUSTING WAS NO MYSTERY. Indeed, Boston batters got to Pete Husting for 11 hits. He never allowed more than one run an inning, but there were four of those innings. Cy Young gave up eight hits, holding the Brewers to two runs. And the whole game lasted just 1:29, even though Milwaukee had to bat in the bottom of the ninth in one last futile attempt to tie the game or go ahead. Criger had tried to play for a while on the 25th, but had to leave and was unable to play at all in this game due to dizziness. Cuppy played left field and Dowd played first base.

July 27—13TH UNLUCKY FOR BOSTONS. Playing in Chicago, Mitchell started the game but couldn't even make it through two innings, the White Sox grabbing a 7-0 lead. Ted Lewis came on after the first, and after giving up two more runs in the second, he shut out Chicago for the next seven innings, which had seen Boston scored four in the seventh and two in the eighth, and tie the game in the top of the ninth. Neither team scored in the 10th, 11th, or 12th. Lewis had ten consecutive shutout innings to his credit. Fred Hartman led off the bottom of the 13th with a bunt toward third base. Lewis pounced on the ball and fired it to first base, but threw it so wildly and hard that it "rolled rapidly toward the right field bleachers, finally struck one of the supports and bounded over the screen and into the crowd. Hartman was nearing second before Criger started for the ball and had won the game before the ball could be found." (*Globe*) Criger had taken over first base for Buck Freeman, who'd broken his toe in the 12th.

July 28—There was no game on Sunday. With the loss the day before, Boston had now fallen 4 1/2 games behind the White Sox, seeing the gap widen by three games in just four days.

July 29—"CY" YOUNG TOO MUCH FOR THEM. Boston cut Chicago's lead by a game, with Cy Young allowing just five hits and only one ninth-inning run, while Boston collected 11 hits, two walks, and two hit batsmen, for four runs (two of them on Young's single in the eighth scoring Parent and Ferris).

> THE BOSTON HERALD — TUESDAY, JULY 30
>
> **YOUNG AGAIN ON EDGE**
>
> Chicago Trails Boston All Through the Game.
>
> A Splendid Victory Over the American Leader.
>
> ---
>
> **CY NEVER IN BETTER FORM.**
>
> Strikes Out Six Men, Is Hit Only Five Times, and Again Gives No Bases on Balls.
>
> [Special Dispatch to the Boston Herald.]
> CHICAGO, Ill., July 29, 1901. The Bostons were easy winners over the White Stockings this afternoon, and the fact

July 30 — LOOKS LIKE WAR. There was no Boston Americans game scheduled, but the *Boston Globe* headline referred to the announcement by American League President Ban Johnson that the league would field a team in St. Louis in 1902. Word of an AL team in New York was not expected to be too far in the future. Charles Somers said he'd like to see a postseason series against Boston's National League team (or any NL team, for that matter). Milwaukee would finish out the season, but was the least successful team and perhaps the leading candidate to move to go head-to-head in St. Louis against the Cardinals.

July 31 — BOSTON DOWNED IN ODD GAME. Boston committed six errors and Philadelphia five. There were only nine earned runs in the game, Boston with one more than Philadelphia, but the final score was 13-10, Philly, in large part due to the Athletics' seven-run eighth inning. Collins was faulted for taking out Winter in the eighth without Lewis having time to warm up. The actual fielding was "far worse" than even the error totals showed, wrote the *Globe*. Particularly egregious was when three baserunners scored on a wild throw from Parent to Criger after the runner on third base had been effectively caught off third. "Not only were the players' arms off in throwing, but their brains took queer streaks … [there were mental errors] as laughable as they were costly, and Dowd dropped a ball that a small boy would be sure of."

At the end of July, the standings saw Chicago on top with Boston back to 4 1/2 games behind. In third place was Baltimore at seven back and Detroit was 8 1/2 out of first. The best of the four clubs in the second division was 16 1/2 behind.

August 1 — BOSTON LOSES TO QUAKERS. Both teams had 12 hits, Cuppy throwing for Boston and staked to a three-run lead in the top of the first. But by the end of the first, Philadelphia had four runs. Parent had his second game in a row with two errors, and two others erred once. There were 11 doubles in the game, three by Collins, and Freeman hit a homer, but Boston's six runs were two fewer than Philadelphia's eight. The *Globe* ascribed the difference to numerous "lucky hits" by the Athletics, balls that dropped in between the infielders and outfielders, more than to the errors.

August 2 — BOSTONS BLANK PHILADELPHIANS. If you guessed it was Cy Young who spun the shutout, you would be correct. Collins hit two more doubles and Freeman hit two, too. Dowd, Collins, Freeman, and Parent all had four-hit games, as the team banged out 22 hits in all — every one of them off hapless starter Bill Bernhard, who was left in for the full game by Connie Mack. Boston committed only one error, by Collins. The final score was 16-0.

August 3 — QUAKERS GET BACK AT BOSTON. Six runs in the third inning off Lewis scotched his hopes for a win. A number of Athletics made great fielding plays, but one of the best may have been the scorching liner Hemphill hit that shortstop Fred Ely leapt for. The ball smacked off his glove, he caught it with his bare hand as it fell, and then threw to first to double off Buck Freeman. It was Ely's first game for Philadelphia. He was 3-for-4 at the plate and "was frequently compelled to doff his cap to the plaudits of the enthusiastic fans." The Athletics won, 7-4.

August 4—Boston 9, Hoboken 4. It was a Sunday and there was no scheduled game, but Boston didn't rest. The Americans played in New Jersey against the Hoboken nine at the St. George Cricket Grounds, with Mitchell and Schrecongost the battery, winning 9-4. The Hobokens committed four errors, and Boston made none.

August 5—AMERICANS LOST AND WON A GAME. The *Boston Post* headline was a bit misleading, in that Boston won the first game (3-1, a three-hitter thrown by Cy Young) and lost the second. The two runs that gave Boston the win in the first game both came on Orioles errors, while Baltimore easily won the second game (9-0) in part because of poor support (including five errors) given Winter. Baltimore scored three runs in the third, three in the fourth, and three in the fifth. Criger complained that Young's fastball was so fast that it blistered his hand through his catcher's glove.

August 6—There was supposed to be another doubleheader at Baltimore but it was rained out.

August 7—BOTH TEAMS SCORED TEN. Two games in Baltimore, and the winning team scored ten runs each time: Boston 10, Baltimore 5 in the first game and Baltimore 10, Boston 4 in the second. The Orioles "threw the [first] game away by hopelessly stupid work on the bases and [shortstop] Keister's miserable fielding and base-running." The stupid work on the bases included running into "a triple play worthy of the Oshkosh League." Singles by Brodie and Jackson, and there was nobody out in the O's fourth. "Bresnahan hit to Lewis, who threw to Collins. Brodie was run down and Jackson hesitated, and instead of reaching third started back for second and was caught by Ferris before he got there. Bresnahan had reached second safely, but seeing Jackson returning he stupidly started back toward first and was caught." Cuppy pitched the second game, and Baltimore's hits were more productive.

August 8—SHY ON RUNS. The *Globe* headline was succinct. Cy Young pitched a good enough game, with the team back at the Huntington Avenue Grounds, and matched Baltimore's Harry Howell. Young was excellent at times—such as when Baltimore's leadoff batter, Jim Jackson, tripled in the fifth but couldn't score. Jackson didn't touch second base, missing by about a yard, but Boston's complaints to Umpire Cantillon resulted in the umpire singing a retort! He started in singing the song "Goodbye, Dolly Gray," and then simply said, "He came close enough." But the O's pushed across single runs in the sixth and the eighth and Boston couldn't score once, indeed couldn't even muster the semblance of a rally. After the loss, Boston was a full six games behind Chicago in the standings.

August 9—EACH TEAM WON A GAME. After doubleheaders on August 5 and 7, the Orioles played Boston for two more doubleheaders on back-to-back days, on August 9 and 10. Four doubleheaders between the same two teams over a six-day period. Every one of the four twin bills was a split. Winter worked the first game on the 9th, and it was far from pretty, with his teammates committing six errors and him giving up 14 hits. That it was as close as it was (an 11-9 loss) was simply because Baltimore's pitching wasn't any better.

Between games, Frank Foreman (the ex-Boston player now with the Orioles) kept taunting his former teammates, shouting out things like, "Come on for your second dose." By the time Iron Man McGinnity took the mound in the bottom of the first, the Orioles offense had already given him two runs. But Fred Mitchell tightened up and allowed only three inoffensive hits in the next eight innings, while Boston batters scored once in the second and then batted around for five runs in the fourth.

August 10—EACH TEAM WINS A GAME. The *Post* headline writer may have forgotten the headline from the day before, and produced the same words but in the present tense. This time the scores were Boston 6, Baltimore 4 in the first game and Baltimore 4, Boston 3 in the second. Lewis won the first game; Young lost the second. Three passed balls by Schreck nearly cost Lewis the game, but he doubled and tripled in his three at-bats. Foreman clowned during the first game from the coaching box and between games as well, throwing kisses to the crowd—which he won over with such antics as furiously rushing at the umpire after being called out at second base, only to halt at the last moment and calmly amble back to the bench. He backed up his bragging with a couple of base hits, driving in one run, and holding Boston to two runs until the ninth, when another run was scored before the brief rally was squelched.

August 11—It was Sunday and, after four games in two days, a day off no doubt felt good. Freeman, Collins, Schreck, Stahl, and Parent were all batting over .300.

August 12—TWO GAMES AND AN EVEN BREAK. The doubleheaders resumed, with Boston hosting the Athletics for a pair of games, again each team winning one. Boston won the first one, 6-0, and lost the second by the same margin, 7-1. Winter was the winner and Mitchell was the loser. Only in the ninth inning of the second game did the Bostons avert a shutout, when Dowd tripled and then scored on a passed ball. They'd been held hitless by Eddie Plank through the first six innings. All the extra-base hits in the first game were Boston's. Stahl doubled and homered.

August 13—COLLINS FOUND 13 VERY LUCKY. It was the 13th of August and the game ran 13 innings. There were six triples in the game, boosted by a new ground rule, implemented the day before, that declared a ball hit into the fans behind the ropes in left field an automatic three-bagger, rather than forcing the fielder to chase down the ball. Philadelphia held a 3-0 lead against Lewis after seven innings. In the bottom of the eighth the pitcher doubled and was retired on a fielder's choice. Collins tripled, driving in one, and then Freeman walked and Hemphill hit a two-run single. The score tied, the game went into the 13th. Jimmy Collins hit a "sizzling grounder" down the third-base line that "became buried among the crowd back of the left-field ropes"—thus a triple. Buck Freeman swung at the first pitch and singled to first base, the ball glancing off the first baseman's glove.

THE BOSTON HERALD—WEDNESDAY, AUGUST 14, 1901.
BOSTON AMERICANS WON IN THE 13TH.
Great Extra Inning Fight at the Huntington Avenue Grounds.
STAR STICK WORK.

August 14—AMERICANS WIN AND ARE BEATEN. Yet another doubleheader, making it 14 games in a ten-day stretch. Cy Young lost to the Athletics 9-0 in the first game, forced out of the game after giving up seven runs in the first three innings. Boston committed four errors. After just ten minutes' break between games, Winter held the opposition to six hits and two runs, and the team woke up on defense, for an errorless 4-2 win in the second game.

August 15—The first-place Chicago White Sox came to Boston, and Young was ready to start again, against Jim Callahan, but rain came just as the game was about to begin. The game was postponed, planned to be made up when the White Sox came back in late September.

People in leadership roles for both leagues laughed off rumors that the two leagues were going to consolidate into one ten-team league for 1902.

August 16—COLLINS MEN DOWN LEADERS. Collins and company began to chip away at the 4 1/2-game White Sox lead. Cy Young threw a five-hit, 6-2 game, beating Callahan. Parent was 2-for-4 with a double and a triple, with four runs batted in.

August 17—RECORD CROWD SAW CHICAGO DEFEATED. Taking the second of two games against the visiting White Sox, Boston moved up to just 2 1/2 games behind the leaders. Ted Lewis allowed seven hits—including two triples and a double by third baseman Fred Hartman—but Chicago scored only twice. The largest crowd of the season, just under 12,000 (11,919), packed into the field on Huntington Avenue, the game delayed by 15 minutes because of the overflow crowd. Clark Griffith gave up four runs, but Chick Stahl was deprived of a home run because of the ground rule that scored a ball hit into the crowd behind the ropes as a triple.

> **CHICAGO OUTPLAYED.**
>
> **Boston Americans Only 34 Points Below.**

August 18 — Sunday. No baseball in Boston.

August 19 — BOSTON AGAIN WINS IN 13TH. Hugh Duffy brought his Brewers to Boston, and the first game pitted Bert Husting against George Winter (though even the Boston papers were still calling him "Winters"—and called the Milwaukee man "Hustings"). Had Boston not committed six errors, the game would likely not have been tied 5-5 after nine. Both pitchers went the distance, and Collins's fielding stood out on defense. A passed ball let Boston score the tying run in the seventh. In the bottom of the 13th Hemphill hit a ball back to Husting, who twice failed to get a handle on the ball and throw to first. Parent singled and sent Hemphill to third base, from where he scored when Schrecongost lifted a low fly ball to Duffy in center field. The White Sox lost to Washington and Boston had pressed to within 1 1/2 games of first place.

August 20 — ROW OF ZEROES FOR MILWAUKEE. Cy Young shut out the Brewers on seven hits, while Boston scored three times in both the second and fourth for a 6-0 victory. Stahl doubled, tripled, and homered but couldn't manage a single. The *Globe* subhead read: Collins and the Rest of the Team Give the Farmer Great Support. There were no errors and one standout play by Jimmy Collins saved the one run that Milwaukee might have scored.

August 21 — COLLINS'S MEN DEFEAT DUFFY'S. Each team had 11 hits (Ted Lewis vs. Ned Garvin), and the Brewers had leads of 2-0, 3-2, and 4-3 before Boston scored four times in the sixth on two-run singles by Dowd and Collins. Boston's sixth win in a row and another loss for the White Sox left Chicago just a half-game ahead of the Bostons.

August 22 — BOSTONS WIN A LOOSE GAME. Cleveland was in town, and the Naps outhit their hosts ten hits to five. They committed only two miscues in the field, while Boston committed six (or seven, by some accounts). But pitcher Moore bunched a couple of walks and two wild pitches into two innings which allowed Boston to score twice in the second and again in the third. Then Boston allowed single runs in the sixth and seventh and eighth, each one an unearned gift. Winter was ultimately spared, and won the game 4-3. It was said to be the worst defensive game Boston had played all year.

August 23 — CLEVELAND GOT ONE LITTLE RUN. Boston Won Out In Badly Played Game. Young allowed six hits and one fifth-inning run on two infield errors. Outbatted and outfielded, averred the *Globe*. Almost every run of the 5-1 game was unearned. There were five Cleveland errors and four by Boston, but LaChance's leap at first base to pull down a sure triple off Stahl's bat was rated "one of the most sensational plays seen in this city for years." Collins had three hits, and Freeman had two, one of them a home run. Boston had won eight games in a row, one shy of the nine-game win streak in June.

August 24 — CROWD MOBS UMPIRE AT AMERICAN GAME headlined the *Post*. THEIR OFF DAY. Cleveland Team Gets Away With an Easy Victory, wrote the *Globe*. Chicago lost, so a win would have vaulted them into first place, but Cleveland won, 4-2. Home runs by Beck and LaChance could well have been outs had the infielders relaying the ball to home taken a bit more time (time that they had); both Parent and Ferris threw the ball over Criger's head. And Parent failed to move into position on a timed pickoff, so Lewis's throw with runners on second and third sailed into center field. And Dowd was out at the plate, when a slide would have seen him score safely. Umpire Cantillon was mobbed after the game by some 50 fans calling him a robber and a thief, and in such a threatening way that Stahl and Lewis had to protect him from the crowd.

It was the first time such an incident had happened at the Huntington Avenue Grounds, though a couple of players had been arrested on the 21st in Washington and another one in Baltimore both for physically assaulting umpires. The *Boston Globe* commented, "It is a well-established fact that Baltimore is the most unfair city in America toward a baseball opponent." That game was forfeited, though the Orioles had already been losing at the time. Apparently, a considerable number of local fans believed that Ban Johnson had instructed the umpires to cause Baltimore to lose games, and the local press was perhaps guilty of whipping up sentiment. Before the game, a "colored man" in Baltimore had come out on the field waving a placard on which was depicted a bottle of whiskey, a funnel, and a sponge. He tried to present it to Umpire Connolly, who turned his back on the placard, while the crowd hooted with excitement.

August 25—THINK PENNANT IS COMING HERE. The *Boston Post* headline actually appeared in the August 26 newspaper, but the story was written on the 25th and there was no game that day (it being a Sunday). In fact, no American League games were held. Boston was just a half-game behind the White Sox after the day. The Beaneaters were 12 games behind the National League-leading Pirates. The season was to end on September 28, just a little more than a month distant. The *Post* wrote that the feeling was that pennant hopes were "daily gaining strength. ... Whatever the outcome, a close finish is in sight, with the odds favoring Boston because of a more favorable schedule. But Chicago in the latter part of its Western trip has not slipped so much as was anticipated, and although most of their remaining games are away from home, there is every indication now that the final leadership lies between them and Boston, with Baltimore a close third."

August 26—FIRST PLACE BREACH WIDENS. Chicago won, beating Philadelphia 11-4. Boston lost, 6-3, to the visiting Detroit Tigers. Winter was hit for 14 safeties and he walked three. Boston seemed to have trouble with left-handers, and Ed Siever held them to six hits. As it happens, six of the Detroit batters hit left-handed as well. The Tigers scored enough runs to win in the first inning alone, with two of the walks and three of the hits producing four of the runs.

The problem of rowdyism in the league was being dealt with firmly by Ban Johnson, who permanently expelled Chicago shortstop Frank Shugart. There was some thought that he'd gone too far, and applied punishment unevenly since both Milwaukee manager Hugh Duffy and Baltimore first baseman Burt Hart had actually slugged umpires on the field and had not been as severely disciplined. The *Post* ran a cartoon that showed Johnson as a "new version of the old woman who lived in a shoe" with a ballplayer over her knee, spanking the player. Shugart had struck Umpire Haskell in a game at Washington on August 21, and both he and pitcher Katoll were arrested by police for their attack on the umpire. White Sox manager Clark Griffith had an odd way of expressing his displeasure, seeming to suggest it might have been better had they jumped the umpire outside the park after the game: "Both Shugart and Katoll made a mistake when they clashed with Haskell on the field. If they wanted to do anything like that they should have waited until some other time. Such actions are a detriment to the national game." (*Chicago Tribune*, August 22, 1901)

August 27—BOSTON WON GREAT 15-INNING CONTEST. It was the longest game of the season throughout baseball, two innings longer than the game of August 19, and a tight, hard-fought 2-1 victory. It was Cy Young for Boston and Detroit ace Roscoe Miller (he finished the season 23-13); both went the distance. It was a well-played game, with only three errors committed, and crisply-played (game time was less than two and a half hours, at 2:25). Boston made two of the three errors, and only eight of the 20 hits, but scored the one run that finally decided the game. Detroit scored first, in the first inning, and then never scored again. Boston matched it when an error put Parent on base and Ferris singled him home. Then it was no runs, despite quite a few baserunners, and even bases-loaded situations to escape from, as Young had in the 14th, with the Tigers executing three double plays and a number of remarkable fielding plays. "Better Game Never Played" read a *Globe* subhead.

In the bottom of the 15th inning, with nobody on and two outs, Lou Criger doubled to right field. He was eighth in the lineup and Cy Young came to bat, already 0-for-5 in the game. He hit a sharp ball to second base, where it took a weird bounce past Kid Gleason and rolled into center field while Criger scored the winning run.

National League President Nicholas Young said he saw no signs of peace between the senior circuit and the new American League. He optimistically believed that there was no way the AL could keep paying as high salaries as it had done to get established in 1901, and that the only reason the NL teams in the cities where there were teams from both leagues (Boston, Chicago, and Philadelphia) was that the National League teams just weren't faring as well in the standings, and that since the Phillies had started to play appreciably better, the tables had turned in that city.

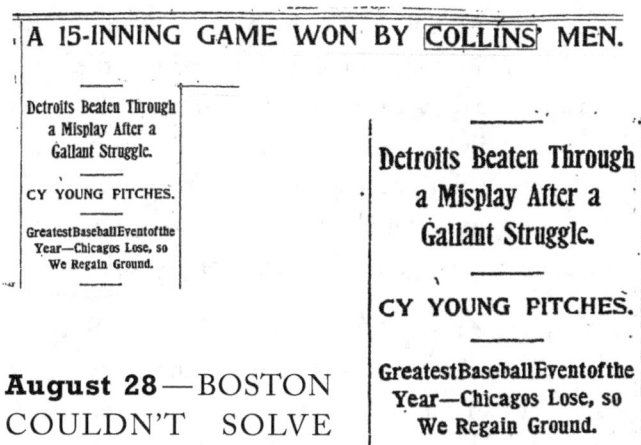

August 28—BOSTON COULDN'T SOLVE YEAGER. They got four hits off him, but Joe Yeager led the Tigers to a 4-2 win over Parson Lewis. When Barrett hit a long three-run homer giving Detroit a 4-0 lead in the top of the seventh, much of the crowd began to leave—it was the largest Wednesday afternoon crowd of the year, over 6,000 fans. Boston scored once in the bottom of the eighth and once in the bottom of the ninth, but it was too little, too late.

August 29—BOSTON WAS AT SIEVER'S MERCY. The two teams continued to play each other, but the venue changed. Both teams left Boston and continued the matchup at Detroit's Bennett Park. It wasn't as uneven a game as the *Post* headline made it appear. The score was 5-3, and Detroit won, but had only ten hits off Winter to the seven Ed Siever allowed, pitching after just two days' rest. All Boston's runs scored in the fifth, however, giving the Americans a 3-2 lead. At that point, Siever buckled down and retired the last 13 batters in a row, save for one base on balls. Boston committed five errors, and Detroit committed none. Chicago didn't play, and the loss dropped Boston to two games behind the White Sox.

August 30—TOOK VICTORY FROM DEFEAT. This was the sort of game that maybe restores a little faith in a team that had dropped four of its last five. Boston scored one run each in three of the first five innings, but Cy Young suddenly gave up four runs to the Tigers in the bottom of the sixth, giving them the lead. It looked as though that sealed it, even after Ferris tripled to lead off the top of the ninth for Boston, because Ferris was unable to score after Criger lofted a fly ball to right field (not all that far behind second base). When Schrecongost pinch-hit for Young, he slapped a ball back to the pitcher, who threw out Ferris at the plate. And Schreck almost ended it when he began to walk back to the bench, forgetting there were only two outs. The game would have been over had the catcher thrown the ball to first base, but by the time he realized the opportunity, Boston coachers had rushed Schreck back to the bag. Whether he made it back in time is debatable; the *Globe* said the throw was in time but that the umpire hadn't realized there was a play and was sweeping off the plate and therefore missed it. Dowd hit a ball to third base, which was fumbled. Chick Stahl doubled, bringing home Schreck, and a passed ball by the same catcher allowed Dowd to score. Ted Lewis threw the last half of the ninth and allowed one hit but no runs.

There was supposed to be a second game—which Lewis would have pitched for Boston—but it was postponed due to a deluge five minutes after the first game ended. The postponed game was pushed back to the following day.

August 31—LOST FIRST, TIED SECOND. A less than pleasing day for Boston, which lost a game it arguably shouldn't have, 6-5, and then played to a 4-4 tie in the second game, while Chicago took two games from Baltimore and finished the month three games ahead of Boston. All credit was due the Tigers, truly. They battled back from 4-1 deficits in both games. In the first game, they scored four runs in the bottom of the eighth to take a 6-4 lead, and then held on. In the second game, they were actually down 4-0 after four, scored once in the fifth, then again in the eighth, and tied it with two runs in the bottom of the ninth. Umpire Cantillon then declared it too dark to continue to play, and called the game. Mitchell bore the loss in the first game. Ted Lewis was the starter in the second. A three-run homer in the first game was the biggest blow.

September 1—After four in Detroit, the Bostons went to Cleveland to play back-to-back doubleheaders on the 2nd and 3rd. PENNANT GOING TO GET AWAY? was the headline in the September 2 *Boston Post*, saying that fans were fearing that the 2-4 (with a tie) performance against Detroit was discouraging, that the team wasn't playing championship baseball. The number of hits per game had fallen by about 50 percent, a hitting slump that didn't bode that well.

September 2—BOSTONS TAKE TWO FROM CLEVELAND. Cleveland scored four runs off Winter in the bottom of the first inning of the morning game, but Boston immediately matched that with four of its own and then continued to add runs toward the 9-4 final score. Winter pitched a three-hit game, but three Boston errors (on a field in very poor condition), a base on balls, and two of the three hits accounted for those first four runs. He allowed only one more hit over the next eight frames. In the fifth inning, he threw three pitches to record three outs. In the 3:30 afternoon game, played to a standing-room crowd drawn by Ohioan Cy Young, Boston won, 4-1, the only Cleveland run off Young coming in the bottom of the ninth while Boston was executing a double play. Both teams had five hits.

Chicago split a doubleheader with Philadelphia.

September 3—NOT ONE RUN IN TWO GAMES. The pitching was good enough for Boston but the bats were back in a slump. Cleveland won 1-0 and 4-0. There was only one time—a bases-loaded situation in the top of the eighth in the second game—when Boston was close to scoring, but a double play squelched that. The first game was a brilliantly-pitched game lastingly only 1:21, in large part because both pitchers (Earl Moore for Cleveland and Ted Lewis for Boston) each allowed only two hits. Each walked two batters. The lone run scored on a throwing error from Ferris to the plate, failing to cut off the baserunner coming home. Mitchell gave up four runs, but with no support on offense had no chance.

September 4—ONE BAD INNING. Sometimes that's all it takes. This time, it was the bottom of the second inning when Winter was banged up for six runs on two walks, then two singles, and then a long home run by Honest John Anderson, and the game was a 6-4 loss to Milwaukee. Boston outhit the Brewers, 11 to eight, and Milwaukee committed five errors to Boston's three. That the game drew only 300 fans was indicative of why Ban Johnson was considering moving the franchise after the 1901 season, but also reflective of the fact that most Milwaukeeans understood the team would be leaving. With three losses in a row, Boston had now fallen four games behind the White Sox. They had a four-game series against Chicago coming up.

September 5—COLLINS MEN TURN THE TABLES. In their final game against the Brewers out west, they ran their record to 12-5 (there were three games against Milwaukee in Boston to close out the season) with a 4-2 win that did indeed turn the tables. It was Cy Young, who allowed six hits while the Boston bats hit double that. Anderson hit another home run for Hugh Duffy's team. Even though Boston started the game with back-to-back leadoff singles, all four of Boston's runs came late, in the eighth.

September 6 — No game for Boston, but Washington beat the White Sox, 5-3. At the end of the day, Chicago was three games ahead of Boston and Boston was in Chicago, ready to play four games against the White Sox. Actually, there had been a game scheduled for Boston to play Milwaukee on this day, but in a rather unusual reversal of the usual they had played the September 6 game back on July 26!

September 7 — BOSTON LOST TO CHAMPIONS. The White Sox won the first of four, and with the opportunities to close the gap running lower, Chicago extended its lead over Boston to four games with 21 games to play—five of them between the two. The score was 4-1 Chicago, with Lewis losing another. Callahan held Boston to five hits. "Outplayed at Every Point, the Wind Taking A Hand," the *Post* observed. The game was played "with a gale of wind blowing straight into the batters' faces." Lewis was at a disadvantage because he depended on his curveball, and the wind was so strong it "straightened them out," while Callahan's fastball was not hindered at all. There was only one error for each team. Dowd was not charged with one, but when he fell a ball got by him and brought in two of the three runs in the Chicago fourth.

September 8 — 20,000 PEOPLE SAW BOSTON WIN, THEN LOSE. The crowd was undeniably a huge one, the largest to see any American League game, a dozen deep in the outfield. The *Globe* suggested that only one National League game, when Baltimore hosted Boston in 1897, had drawn more fans. They had poured out to see Chicago try to prevent Cy Young from getting a win and bringing Boston up a game in the standings, but the headline was misleading making it sound like a doubleheader. What it meant was that Boston had broken a 2-2 tie by scoring a go-ahead run in the top of the eighth. The White Sox had the bottom of the order coming to bat. The shortstop, Jimmy Burke, hit a fairly easy groundball that Jimmy Collins failed to handle—it skittered right through his legs. Burke was thrown out by Freeman on Billy Sullivan's bunt toward first base. Pitcher Callahan pinch-hit for starter Roy Patterson and singled through the right side of the infield, Sullivan going first-to-third. There was a mound conference, but time hadn't been called and Callahan ran to second base. The ball was hastily thrown to Parent, who ran to cover the bag from shortstop, but rather than tagging out Callahan, he threw instead to an unprepared Collins at third, hoping to catch Sullivan off the bag. Collins dropped the ball. Dummy Hoy then drove a ball deep down the left-field line and both runners scored.

September 9 — CASE OF RATTLES. Boston Loses Both Games to the Champions (*Globe*). This was a disastrous day for any pennant hopes harbored in Boston. By losing both games, 4-3 and 6-4, Boston had fallen seven games out of first. Lewis and Winter were the losing pitchers. It was four wins in a row, the White Sox sweeping the Boston Americans. Chicago scored one run in each of the first three innings of the first game, but Boston got one back and then tied it on Buck Freeman's home run in the fourth. But in the bottom of the eighth, Pop Foster hit one of the longest home runs ever seen in Chicago for the 4-3 win. The White Sox made a statement in the first inning of Game Two, with five runs in the first inning.

September 10 — There was no game, and a despondent Boston team traveled to Washington. Meanwhile, Milwaukee welcomed the White Sox, who won yet another game, beating the Brewers, 6-3.

September 11 — BOSTON BATTED GLORIOUSLY. Cy Young held the Senators to three hits and nary a run, while Boston drummed out two runs in the first, five more in the second, and pretty much cruised from that point on. Stahl was 4-for-5, and both Collins and Ferris were 3-for-5. Meanwhile, Washington committed five errors on their own field while Boston had but one. Collins was, in Murnane's words, "at his best, covering an immense amount of ground, and making several plays that seemed beyond the power of man." As was often the case at the time, top-notch defense won the applause of partisans of the opposing team and this game was no exception: "At the start, the crowd was out strong for the home team, but was soon cheering the brilliant work of the Collins boys. ... The playing of the Boston men brought out constant applause." The final score was 9-0.

BOSTON WINS HANDILY.

Defeats Washington, and Capt. Collins Says He Is Confident of Taking the Pennant.

[Special Dispatch to the Boston Herald.]
WASHINGTON, D. C., Sept. 11, 1901. Boston played ball here today to a certainty, and won a victory from the Senators that was r—
the disast—

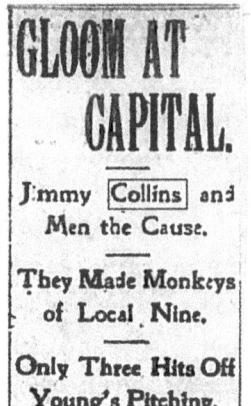

GLOOM AT CAPITAL.

Jimmy Collins and Men the Cause.

They Made Monkeys of Local Nine.

Only Three Hits Off Young's Pitching.

September 12—GAME DRAWN IN 10 INNINGS. The Senators might well have won, except for a collision in left-center field, after which Collins hit a three-run homer in the third inning. That gave Boston a 4-1 lead, and they scored twice more, but Washington kept chipping away at Lewis's pitches and scored three times in the seventh and two in the eighth for a 6-6 tie. Neither team scored in the ninth or the tenth, and darkness prevented there being an 11th.

September 13—THEY LAND ONE. Collins' Team is Lucky to Do Even That. So opined the *Globe* headline writer. There were two games in Washington, beginning at 2:00 P.M. Boston managed a total of seven hits in the two games. The 5-1 win in the first game came because their three hits were bunched with two walks, a couple of errors, and a double steal to score four runs in the fourth. Winter won that one. Mitchell was the victim of a four-run inning, the sixth, in the second game. Boston scored twice in the ninth, but fell short, 5-3. These were the last road games of the season. There were 14 games to play, and Boston was 6 1/2 games behind the White Sox.

September 14—AMERICANS BAT HARD AND OFTEN. Boston and Washington faced off again, this time at the Huntington Avenue Grounds. Another three-hitter hurled by Cy Young held Washington to one run (and he even beat out a bunt to first base in midgame), while Boston scored an even dozen. 12-1. Hemphill had four hits, two of them triples.

September 15—No game. A story in the *Boston Globe* let readers know that the National League had been active early, trying to sign players for 1902 even a couple of weeks before the season was over, but the players were slow to sign, asking for substantial increases or just holding back before committing. The war between the leagues was still on, and without sufficient incentive to sign early, many apparently decided to wait and see what the market might bear.

September 16—BOSTON WON ONE, LOST ONE. Time was running out on the season, and Boston would have to pretty much run the table to have a chance at the pennant. They were seven games out, sinking rather than rising in the standings. Washington was in sixth place, but no pushover. Boston won the first game, 6-5, but lost the second, 7-5. A combined Lewis and Young (in for the last three innings) allowed only six hits in the first game but five runs. The score was tied after nine. With one out in the bottom of the tenth, Collins doubled. With two outs and two strikes on Hemphill, the right fielder singled in Collins with a Texas Leaguer to left field. Winter lost the second, though Boston gave the Senators a scare by batting around and scoring three runs in the bottom of last inning (the eighth) before the rally was brought to a halt, and then the game called due to encroaching darkness.

September 17—SHUT OUT BY DOWD'S CATCH. Cleveland came to town, but played only seven innings. Cy Young started and gave up four hits in between the showers that preceded and then ended the game. It was the third game in a row in which Young had appeared. The 5-0 win might have been marred by a Cleveland run in the top of the seventh. Zaza Harvey singled, then went to third when Ferris badly misplayed a ball hit right to him at second base. "When [Ferris] got through he looked as disgusted as a hobo on the outside of a lunch night cart. After fumbling, Ferris played handball until the runner landed at third." (*Globe*) Joe Connor lifted a high fly ball deep to left field and no one thought there was a chance, but Dowd ran it down and snared it with a shoestring catch. Young saw that Harvey had run home, got himself over to third base, and took Dowd's throw in for a double play.

September 18—RAIN STOPPED LOCAL GAME. There was meant to be a doubleheader at the Huntington Avenue Grounds, but there was rain. The teams started to play and Cleveland scored three runs in the top of the first in the wet conditions. Three outs were recorded, and Boston prepared to bat when the rain became a downpour. Any chance to play the last two scheduled games with Cleveland was washed out, not postponed.

September 19—No game. It was a Thursday, and the first time since April that there was no game anywhere in the league.

September 20—CHILLY DAY FOR DETROIT. Ted Lewis spun a four-hitter during a day so cold that many of the 1,000 heavily-dressed fans walked back and forth in the bleachers trying to keep the blood circulating. The game itself wasn't that energizing and "went on in a cheerless and mechanical sort of way" while a cold drizzle began in the fourth inning. Three of the four hits came in the first inning, when Lewis walked two and was fortunate to only yield two runs. Boston also assembled three hits and one walk, and produced two runs in the first. Boston added two in the first and one in the seventh, while Lewis allowed only two more baserunners—one walk and one hit. The most exciting play was a leaping barehanded catch by Tommy Dowd in the top of the seventh.

September 21—RATTLE WINTERS AND WIN GAME. There was a real contrast in energy on the field, with Tigers players and coaches so vocal and active that it was contagious and the crowd of 4,300 got really into it. Detroit scored three times in the first after Winters walked the first two batters and gave up a pair of scratch bunts, with a third run scoring on the failure to complete a double play. There were no errors charged to the Boston fielders. The Tigers never got a man past second for the rest of the game. There were opportunities for Boston, but only one run scored, in the fourth. Umpire Connolly seems to have had a bad day, but the *Post* said he was "impartially poor." Whatever misjudgments he made did not affect the scoring. Boston was 7 1/2 games behind Chicago, but the Tigers were now just three games behind Boston and threatening to make a run at second place.

September 22—Sunday. The team played its third in-season exhibition game of the season, in Providence, winning the game, 10-5. It was Mitchell on the mound, and Providence scored four times in the sixth inning to take a 5-1 lead. The Boston offense then put up a "9" in the seventh, closing the gap and going up by five.

September 23—SECOND PLACE SLIPPING AWAY. With Boston's two losses this day, the Chicago White Sox clinched the 1901 pennant. It was the last week on the schedule, with eight games on tap in six days. Cy Young took the ball for the first game on Monday. With two more wins over Boston, the Tigers pulled to just one game behind Boston in the standings. Young was hit fairly hard, giving up 11 hits, but it was the worst day of the year for the Boston defense, with so many errors that there were disagreements in the box scores. The *Globe* counted 17 of them—eight in the first game and nine in the second, while the *Post* had five and six, the *Herald* showed four and five, and the *Journal* showed six and five. There were a lot of them.

Pitching the last two innings of the second game was "Wilson"—someone you won't find in the record books if you look up Wilson. The *Boston Journal* wrote, "Wilson of the Albany club relieved 'Ted' Lewis in the seventh inning, and, if he has anything, he did not show it." He walked the first man and then gave up two runs on a triple by Miller, though had there not been one of those errors, there'd not have been the triple. Who was Wilson? He played under the name Wilson in 1901, but by 1902 he was playing as George Prentiss and that's how he's in the books today. For a more complete understanding of this, consult the Prentiss biography in this volume.

September 24—GREAT RALLY SAVED BOSTON. The White Sox, their pennant secured, came to Boston for three games that no longer held the drama they might have had there been a head-to-head battle for first place. Both teams scored in the first, but the White Sox added single runs in the second and sixth and it was looking a little grim until the great rally: seven runs in the bottom of the eighth. It was the eighth win for Boston over Chicago as a visiting opponent. There were five more Boston errors, but Winter won the game, 8-3. The *Boston Globe* had a somewhat obscure line that is far more amusing today as the meaning of words has changed: "Mertes got gay with umpire Connolly in the second inning and was ordered off the field." Apparently, per the *Post* game story, he told Connolly to "umpire right."

September 25—CHICAGO LOST NINTH STRAIGHT. Clark Griffith's men were just playing for pride. The pennant already determined, but having lost every one of the eight games they'd played at the Huntington Avenue Grounds, it would be nice to break the spell. The White Sox scored twice off Cy Young in the first inning (after two Boston errors), but Collins and company got one back right away and took a 3-2 lead in the second. Chicago never scored again, while Boston added two more to its total. It was Cy Young's last appearance for Boston in 1901. He finished with an outstanding 33-10 mark and a 1.62 earned-run average. He threw for a better ERA in 1908, and he'd won more games (36) for Cleveland in 1892, but this was a truly spectacular season. He won more games than any two other pitchers on the Boston staff added together. Both Winter and Lewis won 16.

September 26—TAME FINISH TO EXCITING GAME. It was a hard-fought game. Chicago scored once in the third and Boston scored twice in the fourth. It was a better-played game than many, each team erring just twice. The score stayed 2-1 through eight innings. Boom! Leadoff man Pop Foster tripled to start the ninth, and then scored when Parent made a poor throw to third base. But Lewis buckled down and there was no further damage. In the bottom of the ninth, Freeman singled to right field. Playing by the book, Hemphill sacrificed him to second base. Parent was thrown out at first and Freeman advanced to third. "Then Callahan began to wander from his moorings. Of a sudden he appeared unable to locate the rubber, and to his shortcomings was due the farcical finish. Ferris walked, and then the three corners of the diamond were filled, as Callahan sent the sphere into collision with Criger's elbow." Schrecongost pinch-hit for Lewis but he never even swung the bat. There were three pitches wide of the plate—though Umpire Connolly gave Callahan a bit of a reprieve by calling the fourth one a strike. The fifth pitch was even wider and Schreck walked to first while Freeman walked home.

The game, the *Globe* wrote, was "one of the prettiest of the season." For Lewis, who had already announced he would be leaving baseball, it was a gratifying way to go out. He may remain the only former major leaguer who became a university president after his career in baseball.

For the White Sox, it was the tenth game they lost at the Huntington Avenue Grounds (0-10). Boston was 2-8 at South Side Park. The three wins brought Boston to five games behind Chicago, but there were only three games left on the schedule.

September 27—WILSON'S DEBUT A GREAT SUCCESS. Here was George Pepper Wilson, in his first big-league start—in fact, the only one before he became George Pepper Prentiss in 1902. He pitched an excellent game against Milwaukee, the Brewers in for the last series of the season (and, as it happened, their last three games for many years, since the Brewers were transferred to St. Louis after 1901 and didn't re-emerge under the Brewers name until 1970). Wilson allowed just six hits and two well-spaced runs, one in the first and one in the ninth. The *Post* in particular praised his poise and performance. Collins—who played in every game all season long—left in the sixth to give a shot to Harry Gleason, the younger brother of longtime veteran Kid Gleason. Gleason got one at-bat and singled, batting 1.000 for the season. He did, however, commit one error in three chances, giving him a lower fielding percentage than a batting average. Parent had a 4-for-4 game. Three runs in the second and three more in the fourth allowed Wilson some comfort from that point forward.

Charles Somers had come to town for two days and secured the signatures of several players for the 1902 season: Cy Young and George Winter (still called "Winters" in the newspapers) as pitchers, and Criger, Ferris, Freeman, and Parent. Jimmy Collins and Chick Stahl were already under three-year contracts, so Somers had eight key men set for the coming season. Every one of the men received a raise.

FINIS FOR AMERICANS.

Boston Team's Season Comes to an End.

A Double Victory Won from the Milwaukees.

Volz, the New Pitcher, Is Tried by the Home Nine.

Latter Makes Bunches of Five and Seven Runs.

September 28—COLLINS'S MEN WIN TWO GAMES. The team finished the season with a six-game winning streak, sweeping Milwaukee as they had swept the White Sox, though this pair of games was a couple of higher-scoring affairs, 8-3 and 10-9. Winter pitched the first game and improved his record to 16-12 (with a 2.80 ERA). His batterymate was a Boston native, Jack Slattery of South Boston, in his first major-league game. He was 1-for-3 at the plate, with a base on balls and a run batted in, one of five runs Boston scored in the third inning.

In the second game, there was another debut—Jake Volz of San Antonio. Volz had a hard time putting the ball over, and walked three of the first four batters, the other one getting a single—and then gave up a triple. Five runs scored before Boston got up to bat. And then Jones hit a home run in the second, the longest ball hit on the grounds in 1901. After four innings Milwaukee led, 6-1. Stahl drove in two runs in the fifth, and Collins

hit a three-run homer. Freeman singled and then, with two outs, Parent singled and ran all the way around the bases and scored after left fielder Jones let the ball get by him. The seven-run explosion gave the home team an 8-6 lead. "Volz slipped his trolley again in the sixth," wrote Murnane, and two runs scored, tying the game at 8-8. Volz walked the leadoff man in the seventh—the ninth free pass he doled out—and then fell down trying to field a bunt. A run scored, and it was getting dark. But with a man on and one out in the bottom of the seventh, Ferris tripled to tie the game again, and then scored when Schreck's single glanced off the pitcher.

It was announced during the day that the Chicago White Sox would return to Boston from Washington, where they'd played their final game on the 27th, and the two teams would square off on September 30 for a benefit game, all the proceeds going to the players.

FINAL STANDINGS

The team finished in second place, and all the winning at the end of the season had opened up a 4 1/2-game lead over the Tigers. They were six games ahead of the Philadelphia Athletics. Their best month—by far—was June, when they'd gone 20-5—the first winning month in franchise history (they had been 1-3 in April and 10-11 in May).

They played much better at home (49-20) than on the road (30-37), helped substantially by sweeping all ten games in Boston from the White Sox. The team they played best against was last-place Milwaukee (15-5), and they had a losing record against only one team—the Tigers—with a 9-11 mark. They played .500 ball against both Philadelphia and Baltimore.

With all the errors that piled up, there were 337 in all, with the middle infielders naturally having the worst of it—Parent with 63 and Ferris with 60. Collins had 50 errors. The team's overall .943 fielding percentage was best in the league, however, tied to three decimal places with the Athletics but with 200 more chances.

Four players appeared in every game– Collins, Dowd, Ferris, and Parent. Buck Freeman's .339 led the team in batting average and he had twice as many homers (12) as anyone else on the team; Collins and Stahl both had six. Freeman's 114 RBIs also led the team; Collins was second with 94. Freeman's on-base percentage was an even .400, tops on the team. He had an OPS (on-base percentage plus slugging percentage) of .920. The team homered 37 times, first in the league, but they were fourth in team batting average and fifth in on-base percentage.

Cy Young's 33-10 season ranked him far and away the best among the pitchers, as we've noted. He was the only one with more than one shutout; he had five. His 158 strikeouts were 50 percent more than anyone else on the team (Lewis was second with 103). He pitched 38 complete games. The staff's combined 3.04 ERA was second only to the 2.98 recorded by the White Sox. Boston scored 759 runs, and allowed 608.

Final attendance of Boston AL and NL clubs

In the all-important battle for fan loyalties, as measured by attendance, the Boston Americans clearly outdrew the National League's Boston Beaneaters. The Americans' attendance was 289,448 (ranking second of the eight AL clubs). The White Sox were first, with 354,350—and outdrew the Cubs, who drew 205,071. The Beaneaters still had one more week to play, finishing their season on October 5. By the time they wrapped up their season, they had attracted 146,502 paying patrons, last among all eight National League teams. Finishing fifth, 20 1/2 games behind the first-place Pirates, had hurt them, too.

The *Boston Post* proclaimed the first season for the American League a "big success" despite their falling short in the race for the pennant. Somers had not only broken even—his announced goal at the inception of the season—but had "netted a handsome profit." The paper attributed much of the success to Jimmy Collins:

"His career has indeed been meteoric. Last year he was simply a grand player, the acknowledged king of third basemen. Today he is one of the big men in baseball. And the remarkable feature is that, despite the cares which management and leadership involve, his playing has not suffered. If anything, there has been an improvement, particular in his batting.

"In happy contrast to Clark Griffith of Chicago and John McGraw of Baltimore, he has gone through the season without once attracting the displeasure of those at the head of the American. So gratifying, in fact, has his handling of his team been that President Johnson took occasion once to compliment him. …

"Always modest and unassuming, he has the respect of players as no other leader enjoys, and his popularity with the crowds is so firmly cemented as to endure long after he shall eventually retire."

As to the American League itself, the September 30 edition continued, "There is every indication that instead of weakening it is going to make gigantic strides towards acquiring the supremacy in baseball. This does not mean that the National League is in a state of decay and must, sooner or later, give up the ghost, but that the American is not a second edition of the old Brotherhood or American Association."

THE FIRST POSTSEASON FOR THE FRANCHISE

After taking all of one day off, the Boston Americans played yet another game against the White Sox, and then five more.

The original plan, announced by Business Manager Joseph Gavin on the 25th, was to play a series of six postseason barnstorming games, in Haverhill, Lynn, Manchester, Woonsocket, Worcester, and Marlborough. Within a matter of days, the scheduling changed, though not the number of games.

The first game was against Chicago, which had finished the season in Washington with the scheduled game on the 28th rained out and scrubbed.

September 30 — At the Huntington Avenue Grounds: Boston: Boston Americans 7, Chicago White Sox 5.

CHICAGO AGAIN BOWS TO BOSTON, read the headline in the *Boston Post*. The game — a benefit for the home players — drew 2,868 fans, who saw Boston beat the White Sox for the 11th time in Boston. Boston had won every single one of its ten home games against the pennant-winners during the regular season, and the Americans won this one as well. Cy Young had planned to leave Boston but was talked into staying over and pitching against Nixey Callahan; at the plate Young was the only Boston batter who didn't get a hit. Boston outhit Chicago 13-11 (or maybe 10). Neither pitcher seemed to exert himself much. As the *Globe* generously suggested, they were "allowing the fielders a chance."

The White Sox didn't commit an error, but pitcher Fred Mitchell played second base and committed at least three. The *Boston Journal* said that Mitchell had committed five errors in seven chances. Catcher Osee Schrecongost envisioned a move to first base and so played the bag, and played it well (both Freddy Parent and Buck Freeman had gone home after the regular season concluded, so Ferris shifted the shortstop). A special dispatch to the *Chicago Tribune* noted the "yellow fielding" of Mitchell, "who was allowed to continue throughout the game, to the disgust of the crowd." The "special" to the *Tribune* probably came from the *Boston Globe* writer, since he used the same words. Collins, with two doubles, and Ferris, with a triple, each had three hits.

Chicago scored solo runs in the first, second, third, fifth, and eighth innings, whereas Boston scored twice in the first and then one apiece in every other inning save for the second and the fifth.

Each Boston player netted about $60 for the day's work, all one hour and 35 minutes of it. Presumably the visitors earned a flat fee of some sort. The crowd "was very well satisfied with the game," concluded the *Globe*.

October 1 — In Lynn, at the Glenmere Grounds: Boston 8, Lynn picked team 5.

Lynn is about 10 or 11 miles north of Boston, and had ever so briefly been home to the Lynn Live Oaks of the independent New England League in 1901. The league had begun the season with eight teams and ended with six. The Augusta Live Oaks began the season and were 10-23 when the franchise was transferred to Lynn on June 30. One week later, to the day, the Lynn team disbanded with a 1-2 record. By 1902 the league had Tim Murnane as its president and became a Class B league within Organized Baseball. It was not until 1905 that a Lynn team, the Shoemakers, joined the league. Lynn was the first stop of five as the Boston Americans hit the road to try to garner a little more money before shutting it all down.

The game at Lynn was played on Tuesday at Glenmere Park at 3:30, for an admission price of 25 cents. The Lynn team was a semipro team, whose most recent game had been a loss to the Milfords, 8-0, on the previous Saturday. The *Lynn Evening Item* announced the game the day before and somewhat oddly said it was being held "with the express purpose of showing the Lynns how the game of ball should be played."

WERE RATTLED was the two-word headline on the game story in the *Evening Item*. Boston batted first and scored six runs in the top of the first. A front-page story in the *Lynn Evening News* called it a case of "stage fright," but both local papers noted that once the Lynns got over their first-inning jitters, they actually outscored the American Leaguers for the rest of the game. Dowd (playing second base) led off with a base hit to right field, and Stahl walked on four pitches. A passed ball let both baserunners advance. Collins hit into a fielder's choice at second base, and Dowd scored on the play. Criger hit a long fly ball but it was dropped and Stahl scored. Hemphill hit a sharp ball to second base, and this time the throw came home, catching Criger for the second out. Schreck hit a ball that went only a few yards from home plate and he was safe on pitcher George Bannon's throwing error. Ferris hit what should have been an inning-ending grounder, but the shortstop's throw let two more runs cross the plate. Then Young (playing right field), Mitchell (pitching), and Dowd all singled, and another passed ball let two more runs in.

Mitchell struck out the leadoff Lynn batter, but then a single, a stolen base, and a walk followed. A fly ball went over Cy Young's head in right field and both runners scored. It was 6-2 after the first inning and things generally settled down with Boston scoring solo runs in the fourth and fifth, and Lynn scoring once each in the third, seventh, and eighth. George Bannon's brother Tom played right field, and hit a double and a triple. Their brother Jimmy was the team's usual shortstop but watched from the stands, unable to play. His replacement at short, Charlie Hagen, was 4-for-4 off Mitchell. Cy Young stole one base and was picked off second base another time by a peg from Lynn's catcher. There were about 1,000 people in attendance, and it was a game "played with great snap," a "fine game and the people were well pleased with the remarkable showing that the Lynns made against such a strong team as the Bostons." (*Lynn Daily Evening Item*)

October 2 — In Manchester, New Hampshire, at Varick Park: Boston 6, Manchester 1.

BOSTONS CAME ON IN STYLE. Rode to Ball Grounds in Lordly Barouches — *Manchester Union*.

What's a barouche? It is "a four-wheeled carriage with a driver's seat high in front, two double seats inside facing each other, and a folding top over the back seat." It must have been something to see.

The weather was a little threatening, which hurt attendance, but an estimated 1,000 people turned out to see the American Leaguers play against a team assembled for the occasion by Manchester Indians manager John Smith. The *Union* commented that "every position on the team was taken by a man who would be considered starters in the New England league." There was a little theater after the Bostons disembarked from their barouches? "A half hour before the game was called [then meaning, before the game began], Jimmy Collins and his ten men rode into the park in that style which might be expected to accompany Governor Jordan. … Immediately the men jumped out of the barouches, another jiffy and a half-dozen balls were flying through the air and ten overgrown boys were doing funny things with the leather. The game itself was interesting, but it is doubtful if spectators who witnessed the 'warming up' were not better satisfied with the practice exhibition." It sounds like there might have been a little showmanship along the lines of the Harlem Globetrotters, but in 1901 baseball.

As for the game itself, aside from the five runs Boston scored in its fourth, it was a 1-1 tie. Those runs did, of course, count. The problem the Manchester men faced was on defense. Facing Cy Young, they got seven hits while four struck out. Working the mound for Manchester was Lew Cross, a seven-year minor-league veteran who had appeared briefly in the majors during 1893 and 1894 for Cincinnati. He held Boston to fewer hits, just five, and struck out six. Boston executed two double plays, which helped, but Manchester committed six errors and that hurt badly. In the fateful fourth, Collins led off with a walk. Schreck grounded to the first baseman, who tried to cut down Collins at second but threw wildly. Hemphill singled, and Boston scored the first run of the game. Ferris bunted and reached base to load them up when pitcher Cross fumbled the ball. Criger drove in two with the second hit of the inning, a single to left field. Mitchell's groundball to second was misplayed and Criger came home. Then it was the shortstop's turn to err, and Mitchell scored. Five runs on two hits and four errors.

Two doubles in the bottom of the fourth inning gave Manchester its only run, though both batters were thrown out at third base, one on a fielder's choice and the other while trying to stretch his run-producing double into a three-base hit. In the eighth, Boston scored once more on Schreck's double and an error that followed.

October 3 — In Nashua, New Hampshire, at Lawndale Gardens: Nashua 6, Boston 2

Pitching for Nashua was 40-year-old Eugene Gokey. There was considerable overlap among the position players with those who had played the day before in Manchester: John Smith in right field, McManus the catcher, and Murphy at third and McLaughlin at short.

Two Nashua newspapers marveled at the way the game had turned out. The *Nashua Daily Telegraph* began its game account reflecting, "Just think what might the Nashua team in the New England league have done had the team been managed by a playing manager like John Smith of Manchester this season.... [It was] just the kind of a team that Nashua should have had all summer, the kind of a team that the Telegraph argued for all the season, and the kind that the citizens would have supported and made a paying institution." The game against Boston was "as good a game as was ever seen in this city" but, for all that, "from another standpoint, a farce on the national game, before a crowd of 350 spectators." The paper decried "the rankest kind of errors and sleepiest kind of playing on the part of the bean eaters." The *Nashua Daily Press* bizarrely mixed in some racist imagery in its account, but crowed that "the whole lot of the haughty Boston Americans" had been defeated. The *Press* counted more than twice as many people — 800 — at the game. Malheureusement, the French-language newspaper in Nashua, *L'Impartial*, did not cover the game.

Henry Burns had been the local man to pull together a team to face Boston, and he'd had his fortune read by a palmist the week before. He was told his team would win, but he was the only one in the city with an "atom of confidence." Burns brought Gokey on board; though 40, he'd just played in his first professional season with Nashua earlier in 1901. Barney McLaughlin had played for the Lowell team, and worked parts of three seasons in the major leagues between 1884 and 1890. Frank McManus had played for the Washington Senators in 1899 and enjoyed a career running from 1896 to 1910. John Murphy was just coming off his first season in baseball, at third base with Portland. The Bostons had Mitchell pitching, but several men out of their regular positions. Dowd came in to play second base and Cy Young played left field. Criger (whose name was spelled Crieger in one paper and Crigger in the other) played first base.

Boston scored first, once in the second and once in the third, and the *Telegraph* writer thought perhaps they were toying with the Nashua nine. If so, it came back to bite them in the fifth inning. Gokey led off and was plunked with a pitch of Mitchell's. A double and an error by Dowd let two runs score, giving Nashua a 3-2 lead. A single brought in another run. Four scored in all. Mitchell left the mound after the fifth and switched places with Chick Stahl in center field. Stahl allowed another run in the seventh. Gokey closed the gate after the third. The *Daily Telegraph* declared that Stahl "had a few curves but no speed. He was, however, somewhat of an improvement over Mitchell."

October 4 — In Greenfield, Massachusetts, at Shattuck Park: Boston 3, Greenfield 0

It was a brisk 56-minute game in Greenfield, a 3-0 win nominally for Boston, but an odd one in that Cy Young pitched for Greenfield and threw to his usual batterymate "Creiger," while the Greenfield battery came over to work for the Bostons. The idea was to "make the contest more nearly even." The game had been delayed a bit because it was the Field Day for the Third Regiment Patriarchs Militant (the uniformed branch of the Odd Fellows). There were over 1,000 people in to see the 3:00 P.M. ballgame, but it took some time to clear the field of some of the others. The *Greenfield*

Record believed that some who were on the grounds simply hadn't left, although those who did found it hard to depart because of the press of people wanting to come in. The *Record* also noted that the "crowd behaved very badly outside the gates and it was all the officers could do to handle it. It was a wonder that someone was not injured in the scramble to get into the grounds." It helped, however, that "several of the Boston men with their antics and remarks kept the crowd in good spirits." Apparently, Schrecongost amused many during the course of the game, playing to the grandstand.

Boston scored twice in the second, both runs driven in by Tommy Dowd, and once in the fourth (all three runs off Cy Young, let us remember), and Greenfield never did score off pitcher Dillon. It was Dillon who knocked in the third run, thanks to an error by center fielder McManus. The *Greenfield Gazette and Courier* praised the "brilliant fielding of the visitors," particularly Jimmy Collins. Dillon was, perhaps, the Thomas Dillon who pitched some for Nashua in 1901 but who otherwise never played professionally. The *Gazette and Courier* wondered whether the failure of the Greenfield men to hit him was "perhaps largely from fear of the fielders lines up against them." Yet it was Greenfield that pulled off three double plays in the game, while Boston had none. Two Greenfielders were cut down trying to steal. They got two men on with just one out in the ninth, but couldn't score.

October 5 — In Marlborough, Massachusetts, at the Prospect Street grounds: Marlboro 4, Boston 3

FANS DANCE AND HOWL. Cranks in Marlboro See Boston Beaten — *Worcester Sunday Telegram*. The last game of Boston's 1901 postseason was played at 4:00 P.M. on Saturday afternoon. It was not just Marlboro men who played against the Bostons. Eugene Gokey, who had pitched Nashua to a win just two days before, was announced — the day before — to take the mound once more in hopes of winning his second game in three days against the second-place finishers in the American League. However, the pitcher in the game was Fred Clarkson, who batted sixth in the order.

The Carters of Franklin, Massachusetts, traveled the 20-some miles to Marlborough to take part in the contest and the *Boston Sunday Herald* described the team as "composed mainly of the Carters of Franklin and Marlboro's crack players." Between 600 and 1,000 people attended the brisk 60-minunte game, hurried along a bit because the American League players needed to catch a train back to Boston.

Fred Mitchell pitched for Boston. Cy Young played right field. Criger was at first base, and Schreck caught Mitchell. Boston scored three times, all three runs bunched in the fourth inning. Mitchell kept the Carters scoreless through seven innings. The Marlboro shortstop, Denny Kelly, struck out three times but he excelled at defense; the *Worcester Telegram* wrote: "Time after time his fine playing was applauded to the echo."

In the bottom of the eighth, however, right fielder Boule doubled down the left-field line with one out and then scored on a single by the left fielder, Moran. Second baseman Saul doubled off the center-field fence, scoring Boule, but Moran wisely held at third. The batter who had the most success against Mitchell was first baseman Charley Ganzel. He'd doubled twice, and was the only player hit by a pitch, back in the fourth. Up now in the eighth, Ganzel doubled again, driving in Moran and Saul and tying the game. At this point, "a crowd of screaming cranks then surged onto the field." After the fans returned to their places, Mitchell finally retired the side. There was some talk about stopping the game, so Boston players could get to their train, "but the crowd was in a frenzy of excitement and demanded that the home team have its turn at bat."

Fred Clarkson — born in May 1881 as one of the famous Clarkson family of Cambridge, Massachusetts, which placed three pitchers (including Hall of Famer John Clarkson) in the major leagues — drew a base on balls to lead off the bottom of the ninth. He reached second on a sacrifice. Up came Boule — who had taken away a possible home run off Cy Young's bat earlier in the game by being well-positioned — and he singled to center, driving in Clarkson with the winning run. While the local fans celebrated, "the Boston players seized their sweaters and started for the hotel on the run." (All quotations from the *Worcester Telegram*, except as noted.) Winning pitcher Clarkson later worked in banking with the Irving Trust Company in New York.

One might imagine that the Boston players were a little discouraged to lose two of their last three games, perhaps not the best memory to carry with them throughout the long winter ahead. They'd played well in the championship games, however, and had every reason to be pleased with their play when it had truly counted.

The National and American Leagues didn't meet in the World Series until 1903, and Boston wasn't the only team playing after the regular season was over. The White Sox played several games, starting on September 30 in Boston and then traveling to Worcester on October 1 to play a game against the "American League All-Stars," a team assembled and run by the Athletics' Nap Lajoie. Chicago won that one, 11-7. The White Sox hosted Lajoie's team at South Side Park in Chicago on October 6 for their final game of the year, but Lajoie's plan was more ambitious. The October 7 *Chicago Tribune* said his team would "remain intact nearly all winter and make a tour of the South and West." After heading to Toledo, the plan was to tour cities in Indiana and work their way south to New Orleans, arriving there around November 1, then to travel through Texas to Southern California and then travel north, getting to San Francisco by Thanksgiving. And then keep playing into the winter. How much of the plan the team may have realized is beyond the scope of this book.

THE REST OF THE YEAR

Unlike the intensive coverage baseball in Boston routinely receives a century later, there was little discussion of baseball from October through December. The news coverage on the sports page turned to the other sports of the day—primarily college football, boxing, golf, and bicycling.

October 10—A *Boston Globe* reporter in Cleveland asked Charles Somers if it were true that Hugh Duffy had been signed to play for the Boston Americans. A dispatch from Milwaukee said that Duffy had indeed severed his ties to that club and had agreed to play center field for Boston, but Secretary Gavin said he knew nothing about it and Somers said he was in no position to affirm or deny, that no offer had been made to Duffy, and that Duffy had always been helpful to himself (Somers) and the ballclub.

October 15—It was reported that the American League had decided to place a team in New York.

November 1—Jimmy Collins arrived in Boston for a few days and said he was doing "a little missionary work" for the club, saying, "We need three or four players, and will no doubt have a good strong team when the time comes to start the season. The club tried to get Donovan of Brooklyn and Crawford of Cincinnati among others, but those men preferred to remain where they were at increased salaries. We have one or two surprises in store for the public in the way of players." (*Boston Globe*)

November 7—The *Post* reported that neither Dowd nor Hemphill "would care for the Boston outer garden" in 1902, but added, "Boston needs but three or four good men, as the Somers aggregation is already strong enough to give the other teams a hard fight for the pennant."

November 10—In the morning's *Globe*, Tim Murnane pointed out that the ballclub saved considerable money by having no president and no general manager, while Collins served both as field manager and third baseman.

November 14—COLLINS SIGNS NEW PLAYERS. Collins had to suddenly leave Boston for his home in Buffalo because his father, Police Capt. Anthony Collins, had become seriously ill from blood poisoning. He sent word to the *Post* from Buffalo that, in the paper's words, he had "signed several new men for next year. Just who these men are or how many he declined to tell the *Post* correspondent. He stated that the nine will be stronger than ever next year, and that his new men were among the National League 'stars' of last year."

November 15—Jimmy Collins reportedly offered left-handed pitcher Noodles Hahn a lavish $4,000 for 1902, but Cincinnati acted quickly to secure its ace.

December 1—It was President J.B. Billings of the Boston Nationals who let it out that Bill Dinneen had been signed to the rival Boston Americans. Dinneen had come to Boston for the Harvard/Yale football game and been entertained by the Americans, while avoiding a visit to the NL team's offices. Billings said he just wanted to know for sure so he could make plans for the Beaneaters. Tim Murnane traveled to Syracuse to intercept Dinneen on his return to Boston, but Big Bill wouldn't say more than that once he had signed for 1902, he would let it be known. He did acknowledge that his longtime friend Jimmy Collins had been to visit him in Syracuse. At the same time, incoming Beaneaters manager Buckenberger was a fellow Syracuse resident and was seeing Dinneen almost every day. Murnane said it was a 5-1 bet that Dinneen had already signed with Collins, but cautioned that he'd been signed by the Americans for 1901 and nonetheless stuck with the Nationals.

December 3—BOSTON CAN TAKE DINNEEN. At the American League meeting in Chicago, the Milwaukee franchise was shifted to St. Louis, in an action taken at close to 11 P.M. President Somers said that he was leaving the pursuit of Dinneen in the hands of Collins. Ban Johnson acknowledged that Collins had written him asking that Dinneen be removed from any blacklist but noted that there had never been any league blacklist promulgated and that he had the highest regard for Collins, who had declined a larger monetary offer to return to the National League but held true to his word. Basically, he said he owed him one and wouldn't stand in the way of Collins signing Dinneen. There was some hilarity at the meeting when a National League manager declared that he would go out after all American League players if Dinneen were induced to jump to the AL.

It was reported that Baltimore had offered Boston the contracts of either Frank Foreman or Jerry Nops, without consideration.

In separate action, the American League voted to ban gambling at league ballparks.

December 8—NEW LEAGUE IN LEAD. The *Washington Post* declared that the American League had won the battle for supremacy, beginning, "There is no longer any doubt as to which is the major league in baseball." The coming season, 1902, would resemble "a fight between a lusty youth and a decrepit man." The story went city by city, and concluded that in the four cities that had both NL and AL teams, there was no contest: The AL teams were superior. In Boston, not only did the Collinsmen outdraw the opposition 3-to-1, but the team's leadership "has ingratiated itself with the Boston press, until it is now given the preference over the old team."

The Beaneaters announced that they would not reduce ticket prices for 1902 but would stick with their standard 50-cent price. Rather than compete by cutting prices, they would do so by offering higher salaries for players.

December 14—The Americans' new catcher, Jack Warner, had just spent six seasons with the New York Giants, and looked to be a good support for Criger.

December 16—Jimmy Collins signed Charlie Hickman to play left field in 1902. Tommy Dowd was still hoping to catch on someplace else, but had indeed played his last major-league game.

December 17—Jimmy Collins arrived in Boston at 7:00 P.M. on the train, to spend a few days looking over the team's business, reported the *Globe*. Regarding the battle between the two leagues, he said, "It looks as though the American league had the old league badly beaten, especially in St. Louis and in this city." Talking about the repositioning and competition during the winter months, he continued, "I am not very much interested in the politics of the game, however, and will not worry about the outcome in this winter game. I have been quite busy in rounding up my team and have little more to do in that line. I am satisfied our team is considerably stronger than last season, both in the box and in hitting. With Hickman, Stahl and Buck Freeman bumping the ball through that outfield, I can see fun ahead for the fans." The Huntington Avenue Grounds would be improved, particularly in left field. The team would likely go south for preseason training in the springtime. "We also have two of the greatest pitchers," he added. "Men who can stand the pace and do the work away as well as at home." Tim Murnane inserted a thought about that: "Capt Collins has endeavored to get a crowd of players who will pull together and take care of themselves off the field. This was the trouble with three or four players last season."

Collins wrapped up, "I can't see where any club in the league has anything on us up to date."

December 18—FREEDMAN AFTER BOSTON. A rumor out of New York held that Giants owner Andrew Freedman himself might shift to the American League (even though Ban Johnson said he'd have nothing to do with Freedman). At the same time, the *Boston Post* asked, "The Boston triumvirs, Messrs. Soden, Conant, and Billings, have almost unlimited capital at their disposal, and under present conditions what better move could they make than to buy out the Boston American League club, lock, stock, and barrel?"

December 19—With A.G. Spalding newly elected as president of the National League, AL leader Ban Johnson said it would be the end of the war between the two leagues. He felt that Spalding was someone more interested in saving the game, rather than wrecking it the way Freedman had been doing. Then he seemed to provocatively crow, "You can see how badly stampeded they were when Freedman found it necessary to give Christy Mathewson enough money to take a hunting trip up in Maine so that the American League managers could not get to see him. We can get any player in the National League that we want, and we are going to get quite a bunch."

December 20—Collins had been back in Boston for a couple of days, and then returned to Buffalo. He said he pretty much had the team together, except for the pitching. Dinneen, he said, remained non-committal.

December 22—NEW MEN ON LOCAL DIAMONDS. The *Boston Post*'s last story of the year on baseball summed up where both the local major-league teams stood, looking ahead to 1902. The Americans were in better shape, still wondering about Dinneen but otherwise set. They'd hired Charlie Hickman to play the outfield; Hickman had begun his career in Boston with the Nationals, but worked for the New York Giants in 1900 and 1901. Buck Freeman was going to move from first base to the outfield while George "Candy" LaChance would take over at first. Ferris and Parent would remain the middle infielders, and Collins remained "king of them all" at third base. Warner was signed and Schrecongost had been let go. Criger would be Boston's main backstop.

Cy Young was coming back, and he, Winter, and Mitchell, and Wilson (he'd not changed his name to Prentiss yet) would be the core of the pitching staff.

A LOOK AHEAD TO 1902

The team changed significantly in 1902. The team did indeed go south for spring training, to Augusta, Georgia. There they played intrasquad games. Games envisioned against the University of Georgia and Atlanta never happened. A feeler to Spartanburg came to naught after they asked Collins to guarantee expenses. The team from Hobart College passed through Georgia to play the University of Georgia team in Athens, and wanted to play Boston, but wanted to share the receipts from the game and Collins would not agree. The only preseason games against outside competition were one in Waterbury, Connecticut, two in Hartford, and a fourth game in Worcester. Boston won all four, outscoring the opposition 51-15.

Of the 24 players who appeared in one or more 1901 game, 13 were no longer with the team during the regular season in 1902, a year that also saw 24 players (obviously, there were 13 new players who appeared in one or more games). Three pitchers won the lion's share of the wins each year—in 1901, just two of them (Young and Winter) won 49 of the 79 wins, while in 1902, Young and Winter combined for 43 of the 77 wins. Ted Lewis and his 16 wins in 1901 was replaced by Bill Dinneen and 21 wins.

The team batting average was .278 each year. Team ERA was nearly identical, too—3.04 in 1901 and 3.02 in 1902. The team allowed 608 runs to the opposition in 1901 and 600 in 1902, again almost the same. The main difference was in runs scored—which dropped from 759 to 664.

In 1902, though no longer enjoying the novelty of being a brand-new team playing in a brand-new park, the Boston Americans significantly improved their home attendance, from 289,448 to 348,567—even though their on-field performance dipped a bit (they won two fewer games and finished third instead of second—eight games out of first place). Some of the increase reflected a decline in appeal of the Beaneaters. The NL team had finished last in 1901, but changed managers and improved in their fortunes in 1902 under new skipper Al Buckenberger. They finished third, winning four more games (from 69-69 in 1901, they were 73-64 in 1902 but were 29 games out of first place). The Beaneaters drew 146,502 in 1901 but only 116,960 in 1902, less than half the attendance at the Huntington Avenue Grounds. They weren't the worst draw in the National League, however, ranking seventh of the eight teams.

On average, the Beaneaters drew 2,093 patrons in 1901 but were down to 1,624 in 1902. The Americans had drawn an average gate of 4,195 in their first year, but grew to 4,909 in 1902, increasing their margin over the local competition from almost precisely two to one to close to three to one. The team was clearly winning the head-to-head battle for ticket buyers.

The American League as a whole sold 1,683,584 tickets in 1901, compared with 1,920,031 National League entries—but by 1902, the balance tipped strongly in favor of the American. The AL drew 2,206,454 to the NL's 1,683,012. Only twice more in the first 25 years of the rivalry did the NL come out on top—in 1903 and in 1910. By 1904 the Boston Americans outdrew the Beaneaters by more than four to one. In the 53 years that the two teams were both based in the Hub, the National League team outdrew the Red Sox with any consistency only during the doldrums of the '20s and '30s. The years the NL prevailed were 1901, 1921, 1925, 1926, and 1930 through 1933. The other 47 years, the Americans outdrew them, and often by multiples of 2-1, 3-1, 4-1, and more.

After the 1902 season, Jimmy Collins and his men won the American League pennant in 1903 with a 91- 47 record, and then went on to beat the Pittsburg Pirates in the first World Series ever played. They won the pennant again in 1904, and the New York Giants refused to play against them in the World Series. The franchise was firmly established.

NOTES

The words in capital letters after many dates are the story headlines which ran in the *Boston Post* on the day indicated (unless otherwise noted.) After the headlines there will sometimes be the newspaper's subhead, which is presented in upper- and lower-case letters, as in the January 17 entry, which shows both a *Boston Globe* headline and subhead and the notation indicating that this came from a newspaper other than the *Post*. Likewise, all quotations are from the *Boston Post*, unless otherwise noted.

The information in the entry may come from the following day's newspaper. For instance, the January 14 entry relates to Connie Mack visiting Boston on that date, but the quotation referring to the "baseball situation" comes from the next day's newspaper.

The spellings of names have been standardized here. We have also often inserted serial commas into quotations, even though they were often not in the originals. The spelling of Pittsburg, when mentioned, represents the way the city's name was spelled (with the "h") at the time and until 1911.

By The Numbers

By Dan Fields

1901 Boston Americans:

0.97
Walks and hits per inning pitched by Cy Young, lowest in the major leagues. He led the majors with the fewest walks per nine innings pitched (0.9) and led the American League with the fewest hits per nine innings pitched (7.9).

1.21
Walks and hits per inning pitched by the 1901 Americans, lowest in the AL.

1.35
Ratio of strikeouts to walks by Boston pitchers, best in the AL.

1.62
ERA of Cy Young, lowest in the majors. George Winter, with an ERA of 2.80, finished fifth in the AL.

2nd
Place in the AL by the 1901 Americans, who won 79 games and lost 57. (They also tied two games.) The Americans finished four games behind the Chicago White Sox, who were led by pitching ace (24-7 record) and first-time manager Clark Griffith.

3.04
ERA of the 1901 Americans, second lowest in the AL.

4
Team members who appeared in all 138 games: third baseman Jimmy Collins, outfielder Tommy Dowd, second baseman Hobe Ferris, and shortstop Freddy Parent.

4
Team members with at least 15 triples: Jimmy Collins (16), outfielder Chick Stahl (16), Hobe Ferris (15), and first baseman Buck Freeman (15). Collins and Stahl tied for fourth most in the AL, and Ferris and Freeman tied for sixth most.

4.27
Ratio of strikeouts to walks by Cy Young, best in the majors.

5
Shutouts by Cy Young, tied for most in the AL.

9
Consecutive games won by the 1901 Americans from June 14 through June 22. During the month of June, the Americans had a 20-5 record.

10
Consecutive hits by the Americans with two outs in the ninth inning against Bill Reidy of the Milwaukee Brewers on June 2. The Americans scored nine runs in the inning and won 13–2.

12
Home runs by Buck Freeman, second most in the AL and third in the majors.

12
Wild pitches by the 1901 Americans, fewest in the majors.

19
Runs scored in the second inning (nine runs) and third inning (ten runs) as the Americans beat the Philadelphia Athletics 23–12 on May 2. Thirteen players (nine on the Americans and four on the Athletics) scored at least two runs in the game.

21
Sacrifice hits by Freddy Parent, second most in the AL. Chick Stahl, with 20 sacrifice hits, was tied for third.

33
Wins by Cy Young, most in the majors, against only 10 losses. He won 41.8 percent of the team's 79 wins (Ted Lewis and George Winter each won 16 games). Young had 19 wins at home, still a franchise record for a single season.

37
Home runs by the 1901 Americans, most in the AL.

42
Doubles by Jimmy Collins, third most in the AL and in the majors.

49-20
Home record of the 1901 Americans, best in the majors.

64
Extra-base hits by Jimmy Collins, second most in the AL and in the majors. Buck Freeman had 50 extra-base hits, fifth most in the AL.

114
RBIs by Buck Freeman, second most in the AL and third most in the majors.

158
Strikeouts thrown by Cy Young, most in the AL.

187
Hits by Jimmy Collins, third most in the AL.

279
Total bases by Jimmy Collins, second most in the AL. Buck Freeman, with 255 bases, finished fourth.

281
Strikeouts by Boston batters, fewest in the majors.

300
Career wins by Cy Young on July 3. He would win 211 more games before he retired in 1911.

.339
Batting average by Buck Freeman, third highest in the AL. Jimmy Collins, with an average of .332, finished fifth.

371 1/3
Innings pitched by Cy Young, second most in the AL. He had 41 starts and 38 complete games, both second most in AL.

396
Batters struck out by Boston pitchers, most in the AL.

.520
Slugging average of Buck Freeman, second highest in the AL. Jimmy Collins, with an average of .495, finished fifth.

594
At-bats by Tommy Dowd, second most in the AL.

.920
On-base percentage plus slugging average (OPS) of Buck Freeman, second highest in the AL.

.975
Fielding percentage by Cy Young, highest among AL pitchers.

1,178
Hits allowed by the 1901 Americans, fewest in the majors.

4,195
Average attendance at home games of the 1901 Americans—second highest in the AL (behind the White Sox, with 4,991 per game) and third highest in the majors (the St. Louis Cardinals drew 5,278 per game). Across the New York, New Haven, and Hartford Railroad tracks, the Boston Beaneaters drew only 2,093 per game.

Around the Majors in 1901:

0
Hits allowed by Christy Mathewson of the New York Giants, in a 5-0 complete-game victory over the Cardinals on July 15. He threw another no-hitter in 1905. On May 9, 1901, Earl Moore of the Cleveland Blues allowed no hits against the White Sox through nine innings, but gave up two hits and two runs in the tenth inning and took the loss.

1st
Year of the American League. On Opening Day, nearly two-thirds of AL players were National League veterans.

1st
Career win by Christy Mathewson, on April 26. As a rookie, he won 20 games, struck out 221 batters, and had an ERA of 2.41; he also threw 23 wild pitches, most in the majors. Mathewson's 372nd and last win for the

Giants came on June 26, 1916; he also won one game for the Cincinnati Reds that year.

1st
Career win by Eddie Plank of the Athletics, on May 18. Although he would become the first left-handed pitcher to win 300 games and would win 326 games (284 with the Athletics) during his 17-year career, he never led the league in wins during a season.

1st
Year of 50 consecutive years in which Connie Mack managed the Athletics. During that span, he won 3,582 games, nine AL pennants, and five World Series titles.

1st
Pennant won by the Pittsburgh Pirates, who topped the NL with a 90-49 record. The Philadelphia Phillies finished second, 7 1/2 games back.

2
Steals of home by Honus Wagner of the Pirates on June 20, in a 7-0 win over the Giants. Wagner is the first player known to have stolen home twice in a game.

2
Consecutive games in which Jimmy Sheckard of the Brooklyn Superbas hit an inside-the-park grand slam (September 23 and 24).

2
Grand slams in one game by the White Sox on May 1 and the Superbas on September 23.

2.18 and 2.22
ERA of Jesse Tannehill and Deacon Phillippe, respectively, of the Pirates, who finished first and second in the NL in ERA. Teammates Jack Chesbro (2.38) and Sam Leever (2.86) also finished in the top ten, and the team's ERA of 2.58 was lowest in the majors.

3
Triples by Jimmy Sheckard of the Superbas in an Opening Day (April 18) game against the Phillies.

7
Consecutive games, all at home, in which the Giants gave up ten or more runs, from September 3 through 6 (including doubleheaders on three consecutive days against the Pirates). The Giants lost all seven games and were outscored 90-27.

8
Consecutive seasons in which Willie Keeler had at least 200 hits, from 1894 through 1901. This was a major-league record for more than 100 years: Ichiro Suzuki had ten consecutive seasons from 2001 through 2010.

9
Runs scored with two outs in the bottom of the ninth inning by the Cleveland Blues on May 23, to beat the Washington Senators 14-13.

10
Runs scored in the ninth inning by the Detroit Tigers in their first-ever game, on April 25, to overcome a nine-run deficit and beat the Brewers 14-13. Pop Dillon of the Tigers hit four doubles in the game.

10
Consecutive hits by Nap Lajoie of the Athletics on April 26, 27, and 29, tying a major-league record that was not broken until 1920.

12
Errors by the Tigers in a May 1 game against the White Sox. On September 21 the Blues had 16 errors in a doubleheader against the Senators.

12
Inside-the-park home runs by Sam Crawford of the Reds, still a major-league record for one season. He led the majors with 16 home runs in 1901.

16
Batters struck out by Noodles Hahn of the Reds on May 22, in a 4-3 victory over the Beaneaters. He was the first player to strike out 16 in a nine-inning game since the introduction of the modern pitching distance in 1893. Hahn led the majors with 239 strikeouts in 1901.

19
Runs given up by Bill Phillips of the Reds in the second game of a June 24 doubleheader against the Phillies,

although only seven of the runs were earned. The Reds lost 19-1.

21
Triples each by Bill Keister and Jimmy Williams of the Baltimore Orioles — most in the majors.

21-0
Score by which the Tigers shut out the Blues in eight innings on September 15. The game was called after eight to allow the Clevelanders to catch a train.

23
Wins by Roscoe Miller of the Tigers in his rookie year. He would win only 16 more games in his career.

25
Wins by Bill Donovan of the Superbas, most in the NL. He had won only one game in each of the previous three seasons.

26
Hits allowed by Doc Parker of the Reds in a June 21 game against the Superbas. The Reds lost 21-3.

27
Losses by Dummy Taylor of the Giants, most in the majors. He won 18 games. Taylor led the NL in starts, with 43.

32
Batters hit by Chick Fraser of the Athletics, still an AL record for one season. He also led the league in walks, with 132.

33
Complete games in 33 starts by Red Donahue of the Phillies.

39
Consecutive scoreless innings pitched by Christy Mathewson of the Giants between May 3 and May 21.

41
Complete games (in 42 starts) by Noodles Hahn of the Reds, most in the majors. He led the NL in innings pitched, with 375⅓.

42.3
Percentage of Cincinnati wins by Noodles Hahn, who had 22 of the team's 52 wins. He was one of only three NL pitchers in the 20th century to win at least 20 games on a last-place team.

52
Bases stolen by Frank Isbell of the White Sox, most in the majors and still an AL record for first basemen. Honus Wagner of the Pirates led the NL with 49 steals. As a team, the White Sox led the majors with 280 stolen bases.

57
Batters faced in a nine-inning game by Roy Patterson of the White Sox against the Brewers on May 5. The White Sox lost 21-7.

126
RBIs by Honus Wagner, most in the majors. He would lead the NL in RBIs four more times, in 1902, 1908, 1909, and 1912.

152
Walks given up by Bill Donovan of the Superbas, most in the majors.

181
Singles by Jesse Burkett of the St. Louis Cardinals, most in the majors. The next player to have at least 180 singles in a season was Sam Rice in 1925, with 182. Burkett led the NL in runs (142), hits (226), batting average (.376), on-base percentage (.440), and total bases (306).

277
Career batters hit by Gus Weyhing, who played without a glove and retired in 1901. The number of batters hit is still a major-league record.

329
Wins by Kid Nichols for the Beaneaters from 1890 through 1901. He was the first pitcher to win at least 300 games with one team.

.377

Batting average of Willie Keeler from 1897 through 1901 and Nap Lajoie from 1901 through 1905.

382

Innings pitched by Joe McGinnity of the Orioles, most in the majors. He led the AL in starts (43) and complete games (39).

.426

Batting average of Nap Lajoie of the Athletics, highest in the majors during the 20th century and an AL record that still stands. The runner-up for the AL batting title, Mike Donlin of the Orioles, hit .340 — a difference of .086. Lajoie's BA was more than 50 percent higher than the league average of .277. (Even so, it's possible that Lajoie's BA was inflated somewhat by the fact that foul balls were not counted as strikes in the AL in 1901.) Lajoie also led the AL in home runs (14) and RBIs (125), becoming the league's first Triple Crown winner. And he led the majors in runs (145), hits (232), doubles (48), on-base percentage (.463), slugging average (.643, an AL record until 1919), and total bases (350). In a May 23 game against the White Sox, he was walked intentionally with the bases loaded (an event not to be repeated in the AL until 2008). In a July 30 game against the Blues, he hit for the cycle with a grand slam for the homer.

914

Career stolen bases by Billy Hamilton when he retired after the 1901 season — a record that stood until 1978. His career batting average of .344 and on-base percentage of .455 rank among the best ever.

1,004

Games won by manager Frank Selee with the Beaneaters from 1890 through 1901, including five NL pennants. He was the second manager to win 1,000 games with one franchise (Cap Anson won 1,282 games with the Chicago White Stockings/Colts from 1879 through 1897).

Sources

Society for American Baseball Research, *The SABR Baseball List and Record Book* (New York: Scribner, 2007).

Burt Randolph Sugar (editor), *The Baseball Maniac's Almanac* (third edition). (New York: Skyhorse Publishing, 2012).

baseball-almanac.com

baseballlibrary.com/chronology/byyear.php?year=1901

baseball-reference.com

retrosheet.org

http://thisgreatgame.com/1901-baseball-history.html

Contributors

Dennis Auger grew up in New Hampshire and now resides in Massachusetts with his wife Elaine. Besides being a lifelong Yankees fan and a SABR member, he is a clinical supervisor at an outpatient substance abuse facility. He has written several articles covering baseball during the 1893-1919 era.

Charlie Bevis is the author of five books on baseball history, including *Jimmy Collins: A Baseball Biography* published by McFarland in 2012. A member of SABR since 1984, he has contributed nearly three dozen biographies to the SABR Baseball Biography Project. He teaches research writing at the University of Massachusetts Lowell and lives in nearby Chelmsford with his wife Kathie and dog Kasey.

Maurice Bouchard lives with his beautiful wife Kim in Westford, New York, just a short drive from Cooperstown. Bouchard, a SABR member since 1999, has contributed as an author, editor, and fact-checker to many "team" books, including *The Team that Forever Changed Baseball and America*, *Red Sox Baseball in the Days of Ike and Elvis*, and *Lefty, Double-X, and The Kid*.

As an alumnus of Williams College, **Rory Costello** was first drawn to write about the life of Ted Lewis in 1999. Though Lewis had by far the most distinguished major-league career of any Williams Ephman, Costello still enjoyed writing about the others. A distinguished Eph—former Commissioner of Baseball Fay Vincent—kindly provided the foreword to the pamphlet Costello assembled (http://archives.williams.edu/files/EphsintheMajors2.pdf). Rory lives in Brooklyn, New York with his wife Noriko and four-year-old son Kai.

Dan Desrochers' ventures to Fenway Park began in 1967 as a 12 year-old who had a passionate desire to attend a Red Sox game. Unbeknownst to his parents, he schemed and plotted his "Impossible Dream" Maine-to-Boston venture that combined bicycling, hiking, and bus and train rides to catch his first Red Sox game. He completed the 200-mile trip and managed to get home before dark. He now lives in Portsmouth, New Hampshire though he still considers himself to be a Mainer—and continues to organize Red Sox trips without his mom's permission. He was behind the Red Sox dugout in St. Louis when the Red Sox won it all in 2004.

James Elfers. As a lifelong Phillies fan, he is enjoying the team's current golden age. He is also the author of *The Tour to End All Tours: The Story of Major League Baseball's 1913-1914 World Tour* (University of Nebraska Press), which tells the story of the Giants-White Sox world tour of a century ago.

Eric Enders is a freelance writer, baseball historian, and former researcher at the Baseball Hall of Fame Library in Cooperstown, New York. His work has appeared in the *New York Times*, the *Village Voice*, *Variety*, MLB's World Series program, *Yankees Magazine*, and many other publications. He has also been a reporter for the *El Paso Herald-Post* and a freelance editor and proofreader for numerous publishers including Barnes & Noble and National Geographic. A native of El Paso, TX, and a lifelong Dodger fan, Eric operates Triple E Productions, a baseball research and editing company.

Charles Faber is a retired university professor and administrator, living in Lexington, KY. He has been a baseball fan since 1936, rooting for several teams, but always against the Yankees. A long-time SABR member, he has written 20 biographies for the Bio Project and contributed to books edited by other SABR members. McFarland has published eight of his books so far, and number nine, tentatively titled *Major League Prodigies: Best Seasons by Players under 21*, is due out in 2013.

Dan Fields is a manuscript editor at the *New England Journal of Medicine*. He loves baseball trivia, and he regularly attends Boston Red Sox and Pawtucket (RI) Red Sox games with his teenage son. Dan lives in Framingham, Massachusetts, and can be reached at dfields820@gmail.com.

David Forrester is a nonprofit technology executive and lifelong Red Sox fan now living in exile with the Seattle Mariners. After spending his first 36 years in and around Boston, he is the proud owner of a New England temperament. He joined SABR ten years ago when his research uncovered Allie Moulton, the first person of African American ancestry known to have played in the segregated major leagues.

Donna L. Halper is an Associate Professor of Communication at Lesley University, Cambridge MA. A media historian who specializes in the history of broadcasting, Dr. Halper is the author of five books and many articles. She is also a former broadcaster and print journalist.

Joanne Hulbert, co-chair of the Boston Chapter and SABR's Baseball Arts Committee, spends long hours obsessively gathering baseball poetry when not at Fenway Park. A resident of Mudville, a village of Holliston, MA she occasionally leaves her poetic pursuit to indulge in something completely different. She has found that there's always something poetic about the life of an obscure and often forgotten player who has a story just as important and valuable to baseball history as any hall of fame inductee.

Steve Krah, a SABR member since 1994 and sportswriter at *The Elkhart* (Ind.) *Truth* newspaper since 1990, has thoroughly researched the life and career of Elkhart native Lou Criger. He is a charter member of the Lou Criger SABR chapter. On June 3, 2012 - 100 years to date after Criger's last big league game - a monument to Criger was dedicated in Elkhart as part of SABR member David Stalker's Early Baseball through Deadball Era Memorial Series.

Mike Lackey is a retired newspaper reporter, editor and columnist. He holds a degree in history from Earlham College and has been a member of SABR since 1985.

Len Levin is a Red Sox fan from way back, but not as far back as 1901. A retired newspaper editor, he lives in Providence, Rhode Island, with his wife, a journalism professor, and currently spends a lot of time editing for various SABR publications. He is also the chairman of SABR's Southern New England Chapter.

Jack Morris is a corporate librarian for an environmental engineering company. He lives in East Coventry, Pennsylvania with his wife and two daughters. His baseball biographies have appeared in the books, *The Team That Forever Changed Baseball and America* (1947 Brooklyn Dodgers) and *Bridging Two Dynasties* (1947 New York Yankees). He is not the Jack Morris of World Series fame but, every once in a while, wishes he was.

Peter Nash is the author of *Boston's Royal Rooters* and the writer and producer of the documentary film *Rooters: The Birth of Red Sox Nation*. He is also the co-founder and co-owner of the reconstituted McGreevy's 3rd Base Saloon in Boston, MA, and writes about issues in the baseball artifact trade at Haulsofshame.com, which has helped recover several of Nuf Ced McGreevy's treasured photographs stolen from the Boston Public Library.

Bill Nowlin regrets missing Opening Day at the Huntington Avenue Grounds. This is the tenth "team book" for which he has been a lead editor for SABR, and he has authored or edited another 30-plus books on baseball, and even some on music. He is co-founder of Rounder Records and has served as VP of SABR since just before the Red Sox won the World Series in 2004.

Joe Santry has been the Historian for the Columbus Clippers of the International League since 1987. He is also the Clippers Media Director and the Director of Communications. Joe was only the second Historian in professional baseball history; Joe Overfield of Buffalo was the first. Joe's father was born and raised in South Boston.

Fred Schuld is a native of Cleveland whose father took him to his first game at League Park in September 1935 to watch Cleveland's Joe Vosmik and Washington's Buddy Myer fight it out for that year's American League batting title. He is a retired high school history teacher who has been a member of SABR since he first learned of the organization. In 1945, just after the war ended, he and a friend took advantage of the end of gas rationing and drove down to see the Ohio River. Their car broke down into Newcomerstown and while it was being repaired, the mechanic suggested that they go visit a man who lived nearby—and Fred shook hands with Cy Young.

Ron Selter is one of SABR's top ballpark experts; his area of expertise is 20th Century major-league ballparks. He is the author of the double award winning book *Ballparks of the Deadball Era* (McFarland). He was text editor for the ballpark encyclopedia *Green Cathedrals* (2006 Edition) published by SABR. In addition, he was a contributor to the books *Forbes Field, Comiskey Park,* and *Ebbets Field* (all by McFarland). The author is a retired economist formerly with the Air Force Space Program. A SABR member since 1989 and a member of the Ballparks, Minor League, Statistical, and Deadball Committees, he has made presentations at both SABR regional meetings and at several national conventions.

Tom Simon has founded the Gardner-Waterman (Vermont) Chapter, the Deadball Era Committee, and, most recently, the Buster Olney (Vermont Kids) Meet-Up, with 14 members between the ages of 8 and 14 who gather in his renovated attic every other week for SABR-style meetings.

David C. Southwick is former publicity coordinator of the Boston Chapter of SABR. He conceived and initiated SABR's first team book for BioProject, on the 1975 Red Sox: *'75: The Red Sox Team That Saved Baseball*. When his beloved Red Sox are out of season, he is a dedicated follower of his alma mater's sports teams, the North Quincy (MA) High School Red Raiders. David presently resides in Dorchester, MA.

Cindy Thomson co-authored the only full-length biography on Cubs hall of famer Mordecai Brown: *Three Finger, The Mordecai Brown Story*. Brown is her relative. She has also written fiction and non-fiction books and articles and is currently at work on a three-book historical fiction series. She lives with her husband Tom in central Ohio where she writes full time. You can find her on the web at www.cindyswriting.com.

Frank Vaccaro is a Teamsters Local 812 shop steward for Pepsi Cola workers and distributors for Northern Queens, NY. He lives in Long Island City with his Czechoslovak-born wife Maria and their cat Furgood.

Paul Wendt has lived across the Charles River from Boston for more than 20 years. He co-founded SABR's Boston Chapter in 1998 and served the Society's 19th Century Committee for ten years as right-hand man for internet and as chairman. Paul studied the history of economics and taught ten years in college before joining SABR. Recently he earned a master's degree in statistics. For the 2013 World Series, he foresees 225 possible matchups rather than the familiar 224 and recognizes a weak rooting interest in more than 200 of them.

Illustration Credits

Thanks to the libraries and the historical community for their support on this project, serving as advocates and leaders dedicated to the preservation, documentation, and dissemination of historical information.

A special thanks to Tom Blake of the Boston Public Library and John Horne at the National Baseball Hall of Fame for their ongoing support and to Mark Fimoff and Bill Burgess for their technical expertise and sharing a wealth of knowledge in older baseball images. Appreciations to Nigel Ayres, Carlos Bauer, Dean Faragi, Michael Forino, Alan Gordon, Sarah Hartwell, Joanne Hulbert, David Lowe, Mark Moore, Ann Olszewski, Joe Williamson, Carolyn Quinn, and Charles Yerxa for their support, as well as those listed in the credits below.

Courtesy of the Boston Public Library, Print Department: Cover, 2, 4, 5, 6, 7, 18, 22, 23 (top), 24, 25, 26, 30 (top left), 30 (Center), 30 (bottom), 31 (center), 33 (center), 34, 35 (top), 41, 43, 52, 54, 55, 59 (bottom), 60, 62, 63, 66, c 71, 72, 83, 89, 93, 96, 105, 110, 115, 117, 121, 144, 147, 159, 160, 161, 168, 177, 178, 182, 184, 185, 186, 187, 188, 189, 190, 191, 192, 194, 195

Baseball Fever: 32 (top & bottom)

Chicago History Museum, Chicago Daily News Negatives Collection: 49, 70, 81, 86, 99, 106, 118, 133, 134, 156, 173, 175

Dan Desrochers Collection: 135, 170

Jeanette Criger-Done Collection: 58

Mark Fimoff Collection: 140 (bottom)

Heritage Auctions: 14, 65, 149

Courtesy of Hunt Auctions, www.huntauctions.com: 59 (left), 84, 107

The Internet Archive, Reach Official American League Base Ball Guide for 1905: 15

The Library of Congress, Library of Congress Prints and Photographs Division: 1, 17, 19, 20, 30 (right), 31 (bottom), 32 (center), 33 (top), 38, 39, 40, 42, 94, 114, 124, 158, 166, 171, 174

Peter Nash Collection: 35 (bottom), 179

National Baseball Hall of Fame Library, Cooperstown, NY: 46, 47, 74, 128, 130, 140 (top), 154, 164

Courtesy of Marc Okkonen: 23 bottom

University of New Hampshire Library, Milne Special Collections and Archives: 112

Massachusetts Agriculture College, *The Index, 1922*-Volume 52: 109

Courtesy Bread Loaf Writers Conference Photographs, Special Collections & Archives, Middlebury College: 111

Northeastern University Libraries, Archives and Special Collection Department: 31 (top)

Robert Edward Auctions, LLC: 176, 183, 193,

The Sporting Life, **October 30, 1889:** 77

Join SABR today!

If you're interested in baseball — writing about it, reading about it, talking about it — there's a place for you in the Society for American Baseball Research.

SABR was formed in 1971 in Cooperstown, New York, with the mission of fostering the research and dissemination of the history and record of the game. Our members include everyone from academics to professional sportswriters to amateur historians and statisticians to students and casual fans who merely enjoy reading about baseball history and occasionally gathering with other members to talk baseball.

SABR members have a variety of interests, and this is reflected in the diversity of its research committees. There are more than two dozen groups devoted to the study of a specific area related to the game — from Baseball and the Arts to Statistical Analysis to the Deadball Era to Women in Baseball. In addition, many SABR members meet formally and informally in regional chapters throughout the year and hundreds come together for the annual national convention, the organization's premier event. These meetings often include panel discussions with former major league players and research presentations by members. Most of all, SABR members love talking baseball with like-minded friends. What unites them all is an interest in the game and joy in learning more about it.

Why join SABR? Here are some benefits of membership:

- Two issues of the *Baseball Research Journal*, which includes articles on history, biography, statistics, personalities, book reviews, and other aspects of the game.
- One issue of *The National Pastime*, which focuses on baseball in the region where that year's national convention is held (in 2013, it's Philadelphia)
- Regional chapter meetings, which can include guest speakers, presentations and trips to ballgames
- "This Week in SABR" e-newsletters every Friday, with the latest news in SABR and highlighting SABR research
- Online access to back issues of *The Sporting News* and other periodicals through Paper of Record
- Access to SABR's lending library and other research resources
- Online member directory to connect you with an international network of passionate baseball experts and fans
- Discount on registration for our annual conferences
- Access to SABR-L, an e-mail discussion list of baseball questions and answers that many feel is worth the cost of membership itself
- The opportunity to be part of a passionate international community of baseball fans

SABR membership is on a "rolling" calendar system; that means your membership lasts 365 days no matter when you sign up! Enjoy all the benefits of SABR membership by signing up today at SABR.org/join or by clipping out the form below and mailing it to SABR, 4455 E. Camelback Rd., Ste. D-140, Phoenix, AZ 85018.

SABR 2013 MEMBERSHIP RENEWAL FORM

2013 dues payable by check, money order, Visa, MasterCard or Discover Card; online at: http://store.sabr.org; or by phone at (602) 343-6455

	Annual	3-year	Senior	3-yr Sr.	Under 30
U.S.:	☐ $65	☐ $175	☐ $45	☐ $129	☐ $45
Canada/Mexico:	☐ $75	☐ $205	☐ $55	☐ $159	☐ $55
Overseas:	☐ $84	☐ $232	☐ $64	☐ $186	☐ $55

Add a Family Member: $15 each family member at same address (list on back)
Senior: 65 or older before 12/31/2013
All dues amounts in U.S. dollars or equivalent

Participate in Our Donor Program!

I'd like to designate my gift to be used toward:
☐ General Fund ☐ Endowment Fund ☐ Research Resources ☐ _____
☐ I want to maximize the impact of my gift; do not send any donor premiums
☐ I would like this gift to remain anonymous.

Note: Any donation not designated will be placed in the General Fund.
SABR is a 501 (c) (3) not-for-profit organization & donations are tax-deductible to the extent allowed by law.

Name _____

Address _____

City _____ ST _____ ZIP _____

Home Phone _____ Birthday _____

E-mail: _____
(Your e-mail address on file ensures you will receive the most recent SABR news.)

Dues $ _____
Donation $ _____
Amount Enclosed $ _____

Do you work for a matching grant corporation? Call (602) 343-6455 for details.
☐ Check/Money Order Enclosed   ☐ VISA, Master Card, Discover Card

Card# _____

Exp Date _____ Signature _____

Mail to: SABR, 4455 E. Camelback Rd., Ste. D-140, Phoenix, AZ 85018

SABR BioProject Books

In 2002, the Society for American Baseball Research launched an effort to write and publish biographies of every player, manager, and individual who has made a contribution to baseball. Over the past decade, the BioProject Committee has produced over 2,200 biographical articles. Many have been part of efforts to create theme- or team-oriented books, spearheaded by chapters or other committees of SABR.

THE YEAR OF BLUE SNOW:
THE 1964 PHILADELPHIA PHILLIES
Catcher Gus Triandos dubbed the Philadelphia Phillies' 1964 season "the year of the blue snow," a rare thing that happens once in a great while. This book sheds light on lingering questions about the 1964 season—but any book about a team is really about the players. This work offers life stories of all the players and others (managers, coaches, owners, and broadcasters) associated with this star-crossed team, as well as essays of analysis and history.
Edited by Mel Marmer and Bill Nowlin
$19.95 paperback (ISBN 978-1-933599-51-9)
$9.99 ebook (ISBN 978-1-933599-52-6)
8.5"X11", 356 PAGES, over 70 photos

DETROIT TIGERS 1984:
WHAT A START! WHAT A FINISH!
The 1984 Detroit tigers roared out of the gate, winning their first nine games of the season and compiling an eye-popping 35-5 record after the campaign's first 40 games—still the best start ever for any team in major league history. This book brings together biographical profiles of every Tiger from that magical season, plus those of field management, top executives, the broadcasters—even venerable Tiger Stadium and the city itself.
Mark Pattison and David Raglin, editors
$19.95 paperback (ISBN 978-1-933599-44-1)
$9.99 ebook (ISBN 978-1-933599-45-8)
8.5"x11", 250 pages (Over 230,000 words!)

SWEET '60: THE 1960 PITTSBURGH PIRATES
A portrait of the 1960 team which pulled off one of the biggest upsets of the last 60 years. When Bill Mazeroski's home run left the park to win in Game Seven of the World Series, beating the New York Yankees, David had toppled Goliath. It was a blow that awakened a generation, one that millions of people saw on television, one of TV's first iconic World Series moments.
Edited by Clifton Blue Parker and Bill Nowlin
$19.95 paperback (ISBN 978-1-933599-48-9)
$9.99 ebook (ISBN 978-1-933599-49-6)
8.5"X11", 340 pages, 75 photos

RED SOX BASEBALL IN THE DAYS OF IKE AND ELVIS: THE RED SOX OF THE 1950S
Although the Red Sox spent most of the 1950s far out of contention, the team was filled fascinating players that captured the heart of their fanbase. In *Red Sox Baseball*, members of SABR present 46 biographies on players such as Ted Williams and Pumpsie Green as well as season-by-season recaps.
Edited by Mark Armour and Bill Nowlin
$19.95 paperback (ISBN 978-1-933599-24-3)
$9.99 ebook (ISBN 978-1-933599-34-2)
8.5"X11", 372 PAGES, over 100 photos

The SABR Digital Library

The Society for American Baseball Research, the top baseball research organization in the world, disseminates some of the best in baseball history, analysis, and biography through our publishing programs. The SABR Digital Library contains a mix of books old and new, and focuses on a tandem program of paperback and ebook publication, making these materials widely available for both on digital devices and as traditional printed books.

MEMORIES OF A BALLPLAYER
by Bill Werber and C. Paul Rogers III
Bill Werber's claim to fame is unique: he was the last living person to have a direct connection to the 1927 Yankees, "Murderers' Row," a team hailed by many as the best of all time. Rich in anecdotes and humor, Memories of a Ballplayer is a clear-eyed memoir of the world of big-league baseball in the 1930s. Werber played with or against some of the most productive hitters of all time, including Babe Ruth, Ted Williams, Lou Gehrig, and Joe DiMaggio.
$14.95 paperback (ISNB 978-0-910137-84-3)
$6.99 ebook (ISBN 978-1-933599-47-2)
250 PAGES, 6"X9"

BATTING by F. C. Lane
First published in 1925, *Batting* collects the wisdom and insights of over 250 hitters and baseball figures. Lane interviewed extensively and compiled tips and advice on everything from batting stances to beanballs. Legendary baseball figures such as Ty Cobb, Casey Stengel, Cy Young, Walter Johnson, Rogers Hornsby, and Babe Ruth reveal the secrets of such integral and interesting parts of the game as how to choose a bat, the ways to beat a slump, and how to outguess the pitcher.
$14.95 paperback (ISBN 978-0-910137-86-7)
$7.99 ebook (ISBN 978-1-933599-46-5)
240 PAGES, 5"X7"

NINETEENTH CENTURY STARS: 2012 EDITION
First published in 1989, *Nineteenth Century Stars* was SABR's initial attempt to capture the stories of baseball players from before 1900. With a collection of 136 fascinating biographies, SABR has re-released *Nineteenth Century Stars* for 2012 with revised statistics and new form. The 2012 version also includes a preface by **John Thorn**.
Edited by Robert L. Tiemann and Mark Rucker
$19.95 paperback (ISBN 978-1-933599-28-1)
$9.99 ebook (ISBN 978-1-933599-29-8)
300 PAGES, 6"X9"

GREAT HITTING PITCHERS
Published in 1979, *Great Hitting Pitchers* was one of SABR's early publications. Edited by SABR founder Bob Davids, the book compiles stories and records about pitchers excelling in the batter's box. Newly updated in 2012 by Mike Cook, *Great Hitting Pitchers* contain tables including data from 1979-2011, corrections to reflect recent records, and a new chapter on recent new members in the club of "great hitting pitchers" like Tom Glavine and Mike Hampton.
Edited by L. Robert Davids
$9.95 paperback (ISBN 978-1-933599-30-4)
$5.99 ebook (ISBN 978-1-933599-31-1)
102 PAGES, 5.5"x8.5"

SABR Members can purchase each book at a significant discount (often 50% off) and receive the ebook edtions free as a member benefit. Each book is available in a trade paperback edition as well as ebooks suitable for reading on a home computer or Nook, Kindle, or iPad/tablet.

www.ingramcontent.com/pod-product-compliance
Lightning Source LLC
Chambersburg PA
CBHW051402070526
44584CB00023B/3261